Financial and Monetary Policy Studies

Volume 37

Series Editor

Ansgar Belke
Institute of Business and Economics
University Duisburg-Essen
Essen, Germany

For further volumes:
http://www.springer.com/series/5982

Efthymios G. Tsionas

The Euro and International Financial Stability

Springer

Efthymios G. Tsionas
Athens University of Economics and Business
Athens
Greece

ISSN 0921-8580 ISSN 2197-1889 (electronic)
ISBN 978-3-319-01170-7 ISBN 978-3-319-01171-4 (eBook)
DOI 10.1007/978-3-319-01171-4
Springer Cham Heidelberg New York Dordrecht London

Library of Congress Control Number: 2013946947

Printed on acid-free paper

Springer is part of Springer Science+Business Media (www.springer.com)

Lenin is said to have declared that the best way to destroy the capitalist system was to debauch the currency [...]. The process engages all the hidden forces of economic law on the side of destruction, and does it in a manner which not one man in a million is able to diagnose.[1]

---

[1] Keynes JM (1920) The economic consequences of the peace, ch. VI. Harcourt Brace, New York, p 228

Contents

Chapter 1
Introduction

We are witnessing a fundamental dualism in the eurozone, many "real euros" in place of a single currency (*the* euro) that would maintain financial stability and promote growth. This manifests in countries like Greece and Italy (and also Portugal and Spain to some extent) experiencing problems with their public debt forcing them to adopt austerity measures to manage their public deficits and spending. If a country is unable to maintain financial and economic stability as well as growth in the framework of common currency, then in practice the euro operates differently in the country compared to other members of the monetary union. To state it in simple terms, the euro is not the same in countries with different demand curves for money arising from different fundamental economic conditions.

Why is it so difficult for the EU to maintain the stability of its currency against market forces? Because market forces, in the final analysis, determine the *real economic processes* which affect growth, public debt, deficits and monetary stability. It is, of course, a fact that the EU does not have the cohesion in terms of political processes that we observe in the US. Different US states behave differently and it may seem necessary at times to enforce particular fiscal policies at the state level to maintain financial and monetary stability. But that is not the whole story. It is not only that the US has achieved the political cohesion that the EU is currently lacking: It is also the higher productivity and growth of the US economy that created a real process of convergence at the state level along with more flexibility in factor mobility and free markets. The market forces are largely ignored in the EU with the view that control at the highest level of European Council or the EPC can substitute these forces. *This is, in fact, a sui generis form of quasi-socialist thought* that still survives in certain quarters of the EU at the highest level.

When the EU bureaucracy refers to "markets" more often than not, it refers to "speculators", "speculative attacks on the euro", "profiteers" and the like. But still the markets are the markets and we cannot ignore them. A "speculative attack on the euro" would never happen if speculators did not see a profit opportunity in the first place. A profit opportunity will most likely arise when and if the demand and supply conditions for money or capital differ widely among EU states as the

E. G. Tsionas, *The Euro and International Financial Stability*,
Financial and Monetary Policy Studies 37, DOI: 10.1007/978-3-319-01171-4_1,

result of asymmetric conditions in terms of overall productivity, efficiency, the average rate of return on investment, competitiveness and the structure of the balance of payments.

In the case of Greece, the prototype that we have so far for an analysis of the fundamental problems of the eurozone, the average rate of return on investment is quite low and there is excessive demand for money. The natural way to proceed, if markets were free, would be an increase in interest rates. The artificial way chosen by the bureaucracy was to increase money supply through the various memoranda signed between the EU and the Greek government in the context of EFSF. Of course, the EFSF is simply a bailout programme for the Greek economy, not real monetary policy that could have positive impact in the short run on incomes and aggregate demand. In fact the austerity program in Greece is nothing but the equivalent of a decrease in money supply, which constitutes a suicidal policy in the midst of a severe depression expressed in an expected −6 to −10 % growth rate for GDP in 2012.

If the EFSF was not simply a bailout program, it would have a chance to succeed. But the funds will be used to pay for wages and pensions as well as interest payments on the public debt. So, in fact, it is maintaining the current standard of living and its largest part goes back to foreign creditors. But the current situation calls for an increase in interest rates to maintain financial stability or financial aid to Greece, not bailout schemes. Financial aid as opposed to bailout is, of course, restructuring monetary policy inside the EMU. It requires political determination, which is lacking, but what is really lacking is something deeper: The regional policy of the EU in the past 30 years has been disappointingly misguided. Vast resources have been largely wasted without real effects on cohesion. If that is not so, then we should observe similar patterns of competitiveness and productivity among different countries, regions or sectors.

Under these conditions the obvious answer is that unless economic cohesion is achieved, and that unless different comparative advantages are allowed to arise, there is no way for the euro to survive.[1] However, this view is naïve and inconsistent. Indeed, if comparative advantages exist, and as we know they exist always, disparities and differences are likely not only to arise but also persist over time. Therefore, it is not cohesion or similarity of industrial or production structures that guarantees monetary stability and stability of a given currency. One may object to that as follows: After the Maastricht Treaty the EU has set strict goals for deficits and the ECB follows very strict policies in terms of monetary policy and financial or monetary stability. This provides with maximum freedom the private sector and the market forces to operate freely in a stable environment of economic policy. What then went wrong?

---

[1] Bagus (2010) provides the first coherent theory of the eurozone based on political considerations, see in particular chapter V, especially pp. 56–58.

Reference

Bagus P (2010) Why Germany gave up the DeutschMark, Chap. 5. In: The tragedy of the Euro. Ludwig von Mises Institute, Auburn, Alabama

Chapter 2
What Went Wrong with the Euro?

The first fact has to do with the "creative accounting" of EU bureaucracy. The creation of the euro zone was largely a political decision in the altar of which they sacrificed actual deficits, actual rates of inflation and public debt as a percentage of GDP. These aggregate indicators are easy to monitor but they are not always transparent to the public. More importantly, as aggregate indicators are only rough measures of the fiscal burden or economic efficiency.

The second fact is that to talk about markets and competition or contestability, one must first and foremost have, and apply, for a long period, anti-monopolistic laws and anti-monopolistic practices. But nowhere in the EMU such practices were ever adopted or applied. The Greek economy, for example, is completely under the influence of monopolies or cartels and the actual work produced by the Competition Committee is quite small. Five hundred job descriptions or occupations are "protected" in Greece, since the 1920s, including for example taxi drivers, dentists, pharmacies, lawyers etc. In industry or retail, oligopolies rule freely the entire market. It is not surprising then, that since 2008 prices have remained high for most if not all retail products without any tendency to fall, despite the dramatic reduction in household incomes.

Nominal wages in Greece are beginning to slide, three years after mid 2008. With prices staying the same, real wages will of course go down. In that sense, productivity is expecting to rise but most importantly, new comparative advantages will begin to develop. This makes it more likely for prices to increase, not decrease, in the next few years, given the cartel structure of most Greek markets. This will put even more pressure on actual Greek inflation (estimated to be around 10 %) but it is hard to claim that this bad for short-run costs of the industry. This is one side of the coin. The other side is that with falling demand most firms find themselves operating at higher levels of short-run average costs, a tendency that will be reinforced through reduction in real wages. What is the resolution of this puzzle? None other than restructuring of the production conditions to lower average short-run costs—innovation, different forms of factor substitution etc, overall restructuring of relative prices.

To conclude this discussion, in terms of increasing inflation in one country member of the EMU, like Greece, and stable inflation in other members, the euro

E. G. Tsionas, *The Euro and International Financial Stability*,
Financial and Monetary Policy Studies 37, DOI: 10.1007/978-3-319-01171-4_2,

cannot be sustained since the initial exchange rates of national currencies against another are now completely wrong, they are artificial and bureaucratic and the markets do not in fact work. Is it probable then that *the Euro might be restructured into more stable currencies*? This question is superfluous. Of course if the Euro were to dissolve a number of currencies would arise, some of which would necessarily be more "stable" than others. But what does this *mean*? Private agents are already free to choose the currency in which they complete their most important transactions and there is no lack of "stable" currencies or, at least, stable contracts in which such transactions can be completed. In addition, under conditions of increasing inflation in one country and stable inflation in other members, it is certain that relative prices have adjusted extensively to reflect the correspondence between the distribution of resources and consumption. The question remains whether this is a structural phenomenon, a necessary implication of the common currency, or merely an effect induced by specific monetary and credit policies.

These inflationary pressures are associated to a large extent the explosion of the public debt and the inability of countries like Greece, Spain, Italy, Ireland and Portugal to commit to solvency. Not because there is an inherent relationship between the two but rather because they both signal the same underlying phenomenon. The adoption of common currency did not change the fundamental factors that determine the national demand and supply for goods and services. Monetary stability, of course, helped to consolidate the South and make economic policies more predictable, which is essential in several respects. But the common currency by itself cannot change underlying economic structures, harmonize incomes and prices or equate rates of profitability in the Eurozone. Tendencies that were already there to move resources across Europe were affected only slightly by the introduction of the Euro. The abolition of tariffs in earlier years was far more important from this perspective.

Relative inflation rates will not only determine relative nominal interest rates but also exchange rates, if national currencies were allowed to exist. Of course, interest rates also determine inflation through aggregate demand, and if the mechanism is allowed to converge to the market solution, the outcome will be a stable national currency, ceteris paribus on foreign trade. When the markets are not left to operate freely, all sorts of imbalances arise. The actual interest rates are too low, the actual exchange rate is too large, and inflationary pressures are accumulating.

In that sense there is no question of how to restructure the euro. By itself any monetary union is "stable" provided economic policies are not adopted that adversely affect one member but not others. An optimal currency area implies the full operation of market forces to yield stable rates of inflation, reasonable *but not necessarily stable* exchange rates, and market—determined interest rates of all sorts. This is easier said than done. What is a *mechanism* that can yield the dissolution of the euro into different national or group currencies? Independently of the specific economic policies that will be adopted, the question is impossible to answer and has little meaning.

The point of this essay is to suggest that creating such a mechanism is not the business of EU bureaucracy but the European and world market itself. Otherwise, any artificially created currency groups (one of which is a "two-speed euro") will be destroyed in practice by the operations of the markets. What the bureaucracy does not understand is that there are deeper, real economic forces behind "speculative attacks" on the euro. These forces, in the final analysis, are reflected in actual inflation, interest rates and exchange rates. As long as the "fundamentals" of a given group are at odds with the common currency, *and economic policies are adopted whose affects adversely affect the different groups*, the common currency is not sustainable. To the extent that affects cannot but be different and adversely affect the different sectors of the European economy, the sustainability of the euro depends on avoidance of such policies which, in the final analysis, relate to policies of money and credit.

The mechanism that will lead to more stable and reasonable currencies depends on the "fundamentals" of a given group. If we allow, for the sake of discussion, each country of the EMU to choose its own currency and abolish the Maastricht Treaty, then in the long run there will be so many currencies as it is necessary, and *market-based currency groups* will be formed. Yet the "fundamentals" cannot but be different. The whole discussion about different currencies boils down to different economic policies that will be adopted in terms of fiscal, monetary and credit configurations. In the absence of such policies the markets can establish easily stable exchange rates. In this context a stable currency is a source of financial stability for the entire global financial system and the source of its own stability lies at the commitment of abstaining from harmful economic policies. Without coordination there is always the danger that one government can deviate from the common practices in terms of economic policies whose harmonization is, more or less, ensured in the context of a monetary union. But even under harmonization, for example the one set forth by the Maastricht Treaty, the monetary union can still embark on monetary and credit policies whose effect can be detrimental.

For example, Greece will revert back to the drachma, with an initial exchange rate of GRD/EUR = 1:1 relative to the euro, assuming only Greece leaves the eurozone. In a short time the exchange rate will stabilize at the actual exchange rate *dictated by economic conditions and market forces* which will be, say, 5:1. The devaluation will allow a quick recovery of the Greek economy and less strain will be placed upon public deficit and public spending. Exports will improve and the much desired reduction in exports will be accomplished. Of course the new exchange rate will be compatible with a higher equilibrium level of nominal interest rates. It is quite possible that expansionary monetary policy will be used along the path of the transition from the old to the new exchange rate equilibrium. At work is also the mechanism of the so-called "J-curve" which implies a temporary worsening of economic conditions before recovery.

Will the euro devaluate relative to US dollar? The answer is yes. Nothing is wrong with this in terms of the European economy since exports will increase and imports will decrease. This, of course, will increase actual inflation in the eurozone and the ECB might increase interest rates or reduce money supply but it is highly unlikely that a reduction in money supply (suicidal during a deep depression) will be necessary: The exit of Greece will guarantee that automatically. The only problem for the new eurozone will be its own structural imbalances, not the "announcement effect" before or after Greece's way out of the EMU. *The misconception of the EU bureaucracy is that appearances and "announcement effects" affect the euro more than the fundamental features and structural imbalances of the eurozone.*

The exit of Greece from the EMU *might* devaluate the new currency. We know, of course that, in the short run, this will relieve the current account, and improve the exports of certain goods and services. Provided the exchange rate is free to float, the international markets will reach a new equilibrium between demand and supply. But unless import substitution takes place in the sector of capital goods and energy, the current account will deteriorate and there will be detrimental for output and employment effects from the price of imports that will rise considerably. In fact, under the inflationary pressures of a devaluation, interest rates will have to raise, favoring the concentration of production at the later rather than the earlier stages, thus making the pressure from imports even more significant. The situation is likely to be made worse by Central Bank interventions favoring lower interest rates and / or a credit expansion that will create malinvestments in the earlier and more "capitalistic" or intermediate sectors. Moreover, there is no guarantee that the new Central Bank will follow a policy of commitment to stable monetary and credit conditions or conditions of price stability. Therefore, *it is not to the best of interest of Greece to abandon the euro unilaterally.*

We claimed that the exit of Greece from the EMU *might* devaluate the new currency. It has been shown by Rosa (2011a) that, in fact, a depreciation of the euro relative to other currencies, for example the US dollar, *preceding* the exit from the euro would make a major devaluation unlikely. In fact the announcement effects that will precede the exit will impact so negatively on the euro that any short—run advantage from increasing exports will disappear since the *ex post* devaluation of the national currency will be significantly smaller, if it happens at all. As Rosa (2011b) argues:

> The euro lost about 25 % of its value between 1999, when it was introduced, and its lower bound of 2001. What is required today, after its 12 % decline since the beginning of 2010, is a further decline from $1.30 to $1.00 for instance (a 23 % decline) or even better to $0.85 (a 34 % decline).

Rosa's argument seems to be quite convincing. Furthermore it offers an alternative to what would happen with the increased public debt burdens after a possible exit from the euro and the subsequent devaluation of the new currency. The *extent* of devaluation would have to be rather small, if any at all, especially for France and other major economies of the eurozone. For the South we have some evidence from the purchasing power parity of the euro against the dollar from Mongelli (2008, p. 32) so in fact *we can quantify Rosa's argument in more precise terms*. As of 2007, one US dollar would be equivalent to about € 0.60 in Greece and Portugal, € 0.83 for Italy and close to € 0.85 for Germany, Austria, Belgium and France. This purchasing power is remarkably close to Rosa's prediction for what would be a natural exchange rate of the euro, and justifies his argument that, in fact, there can be no excess burden from servicing the public debt of countries that leave the eurozone.

Let us look at this argument more closely. It is based on the fact that the euro has already lost 25 % of its value and that it might end up at an exchange rate of $0.85 which is "optimal". In what sense it is optimal we are never informed. We are informed that it is "likely" or even "desirable" to end up with an exchange rate of $0.85 and after all, a depreciation of "only" 34 % is required. However, this analysis is quite simplistic in that the simple algebra is, in fact, refuted in case a drastic reduction of demand for euro takes place. Such shifts of demand are quite possible and take place almost instantly making it possible that devaluations of more than 34 % are possible. It is unlikely that other national governments will tolerate their drastic over-valuation with detrimental effects on exports and the balance of payments despite the fact that, for example, German exports will increase considerably. A "balance" of policies will be adopted in the short-run to minimize the fluctuations of the exchange rate close to what Rossa suggests—although for reasons that have nothing to do with his algebra.

Even slight fluctuations of the euro exchange rate will make it impossible to accommodate interest payments for the debts of the South. Fiscal consolidation will be put in danger and additional austerity measures will have to be adopted to restore the fragile fiscal equilibria. Of course there are other issues as well: Although it is in the best interest of the South to remain within the eurozone, the accumulation of public debts and their accommodation by the ECB cannot continue forever. The debts of the South necessitate a diversion of credit from the North which, in fact, is nothing else but a policy of protection of their own commercial banks, exposed to the Southern debts. What, according to the ECB, appears to be financial contagion of destruction of northern European banks is, in fact, the result of risks taken by the commercial banks in the past. It would be reasonable to let some banks go bankrupt *rather than proceed with credit expansion* letting the commercial banks conduct business as usual. The consumer savings can be guaranteed, but it must be explicitly recognized that some investment decisions of the commercial banks were totally wrong. Unless such decisions are to be made by the ECB, financial contagion will continue since public debts are accumulating at alarming rates and the eurozone will not be able to survive.

Since a large part of the public debts of the South is, in fact, malinvestment on the part of European banks and European governments, *the markets should be allowed to correct the financial malinvestment*, through new contracts, or by erasing part of the public debt, recognizing explicitly the losses that were incurred in the process of bad financial decisions. In actual markets, firm that were involved in unsuccessful investment will close, and the banks that financed their investment plans will, naturally, incur a loss. There is no point for a government to prefer bailing out a bank instead of bailing out the firm, since both failed on the same ground. If the government intervenes by expanding credit to the firm just to repay the bank, and investment plans are not profitable, the situation cannot lead to a satisfactory equilibrium. The firm will keep borrowing, increasing its debt, while the bank will appear profitable and solvent. The expansion of credit is a bad idea, as always, since it inflates the malinvestments instead of providing a solution to the problem.

Of course, a country is different compared to the firm, not only from the political standpoint but also because there are thousands of investment plans and investment decisions that took and still are taking place. Some of them are profitable and others are not, thus suggesting that commercial banks should, first of all, make sound and informed decisions. In the case of Greece, the bail out plan was confined solely to facilitate the Greek government to pay pensions and wage bills in the public sector; this is an unprofitable "investment" and works only to the best interests of European commercial banks and the ECB. *The bailout plan supports government consumption and the European commercial banks but not the stability of the euro.*

In the theory of optimal currency areas, Mundell (1961, 1969) three conditions are known to be necessarily for optimality. First, labor mobility. Second, wage flexibility. Third, in the absence of these two conditions, there is a case for flexible exchange rates and separate monetary policies. Kenen (1969) has also argued for the necessity of similar economic structures, fiscal integration, and the degree of product diversification. Incidentally, Mundell argued that currency competition would result in high transaction and informational costs, so it would not be a practical solution unless there is "money illusion". The argument is hard to accept. If consumers can rationally choose bundles of goods and services and portfolio, why should not they be able to choose an optimal composition of currencies to hold at any given period given their expectations about future exchange rates?

Of course, "shocks" will always be asymmetric and inherently unforeseen, for the most part. In this environment, the shock can be absorbed by a system of flexible exchange rates but it will otherwise have a detrimental effect. Consider for example two countries as in Mundell (1961), the East that produces cars and the West that produces lumber. Suppose there is a positive productivity shock in the East. According to Mundell (1961) this leads to *increased demand* for lumber in the East. There will be current account surplus and excess demand for labor in the West, and the opposite effects in the East. This has been criticized by Dellas and Tavlas (2009) who argue as follows: The positive productivity shock in the East, will increase the marginal productivity of labor and the demand for labor, and will shift to the right the aggregate supply curve, along with a raise in the marginal product for capital. The net effect will depend on the underlying parameters of the two structures, as the authors conclude.

Under conditions of labor immobility, the increased production of cars should be followed by a reduction of their price, as well as an increase of the demand of lumber from the West, if lumber is an input in the car production. If exchange rates are flexible, it is clear that the Eastern currency will devaluate and the Western currency will appreciate. Since cars are exchanged for lumber in the international market, the positive shock will be beneficial for all and similarly a negative shock will be detrimental to all.

If we allow for free capital flows the situation is somewhat different. The positive shock in the East increases the marginal productivity of capital and interest rates, making investment in more "capitalistic" or "round about" processes (like cars) more profitable compared to the near—to—final products, like lumber. Capital will shift from the West to the East, and more capital from the East will be invested in the car industry. The structure of relative prices will change accordingly to signal to the investors the different profitability opportunities that arose. More cars and less lumber will be produced resulting in increased employment in the East and unemployment in the West, if the wage rates cannot be adjusted immediately. If the shock is permanent, the increased production of cars will require more lumber as well, making the situation better in the West, requiring more labor and an increase of wage rates. If the shock is only temporary, the East will find itself with considerable malinvestment (if the expectations were the shock to be permanent) and a corrective movement will take place: The decrease in the marginal productivity of capital and interest rates, will imply a flow of capital from the East to the West, since the production of close—to—final or less "capitalistic" processes is now more profitable.

If expectations are "correct", temporary shocks cannot have an immediate effect and persistent or permanent productivity shocks will generate business cycles, similar to those produced from real business cycle models. However, the reason for the fluctuations is the change of relative prices and the resulting change of profitability in the various sectors of the international economy. Without changes in the relative prices or the rate of interest, it is not possible to have capital flows as a result of a positive productivity shock. All investors, domestic or foreign, make their calculations in monetary terms including prices, interest rates, and exchange rates. It is true that the final or equilibrium value of exchange rate may well stabilize to a level similar to the previous one, but this cannot come about unless there are first movements in the exchange rates and prices that are consistent with the changes in the relative marginal productivities of the factors of production.[1] These movements can, of course, be considerable.

Under a system of fixed exchange rates or a common currency between the East and the West, as in Mundell (1961), the free flow of capital between the two regions will necessarily show up in the form of distortions in the money and credit markets, if the interest rates are predetermined. Accommodating the inflow of funds in the car industry (East) will result in a credit expansion. If the shock is persistent but not permanent but expected to be so, the credit expansion and growth will soon revert to their opposite as the result of changes in relative prices and relative marginal productivities. The malinvestment will be corrected with capital outflow and detrimental effects on output and production. To the extent that the credit expansion was not artificial, in the sense that world savings cover world

[1] In that sense the argument of Dellas and Tavlas (2009, p. 23).

investment, the economy will correct the mistakes through fluctuations in outputs and relative prices. *In a monetary union, it is exactly the goal of price and monetary or credit stability that cannot be achieved*: The fluctuation of exchange rates, in a flexible environment, would reflect the changes in relative prices but with a common currency inflationary pressures will arise and the burden of correction will fall (1) on capital markets and (2) on money and credit.

Even in a monetary union, one may claim, that different resources like capital and labor, denominated in a common currency, still provide the markets with the right signals for relative profitability of activities in different countries and sectors. In the Mundellian universe there is, of course, little problem with that. But the hidden issue is that, under free capital mobility, chances are that investors would prefer to conduct operations using a third, more stable currency, if the currency of East-West is likely to depreciate relative to another currency, say that of the North. With a positive shock in East (cars) that raises the prices of Eastern relative to Northern cars, the malinvestment will correct itself sooner via the importing of cheaper Northern cars and a switch to less "capitalistic" methods of production. The East-West will appreciate at first relative to North, but will depreciate in the immediate future, reflecting the relative profitability of investing in the North. Much depends, naturally, on the time structure of producing cars in the North relative to the East-West union. Part of the correction of investments, involves the changes of exchanges rates of the East-West (say EW) relative to North (N). The demand for N will rise after the depreciation of the EW, and this will affect the reserves of foreign currency in East-West. To appreciate the EW, the Central Bank is likely to make various mistakes, including a credit or monetary expansion, whereas in fact nothing of the sort is required, besides letting the international markets clear at a point where the demand for currency reflects current demand for the various activities or "aggregate demand" and "aggregate supply".

The reason why the Central Bank is worried by this situation is that a large portion of the increased reserves in foreign currency might be the result of "speculative" considerations. The Central Bank believes that speculative attacks on its currency are conducted, in order to profit later on from the appreciation of the currency. This notion is consistent with a scenario where the EW (or the euro) has depreciated as the result a change in relative marginal productivity of capital relative to the North (or the US) but this change is expected to be temporary. If the deterioration in relative marginal productivity of capital is persistent then so will be the depreciation; but what is of concern is the opposite: The euro has been "attacked" in order to depreciate and then let it appreciate freely, so that speculative gains can be realized. But the question is, why should the euro appreciate after the speculative attack? An increase in "aggregate demand" or a positive productivity shock must be forthcoming and expected in order for things to happen in that way. But there is no rational foundation for this expectation particularly when economic policy is organized around austerity measures.

From the recent literature it turns out that a monetary union is recommended mainly to avoid inflationary pressures or biases (Barro and Gordon 1983) or monetization of debts and accommodation of the financing needs of the national governments (Alesina and Barro 2001). This involves two (related) assumptions: *First*, that the Central Bank is, somehow, better equipped than national governments, to accomplish these goals. *Second*, that a system of freely floating currencies is worse than a monetary union. Of course, the Central Bank of an economic union can solve the coordination of national policies only to the extent that the political and economic authorities of the Union can do so. Commitment in this game of coordination, is a problem that is to be solved by the political and economic authorities themselves. However, commitment is not the only problem to be solved in this game, and the Central Bank may have its own objectives; an issue that we examine later on in this essay. The other problem concerns the effects of asymmetric shocks and also the recent problem of explosion of public debt in certain European countries.

The adverse effects of "asymmetric shocks" can be corrected by the markets in a system of floating exchange rates. This is common knowledge but it is also precisely why an economic union encompassing different economic structures cannot be sustainable. Suppose a member of the economic union (like Greece or Spain and Italy, the South in short) is hit by a negative productivity shock which implies lower marginal productivity of capital across all industries. If the shock is expected to be highly persistent, and interest rates are harmonized, it would take some time to realize this development. Effectively, interest rates in the South should be lower in order to maintain profitable current investments in the margin. Since this is not possible, planned investment will be postponed but at the same time, less "capitalistic" or less "round about" processes will be favored implying negative net capital flows for the South. The concentration of production near the later stages will decrease the demand for capital from the North and will increase the demand for intermediate materials or products that are closer to the final product sector. Employment, in particular, will shift from the early to the later stages. In the process, the demand for capital will also increase but since the sectors producing goods close to final require less capital, the net increase will not be sufficient to compensate for the reduction in investment.

The reduction in investment can be detrimental for the Northern industries, so the Central Bank in likely to respond by announcing lower interest rates and also a credit expansion program, as the ECB recently did. The lower interest rates will sustain a portion of investments at the margin but if the shock is severe it is unlikely that it will be sufficient to attract new investment in the more "capitalistic" sectors of the North. Prices of consumer and intermediate or close—to—final goods will increase in the South, and prices of investment goods in the North will decrease. It is clear that depression and inflation will prevail in the South, a fact that appears to be puzzling to many. The changes in relative prices will affect the relative profitability of different stages of production and different goods in the Union, and will imply capital flows to the service or close—to—final goods in the South, but only with considerable time lags. Lower interest rates announced by the ECB will, of course, shorten the amount of time required for the shifting of capital to the South and the lowering of the "average length of production" in the Union as a whole.

To conclude, a negative productivity shock will initially be detrimental to the country that experiences it and the countries that supply goods necessary for production, in proportion to the importance of the country in total exports from those that did not experience the shock. To an extent, the shock will affect all members of a Union, but the country that received the shock is likely to move towards less "capitalistic" processes of production, enlarging its close—to—final goods sectors. The initial outflow of capital from its capital—intensive sectors will be followed by inflow of capital or increase of investment in the service / final goods sector. In the absence of other shocks or policy changes from the ECB, the shock will be "absorbed" by the shifts of capital across the Union.

What then is *the* problem? Moving towards less "capitalistic" processes of production for the Union as a whole, makes it necessary to increase imports of capital from countries outside the Union, at higher prices. In the short—run, this is equivalent to a positive shock in the marginal productivity of capital for the US or the UK. But if the restructuring of the time—profile of production is not to the liking of the political authorities, the necessary corrective actions in the international capital markers will not take place, and the appreciation of the dollar or the pound, resulting from the increased imports of capital goods, is likely to imply policy measures by the ECB. *There lies, finally, the danger for a monetary Union: The monetary authority is likely to find the short run effects of a negative "asymmetric shock" too important to let the interest rate move freely, or the exchange rate to float freely relative to the currencies of the US or the UK.*

The issue for a monetary Union is not so much what happens internally, but what happens in relation to the rest of the world. Inside the economic and monetary Union, free movement of capital (and other resources, to the extent possible) may guarantee a structure of production that is compatible with the given system of relative prices, interest rates, and marginal productivities of capital (or factors used early on in the time structure) in the absence of policy distortions. The fact of the matter, however, is that capital may also move freely between the Union and the rest of the world. This will, naturally, affect the exchange rates, as well as the real pressure exercised on its debt and the current account.

After all, a monetary Union is primarily a political decision. If the Union is sustainable or not, it depends on how the political authorities and / or the Central Bank will react to a shock (asymmetric or not, has no significance) when its currency is devaluated relative to a foreign, important currency like the dollar or the pound. In nominal terms, the exchange rate of the euro relative to the dollar is free to float, but the exchange rate appears also to be a main concern for the ECB. Policy measures on behalf of the ECB, under the influence of shocks, are likely to propagate the volatility of the shock among its members, when a policy of "competitive euro" is adopted: *In fact, the euro should be allowed to float as a result of a shock, asymmetric or not, in order to maintain relative profitability in the different stages of production in the international markets, and thus absorb the greatest portion of the adverse effect of the shock.*

We will argue later on that there is no such thing as an "asymmetric shock". The concern with exogenous shocks at the expense of ignoring policy shocks is quite detrimental for an economic analysis of monetary unions and currency areas. Mundell's argument that in the absence of capital and labor mobility it is optimal to have different monetary policies should be read in a different way: In the absence of resource mobility monetary policies *will* be different because governments have every incentive to do so. However, resources that are internationally less mobile or no mobile at all (a) cannot become more mobile because common currency is adopted, and (b) they are mobile within a given country. The international movements of resources that cannot take place will be made under a different form through movements across various uses in the same country, through shifts across the time-distribution of investment and also via liquidation and crises.

References

Alesina A, Barro R (2001) Dollarisation. American Econ Rev 91, 381–385

Barro R, Gordon D (1983) Rules, discretion and reputation in a model of monetary policy. J Monetary Econ 12, 101–121

Dellas H, Tavlas G (2009) An optimum-currency-area odyssey, Bank of Greece, working paper

Kenen PB (1969) The theory of optimum currency areas: an eclectic view. In: Mundell RA, Swoboda, AK,(eds) monetary problems of the international economy. University of Chicago Press, Chicago, pp 41–60

Mongelli FP (2008) European economic and monetary integration and the optimum currency area theory, ECB working paper

Mundell RA (1961) A Theory of Optimum Currency Areas. American Econ Rev, 51, pp 509–517

Mundell RA (1969) Discussion: the currency area problem. In: Mundell RA, Swoboda AK (eds) Monetary problems of the international economy. University of Chicago Press, Chicago, p 111

Rosa J-J (2011a) The coming euro depreciation, http://jjrosa.blogspot.gr/2011/11/comingeuro-depreciation.html

Rosa J-J (2011b) More plans to save the euro, http://jjrosa.blogspot.gr/2011/12/more-plans-to-save-euro.html

Chapter 3
Public Debt: Introductory Remarks

What will happen with Greece's public debt? In fact, the EFSF is nothing but a set of consistent policies aiming at full repayment of the debt using bailouts. In fact, the scheme is apparently a bailout for European banks and the European financial sector as a whole. Greece's failure to pay will destabilize the European financial sector and would call for (possibly huge) interventions by the ECB. Will Greece's debt be convertible to drachmae or another currency that Greece can freely choose? In the short run, the question is irrelevant because Greece will choose to repay current obligations in terms of a currency relative to which the drachma will devaluate the most. In the long run, the question depends on which currency will appreciate more relative to the drachma. Without precise knowledge of policies that will be followed to result in new actual inflation rates, the question is impossible to ask. If US productivity proves better than productivity in the new eurozone, the dollar will appreciate so again the USD will be Greece's choice. If the ECB accepts that, the euro will devaluate even more since its demand for USD will increase, so it is unlikely that the new eurozone will accept anything less than full repayment of *current* obligations in *current* euros.

Is it possible to reach an agreement so that full repayment of *current* obligations in *the old exchange rate of the euro*, will be possible? To most people this would seem reasonable. After all these obligations were created under the old euro so they should be paid back in terms of that currency. What this means, is to repay in terms of the old euro and therefore in terms of current, inflationary drachmae! Effectively, the Greek central bank can increase money supply to pay back or bail out itself at the cost of higher inflation. Additionally, *this amounts essentially to an effective "haircut" of the Greek debt.* Why is it so bad when the EU at the highest level of the bureaucracy has already accepted as reasonable a 50 % haircut of Greek debt? Moreover, as we have seen, J.-J. Rosa's (2011a, b) arguments suggest that the extent of devaluations will be small and therefore the excess burden of public debt will be small.

The only real problem with this policy is the increase of Greek inflation, but *this is a Greek problem.* The EU would probably accept the additional effective haircut if the benefit of having Greece out of EMU would be forthcoming. The burden of the haircut upon the European banking sector is usually greatly exaggerated

E. G. Tsionas, *The Euro and International Financial Stability*,
Financial and Monetary Policy Studies 37, DOI: 10.1007/978-3-319-01171-4_3,

because the haircut does not affect the obligations of Greek social insurance funds, which constitute substantial part of the debt. These cannot be subjected to an immediate haircut or else the economic and social system would collapse. But *an implicit, inflationary—based haircut is the only possible solution in the short run.*

After Greece's exit from the eurozone, the inflationary pressures will have to be considered and this lies indeed at the heart of the issues of a new, stable eurozone. Because a set of consistent policies that will be used to combat Greek inflation will set a standard for other countries that will be forced to abandon the eurozone as well. Not only that, but this set of consistent policies, if it exists, is related to the source of inflationary pressures in any monetary union with asymmetric or widely differing constituent parts.

We noted before that currency groups should be formed for "similar" economies. At the very least, *this requires identical or near—identical actual inflation rates*. These "*actual inflation rates*" are objective measures of the percentage increase of prices for the most important commodities in each country of the group. So, we are not referring to overall measures like GDP deflators or questionable price indices that can be manipulated at will. Objective measurement of inflation is required if we want to *predict* in the long run, these currency groups that will endogenously follow from the free operation of markets. Purchasing power parity is one way that can be used, *grosso modo*, to allow predictions of group formations in the long run. One might object that the short run is important because the "implied" unrest in the financial sector will be detrimental for the real economy. Such views exaggerate the problem and, in the final analysis, we are interested in stable currency unions. Stability is, however, a long—run property of currency unions and constitutes, of course, the heart of the problem for European economic policies.

But it would be a mistake to rely on a long-run solution, under which the ratio of prices is approximately equal to the exchange rate. The reason is that, because of *persistent asymmetric shocks*, the ratio of prices in two countries can deviate systematically from their actual exchange rate for a considerable time period which is relevant for practical purposes, but mostly irrelevant for the long-run equilibrium itself. It is true that the argument of asymmetric shocks has been used before as a criticism of the EMU but such views have been largely ignored. The argument takes a new significance now, after the 2008 recession, but persistent asymmetric shocks do not fall out of thin air. They are produced endogenously by the real, market processes which operate in the background and they are responsible for the dynamics of the world economy.

To solve such problems in the world of academics is highly important but we also need to think about the relevance of the propositions. The Maastricht Treaty was correct in one respect. That in order to put the fiscal situation under control there should be an independent central bank that would refuse to accommodate the government's need of funds. The argument was forcefully put forward by Sargent (1986, pp. 100–101) in his analysis of European hyperinflations in the 1920s. But the Maastricht Treaty was totally incorrect in placing the same straightjacket on all economies of the eurozone, no matter how different they were and despite the fact that *Sargent's careful analysis focused on stabilizing inflation, not on maintaining such policies forever in the indefinite future*. For one, persistent asymmetric shocks propagated through the EMU system can have adverse effects, as we now know well. The Maastricht Treaty was not concerned with the problem of public debt and its long—term prospects so it did not consider that nearly Ponzi schemes could be run from a single member counting on the forced solidarity of others. Of course, the Ponzi schemes were not intentional but they arose from the different time horizons at which pre-existing obligations would end and thus they would have to be paid back.

It is possible that if "creative statistics" were not adopted when the EMU was decided, these situations would not arise. Of course, a monetary union is started with the best of intentions and the best of expectations, as in any exchange of wedding rings, although we know that people do set themselves apart at some point in time with certain probability. However, *with the EMU the situation was totally different*. Different economies with widely differing long—term prospects, highly likely to be adversely affected by persistent asymmetric shocks, with fundamentally different economic structures, were put together anyway in the interests of European bureaucracy. It was quite certain (or it should be so) that at some point in time (1) asymmetric shocks would produce widely differing actual inflation rates putting substantial pressure on intra-EMU terms of trade, (2) maturing debt would be difficult to pay back under such conditions and (3) the EMU was not a practically closed economy as some optimists would like to think. Indeed, *the burst of the housing bubble in the US set the stage* in which the recent European drama, with distinctly Greek aspects, took and is still taking place.

References

Rosa J-J (2011a) The coming euro depreciation, http://jjrosa.blogspot.gr/2011/11/comingeuro-depreciation.html

Rosa J-J (2011b) More plans to save the euro, http://jjrosa.blogspot.gr/2011/12/moreplans-to-save-euro.html

Sargent TJ (1986) Rational expectations and inflation, Harper and Row

Chapter 4
Was the Eurozone an Acceptable Currency Union?

What should have been done instead of the EMU? Or, what would have been a reasonable basis upon which to base a sound monetary union? We do not intend to pose this as a historical question but rather as a way to understand the best way to form stable currency unions in the future. From the long-run perspective, but also from the perspective of considering seriously the adverse effects of asymmetric, persistent shocks, viable monetary unions rely upon the foundation of:

(1) approximate equality between *actual* inflation rates and *actual terms of trade* or exchange rates, *even* under a common currency,
(2) an arrangement (cancelling out) of mutual debts, and the common present value of debts to all third parties,
(3) independence of the central bank from the fiscal needs of the government or to state it differently, *drastic control over fiat money* that is not backed in *some* way.

All three conditions were and still are absent in the EMU. The ECB is, after all, another mechanism of the Bureaucracy to manipulate the economy. Competition laws are nowhere to be seen in the horizon despite declarations and enforcement of opening several so called "closed professions". Apparently, (1) and (2) were never considered. What about fiat money, in condition (3)? Under the EFSF, the EMU took it upon itself to bail out the Greek economy. If Greece were to repay current interest burden on the public debt, the payment of wages and pensions was at stake. The transfer of funds to Greece was not creation of new money but this transfer was not backed at all. In principle, it was backed on future tax collections of the Greek government but this soon proved to be an unfounded expectation. Effectively, money supply was increased in Greece without any backing so from the point of view of Greece the bailout plan was fiat money creation for all practical purposes.

There is a solidarity aspect to the option of the bailout plan which is a priori admirable, but the fact remains that inflationary pressures must have gone up in Greece—of course, we have no way to measure it, other than the fact that, by casual inspection, prices of important commodities did went up. If inflationary pressures went up for Greece the same is true, and even 1:1, for the EMU as a

E. G. Tsionas, *The Euro and International Financial Stability*,

Financial and Monetary Policy Studies 37, DOI: 10.1007/978-3-319-01171-4_4,

whole. In addition, the "haircut" of Greek public debt resolved the problem for French and German banks but not for the Greek social insurance sector, a significant holder of Greek government bonds.

Chapter 5
Preconditions of a Monetary Union

Several people pose the question: Why would the EU not accept the conversion of all government bonds to the so called Eurobonds? That would be a reasonable idea, if the Bureaucracy of the EU did not have its own objectives which are quite different from national objectives, a fact that would never occur in the US or the different regions of the UK. For the Bureaucracy, the objective is to accommodate first and foremost the banking sector of the "hard core" of the EU. This is, of course, quite reasonable and no sensible person in his or her mind would ever think that unilateral cancelation of the Greek debt is a reasonable option. What is the problem then? The problem is that the EU and the EMU in particular face an unprecedented historical situation: The formation of a monetary union in which government bonds of a nation A held by a nation B, cannot be repaid or arranged in *some* way over a time horizon. Surprisingly, there was simply no provision for that.

The EU focused so much on "growth enhancement" policies, "knowledge based" technologies and "structural reforms" (Mongelli 2008) that took many things for granted. It also placed limitations on public finances and effectively removed national monetary policies (although ECB's monetization of part of the public debt constitutes active monetary policy). One of the things taken for granted, was that the public debt of Greece or other Southern European countries was sustainable based on *ex ante* calculations about growth and public finances. *When these calculations proved wrong, monetization of the public debt was and still is the only solution—a solution that if continued will dissolve the euro sooner than later.*

In that sense the historical experience is that the formation of stable currency unions involves an arrangement of public debts of the constituent members between them, and also a provision for the outstanding public debt of the union as a whole to third parties, after the "clearing" inside the currency union. This historical experience is not available if we consider exclusively the European hyperinflations upon which the EMU was apparently founded. New historical evidence is now available.

The fact of the matter is that Greece has an *average* debt/GDP ratio in the EMU! Greece's importance in the EU is about 2 % by all measures. If other countries are worse off compared to Greece, why the stage of the European drama

E. G. Tsionas, *The Euro and International Financial Stability*,
Financial and Monetary Policy Studies 37, DOI: 10.1007/978-3-319-01171-4_5,

had a distinctly Greek character? The Irish and Portuguese problems appeared almost concurrently and currently (end of November 2011) the Italian bubble is about to explode. The Hungarian government tried at first to follow an alternative path (saying no to IMF, taxing bank activities, refusing the debt etc.) but currently it experiences exactly the same problems. The crisis is spreading all over the EU like a plague. Spain is at the threshold, and the whole master plan behind the Maastricht Treaty is at stake.

But if fiat money creation is prohibited and if fiscal policy is subject to backing or the government budget constraint, why should the EMU fail and what are the lessons? The EMU failed because *the Greek crisis created a deeper crisis in the credibility of the European authorities and the EU bureaucracy itself as a policy maker*. Most of the measures taken were anticipated by the markets in a rational expectations setting. As Sargent argues:

> …the substantial changes in ways of formulating monetary and fiscal policy associated with the end of the four inflations studies here can themselves be considered to have been caused by the economic events preceding them (Sargent 1986, p. 107, footnote 27).

Arguably,

> …previous attempts to stabilize the exchanges in Hungary […] and also in Germany, failed precisely because they did not change the rules of the game under which fiscal policy had to be conducted (Sargent 1986, p. 101).

The "rules of the game" in the EMU were compatible with a central bank that could, in principle, refuse inflationary finance according also to the Treaty of Maastricht. *First*, when it became apparent that inflation measures are changed at will, this promise became empty. *Second*, when it came to pass that individual state debts are not backed, but bailout plans could be developed on an *ad hoc* basis, the "rules of the game" became *more* uncertain, not *less* uncertain. The EFSF could bail out Greece, but what would happen if Italy, Spain and Portugal or Ireland were in the same position? More funds would need to be transferred and this could have a detrimental effect on financing, at low interest rates, German and French investments.

Portugal and Ireland avoided being members of the *chorus* in the Greek tragedy of the EMU, simply because the major political parties reached an agreement over the basic issues quickly, a fact that took some time in the idiosyncratic Greek political scene. But politics is not enough when it comes to the fundamental determinants of the crisis. These are, to a first approximation, widely differing terms of trade or *actual* exchange rates, in turn widely differing *actual* interest rates and therefore, widely differing *actual* inflation rates. Of course, this is not the end of the story. Even behind these factors, lie other fundamental causes, which amount to intra-EMU widely differing interest rates compared to profit rates or actual rates of return on investment. For example, preceding the crisis that started in 2008, there was considerable overproduction and optimism in the US economy that lowered the rate of return. Restructurings would have to take place that would be consistent with an increase in that rate. The US economy recovered swiftly from the crisis but this is not happening in the EU. Apparently, the necessary restructurings and the "creative destruction" did not appear or, to be more accurate, such restructurings are taking place slowly and implicitly through the market forces coming at odds with non-competitive markets, a whole series of bureaucratic restrictions and a lot of politics.

Given the historical experience, the European debt crisis could have been resolved if (1) fiat money and inflationary finance was to be excluded and also if (2) upcoming payments of matured debt could have been secured through tax revenues or

> an independent special fund to pay off outstanding government debt [...] a newly created agency independent of the treasury and with its own earmarked revenues... (Sargent 1986, p. 119).

Sargent refers to measures taken by the R. Poincare government in France (1926). Poincare took many additional measures like raising taxes to balance the budget, raise of indirect taxes and reduction of the highest income tax from 60 to 30 %, increase of customs duties, increase of basic income taxes from 12 to 18 % on income from land, from 7.2 to 12 % on income from securities, and a once-for-all tax of 7 % on the first sale of real estate or a business. The debt agency which was created to accommodate the public debt had

> ...its own earmarked revenues from the tobacco monopoly, the total receipts from the inheritance and estate taxes, and the new 7 % tax on the first sale of real estate and businesses (Sargent 1986, p. 119).

Some of the Poincare measures in 1926 are quite similar to the measures taken by the Greek government. The fundamental difference is that it is not clear that the Greek measures are oriented exclusively towards repayment of the outstanding public debt. In fact the bailout plan secures repayment of the outstanding public debt so the additional "austerity" measures seem out of place. In principle, they are not since they complement the bailout plan. However, it is not clear that this is indeed so. In other words it is not clear what is the proportion of future tax revenues and the proportion of revenues from austerity measures that will go towards servicing the public debt. It seems that the bailout plan is aimed towards servicing interest payments, and pensions/salaries of social insurance, and the additional funds will be used towards servicing capital payments. On the one hand this is not clear at all, and on the other hand the extra revenues do not seem possible to collect at all. Certainly, there cannot be a continuation of the bailout plan in the indefinite future. The purpose of any bailout plan is to help the economy in the short run, provided that the government can secure, in the medium run, the necessary funds for pensions and salaries as well as interest payments of the debt.

The Greek experience may seem to be rather idiosyncratic and not representative of what might have happened in Italy or Portugal and Spain. This is true, considering the innumerable ties between the public and the private sector, the interplay of political bureaucracy with business and banks, the reciprocal relations between political parties and special interest groups etc. Despite the idiosyncratic character of the Greek case, we cannot nevertheless see how similar debt problems can be resolved in Italy or Spain and Portugal without special—purpose Funds to service the public debt, *independently* of government bureaucracies and with *secure* holdings of revenues from taxation of various sorts.

As we pointed out, a stable monetary or currency union without an arrangement of intra-union debt is impossible. This has to be cleared out before one even considers the *formal* establishment of a union. Joint dents to a third party, depending on the amount and the time to mature, should be –along to Poincare's experience in France- the business of an independent Fund that can secure its own revenues from well specified, risk-free economic activities. Without this condition, the union will not be credible and therefore, this will reinforce the so called "speculative attacks" against its common currency.

However, there is an additional conclusion that Sargent draws:

> The essential measures that ended hyperinflation in Germany, Austria, Hungary, and Poland were, first, the creation of an independent central bank that was legally committed to refuse the government's demand for additional unsecured credit and, second, a simultaneous alteration in the fiscal policy regime (Sargent 1986, pp. 99–100).

Regarding the change in the fiscal policy regime, we have little to say beyond Sargent's competent historical presentation. However, *Sargent places too little emphasis (if at all) on the "creation of an independent central bank" that, after the hyperinflation, soon forgot its "legal commitment" and embarked on monetary and credit expansion*. This shows the value of "legal commitments" and the political interplay that can be effected between an "independent" Central Bank and the government.

References

Mongelli FP (2008) European economic and monetary integration and the optimum currency area theory, ECB working paper

Sargent TJ (1986) Rational expectations and inflation, Harper and Row

Chapter 6
What was the Theory Behind the Formation of EMU?

The author has been an alternate member of the EPC (Economic Policy Committee) representing Greece (along with the governor of the Bank of Greece and the chairman of the Council of Economic Advisors of the Ministry of Finance) during 1997–2000. Although, in this capacity, one cannot possibly know everything that happened in the "inner circles" of the European bureaucracy, one thing was clear. The bureaucracy was trying to maximize the "sphere of influence" of the euro aiming at maximizing the demand for money of this currency. The objective, at that time, was solely by revealed preference the maximum possible appreciation of the euro against the US dollar to establish euro as the world currency or one of the leading currencies. Apparently it succeeded in that, if we consider the special efforts that went into adopting the euro explicitly in Malta, the Vatican state, Monaco, San Marino etc. The prospect was also that other states in the Balkans and the North Africa will follow.

Presumably due to optimism, the appreciation of the euro was not a concern since a raise in productivity was also expected to follow, magically so to speak, from the formation of a large monetary union. Fiscal and monetary consolidation through the Maastricht Treaty was considered to be a tight budget constraint that would set the foundations for fiscal, monetary and financial stability necessary for growth. Growth was supposed to be guaranteed through the Common Support Frameworks (CSF) whose principles and layout could be traced before the 1980s.

The optimism of the Bureaucracy was not founded on the facts. The CFSs did not produce the desired results–for example they did improve local infrastructure but they did not have a noticeable impact on regional investment so they left cohesion pretty much where they found it. Without cohesion one cannot even think about a common currency but the politics of the Bureaucracy were so grandiose that, apparently, overwhelmed any criticisms. In a sense, *the magnificent vision of a unified Europe provided the ideological support for all sorts of unreasonable and misguided economic policies that led to the Maastricht Treaty and the EMU.*

In this restrictive frame of thought, no one would seriously consider to question the necessity for balanced budgets, low inflation, and tight and stable monetary policy under an "independent" ECB. That would be reasonable for a *single* nation after all, so extending it to a *whole* monetary union like the EMU was natural.

E. G. Tsionas, *The Euro and International Financial Stability*,
Financial and Monetary Policy Studies 37, DOI: 10.1007/978-3-319-01171-4_6,

After all, a nation has widely differing regions and in the context of the EMU one could think of different states as different regions of the same state.

Where was then the "fallacy of composition" in this seemingly reasonable argument? The fallacy of maximizing the demand for the new currency was similar to convincing people of the same region or state to adopt the same currency instead of, say, US dollars, gold, silver etc. At fixed exchange rates, also expected to be fixed, and *provided* the expectation was rational, there would be no real problem as any currency would be as good another. The rationality of the expectation was *not* there in the first place–in fact *all fundamentals* were against it, but nevertheless the expectation was forced by the European Bureaucracy. When the expectation turned out to be at odds with the national realities and idiosyncrasies, cohesion was still enforced: After all, what was the difference between states of the EU and states in the US?

The difference turned out to be quite significant and was located at the very foundations of the ideological misconceptions of the European Bureaucracy: Californian debts can be secured by US government bonds and they are backed for all practical purposes. But Greek debt was not intended to be backed against European tax revenues. When Greece failed due to maturing of major payments, Greece was left alone, the Commission was embarrassed and the best the EU could do was (1) to bail out the economy as far as outstanding payments were concerned (to other members of the same currency union!), and (2) impose severe austerity measures so that in the immediate future the Greek government could repay on its own these obligations, net of outstanding and forthcoming wage, salary and pension payments in view of the extreme pressure put by social insurance's holdings of Greek bonds.

The Bureaucracy usually blames the rating companies. But the rating companies follow the events, they do not create them. When outstanding debt is not backed the rating agency will naturally *recognize* the fact and it *will* give a lower rating. Taking that as a "signal" that the markets attack the euro, has so much sense as blaming illegal trading in markets with controlled prices: It is anticipated. Of course the Bureaucracy acts in a political way and cares only about the politics of the eurozone. *But the politics of the eurozone and its economics are two entirely different things.*

To be sure, this fact is historically unprecedented, given the size and importance of the venture. The desire for a political union is noble and admirable but it *cannot* be the result of an economic union. In such processes, politics have a prior and dictating role, and the economics will follow. If one lets the economics lead, then in all likelihood, one will end up with groups of political entities that are economically the same in the long—run, an event that has a very small posterior probability, so *it is likely that one will end up with as many groups as the nations involved.*

Chapter 7
Will the Eurozone Dissolve into its Constituents?

The short answer is not necessarily. First of all, the markets dictate competition of currencies in order to result into endogenously formed currency unions. When money was introduced, it had to compete with all sorts of alternative exchange media like furs, corn or clay vases and jewels. It prevailed not because someone ordered it. In fact, someone ordered gold and silver coins with his face upon it (kings, emperors etc.) precisely because that sort of money was already in use, in one form or another, in the vast majority of exchanges.

This sort of thinking makes one conceive that there is intrinsic value in gold, silver, furs, the US dollar or the euro. In fact this is not true. The emergence of money and therefore the emergence of currency is endogenous in any economy based on transactions. The same way of thinking led people think that they should peg their currency to gold. The idea seems to be outdated but it is so only with respect to what you peg in, not pegging itself. One can peg to the US dollar but we are well aware of the negative Latin American experience. One can peg 1:1 to the euro (or adopt the euro) but we are now well aware that this could prove a disaster for economies like Greece. One can even peg to gold reserves but that would be, apparently, old—fashioned.

Although old—fashioned, is it wrong? After all it will provide monetary stability and will save an economy from hyper-inflations that will necessitate restrictive monetary and public measures plus an independent Debt Fund authority that would barely survive the manipulations of bureaucracy in most European countries.

Pegging the currency to a measure of real wealth would seem to be the way out of most problems of pegging. Constraining the currency to follow mechanically another form of currency that is considered an absolute standard can prove detrimental for domestic production. By relating a national currency to the net formation of capital stock or productivity is a much better alternative. The idea is that in order to have another country's investment or another country's productivity, a country should be able to do so at some prices. These prices, in turn, should reflect the overall real terms of trade, and the effective exchange rate. Alternatively one may consider average costs at the industry level. Appropriately weighted, differences of short—run average costs should reflect the required adjustments in

E. G. Tsionas, *The Euro and International Financial Stability*,
Financial and Monetary Policy Studies 37, DOI: 10.1007/978-3-319-01171-4_7,

effective exchange rates that can be used as a rough guidance to short—run adjustments in exchange rates. If long—run average costs can be estimated, then these should be used to infer more precisely the required adjustments and in that way, a prediction about likely to be successful and stable currency unions.

One may be mislead to think that even when long—run average costs can be estimated accurately, one could come up with certain rates and these rates could be used to scale the money supply appropriately in order to secure a single currency. However, that would be impossible in the global economy with near perfect mobility of most resources. Hence, nearly identical long—run average costs in most industries would determine nearly identical exchange rates and thus a nearly stable monetary union.

But no one can preclude in advance technical change in some sectors of one country of a union that would imply a significant decline in long—run average costs. If imitation and adoption of best practice technologies is possible and relatively costless in the short—run, long—run average costs will decline accordingly in the relevant sectors of all countries in the union, if not in the whole world. In that case, perfect mobility of innovation and its adoption will not influence terms of trade or the currency union. If, to be practical, adoption of innovation by other countries takes a couple of years, the constraints that will be imposed upon fiscal and monetary realities, can be severe in that time range. These constraints are real in the EU through the complicated patent and industrial competition schemes.

Therefore, relatively costless and timely diffusion of innovation in terms of reducing long—run average costs would be the necessary and sufficient condition for a stable monetary union in the long—term. Of course, the practical question is how a central authority could "peg" its currency to long—run average costs, when innovation is uncertain and its adoption is not always costless and timely. In fact, no central authority can do that in the sense of prior planning. In that sense, all monetary unions face non-trivial risks of dissolution in the long—run, even in the absence of fiat money creation and in the absence of irresponsible fiscal policies or non-backed public debt policies.

What prevents nearly costless and timely diffusion of innovation and reduction of long—run average costs? The primary factor is, of course, the nationalist barriers that exist in any currency union that involves different state entities that are not part of the same state. The essence of *national* competition in a monetary union is to gain *relative* comparative advantage, even in the short—run, and thus capitalize on lower relative prices that imply, in effect, a national advantage in the currency union or for that matter, relative to any other state in the world. A firm in a particular section of a country would think in the same way; to gain an advantage and increase its profits.

The relevant question is not how to contain the firm in question, the sector, or the country inside or outside a currency union but why the given firm chooses a particular currency to realize its profits. Since profits are calculated in real terms, the particular currency is of no concern *provided it will remain stable* during the time period in which production starts until the realization of nominal profits. If the firm deals with clients who use a currency pegged to a long—run quantity, like long—run average costs, it is reasonably safe to assume that the time horizon of the firm falls well within that interval. Highly volatile currencies will, apparently, be avoided, and volatility expectations are formed based on past information. Moreover, a currency pegged to a long—run quantity, is highly likely to allow enough time for the innovation to spread in all sectors and regions according to factor endowments and/or relative prices. In that sense, the long—run peg allows enough time for the whole currency union to adjust to the new situation and thus lay the real, technically-based foundation for the endogenously determined survival of the monetary union.

But a "technically-based foundation" is not the same as "*market*-based foundation". In other words this is only a supply-side argument, not an argument from general or even *partial equilibrium*. Partial equilibrium after technical innovation is not general equilibrium from the point of view of the currency union or the world as a whole. Such considerations are unavoidable. If all currencies are gold-pegged and Spain discovers new gold mines in Latin America, the relative trade position of Spain will improve, and the price of gold will go down, allowing for the necessary time. Similarly, if all currencies are productivity-pegged and Greece suddenly improves its productivity, the relative trade position of Greece will improve, and the price (average cost) of innovation will go down, giving the motive for other countries to follow on the same path, *grosso modo*.

The comparison of gold to productivity is rough. Using gold to produce more gold coins with the face of king Ferdinand or queen Isabella on them, and throw them into circulation to pay the bills of the palace, does not mean a whole lot. But a productivity enhancement by the Greeks, in providing cheaper solar or aeolic (wind-based) energy, for example, is quite different. Any fund (a public debt fund is only the obvious example) could use the future revenues of the Greeks but not the new Spanish gold coins, anticipating higher inflation and price level. In the very short—run one could profit from arbitrage in Spanish currency, but this very short—runs would be really short. In the Greek case, instead, the drachma would appreciate and drachma-pegging would be a reasonable choice in the long—run. Any union that involves the drachma would be sustainable in the foreseeable future.

In a situation of detrimentally high inflation and continuous devaluation, it is reasonable to relate the currency to anything fixed and peg it. Even communist commissars like Trotsky have suggested that in all seriousness. After a period of detrimentally high inflation and continuous devaluation, the drachma or the liretta and peseta could be pegged to the US dollar for a short period of time to make sure that exchanges and trade are stable. After that period the actual terms of trade will be determined by relative prices and thus, relative productivity. Without improvements in productivity, the currency cannot appreciate and reach an equilibrium level, given that the government is determined to orient its policies towards balanced budget and exclude creation of fiat money.

The argument seems to be dated at first sight: Devaluate the currency or impose import and exchange controls to gain time in order to improve productivity. The qualification is that, in fact, this has never happened in the past and most governments felt comfortable with devaluation or foreign trade controls of all sorts. Will there be a political authority that will follow a devaluation and inflationary policy mix to address the public debt and deficit issues, *and then* provide all the initiatives necessary for a substantial improvement of productivity in sectors with the newly created comparative advantages? Although it is hard to tell, this constitutes a *condition* for sustained growth and eventual resolution of all the puzzles that it will face during a depression; for example higher tax rates that will, fortunately, yield higher tax revenues versus the depression of total demand that will actually yield less tax revenues.

Backed against riskless revenues from newly created comparative advantages, servicing the public debt (after a possible restructuring) should be feasible. This action would give the necessary time for the government to restructure its public finances, including more rational or optimal tax rates, and an improvement in the tax collection mechanism. Moreover, "newly created comparative advantages" do not necessarily mean discoveries of oil or natural gas reserves, or the willingness of the German industry to invest in cheap solar energy, whose price in Germany is extremely high. New comparative advantages *always* emerge from a crisis, as the result of changes in relative prices that affect significantly the short—run and long—run average cost curves. *Assets or services created from these comparative advantages can always serve as backing of new money creation*, as in the Poincare paradigm in France.

To the Classical economists money was merely a veil of economic activity. The Austrian economists like Hayek and von Mises did not make the same mistake, and of course Keynes did not make the same mistake either. Active monetary policy to increase the price level and lower real wages is a well known prescription of the Keynesian agenda. Credit and money was also high in the agenda of Austrian economists.

In a world in crisis, where different currencies compete, credit in one currency is not the same as currency in another. The firm will always prefer to borrow funds in terms of a stable currency that is also expected to be stable until repayment. Furthermore, borrowing in terms of currency that is expected to depreciate in a few years, is also a good option, particularly if expected productivity of the new projects of the firm is large. Of course, depreciation has to be understood from the point of view of actual inflation. New investment opportunities will most likely arise in members of a monetary union, whose actual inflation is expected to rise considerably in the future.

Does it mean that we should expect huge investments in Greece? Probably not. Of course during the crisis, credit is also limited so the financing of new projects from the Greek financial system will also be limited. But since interest rates are well below the "natural" rate of interest (the one that imply satisfaction of the excess demand for cash) investment opportunities do exist that are not available elsewhere in the Eurozone. *This sets Greece apart from Eurozone in terms of future investment and growth prospects.*

For the Eurozone or any monetary union, the imposition of a fixed interest rate as an administrative measure, means that actual interest rates (determined from the internal rates of return for worthwhile projects and the demand for cash) will differ and thus capital mobility must take place until *actual* interest rates are equal among themselves. But the problem remains that nominal interest rates will be different since there will always be excess demand for money due to the credit restraints and the tight monetary policy of the ECB, which affects countries like Greece, Portugal, Spain, and Italy or Ireland with a significant overhead in terms of capital and interest payments on the public debt. But then *the monetary union, in order to be sustainable, has to leave interest rates to be determined by the money market,* via *the equilibration of supply and demand for euro in the different member states*.

The problem with this operation of market forces is that the average interest rate at the level of the Monetary Union will not necessarily equate supply and demand in no specific country but for the union as a "whole". Part of the reason is that actual rates of inflation are quite different. Another reason is that the demand of money is quite heterogeneous in the EMU. But is it not the same with regions of a given country with large regional differences, different steady states of growth etc.? It is indeed the same, but nobody ever claimed that the *political* union of regions is also a good *economic* union. This is and still was a *political* issue ever since the first national states were formed. To use the *same* argument for the EMU, even when a common currency is apparently catastrophic, cannot be a good argument.

In that sense, the currency is not so much the problem. The problem, as we remarked on several occasions is much deeper. It does not even have to do with the fundamentally different institutional and economic structures in the EMU. It has to do with misguided policies and mistakes of the European Central Bank. In that sense currency is a veil, from a new perspective (that is, other than the standard neoclassical view.) It hides the deeper reasons that contribute to the essence of a successful monetary union. From the economic theory point of view, it is not so much the absolute price level (denominated in some currency) but what the common currency implies about the *relative* prices. *The answer is that it will distort the relative prices, producing allocative inefficiency, if and when the equilibrium in the credit markets is distorted.* Most banks in the EMU would prefer to lend in USD of GBP under the expectation that these currencies will appreciate. If investors have no choice but to accept these terms, *the new credit market equilibria will imply further depreciations of the euro, until this currency is useless for practical purposes.*

The driving force behind this equilibrium is not the productivity differentials between the EMU and Great Britain, the US and other major competitors. Such differentials always exist but tend to converge over time. The real driving force is that economic policies change relative prices so that false productivity differentials arise that make certain investments look profitable when, in fact, they are not. If adjustment of productivity takes approximately as much as the completion of a marginally profitable new investment plan, it is clear that currency matters and it is much better that currency clubs also reflect productivity clubs in a world scale. It seems that the EU was aiming to maintain *approximate productivity convergence* among country members. With the Treaty of Maastricht we have nothing of the sort but regional funding and support for infrastructure investment has been quite extensive. Another factor that affects negatively the whole process is, of course, the rigidity of almost all European markets, and the absence of the private sector from its regional cohesion plans. We must reiterate: A condition that was ignored in the formation of the EMU but also in academic literature was the question of public debts. It was assumed that the inter-temporal government budget constraint will approximately hold in view of the Treaty of Maastricht, but the policy authorities ignored the fact that there is also a side or transversality condition: The condition for "no Ponzi schemes". The experience with the EMU has not been so bad but *it was precisely the non-satisfaction of the transversality condition, or mounting public debts in the South, that effectively puts the EMU before the danger of dissolution.* Part of the problem was, of course, the "creative statistics" of several countries but nobody can deny that the political authorities knew and problem and largely ignored it until it exploded after 2008.

The policy of easy and cheap credit, contributed to the accumulation of public debts even more. Moreover, a fundamental concern was ignored in the formation of EMU: Different countries have different obligations to the commercial banks so unless debts are contained or they can be mutually canceled out, they are bound to explode at some point in time. To sustain these debts, the ECB should proceed with credit expansion but after some point this expansion will no longer be possible without creating inflation and business cycles or more "asymmetric" shocks. We thus come to the crux of the matter: *"Asymmetric shocks" will be distributed among the countries of an economic and monetary union so they do not present deadly dangers: The real problem is with the inter-temporal government budget constraints.*

Besides, *there is no such thing as a "shock" since everything is endogenous in the international economy and can be traced back to the marginal productivity of capital in the time-profile of production.* The idea that given the factors of production, the production functions shifts up or down as the result of "random" causes is, for the most part, totally foreign to entrepreneurial reality. What is in fact a "shock" is nothing else but a re-allocation of the factors of production among different activities; this fact, of course, escapes the attention of standard "production functions" and particularly the "aggregate" production function. The idea of shocks themselves, suggests a fundamental misunderstanding in the interdependence of the various stages and sectors of production, which depends on demand and the configuration of prices. Abstracting from this fact and blaming it all on "productivity shocks" is a lame excuse for doing partial equilibrium analysis whereas, in fact, general equilibrium would suggest that shocks come only from truly exogenous factors like technological innovation, which of course does not happen on a regular basis and not on a persistent or cyclical basis. To be more precise, for the European economy, a change in demand could be a shock and the same is true for a change of demand from the US, but productivity per se cannot be shocked unless there are deeper reasons relating to technological innovation.

Marginal productivity of capital can indeed change, but only as a result of deeper reasons as well, like for example changes in the interest rates or relative prices.

So *the question of an effective monetary union was addressed in the wrong manner, from the very beginning*. Any "shock" can be truly absorbed by the system if prices and interest rates are free to adjust. Since interest rates and relative prices were relatively free in the EU suggests that the effect from adverse "asymmetric shocks" would have been mitigated. Even with limited capital mobility the structure of production would have been changed in view of changes in the relative prices of goods in the different stages (including factors) and the markets would easily achieve a new equilibrium. The fundamental problem was that the public sector was not controlled and the problem of balanced budgets or reductions in deficits and debts was mostly left to the individual governments. In effect, a balancing problem was created where some countries S were more exposed to the banking sectors of other countries N, without a similar exposure of N or a positive stance of N with respect to main creditors of S. In that sense, the budget constraint at the EU level could not be met since the debt markets would not clear.

Chapter 8
Can There be an Efficient Dissolution of a Monetary Union?

Historical experience with monetary unions suggests that they were dissolved when it was found advantageous to inflate the currency by changing the silver content of the papal coinage. The Latin Monetary Union of 1865 undermined its own foundation before it adopted the gold standard in 1878 and was sustained, formally at least, until 1927. It is no accident that it the gold standard was found to be the only way to preclude individual members from engaging in inflationary policies. The union was dismantled as the result of the First World War and its financing. That was hardly an efficient way to dissolve the monetary union and suggests that returning back to national currencies is not a way to ensure international financial stability.

Any efficient dissolution must be subject to some constraints for the individual currencies. *First*, no fiat money creation. *Second*, backing on future tax revenues, or real assets, and its services. *Third*, almost balanced budgets. *Fourth*, fully independent central banks, that will refuse to accommodate the government's need for inflationary finance. It is unlikely that these four conditions will be met as the dissolution of the union will be effected precisely because the discipline imposed forbids embarking on this enterprise whose future is, most certainly, gloomy. The question is twofold: (1) How will this affect the EU as a whole, and (2) how the international financial and banking system will be affected.

A European—wide depreciation of its new currencies against the dollar will increase European exports in the short-run since terms of trade will be affected. This will provide the necessary funds in terms of taxation to set into motion new growth plans for most European countries, provided they will also actively seek to reform their institutions and their markets towards more transparency, simplicity and competition.

In turn, a short-run European—wide depreciation will mobilize new investment affecting positively the flows of the international financial and banking system. The need for more credit will undoubtedly bring new American or Asian banks in the European stage, until international credit markets complete the process of flows necessary to attain a new equilibrium. Of course, one cannot "speculative attacks" on certain currencies. Speculative attacks are only possible when the fundamental determinants of the equilibrium in foreign exchange markets differ considerably

E. G. Tsionas, *The Euro and International Financial Stability*,
Financial and Monetary Policy Studies 37, DOI: 10.1007/978-3-319-01171-4_8,

among countries. If exchange rates are allowed to float freely, any speculative attack can only be a very short-run phenomenon. The misconception is that buying and selling one currency for another, is a bad thing. In fact, it is the only way to lead towards equilibrium in the foreign exchange markets, *when currencies are not exchanged according to the "law of one price"*, that is when arbitrage opportunities are allowed because of government interventions or international agreements.

Destabilization of the international financial system because of dissolution of the euro is simply not possible. *In fact, the destabilization of the international financial system after mid 2008 is precisely due to the failure of the euro* to solve a simple problem: The problem of public debt. This mounting problem was left to be solved by the European Council and the ECB where, in fact, an independent institution should be in charge of dealing with this problem at the national level. It is inconceivable why a national problem was allowed to become a problem for the Euro itself and, moreover, why allowances were not made for the payment of the forthcoming debt obligations. The substantial upward revision of the Greek deficit from 6.5 % to almost 13 % could not have been a reason since the debt was unsustainable given any amount of public deficits. This complete lack of foresight was hidden only because it was intermingled with another problem, the bailing out of European commercial banks and the simultaneous budget crisis in Portugal, Spain and Ireland.

From that viewpoint fiscal consolidation revealed an unprecedented lack of foresight and a rather hasty treatment of the problems of the budget constraints. Fiscal solvency ignoring the forthcoming debt payments, that is fiscal solvency over a time horizon, was apparently ignored by focusing on the "aggregate" statistics of deficits as a percentage of GDP.

Following a possible dissolution of the euro, there will necessarily be a transition period to a new equilibrium of international credit markets. Not all markets will adjust with the same speed and this will, of course, affect different countries at differing degrees. *The fact is that we will be moving towards a new, healthier equilibrium* of credit at the international level, which is the essence of globalization. The adjustments during the transition period can be mitigated by the constraints we have posed (nearly balanced budgets, no fiat money etc.). A mandate that enforces these constraints, accompanied by a mandate on a fully independent public debt authority will place a constraint upon the appetite of national governments for inflationary finance and, from that point of view it will minimize the probability of destructive economic policies with adverse effects on welfare.

An Independent Public Debt Authority *will repay* capital and interest payments timely and to full extent. Of course, the authority will have to rely on backing that is, existing and future tax revenues, capital services, new revenues etc. Will national economic policies accommodate the independent authority in that respect? For one, expected tax revenues will also be used to create money so it might seem that there is a conflict of interest here, in which the national government, naturally, has the upper hand. Of course there are trade offs here but the independent public debt authority must be given the priority. The authority cannot use the entire amount of backed—up funds but it should be given the right to a certain percentage of these funds, say 50 %. Some financing processes must also be developed to accommodate the independent authority. For example claims on export revenues and, more importantly, clearing procedures on mutual obligations between bank holders of the debt in another country with the latter country's claims on foreign titles. It seems that *the biggest anomaly in the recent debt crisis of the EMU is precisely* the fact that such financing or clearing procedures were not used. Certain European countries thought that full repayment in cash of their banks' claims on Greek titles could not be arranged by other means. They also thought that it is not wise to do what is done in the private sector when a firm cannot repay immediately; extension of maturity. This would constitute a "credit event", they thought. *In fact the credit event itself was the inability of the EMU to deal with a problem that the Bureaucracy never anticipated*, the problem of public debt itself which, of course, was there since the creation of the euro. Intertemporal fiscal consolidation was largely ignored, apparently and this lead to immense problems when it was realized that beyond the aggregate statistics one has to consider several other facts that would signal to the international markets that the euro was weak.

The EMU authorities need only look at maturities of the debt to realize that a major problem would indeed explode at the end of 2008 and the beginning of 2009. The mere fact that there are deficits which are incompatible with debt payments maturing at a given date should have provided a clear signal to the monetary authorities that major problems are likely to emerge irrespective of the exact deficit-to-GDP ratios. Another variable that went out of proportion in formulating the hectic policies of the bureaucracy was, undoubtedly, the credit ratings by certain experts, too well known to name them here. These experts provide an average econometrician's estimate of the probability of default using textbook—based methods for the most part, apart from subjective judgments. Such ratings will, naturally, affect an investor's willingness to buy Greek or Italian bonds. The Greek and Italian governments apparently want the revenues from these titles badly, because they run large deficits and, in the Greek case, they cannot even pay the wages of public servants and the pensions of retired individuals.

To borrow (irrespective of maturity) to pay salaries and pensions does not look very good to foreign buyers so they demand higher interest rates which is, of course, responsible for the large spreads of Greek government bonds. For example, the 10-year Greek government bonds paid, on the average, 12 % as of October 2011. But on the other hand, the end of November 2011 auction of German government bonds did not go well either. In a monetary union, it is likely that spreads might be affected by the spreads of the country which is in trouble.

Would it be a better plan to issue Eurobonds well before the explosion of the debt crisis? That would have been a wise provision but in the aftermath of the debt crisis it would not provide the right signals to the international markets. It would have been a destabilizing act whereas other measures were called for. Bilateral settlements of debt payments would have been preferable, as in the case of the

Latin American debt crisis of the 1980s and the necessary time horizon to complete the agreements would not have been much greater compared to the time that it took to "bail out" the Southern economies.

To co-ordinate all the relevant data and all bits of information that are necessary in order to solve the problem of an optimum currency area, appears overly difficult. This is not because the economic theory is lacking but because the collection of necessary data and information is enormous. We have *certain* degrees of labor mobility among sectors and countries—that differ depending on both—, we have *certain* degrees of wage flexibility, *certain* degrees of fiscal coordination, and *certain* degrees of flexibility against the euro, depending on the policies of the ECB. All these "certain" degrees are, of course, totally unknown in advance, and we cannot claim we are in a position to predict the flows of capital that will result from a given shock. *If the task of absorbing the shock should be left to the market, so should be settled the question of policies to maintain the stability of the euro.*

The question of a stable economic and monetary Union is a function of several variables. *First* and foremost, the Central Bank should not intervene in terms of interest rates or creating artificial credit (and, of course, "money"). *Second*, the optimal configuration of currencies, or the optimal and stable economic and monetary Union itself, should be determined by the markets. *Apart from the problem of commitment, the game of unions involves many other factors, which boil down to a single question: What will the Union do when "shocks" ("asymmetric" or not) are experienced.* Policies that change the interest rate or expand credit, beyond savings, will result in malinvestments that will propagate the recession, and create severe disequilibria in the labor, goods and capital markets via the artificial distortion of expectations of profitability in the time—sequence of production. In the first place, such shocks are really induced by the very same policies that are proposed to solve the problems.

If the optimal economic and monetary Union is to be determined by the markets, the requirement is to let the international financial system work under a configuration of freely floating and freely substitutable currencies, so that transactions can be performed in any number of given currencies. *From the system of competing currencies, the markets itself will determine the optimal configuration of a currency Union.* We are not to deny that the prescription involves informational and transaction costs, but it is not a system that is unheard of. For example, European mortgages could be denominated in several currencies in the past, including the Swiss franc and such options were offered readily by the banks. More flexible products could be developed to accommodate the need for diversification and insurance against risk, on the part of the consumer, but also the business sector. Under competing currencies, the development of such programs could be made endogenous, fully insuring against macroeconomic risks.

The informational and transaction costs are present when adoption of new currency is involved. Freely competing currencies, resulting in the adoption of more stable currencies, can work in the long—run if the Central Banks refrain from arbitrary changes in interest rates and arbitrary changes in money supplies or credit. This is, of course, difficult to achieve, but it is difficult precisely because the policies of Central Banks are hard to conceive as "commodities" in the international markets. Since the policies of Central Banks affect the value of money, and its relative price compared to other denominations, eventually the more stable currencies will be chosen by economic agents to realize their plans. If the stability of currency is altered, the Central Bank will realize that it can gain a *short-run* advantage that cannot be maintained in the *long run*: The short-run appreciation will be followed by depreciation, and conversion of obligations to other currencies, that maintain the initial configuration of relative prices for the investment plans of the private sector.

If, indeed, a number of countries can converge to adoption of common currency in an *endogenous* way, that would constitute an optimum currency area which, in fact, could not have been found by other means (political, for example). Several groups of countries could, in principle, form unions in that manner. Will these currency groups be stable? If the Central Banks are committed to freely determined interest rates and a credit policy that respects available savings, there is no reason why a country should abandon the monetary Union if indeed all contracts can be freely agreed, and accommodated, in different currencies. The problem is that the Central Banks will have no incentive to do so and, in fact, they have the incentive to depreciate temporarily the currency. Since their currency will be soon abandoned, in part, depending on informational and transaction costs, eventually the Central Banks will opt for a floating system without interventions. Because of political priorities, this obvious optimum is not likely to prevail soon, but *it is useful to realize and know that it is the only available action in the long run.*

Incentives and constraints are not given; they have to be learned over a period of time, and what is true for firms is also true for the Central Banks, as well as for political authorities. Unfortunately, the horizon for a firm and a political authority, are quite different so, contrary to business games, political games have a much shorter horizon. Although the case of monetary Unions is open, because of that, the case for freely competing currencies in international markets is more determined: No currency groups can "gain" by artificial means, in terms on interest rate policies or credit and monetary policies, unless there are *permanent* productivity shocks or favorable (relative to others) *permanent* changes in the structure of technology.

The practical question is why the US dollar or the UK pound is not adopted in transactions, at least in medium—term or long—term projects, instead of the euro, when the euro is depreciating and is losing confidence. In fact, the answer is that the euro is depreciating *precisely because* medium—term or long—term projects are less profitable relative to the marginal productivity of capital in the US or the UK. One could, in principle, borrow or lend in terms of any currency, but the uncertainty resulting from the policies of the ECB or the Fed, is overwhelming. Without a credible solution to the game of Central Banks, the denomination of contracts to another currency would involve too much risk, *given* the pre-commitments of the ECB. If and when these pre-commitments prove themselves wrong, we should expect a "flight from the euro" and its further devaluation.

Apparently, the stability of the international financial system rests upon a broader issue; the co-ordination and commitment of Central Banks. If this cannot take place, the markets can self—correct, without too much volatility, if currencies are freely competing. In fact, the markets are self—correcting, implying fluctuations of the exchange rate of the euro relative to US dollar. *If these fluctuations are "too large", this is not a problem of the markets themselves, but a problem inherent to the marginal productivities in EU relative to the US.*

Currently, it is unquestionable that the economic situation in Southern Europe, places a burden upon the euro. Public debts in the South are too high, "productivity" is relatively "low" compared to the North and fiscal harmonization seems to be questionable. Witnessing the fact that contracts in the South are still denominated in terms of the euro, instead of a more stable currency, is naturally a puzzle. But *what is a "more stable currency" in Southern Europe?* One could abandon the euro, but what currency would be its substitute? The recent upward trend in gold prices provides an answer. As this does not relate *explicitly* to the issue of new contracts, or re-domination of existing ones, it is natural to expect "flight from the euro" in the form of abandonment of investment projects and the subsequent reduction in output and employment. In fact, this is nothing but a restructuring, at the EU level, of production in favor or less "capitalistic" processes and methods of production.

The reason why this does not relate *explicitly* to the issue of new contracts is the *expectation* that the ECB will do *something* to appreciate the euro. The ECB, indeed, announced a decrease of interest rates to 1 % accompanied by a credit expansion. It will take a year or two to evaluate objectively the effects of this policy, but the results are clear: The decrease of interest rates facilitates an artificial expansion of the "capitalistic" sectors whereas in fact, the shortening of the average length of production in the EU, as a whole, *requires a re-direction of investment to the later stages or close—to final—sectors, necessitated by the negative asymmetric shocks in the South.*

The final sector has to compete *internationally* in order to provide real, overall, benefits for the EU. Whether this is possible is an open question, and depends on the relative prices of the service sector in the EU relative to the *international competition*. The process of adjustment may imply a relative strengthening of the competition, thus exposing more the close—to—final sectors of the South, and depriving the Union, as a whole, from its relative advantages in that respect. Therefore, the possibility of shifting resources to the more profitable close—to—final sectors *outside* the South arises.

The fact that there is international competition not only in the favored (by the shock) close—to—final sectors of the South but also in the early stages of production located in the North—whose prices fall and *cannot* attract investment in the *long run* under certain conditions, including price stability- has certain implications. In the short-run, the service or close—to—final goods sector cannot recover if international competition can provide similar services at lower prices (for example, tourism). In the *long run*, the international capital flow and reallocation of investment will not be favorable for the EU. In a *long term process of adjustment*, the lower prices of European capital goods will be absorbed by the international markets, followed by a *gradual* increase of their prices etc. In the process, the euro will tend to depreciate at first, and *after a long period of time*, it will tend to appreciate as the result of the recovery of the demand and prices of capital goods. The depreciation in the long-run, will be felt more strongly as the result of the lower prices of capital goods and the fierce competition of the South in terms if its close—to—final or service sectors.

Chapter 9
Complete Fiscal Freedom in the Transition Period?

The question whether to allow complete fiscal freedom for national governments in the immediate period following the dissolution of the euro is not so much related to stability of the international financial system: Most Europeans governments *will not* do so. Electoral and other motives might, of course, make *some* of them resort of inflationary finance. The economic history of Greece in the 1980s shows us that inflationary finance has a limit and, after that, governments rely on borrowing. In the transition period or after, that will not be possible since it is already anticipated by the international markets.

Allowing some inflationary finance might seem beneficial in the short run for certain governments (in Greece and Italy mainly, but also Portugal, Spain, and Ireland) to put their budgets "on track". For example the Greek Budgets after 2009 were proved to be totally incorrect, and the same is true for the Greek budget of 2012 which shows as additional feature, in that it is inconsistent even in its basic arithmetic. The fact of the matter is that *the Greek economy is in need of several institutional changes*:

Competition is unheard of in several if not all markets, tax evasion is as large as GDP itself, the Greek Revenue Service cannot collect revenues anymore, the information and computer systems are inadequate to deal with cross-checking, government spending is still going up, there is no accounting (balance sheets) for public hospitals or regional and prefectural administrations. The government did not even know the precise number of public employees in 2010 and it was necessary to perform an internet-based survey just to figure out the *number*. This state of affairs has apparently to change. To many economists this might seem like an unreal situation but *in fact it is a problem of lack of incentives and lack of mechanism design*.

One, in principle could allow complete fiscal freedom. But the fundamental principle behind this generous act must have an objective: To change institutions and mentality of individual economic agents with a well defined system of rewards and punishments which is, in simple term, the essence of mechanism design. The critical issue (often ignored in the theory of mechanism design) is that rewards and punishments must have a probability of realization close to one. This can only be

E. G. Tsionas, *The Euro and International Financial Stability*,
Financial and Monetary Policy Studies 37, DOI: 10.1007/978-3-319-01171-4_9,

enforced and can be learned by individual economic agents only through its actual application in practice.

Of course, changing institutions and mentality is inherently difficult. Even when this is not so, the government will try to maintain what is, in fact, to be abolished. During the great depression, for example, Hayek argues that the government:

> …succeeded, by means of an easy-money policy, inaugurated as soon as the symptoms of an impeding reaction were noticed, in prolonging the boom for two years beyond what otherwise would have been its natural end. And the when the crisis finally occurred, for almost two more years, deliberate attempts were made to prevent, by all conceivable means, the normal process of liquidation (Hayek 1935, p 162).

Preventing what is bound to be destroyed in the creative process is, of course, no positive action. But Hayek continues on to provide guidance on credit policy during expansions and recessions, stating the obvious –obvious, after observing what has happened in the recent financial crisis:

> … the simple fact of an increase of production and trade forms no justification for an expansion of credit, and that –save in an acute crisis- bankers need not be afraid to harm production by overcaution (Hayek 1935, p 125).

In an acute crisis, therefore, overcaution of the banking sector is not justified at all. Part of the reason is that new opportunities will arise. After the recent financial crisis of 2008, another part that completes the arguments is that explicit guarantees were given to the financial sector, securing its deposits and promising bailout plans for individual plans. But such plans are only useful if the financial sector is willing to take more, not less risk, in financing new investment. Without this provision, the explicit guarantees (amounting to almost 120 billion euros in Greece) are empty of content. Of course, it is the business of *national* commercial banks, not the business of a *Central* Bank, to calculate the risks of individual banks or individual investment projects.

Hayek preferred an international monetary authority thus opposing the Keynesian idea of national, independent monetary policies stating that:

> … any mechanical principle (such as the gold standard) which at least secures some conformity of monetary changes in the national area to what would happen under a truly international monetary system is far preferable to numerous independent and independently regulated national currencies (Hayek 1939, p 93).

Even the gold standard would be far better, for Hayek, and it would be as good as *pegging to anything relatively constant* as long as monetary changes are synchronized at the international scale. Indeed, "*any mechanical principle*" would be as good as another. But we have to look deeper into Hayek's thought for Hayek did not favor monetary stability for its own sake. Hayek, in fact, looked into raw material or wholesale price stabilization (White 1999, p 177) and he did not advocate low inflation or inflation targets as in the EMU. In fact, *Hayek was looking for the principal sources of price fluctuations to be identified as common factors of the variability of relative prices.* In this essay, we have argued for nothing less or nothing more.

In Hayek's thought the idea of creative destruction is present in that a depression will destroy malinvestment or "maladjustments of the industry" that were made during the previous boom of an unwarranted business expansion (Hayek 1933, p 19) caused by an unwarranted credit expansion. The final conclusion is reasonable:

> … discrepancies in demand and supply in different industries, discrepancies between the distribution of demand and the allocation of factors of production, are in the last analysis due to some distortion in the price system that has directed resources to false uses (Hayek 1975, p 7).

The role of relative prices is identified in Hayek (1933, p 43): Monetary shocks that change the rate of interest, subsequently alters relative prices and triggers a boom that will be necessarily followed by a recession to clear out the created "malinvestments". Before the crisis of 2008 we had, beyond any doubt, an investment boom created by an expansion of credit. *Although the monetary expansion in the US was not the single explanatory factor, it is certainly true that this was one major factor of the 2008 depression.*

It is well known that general price level stabilization meant *nothing* to Hayek (since relative prices were the key variables) and that he also believed that creating new employment through monetary policy "… *we lay the foundations for a future period of worse unemployment*" (Hayek 1975, p 7).

In addition Hayek put forward the idea of free competition among currencies (Hayek 1978, esp. p 19). The idea is that strong currencies will eventually dominate and will be used as means of transactions, by free dealing in currencies of other nations within the territories of a given nation so that consumers will determine the equilibrium currency allocation as for any other commodity. Finally, Hayek (1991, p 29) comes to the concept of private money, as a natural consequence, which requires "…*a common composition of the standard index number*". In a sense, Hayek's proposition is directly comparable to our proposal of dissolution along the lines of "productivity" or other similar measures, provided money is backed by risk—free future returns on assets.

From Hayek's point of view we can say that the EMU focused too much on "macroeconomics" as developed or understood by the Keynesians. The interpreters of Keynes, and perhaps Keynes himself, believed that an all—powerful central authority can perform fiscal and monetary policy to increase employment and income at practically no cost. Hayek opposed that view on microeconomic grounds, based on the subtle operations of credit expansion and monetary policy through the channels of the economy. In a sense, the Keynesian arguments call for a "quick and dirty" dealing with the recession whereas the more subtle Hayekian arguments deal with the causes of the depression which can be traced back to credit expansion and monetary policy *before* the recession. Of course, the all—powerful central authority of Keynes materializes in the modern Bureaucracy of the EU and the roots of the Keynesian idea, in that respect, can be traced back to the Soviet paradigm of the early 1920s. The tracing of ideas, apparently made

Hayek (as well as others) to relate to fascism and totalitarianism of the same era and finally produce an economic theory of freedom.

In that sense we need to go back to relative prices as opposed to *general* price level stabilization. But relative prices reflect marginal productivities which, in turn, guide profit—based business decisions, in the absence of monetary and credit distortions (of the average interest rate). Hayek's suggestion to focus on money or monies, is orthogonal to central government control, essentially imply that money is not neutral, and authentic investment plans with non-negligible probability of positive return, should be allowed to perform freely in that environment; where authenticity means that credit or arbitrary money creation does not alter the interest rate based on which all calculations for non-trivial investment plans take place. Apparently, we do not have to take private monies for granted, as we do not have to take for granted the full convertibility of currencies. The essential point is to secure minimal interference to relative prices, avoid artificial credit or monetary expansions that will, at some point in time, with probability one, lead to a recession.

With the EMU and the Maastricht Treaty, monetary and credit expansion were made much more subtle compared to Keynesian policies. Hayek notes that:

> … the present expansion of money […] has gone into entirely different channels. The additional expenditure has been much more widely dispersed (Hayek 1975, p 20).

In the past, the sequence of money and credit expansion could have been traced entirely to investment and the capital producing sector. But "*the present expansion of money*" can be traced to regional cohesion funds, capital transfers to the southern Europe, and even the ability of the Greek government to provide its banking sector with an insurance fund amounting to 120 billion euros. When this amount can be used by an independent Public Debt Authority to repay the debt fully and timely, what is the purpose of maintaining it?

Hayek expressed the simple idea that some banks can fail because they supported investment plans that were not really profitable; they only appeared so after a credit expansion and an artificial boost of their productivity. Apparently such banks need to suffer the consequences precisely like the investment plans that failed since banks have unwisely financed these projects (Spring 2005, p 8). This is a healthy outcome of the depression; not a bad outcome that needs to be corrected by economic policy.

But the whole EMU—based idea of international financial stability seems to rest on the unreasonable proposition that the EFSM needs to finance *every* bank that failed, in order to protect consumer's savings. The healthy response is that the central bank can guarantee and protect the savings but not the entire portfolio of the bank. If, after paying savings plus interest, the bank is not profitable then the bank needs to be left out of the financial system at least temporarily. This is what financial stability is all about after all; not having to deal with highly risky banks or other financial intermediaries.

References

Hayek FA (1933) Monetary theory and the trade cycle. Harcourt, Brace & Co, New York
Hayek FA ([1935] 1967) Prices and production, Kelley AM, 2nd edn. New York
Hayek FA (1939) Price Expectations, monetary disturbances, and malinvestments. In: Hayek (ed) Profits, interest, and investment. Routledge and Kegan Paul, London, pp 135–156
Hayek FA (1975) Two Types of Mind. In: Hayek (ed) The trend of economic thinking and Bartley WW III, Stephen K (eds) The Collected Works of Hayek FA, Vol. 3. Routledge, London and University of Chicago Press, Chicago 1991, pp 49–55
Hayek FA (1978) New studies in philosophy, politics and economics. University of Chicago Press, Chicago
Hayek FA (1991) The trend of economic thinking. In: Bartley WW III, Stephen K (eds) Essays on political economists and economic history. University of Chicago Press, Chicago and Routledge, London
Spring (2005) Hayek's theory of money and cycles: retrospective and reappraisal. Quart J Aus Econ 9(1):3–14
White LH (1999) Hayek's monetary theory and policy: a critical reconstruction. J Money, Credit and Banking 31(1):109–120

Chapter 10
Understanding Crises and Recessions

To understand the essence of a crisis or depression, as a basically monetary phenomenon, is necessary. If the crisis has been the result of a credit expansion then proposing credit expansion as a cure, would be an absurd idea. Indeed, the 2008 crisis resulted from an unprecedented expansion in the housing market in the US but it was transmitted to Europe only because credit was already loose, given tight monetary policies. Indeed, European and US investment and inventories were huge just before 2008 (and for the whole period 2000–2008), the same was also the case in Greece, and Greece in particular experienced and unprecedented expansion of credit on all fronts (household, business, etc.). As Hayek writes:

> Once the monetary causes have brought about that development in the whole economic system, which is known as a boom, sufficient forces have already been set in motion to ensure that, sooner or later, when the monetary influence has ceased to operate, a crisis must occur. The "cause" of the crisis is, then, the disequilibrium of the whole economy occasioned by monetary changes and maintained through a longer period, possibly, by a succession of further monetary changes—a disequilibrium the origin of which can only be explained by monetary disturbances (Hayek 1935, p 67).

For good or bad, therefore, the prediction is that a monetary or credit expansion, produces a mismatch between expected and actual relative prices, which gives rise to allocative inefficiency in the short run, and misdirects investment resources to activities that appear to be profitable but in reality they are not. In turn, a crisis must occur, which amounts to nothing more or nothing less than destruction of capital that has been misallocated as the result of the artificial change in interest rates, and the subsequent distortion of relative prices.

Given tight monetary policies one may wonder whether the commercials banks or the central bank can "create" additional credit to accommodate what they perceive as higher demand for cash. At first sight this may seem impossible but it is not inconceivable as Hayek has shown:

> What interests us is precisely the question of whether the banks are able to satisfy the increased demands of businessmen for credit without being obliged immediately to raise their interest charges—as would be the case if the supply of savings and the demand for credit were to be in direct contact, without the agency of the banks (as, for example, in the hypothetical "savings market" of theory); or whether it is even possible for the banks to

E. G. Tsionas, *The Euro and International Financial Stability*,
Financial and Monetary Policy Studies 37, DOI: 10.1007/978-3-319-01171-4_10,

raise their interest charges immediately the demand for credit increases. Even the bitterest opponents of this theory of bank credit are forced to admit that there can be no doubt that, with the upward swing of the trade cycle, a certain expansion of bank credit takes place (Hayek 1935, p 89).

The forces of competition will provide the commercial banks with enough motivation to expand credit, and the credit reduction would be enough to restrain the forces of recession:

Only so long as the volume of circulating media is increasing can the money rate of interest be kept below the equilibrium rate; once it has ceased to increase, the money rate must, despite the increased total volume in circulation, rise again to its natural level and thus render unprofitable (temporarily, at least) those investments which were created with the aid of additional credit (Hayek 1935, p 94).

Consider in this respect the EFSF and European regional funding to the South. The EFSF is based on the idea that banks who exposed themselves to Greek securities must be bailed out or saved. The European regional funding is purely credit that can be used one way or another. In essence this amounts to credit expansion by the EU, when in fact credit expansion and monetary expansion was the main problem in the first place. We must realize that, in the course of the economic process, some European banks backed overly strong the expansionary plans of the Greek government or the Greek business sector. These banks must suffer the same consequences as the unprofitable investment plans that they financed.

The banking bail out has as much sense as bailing out the unprofitable investment plans that turned out to be disastrous. If the private sector assumes risk to full extent, the same must be the case with commercial banks. It is inconceivable to assume that commercial banks are supposed to survive when the unprofitable investment plans they financed, failed. The European Bureaucracy does not even realize that a new banking sector must emerge out of the crisis, exactly as a new private sector is emerging especially in the market for capital goods which is under heavy reconstruction.

Of course, the US more or less dictated the EFSF by their policy on bailing out their own banking authorities. This policy is incomprehensible. In the course of the business cycle not only physical but also financial capital must be destroyed to make relative prices and financial returns approximately equal. The idea of bail outs is reinforcing the very causes of the crisis, which is credit expansion in the wrong direction. If an investment plan can fail as the result of a credit expansion which provided the wrong signals, why should one bail out the bank that financed this project? The commonplace objection that deposits must be secured is, of course, unwarranted.

We should emphasize that bail out plans on the scale of EFSF are dangerous and fundamentally misguided. The problem is not more credit for Greece, Portugal or Italy, but a fundamental, immediately restructure along the lines of the Poincare plan in France—to pay for salaries and pensions. More credit along the lines of the

EFSF reinvests in the fundamental causes of the crisis, which were credit expansion in the first place:

> By creating additional credit in response to an increased demand, and thus opening up new possibilities of improving and extending production, the banks ensure that impulses toward expansion of the productive apparatus shall not be so immediately and insuperably balked by a rise of interest rates as they would be if progress were limited by the slow increase in the flow of savings. But this same policy stultifies the automatic mechanism of adjustment that keeps the various parts of the system in equilibrium and makes possible disproportionate developments that must, sooner or later, bring about a reaction (Hayek 1935, p 94).

In that sense, fully predicted by Hayek, what the EFSF does not realize is the developments and processes that will lead to a reaction. Of course, the commercial banks that are bailed out may choose to hold less risky portfolio but sooner or later the additional credit, which keeps their profit rates approximately the same compared to the pre-crisis situation, will find them tempted to finance equally risky projects since the crisis uniformly lowers, more or less, the profitability of investment plans. From the point of view of economics what matters is the *automatic mechanism of adjustment that keeps the various parts of the system in equilibrium*, at the European and the national level. These adjustment mechanisms have been practically destroyed by the EFSF, but also the Treaty or Maastricht as well.

Let us expand on this point. After all, the Treaty or Maastricht is about monetary stability focusing on the general price level. The stability of the "general price level" was shown to be an illusion ever since Hayek's *Prices and Production* (1935). Monetary stability is really about credit and money expanding in accordance with the profitability of private plans in the absence of monetary policy and *expansionary* credit policies by the commercial banks. Yet the commercial banks opened themselves to all sorts of risks for a simple reason: Investment demand for credit was accumulating long before the 2008 crisis and the banks accommodated this tendency. ***The reason was the explicit monetary expansion in the US and the accommodation provided by the ECB.*** In that sense we have had a classical Hayekian crisis. If that was all and the ECB showed some restraint there would be no problem, but the political decision of the EU Bureaucracy was to accommodate the expansion. Now the Bureaucracy attempts to save the situation by bail out plans, thus fully monetizing its wrong economic policies. Let us rely on Hayek again:

> The determining cause of the cyclical fluctuation is, therefore, the fact that [...] the rate of interest demanded by the banks is not necessarily always equal to the equilibrium rate, but is, in the short run, determined by considerations of banking liquidity (Hayek 1935, p 96).

Apparently, the credit expansion, implicit or explicit, will make interest rates deviate from their equilibrium rates and set in motion micro or macro credit policies that will be suboptimal. *Currently, we are precisely in a situation where banking liquidity determines interest rates.* The EFSF put the banks in such a dominant position that they themselves have a more pronounced role in the determination of interest rates through liquidity. But given the EFSF's support the banks may get the wrong impression not only on available liquidity but also on their total risk position. ***As a result the EU bailout plans are totally in the wrong direction***.

The crisis should have allowed for a reallocation of resources in the direction of more profitable plans to overcome the crisis. *But the EFSF made that impossible, primarily because it did not allow for a reallocation of resources and funds in the financial sector.* A new financial and banking sector that would emerge from the crisis *would have been the healthiest indication that the European capital market itself is moving in the right direction*; yet a unique opportunity was lost.

As argued by Prychitko (2010) in an attempt to understand the bubble in the US:

> The housing bubble developed between 2001 and 2006 when the Fed lowered the federal funds rate and government agencies (through the Community Investment Act and other devices) encouraged and targeted credit toward the housing industry in particular. During those years, credit-induced demands for new homes caused a doubling of their values—an historically unprecedented event. The housing industry, of course, is a latticework of timely production projects and draws a wide variety of specific (yet complementary) higher-ordered inputs into the housing market. Too many to list in detail, but such resources obviously included real estate, lumber, iron ore and its shipments, copper and wiring, PVC materials, and so on. Equally important, it included skilled and unskilled labor in these and other industries, as well as the financial sector itself. Higher relative prices and wages, salaries, and bonuses attracted millions—today the cyclically unemployed—into the housing and finance industry and away from sectors that would have maintained jobs without Fed generated interest rate reductions. The Fed-induced credit expansion prior to 2006 altered the saving–investment link and had real consequences that influenced relative prices in such a way that the change in prices—not the price level—mislead workers, firms, and investors.

We should note that the Fed lowered interest rates from 6 % to an unprecedented 1 % between 2001 and 2004. The resulting misallocation of resources should have been quite predictable, since nothing has changed in terms of consumption and savings decisions or time preference on the part of the consumers. It is thus the changes in *relative* prices, not the change in the *general* price level that created the artificial boom and the subsequent crisis. Of course the banks engaged in an unprecedented credit expansion, willing to make too much risk and finance the new investment plans that were focuses on the more "round about" methods of production.

But what is true for firms, finding new profit opportunities in the production of goods further removed from the consumption sector, is also true for national governments. When Greece and other Southern European governments joined the euro, they had to follow in advance, policies that reduced the interest rates considerably. This is turn made public borrowing easier and cheaper and provided an additional motive for financing public sector activities and the welfare sector in particular through increases in public debts. *The lowering of interest rates shifted the attention from sound public finances to running Ponzi schemes with the expectation that the new debts can be easily repaid irrespective of maturity.*

The very foundations of the euro thus allowed certain governments to run large public debts which, eventually, exploded when the economic conditions changed, following the failure of long-term investments that were misdirected due to artificial lowering of interest rates. Monitoring the debt to GDP ratio is not a sufficient criterion for policy. Industrial structures with the same debt to GDP ratio are not equally exposed to *mal*investment or maturity of old debt at a given point in time. Of course "toxic" government bonds could easily destabilize the system since they are hold by many European central banks and the ECB has announced its commitment to accept Greek government bonds irrespective of rating, that is even if they were junk.

The running of Ponzi scheme on the part of national governments in the Eurozone or more precisely the accommodation of large public debts in view of the historically low interest rates in Europe, was not predicted and was in fact the Achilles' heel in the EMU. The emphasis was put on sound public finances and the debt/GDP ratio which was however inappropriate in view of the low interest rates. What is worse is that there is no automatic mechanism to allow markets to work and lead to a new equilibrium as in the era of the gold standard, where gold flows would work quickly to re-instate an equilibrium.

References

Hayek FA ([1935] 1967) Prices and production. In: Kelley AM, 2nd edn. New York

Prychitko D (2010) Competing explanations of the Minsky moment: The financial instability hypothesis in light of Austrian theory. Rev Austrian Econ 23:199–22

Chapter 11
Will Bailouts Lead to a Dissolution of the Euro?

As we remarked, there are bailouts at several levels. To bailout the public sector wages and salaries or pensions in Greece, Greece needs a plan according to the Poincare lines. A public debt authority and a pensions authority that will consolidate obligations and revenues, backed on real resources. This is a matter of short run importance and immediate consideration must be given to it.

The consolidation of public debt is intimately related to the consolidation of the financial situation of commercial banks. The government took it upon itself to bail out all banks and guarantee (up to approximately 200 billion euros) the net financial position of its commercial banks. This guarantee is unconditional on what these banks did in terms of investments and risk taking of past and existing investment plans. The question arises as to why the government did not also provide guarantees to bail out the financial accounts of major corporations. Apparently, these corporations did not perform very wisely in terms of investment plans—but banks which financed them indiscriminately performed equally bad. What is it so special about the financial sector that we cannot encounter in the real, private business, investment sector? Apparently, not much.

If we look into the specifics of the Greek banking sector we see that banking Boards and CEOs were not very keen to cooperate and agree with merging. Instead of sharing risks they chose to remain independent, being certain that the government guarantees would bail them out of any rough situation they might face. Unheard of in the rest of the private sector, the commercial banks were given a free hand on oligopolistic competition, making them totally indifferent to the general economic conditions but with a guarantee on rates of profit.

This is just one occurrence of the fact that the ECB and the EMU are in favor of "financial stability"—translated to the axiom that banks are bailed out. Another craziness of our times is the "Taylor rule" followed by the Fed for far too many years, aiming at general price level stability. To such axioms and propositions little faith can be placed any more. Behind the "general price level" there are far too many relative prices which determine resource allocation and allocation of investment. Behind "financial stability" there are far too many banks that ought to be closed.

One author put it clearly as follows:

E. G. Tsionas, *The Euro and International Financial Stability*,
Financial and Monetary Policy Studies 37, DOI: 10.1007/978-3-319-01171-4_11,

> When the dot-com boom came to an abrupt end in 2000–2001, the Fed responded quickly, cutting interest rates and injecting liquidity into the financial sector, as they had done before on several occasions. Investors, politicians and voters could breathe a sigh of relief. The monetary response cushioned the downfall, and only a modest recession followed. However, the Fed's monetary response gave immediate rise to a new credit cycle, even more vicious and destructive than the last one (Gustavson 2010).

Of course it was not solely the dot-com boom but the bubble in the housing market as well. As Haberler says:

> If in a growing economy the central bank follows a monetarist policy of increasing the money supply to keep the price level stable, it imposes unsustainable forced saving. We have seen that this, according to Hayek, was supposed to have happened in the 1920s with disastrous consequences.

Although this is closer to a "Taylor rule", nevertheless it describes well the *unsustainable forced saving* implied by the ECB and national European banks as a result of the recession, under a nominal regime of constant general price level or constant inflation. Now, what is more disturbing is that in a depression the central bank reallocated funds so as to allow *increasing the money supply* in certain countries. The *disastrous consequences of this counterfactual policy are yet to be observed but they will be, nonetheless, disastrous.*

Unless resource and investment re-allocation is allowed to take place, in full, the disastrous consequences from resource allocation in the "South" will continue to place a financial burden upon the rest of the EMU. The euro will not be sustainable unless these fundamental disequilibria are diminished though (1) a coordinated policy in the South and (2) a healthier financial sector in the EMU as a whole.

From that point of view, insisting on bank bailouts to maintain "financial stability" is the worst thing that the EMU can do to its real stability: ***Its real financial stability lies with the stability of relative prices and profitable investment plans, not the phantom of misguided "financial stability" for the euro as a whole***. The phantom of misguided "financial stability" for the euro as a whole is multidimensional. It has to do with (1) unprofitable investments at the level of the EMU, (2) the misguided plan of bailing out all banks and countries, (3) credit misallocations at the EMU level that disregard relative prices, (4) the misguided allocation of huge regional funds for cohesion, (5) the painstaking structural adjustment plans imposed by the IMF on members of the EMU.

A bailout program is primarily a program to rescue the profitability of commercial banks or what is known as "big players" in the terminology of Prychitko (2010). As he argued:

> Big players create big unintended consequences as they, too, act only under conditions of uncertainty and ignorance. The Greenspan Put (now evolved into the Bernanke Put) serves as a stark example. By announcing in the midst of the housing bubble that speculative investment banks could retain their extraordinarily high profits and count on the possibility of a loss-floor, those firms evolved into Big Players themselves. They placed higher bets as the discipline of profit and loss—especially loss in this case—was systematically weakened. The unintended consequences behind the Put—the moral hazard—became all too clear.

> Their waves of failure beginning in 2007 were a direct result of adjusting their speculative and Ponzi-financed plans in light of the monetary expansion and the promises made by the Greenspan Fed.

The public debt explosion was no different in that respect, and laid at the foundation of the EMU. Not only the commercial banks themselves, the primary concern of the ECB, but governments running huge public deficits could safely count on a bailout. In fact, the bailout did not come in the explicit form they were probably expecting, because they are not "big players". The big players are only the commercial banks and the ECB that could lose from a possible bankruptcy of a country – member of the EMU.

According to a Working Paper of the ECB:

> The empirical evidence on the real interest rate channel thus far points to the fact that real interest rates have fallen across the whole euro area since the early 1990s and, in particular during the run-up to the launch of the euro. ECB (2004) suggests that the natural real interest rates is likely to have declined in the euro area (as a whole) over the last decade and may be lying in the range of 2–3 %. Compared with the euro area average, the reduction was particularly important in Ireland, Spain, Portugal, Italy, Greece, and also the Netherlands. After the sharp decline in the 1990s and particularly in the run-up to EMU, real interest rates changes were more modest. Hence, the real interest channel per se seemed to have played a relatively small role after the launch of the euro as an asymmetric transmission channel leading to growth and inflation divergences, except Ireland (Mongelli 2008).

In fact the real interest rate did not play a small role at all as in fact the greatest reductions took place in the countries that precisely have public debt problems after the subprime crisis. The low productivity and the fiscal deficits can, in fact, be explained by the redirection of investment into unproductive and unprofitable uses, ex post, resulting from the diversion of resources to long-term investment, similar to the housing bubble in the US. Additionally, the EU has followed some general "growth fostering policies" consistent with the lowering of interest rates, for example the telecommunications sector, the "information economy", "knowledge-based economy" etc.:

> The Lisbon Agenda is one of the clearest examples of the exogeneity of OCA [Optimum Currency Area]. It was first adopted by the European Council in Lisbon in March 2000, and sets out a strategy which aims at addressing the issues of low productivity and stagnation of economic growth in the EU over a ten-year period. The purpose of the Agenda is to make the EU the world's most dynamic and competitive economy by 2010: a goal that is to be achieved by transforming Europe into the world's largest knowledge-based economy. The initiatives in the Agenda are organised under three pillars: an economic pillar, a social pillar, and an environmental pillar. This postulates that enhancing knowledge generates direct and indirect benefits. The belief is that various high-technology businesses, especially computer software, telecommunications and virtual services, as well as educational and research institutions and other aspects of an "information society" can contribute to boosting creativity and innovation, enhancing productivity, and propping up the economy (as shown by New Zealand) (Mongelli 2008).

The view that *enhancing knowledge generates direct and indirect benefits* depends on the overall structure of the economy. Long-term investments will, of course, utilize beneficially the produced “knowledge”, provided these investments turn out to be profitable in the long run. If not, “knowledge” simply cannot *contribute to boosting creativity and innovation, enhancing productivity, and propping up the economy*. Thus the naïve view that all knowledge enhancement, no matter to what degree, is beneficial for productivity, does not have a real foundation. This effect is amplified when artificially low interest rates and the deconstruction of relative prices have taken place, especially in markets, like the ones in Europe, which are heavily regulated and still require structural reforms.

References

Gustavson M (2010) The global debt crisis, http://mises.org/daily/4151/The-Global-Debt-Crisis

Mongelli FP (2008) European economic and monetary integration and the optimum currency area theory, ECB working paper

Prychitko D (2010) Competing explanations of the Minsky moment: The financial instability hypothesis in light of Austrian theory. Rev Austrian Econ 23:199–22

Chapter 12
On the Destabilizing Effects of Bailouts

The destabilizing effects arising from bailout programs can be found in the massive re-allocation of resources that they induce and divert from other uses that, normally, would have a priority. The underlying motivation for a bailout lies in preventing large banks to fail and thus prevent a collapse of the entire banking system. The amount and extent of the bailout depends on: (a) the amount artificial credit created by the entire banking system, induced by the ease of credit and low interest rates imposed by the Central Bank, and (b) the extent of malinvestment induced by the artificial credit expansion. In this sense, it appears irrational to create an artificial expansion and then use more credit expansion to rectify the adverse effects on commercial banks arising from the liquidation of unprofitable investments that they financed.

This is, precisely, the massive re-allocation of resources that was induced first by low interest rates but—despite the liquidation—persists and enhances further because large commercial banks are allowed to expand based on the principle of the Marshallian banking multiplier (de Sot 2009). The remark that large banks will become wiser in their investment decisions is irrelevant: The bailout funds are largely based on credit expansion based on the banking multiplier on the part of the European Central Bank. It would be impossible to argue that these funds result from savings of European consumers (diverted to profitable uses) so, in fact, the bailout is a stage in the credit expansion that has been created and is, therefore, still present.

The "collapse" of the banking system and the putting in "danger" of "financial stability" refer to the fact that banks have expanded credit well beyond their deposits but the deposits themselves are secures even if 90 % of the loaned funds plus interest are non-performing. A bank that received €100 million in deposits at rate 2 % but lent €1,000 at rate 3 and 90 % did not perform can still make a profit of €1 million after repaying deposits plus interest. Even if the loan rate was only 0.5 % the bank would incur losses of €1.5 million if all deposits were requested at once during a bank-run. If only 30 % of the deposits plus interest were withdrawn the bank would, in fact, have as *profit* of €39.5 million or 39.5 % over deposits! As a matter of fact, in this situation, the bank would be solvent if it could keep just 1.5 % of its deposits, which is possible even during a bank-run.

E. G. Tsionas, *The Euro and International Financial Stability*,
Financial and Monetary Policy Studies 37, DOI: 10.1007/978-3-319-01171-4_12,

It is, therefore, clear that the bailouts are not about securing deposits but about rescuing bank profitability which is quite excessive anyway. The purpose is to maintain the ability of commercial banks to keep deposits, and expand credit beyond this level thus, effectively, increasing money supply. Bearing in mind that stable monetary conditions constitutes the founding objective of the European Central Bank it is hard to see how the bailouts serve this objective when, in fact, credit and money supply should be *reduced* in the aftermath of the sub-prime crisis. The available statistics show, indeed, such a reduction which is, however, offset by the bailout program for the large commercial banks which is a disguised form of actually increasing credit and money during the recession. The distortions in relative prices, interest rates and the distribution of resources that has been effected by the original pre-2008 credit expansion, continues in the form of increasing artificially the deposits of large banks and enabling them further to engage in monetary expansion at low interest rates. Although there is an effect on banking expectations about the overall profitability of new investment projects or consumer loans, there are other effects (a) from the increase of deposits through the bailout programs, and (b) through the interest rates which are still quite low.

As long as banks continue the expansionary policy—and they have every reason to do so at low interest rates—and interest rates are low, further corrections in the form of liquidation of malinvestment are impossible. The fear is that further liquidation will result in an increase of non-performing loans and it would place additional burden on the profitability of all commercial banks. However true this may be, the actual effect on the profitability is much smaller compared to the one that is usually thought and profitability per se is not endangered, only its level. The recipe of low interest rates and bailouts is, in reality, a policy in the wrong during a recession as it does not allow the private sector to obtain precise signals about the relative profitability of alternative investment plans. Among its many adverse consequences is the fact that labour is not allowed to move into the sectors that are most profitable and, in that way, it creates structural unemployment through the induced imbalances between the demand and supply for labour at the micro-economic level, that is in its various sources of demand.

Through the partial "flight of savings" that we have witnessed in many commercial banks of Southern Europe, another mechanism of credit expansion can, I fact, take effect. To the extent that this "flight" ends up in the savings accounts of Eurozone banks, the net effect for the European Central Bank is null. Yet other commercial banks, say in the "North" can take advantage of their increases of deposits and use the multiplier principle to extend credit even more. Although there are no immediate "aggregate" effects, there are important effects that work their way through credit expansion by *different* commercial banks. Since the northern industry enjoys relative prosperity—because of the depreciated euro and the credit expansion that works through the totality of industrial sectors—this expansion of credit at low interest rates is, in fact, quite welcome and cannot but be sustained by the northern commercial banks and the European Central Bank. In the medium-term when the two effects (recession in the South and temporary prosperity in the North) work through the European economy, they set in motion overlapping business cycles arising in different industries and different countries that definitely prologue the classical trade cycle that resulted from the original pre-2008 credit expansion.

These effects take a number of years to work through the European economy and can mask a fact of immense importance: The fact that two effects are at work may give the erroneous impression that the Southern economies suffer the consequences of their "actions" while the North is safer because of its sound policies and industrial structure. Therefore, this provides no indication to the policy authorities that wrong and inappropriate policies are used. In fact, higher interest rates and a solid banking system—in the form of a system closer to 100-percent reserve requirements—is called for instead of further, masked, active monetary policy through the commercial banking sector.

Reference

de Soto JH (2009) Money, bank credit, and economic cycles, 2nd edn. Mises Institute, Auburn

Chapter 13
On Sound Money and Credit Conditions

It may appear at first sight that the EMU has done everything possible to maintain stable monetary and credit conditions. National currencies were substituted for a common currency whose stability rests upon restrictions on fiscal deficits and inflation. Yet it is doubtful that the euro brought stable credit conditions, because:

> ... most of the supporters of sound money do not want to go beyond the elimination of inflation for fiscal purposes. They want to prevent any kind of government borrowing from banks [...] [b]ut they do not want to prevent in the same way credit expansion for the sake of lending to business. The reform they have in mind is by and large bringing back the state of affairs prevailing before the inflations of World War I. Their idea of sound money is that of the nineteenth-century economists with all the errors of the British Banking School that disfigured it. They still cling to the schemes whose application brought about the collapse of the European banking systems and currencies and discredited the market economy by generating the almost regular recurrence of periods of economic depression (von Mises 1912, Chap. 23, Part 2).

Unrestricted credit expansion is as sound as inflationary monetary policy, which has been condemned by the EMU. In the credit market, the reader will be well aware of policies in terms of banking regulation such as the Basel Agreements in various phases aimed at controlling "global risk" or "systemic risk", and thus "protecting" commercial banks from taking "excessive risks". As von Mises describes concisely his business cycle theory:

> The inevitable eventual failure of any attempt at credit expansion is [....] the outcome of the fact that it is impossible to substitute fiat money and a bank's circulation credit for nonexisting capital goods. Credit expansion initially can produce a boom. But such a boom is bound to end in a slump, in a depression. What bring about the recurrence of periods of economic crises are precisely the reiterated attempts of governments and banks supervised by them to expand credit in order to make business good by cheap interest rates (von Mises 1912, Chap. 21, Part 2).

In fact that was exactly what happened in the few years past 2008, since the beginning of 2000. The credit expansion facilitated an expansion of business, which was "over-production" in some sense. Business investments increased dramatically at the expectation of high profit possibilities which were then refuted by the facts, when it became evident that the lowering of interest rates was not due

E. G. Tsionas, *The Euro and International Financial Stability*,
Financial and Monetary Policy Studies 37, DOI: 10.1007/978-3-319-01171-4_13,

to plenteousness of capital goods but it was rather an artificial decrease caused by the banks and the government. This explains not only the recent crisis but the recurrence of crises in general which, at the final analysis, are produced by the recurrent monetary and credit policies of the government or the banking system.

When the credit expansion can no longer work because the recession is rather deep, we are informed that the eurozone is about to decrease interest rates to 1 % (as of December 2011). The eurozone might as well proceed to increasing the money supply or the banking sector could proceed with credit expansion. The only reason these authorities do not do so is because the recent crisis is still very new and its lessons cannot be forgotten so easily. So they adopt the alternative, a decrease of interest rates which, according to standard analyses, will boost the economy, yield some inflationary pressures that can be minimized using fiscal measures etc.

The current depression is a correction of the mistakes of the boom of the period 2000–2008, whose cause was the credit expansion. By lowering the interest rates and creating another artificial credit expansion, the mistakes will only be left corrected only half-way through, and new investment mistakes will be produced. What is fundamental to understand is that credit markets and investment markers must be left free to achieve a new equilibrium for the EMU as a whole. Otherwise, the systematic intervention of the ECB and its "guidance" of the commercial banks will produce a temporary recovery that will be followed, almost surely, by another slump. Any correction of mistakes, involves some annihilation of investments and jobs, and other resources. If credit was not made artificially cheap, such mistakes would not occur in the first place. By insisting *now* on *cheaper* credit, the Eurozone and the ECB are bound to make the state of affairs even worse.

The chaos that the Eurozone and the ECB face, is a dual image of the disequilibria in capital, money, credit and product markets. *The interaction of these disequilibria is disastrous*. The chaos reveals itself in a rather blatant way in terms of the explosion of public debt in nearly all countries of the Eurozone—despite the fact that this more apparent in Greece, Spain, Portugal, Ireland and Italy. Germany and France do not face lesser problems. If borrowing for international credit markets is possible only at high interest rates, producing the rising spreads, why should domestic borrowing become *cheaper*?

Of course, one can blame the "speculators" that "attack" the euro through its "weak links" like Greece, but the fact remains that no speculation would be possible if European central banks and monetary authorities could agree on how to handle collectively their debts and of course, if European productivity was expected to raise in the near future. Stable currency without stable productive conditions is unheard of in the past and it will be so in the present and future.

We have seen that Hayek was in favor of "any mechanical principle" by use of which, money would retain its value in transactions independently of the government's intervention and, in fact, against government's intervention in monetary affairs. His argument is presented as follows:

> My expectation would be that, at least for large regions much exceeding present national territories, people would agree on a standard set of wholesale prices of commodities to treat as the standard of value in which they would prefer to have their currencies kept constant.

> A few banks that had established wide circulation by accommodating this preference, and issued currencies of different denominations but with roughly constant rates of exchange with one another, might continue to try and refine the 'precise composition of the' standard 'basket' of commodities 'whose' price they tried to keep 'constant in their currency!' But this practice would not cause substantial fluctuations in the relative values of the chief currencies circulating in the region. Regions with different compositions of the currencies in circulation would, of course, overlap, and currencies whose value was based chiefly on commodities important for one way of life, or for one group of predominant industries, might fluctuate relatively more against others but yet retain their distinct clientele among people with particular occupations and habits (Hayek 1990, pp. 75–76).

The practical implication of Hayek's proposal for free circulation of different currencies in the context of an economic union, is pegging currencies to "*a standard set of wholesale prices of commodities to treat as the standard of value in which [people] would prefer to have their currencies kept constant*". It is clearly not easy to define the "standard set" but once defined by the market, it is a matter of supply and demand to stabilize the exchange rates between different currencies and hopefully lead to a common denomination when and if "ways of life" have approached a common level. Under different conditions, an artificial common currency cannot sustain itself—if productivity, preferences and "ways of life" are different.

A monetary union is not by itself a good thing, and the same is true for a common currency in any given country, where there is different demand for money across regions. Money and its substitutes can be used freely by economic agents to adjust their plans to the changing economic conditions. These agents will form their expectations, and thus their plans, on relative prices but they will have to execute them in terms of nominal prices denominated in a currency that best suits their needs. As Hayek says:

> Though we are apt to take it for granted, it is by no means of the essence of money that within a given territory there should exist only one kind, and it is usually true only because governments have prevented the use of other kinds (Hayek 1990, p. 77).

No doubt, a multi-currency system adopted in a given, single country, will create confusion for *some* time but the market forces, will quickly reduce to zero the demand for depreciating currency and increase the demand for stable currencies. What might be confusing for a single nation, *it will be, as a matter of fact, therapeutic from the point of view of an economic union, like the Eurozone, provided economic agents are free to choose the currency they adopt for trade or the realization of their plans, more generally*. Under this condition, it is not necessary to dissolve the economic Union as such, but it is a condition that the common currency, the euro, must be abolished in favor of national currencies. The economic unification can go on despite the fact that currencies are left to compete freely in the European or the international market. It is not even necessary to require national governments and central banks to refrain from inflationary money creation: The temporary advantages of this action (if any, in view of the fact that most agents will transact in stable currencies) will be outweighed by the quick depreciation of the national currency and the flight from it. In that way the government that resorts to inflationary finance, will find itself without the necessary means to perform the task.

To re-iterate, our proposal for a new and sound monetary system is quite simple: Return to the national currency system in the Eurozone, without any restrictions at all. No restrictions on how the government behaves, but also no restriction on the convertibility of a currency to another in any former member of the EMU. For all it matters, practically, a nation can choose to peg its currency to the German mark, the US dollar or the sterling, or not have a national currency at all and adopt initially the German mark or the Swiss franc, ensuring full and immediate convertibility to any other European currency.

Speculative "attacks" will be endogenized, by definition, in this scheme. In fact, it will not be speculative attacks that change the exchange rates but the demand for money denominated in different currencies—which is, in reality, the only demand for "money" that economic agents have, if left alone to pursue their plans. The credit markets will find their equilibrium very quickly, since most exchanges, current or future, will be arranged in terms of currencies that are *expected* to be stable. Only unexpected government interventions might disturb this equilibrium, but the outcome will be rather apparent on the demand for national currency.

From that point of view of arranging a new financial and monetary order, we can see immediately the flaw in the short-sighted argument that fiat money creation can improve the balance of payments, even in the short run. The whole argument rests upon the supposition that a depreciation of the national currency, say the *drachma*, will improve exports and discourage imports. But if the process of exporting and importing goods and services takes some non-negligible time, its effect will disappear immediately from the flight away of *drachma*, and the conversion of *drachmae* into a stable currency, say the mark or the dollar. If most exports and imports are from and to German or American markets, economic agents will fully and immediately cancel out the effects of the depreciation by causing a drop in the demand for drachma. So the only temporary positive effect on exports from a depreciation of the *drachma* essentially lies upon the *monopoly* of *drachma* by the Greek government. Once this monopoly is taken away and currencies are free to compete we see immediately that: The increased demand of *drachmae* by foreign importers of Greek goods and services—who might see an opportunity here—will disappear *immediately* when domestic (Greek) agents will demand more German marks or US dollars, which *the Greek government or an international authority* will have to provide to them. Additionally, foreign importers will have to anticipate these actions and, therefore, they are not likely to proceed with increased orders of Greek goods and services. Of course, before even they begin to think about the question, the flight from the drachma will present them with additional evidence that nothing has, in reality, changed in terms of short—term productivity and competitiveness of Greek goods. As Hayek argued:

> Indeed it would be discovered that 'balance of- payment problems' are a quite unnecessary effect of the existence of distinct national currencies, which is the cause of the wholly undesirable closer coherence of national prices than of international prices. From the angle of a desirable international economic order the 'balance-of-payment problem' is a pseudo-problem about which nobody need worry but a monopolist of the issue of money for a

> given territory. And not the least advantage of the disappearance of distinct national currencies would be that we could return-to the happy days of statistical innocence in which nobody could know what the balance of payment of his country or region was and thus nobody could worry or would have to care about it. (Hayek 1990, p. 109).

It seems that the ECB, the EPC of the EU, and the Fed as well, think along some very basic monetary theory: Increase the quantity of "money" and this produces inflation. In order to stimulate "economic activity" lower interest rates. Such simplification is quite dangerous. The recent reduction of interest rates to 1 % or a future increase in fiat money supply of the euro, which is forthcoming, in one form or another (through banking "supervision") is fundamentally flawed in this sense: Changing the aggregate money supply or the interest rate has immediate implications for relative prices. Increases in money supply:

> are then often regarded as harmful chiefly for this reason, as if they raised or lowered all prices *simultaneously* and by the *same* percentage. Yet the real harm they do is due to the *differential* effect on different prices, which change successively in a very irregular order and to a very different degree, so that as a result the whole structure of relative prices becomes distorted and misguides production into wrong directions. Unfortunately, Lord Keynes made practically no use of this most important contribution to monetary theory of the Cambridge tradition deriving from Marshall (Hayek 1990, p. 97).

In that sense, the chief problem is not inflation *per se* but rather the real distortions that are implicit in a general inflation, which are none other but the wrong messages that are sent to the producers of capital goods at first, and to the certainly expects an increase of inflation in the Eurozone—which, after all, might be acceptable, in view of the deep recession. It does not matter, for practical purposes, whether the ECB reduces the interest rate or increases money supply. A monopoly on currency implies also that the central bank(s) and the commercial banks are in agreement regarding the fundamental issue of "shortage" or "excess" of money in the "market". After all, the commercial banks, the central banks and the ECB are not antagonistic. Therefore, they seem to think that they can control the rate of interest as well. By lowering the interest rate, "total investment" must go up and "aggregate demand" must go up as well, by standard textbook arguments.

In fact, this idea is flawed, in the sense that *an artificial reduction in interest rates must be, eventually, followed by a recession that will clear up the misallocations of excess credit in the capital markets.* Interest rates, of all varieties and kinds, like any other price, must be left to be determined by the capital markets and the markets for all products, in the general—equilibrium sense. However, the fact of the matter is that disequilibria in several markets are left intact while interest rates are reduced and these disequilibria will be *propagated* by an artificial change of relative prices for all goods and services induced by a change in interest rates—or an increase in money supply.

The flaws of a textbook-like approach of the EMU and the ECB, can be traced back to both the Keynesian and Monetary traditions in which the dominant role of "the" money supply and its effects upon "inflation" are greatly exaggerated. As Hayek emphasizes, once more regarding Friedman's approach:

> It's chief defect in any situation seems to me to be that by its stress on the effects of changes in the quantity of money on the general level of prices it directs all-too exclusive attention to the harmful effects of inflation and deflation on the credit or debtor relationship, but disregards the even more important and harmful effects of the injections and withdrawals of amounts of money from circulation on the structure of relative prices and the consequent misallocation of resources and particularly the misdirection of investments which it causes (Hayek 1990, p. 80).

This misdirection of investments is, of course, the chief cause of anomalies in capital and investment markets which, in turn, adversely affects the credit markets and the access of firms to new capital in the stock markets. In essence, the financial turbulence is nothing but a predictable effect of interest rate or money supply policies on the markets—that is the global set of plans and expectations of economic agents.[1] This can be compared directly to the practice of price controls who are supposed to benefit the "general public" but in turn, they only create excess demand to be covered by other means, legal or not.

This interference with global resource allocation is totally foreign to the managers of the ECB or the Bureaucracy in EU, the EPC, and the EMU. Although it is convenient for them to think in terms of a single market of goods and services, and even a single market where money demand for the euro is well defined, in fact, this is absolutely flawed. In the context of global turbulence and disarray, the policy makers insist on thinking in terms of textbook models, without regard for the real processes of resource allocation in Europe. In fact, the whole idea of economic policy in the Eurozone is surprisingly similar to the role of a planning authority in a socialist economy. Since relative prices cannot be dictated to coordinate perfectly the global set of expectations and transactions, the whole task is flawed from the beginning. In particular:

> No authority can beforehand ascertain, and only the market can discover, the 'optimal quantity of money'. It can be provided only by selling and buying at a fixed price the collection of commodities the aggregate price of which we wish to keep stable (Hayek 1990, p. 81).

Admittedly, this looks easier compared to the problem of socialist planning. After all, given a basket "*of commodities the aggregate price of which we wish to keep stable*", monetary policy can accommodate this objective. In fact, the idea goes back to Fisher (who proposed an "index number" to peg the currency, and provoked the severe criticism of von Mises). The problem is solved once we allow for the miraculous "*collection of commodities*" to be part of the market's learning process as well. But this, in turn, is nothing more and nothing less than freely—competing currencies not only in the context of the EMU but inside national borders as well. Of course, the market can always discover the "*optimal quantity of money*", but the solution has to be optimal in a broader context than systems of national currencies, inside closed borders, without allowing for competition.

[1] For a lucid treatment, see Kirzner (1979), pp. 146–151, also pp. 26–29.

If we take seriously Hayek's conclusion that "*[n]o authority can beforehand ascertain, and only the market can discover, the 'optimal quantity of money'*", then we have to wonder about the nature of "money" implicit in this conclusion. Apparently, the value of "money", like any other commodity has to be determined eventually by the processes of the market. In that sense, the only reasonable recommendation for a sustainable and reasonable financial system following the dissolution of the Eurozone, is *market determination of currency zones or "optimal currency areas"*. This is to be discovered by the markets, and there is really nothing more we can say on that. As Kirzner put it, the function of the market is to facilitate learning about that which is not known as of yet (Kirzner 1979, p. 138).[2] The role of the market is to coordinate expectations about others' plans, so as to facilitate learning about things that do not exist (as of yet) and to allow certain agents to capitalize, and thus make profits, during the process of coordination.

Given a monetary union, whose members wish to favor monetary stability, for the reasons stated, above, Hayek argues that:

> … the nearest practicable approximation would seem to be precisely that stability of raw material and perhaps other wholesale prices which we could hope competitively issued currencies would secure (Hayek 1990, p. 88).

The proposal is quite reasonable, albeit it is only hoped for that competing currencies will tend to equilibrate around such wholesale prices. Hayek, in his discussion, explicitly excluded the prices of labor or land, since "*the average price of land and labour is hardly something for which we can find a statistical measure*" (op. cit.) but the same is true for all prices inclusive those "*of raw material and perhaps other wholesale prices*". Perhaps raw materials are much more delineated and discretely identified compared to concepts of "land" and "labor", in general. Naturally, this presupposes competitive conditions in the markets of raw materials, conditions that are not altered by immediate interventions, collusion, or cartelization. A nation that can control markets for raw materials, in one way or another can artificially increase its supply of money and thus, distort relative prices in international and intra-national trades to its benefit.

But this is not a real issue once the Eurozone is dissolved back to its constituents. The markets need a stable currency, at least in the medium run. If the stability of currency is brought about by controlling the markers for raw materials, nobody would care provided this control is not a caprice of chance or political power, expected to disappear sooner or later in the medium run. Convertibility can assure the more or less accurate realization of plans, and that is all we need (and hope for) the markets to perform their role. Pegging to wholesale prices is a starting condition. One might as well move to a gold standard if deemed necessary. The crucial factor, which has been emphasized by Hayek, is quite different and concerns *the wholesale conversion of international currencies from monopolies to competitive markets, as nearly as possible*.

---

[2] "Subjectivism suggests that things about which men are completely ignorant are things that, in the sense relevant to economic theory, *simply do not exist*".

It should be clear that the purpose of the ECB, and any Central Bank in its position, would be to ensure the stability of the financial system, which is understood in terms of bailing out commercial banks that failed to accommodate the credit expansion made by the Central Bank. It is very hard to believe that the Central Bank is unbiased in terms of its theorizing. In fact it is a cartel of the commercial banks and this affects in an essential way the current depression in the EU. It is very useful to examine Rothbard's view on the matter:

> The bleak record of accelerating inflation and recession since the inception of the Federal Reserve in 1913 may be seen in a different light if we reevaluate the purpose that this central bank was intended to serve. For the Federal Reserve was designed not to curb the allegedly inflationary tendencies of freely competing banks but to do precisely the opposite: to enable the banks to inflate uniformly without worrying about calls for redemption by noninflating competitors. In short, the Federal Reserve was designed to act as a government sponsored and -enforced cartel promoting the income of banks by preventing free competition from doing its constructive work on behalf of the consumer. The Federal Reserve emerged in an era when federal and state governments were embarked on precisely this kind of program in many sectors of industry, and it was designed to do for the banks what the ICC had done for the railroads, the Agriculture Department for the farmers, and the FTC for general industry. These actions of the Progressive era came after widespread attempts, in the late 1890 s and earlier, to cartelize or create monopolies voluntarily, attempts that almost all came to swift and resounding failure. Various large business groupings, therefore, came to the conclusion that government would have to play an active and enforcing role if cartelization was to succeed. (Rothbard, p. 135)

> The Federal Reserve System, like all central banking systems, is inherently inflationary. In the first place, the central bank acts as a lender of last resort, a giant governmentally privileged institution standing ready to bailout banks in trouble. Second, by coordinating bank activities, the central bank can pump in new reserves throughout the system and thereby induce a multiple expansion of bank money and credit. Since the banks can inflate uniformly, individual expanding banks no longer suffer from the constraining redemptions by nonexpanding banks that prevail in a regime of free and decentralized banking. If a bank expands credit on its own, it will soon find that its expanded notes or deposits will be passed on from its own clients to clients of other banks and that in the normal course of business they will be returned to the expanding bank for redemption. Yet the expanding bank will not have the funds to redeem these claims. There is also a third reason, which might not be as evident: Even if legal reserve requirements remain the same, the centralizing of reserves into the hands of the Fed by itself permits a considerable inflation of money and credit. (Rothbard, p. 105).

It is evident that the ECB has been acting in precisely this way. Although the ECB stands for monetary and credit stability, it did not hesitate to expand to redistribute credit to maintain the stability of the euro by devising bailout plans for Greece or Ireland. But the credit expansion—bailout plans are not designed to stabilize the euro but maintain the profitability of the commercial banks—the real foundation of any central bank. The important question is why the Central Bank should not allow certain commercial banks to fail as the result of their bad investments. The reason is, precisely because, the ECB does not see the financing of these bad investments as the real problem; it considers it merely a problem of public debt that somehow got out of control. Of course we should not forget that "*[v]arious large business groupings [...] came to the conclusion that government would have to play an active and enforcing role if cartelization was to succeed*" but cartelization alone is not sufficient to explain the details of public debt explosion although, arguably, it can explain the behavior of the Central Bank.

The second point is that the notion of an independent Central Bank is, indeed, quite arbitrary. Its independence must be tested and judged in the light of the available data. If the Central Bank were to act solely on the basis of an insurance fund for the commercial banks, under strict terms, and under competition in the banking system, it is quite unlikely that the government or the commercial banks would ever proceed with credit expansion beyond the limits of their reserves. But the limitation of competition by the ECB or any other Central Bank creates are the conditions necessary and sufficient for money and credit expansion; it does not enforce the competition of the sector and, certainly, it does not guarantee financial stability.

The explosion of public debts, almost worldwide, is the natural outcome of credit expansion through government bonds at first sight, but only because certain commercial banks and certain Central Banks were willing to accommodate this credit expansion. One could argue that since this seemed like a profitable investment, the commercial banks and many Central Banks should proceed with buying government bonds, re-selling them in the international markets etc. From the point of view of the borrowing countries this was a disastrous idea, not because of the final explosion of public debt, but right from the beginning. The borrowed funds were allocated in the economy by the government itself or by the Central Bank and its credit channel. Since many investment projects that were financed began to fail after a few years, it is hard to understand why the ECB did not spot the problem in the mid 1990s when Greece joined the eurozone. What were the profit expectations for existing and new projects? What was the situation of government finances? How well did the public and private sectors in comparison to the rest of Europe in terms of productivity, profitability and competitiveness? Why would one accept to buy Greek bonds if it was evident that Greek, and indeed most Southern economies needed major restructuring and savings accumulation before being able to borrow at alarming rates?

These were the data at which any investor should look into before financing any existing or new projects, but the ECB did not. Apparently, the ECB was aware of the inflationary pressures that the South could create or underestimated to a large extent that the South could create significant inflationary pressures, resulting from credit expansion and irrational allocation of credit through its channels. But the "cartelization", in Rothbard's terms, manifested its disastrous effect through another channel after 2008: Given the policies of low inflation, ***credit expansion manifested in terms of exploding public debts, and deep recession***.

In terms of economic theory, the Austrian school predicted successfully the recession that would result from credit expansion and the subsequent malinvestments in the various sectors of the economy through the artificial reconstruction of the constellation of relative prices and interest rates. It did not concern itself with the problem of public debt and its explosion for a very good reason: There was no reason to assume that a government would rely on foreign borrowing instead of monetary expansion. But if monetary expansion is not possible, as in the eurozone, the building up of public debt becomes the *only* solution *before* the commercial banking system collapses. In a situation of this kind, the interest rates on government bonds should sky—rocket almost immediately, and thus borrowing would become impossible. The fact did happen, but only after 2008, and in the beginning of 2009, in Greece.

Why did it not happen previously? The arguments about public debt sustainability were ignored by the various credit rating agencies and became relevant only after early 2009. In 2010 the biggest (at least since 2000) credit expansion took place and put the economy into a trajectory of depression with the accompanying deterioration of public finances. During the same period, Greek commercial banks passed all the "stress tests" required by the ECB and the Basel agreements. Apparently, the ECB, credit rating agencies, governments and commercial banks *were looking at the wrong "fundamentals"*, and did not have any *accurate predictors* for the upcoming crisis.

The most significant part of the problem is that the credit expansion in Europe took the form of government bonds (bought by the major French and German commercial banks, with the blessings of the ECB) from the mid 1980s. In mid and late 1990s Greek public debt began to increase steadily again after a short intermission in early 1990s. Public debt was not considered a problem at all after Greece's successful completion of the "stabilization pact" after 1996–1997. Whereas, in the US or the UK, the policy makers would use interest rate or credit expansion policies, the South of eurozone resorted to new debt. Inflation and growth would, naturally, absorb a certain part of the burden created by interest payments and the financial system would not be put at risk. However, *credit expansion in the highly regulated eurozone, could only result in explosion of public debt, and the increased risk of Greek commercial banks by their holdings of Greek government bonds. The purpose of the bailout was precisely to secure interest payments for Greek and other major European commercial banks, through new credit expansion.*

Apparently, public debt enters the two—dimensional picture of problems after the 2008 crisis. Inflation and growth—the two dimensions so far—can be controlled, of course, by monetary and fiscal policies, but since credit expansion lies at the heart of Central Banks, and so does inflation, weak and non—competitive economies can only rely either on discretionary funding from the ECB or, alternatively, on new credit through government bonds and public debt. Since discretionary funding is limited (although it was exploited heavily through the European regional cohesion funds) credit expansion in the eurozone system has to appear in some form as malinvestment; this form is the explosion of public debt. In a single economy this would appear as non-performing loans by the commercial banking sector as a result of financing enterprises that eventually failed after the market adjustments taking place after a credit expansion. The deep recession in the South and the EU is, indeed, one aspect of the disastrous effects of ECB's credit expansion. The other aspect is, of course, bank failure that is prevented through the bail out plans. *If bank failures cannot be contained, either a bigger package of credit will be necessary or another way must be sought to salvage the European banks.*

Most economists put the problem in these terms: If bank failures cannot be contained, either a bigger package of credit will be necessary or the eurozone will dissolve. But even if the eurozone is dissolved, a way must be found to maintain the profitability of European banks that are exposed to Greek public debt. The Southern banks will be on their own (if we assume that certain Southern countries join Greece in its exit from the euro) but the commercial banks of the new eurozone must be sustained. In principle the ECB can sustain them through a different bailout plan of credit expansion before the South becomes able to pay interest and capital at maturity—even after a "haircut".

The questions here are: What *will* happen and what *should* happen. *What should happen* is clear from the point of view of economic analysis. Credit expansion in the form of bailouts, new debt, money creation or any other form is absolutely disastrous for the eurozone. It puts the monetary union into wide fluctuations and destroys the prospect for future, healthy growth. Some commercial banks should bear the loss, while others (mostly Greek) should be allowed to fail. The common currency has nothing to do with the process of re-adjustment that takes place after major malinvestments and repeated credit infusion into the system. The same effects would materialize with a common currency or different currencies under floating exchange rates. However, the monetary union and the dominant role of the ECB can only be retained only as long as there are no bank failures; the chain effects from this natural market outcome would be disastrous for the financial system as it currently stands in the eurozone.

A common currency area such as the EMU with the huge concentration of reserves into the hands of the ECB, can only result in *effectively inflationary*, that is credit—expanding policies. The bailout policies are very likely to continue in the future, to maintain the profitability of commercial banks in the EMU, which are intimately related to Greek public debt. From that point of view, *what will happen* is that the ECB *will try* to keep Greece in the EMU and *try* to reform the entire public sector so as to use the *possible* surpluses to the interest of the commercial banks.

On the question of *what should happen*, first of all, more competition should be allowed in the EMU along with a minimal role for the ECB, ensuring no credit expansion in every country beyond the level of reserves. Second, containment of public debts through more effective fiscal measures. Third, considerably less emphasis on bank profitability and focus on true monetary, credit and financial stability.

From that perspective, the question on whether the euro will dissolve or not boils down to a single and simple question: *For how long will the ECB be able to bail out Greek or other Southern (but not exclusively) commercial banks through credit expansion, which is known to have depression effects*? Up to 2020 there are important outstanding obligations of the Greek government, in terms of public debt, and the situation is no better for Southern Europe as a whole. Public debt is mounting for the eurozone as a whole so maturities determine also the dates for major expansions of credit, or inflation. Since the constellation of prices and interest rates is out of synchronization by far, the growth prospects for the eurozone are gloomy. *Assuming that the ECB is reaching its limits in terms of credit expansion, major problems for its banking sector will appear in the horizon.* We are likely to see mergers and acquisitions to prevent the collapse of the financial system, renegotiation debts etc. but the fact remains that without major credit expansions (and thus further more severe and volatile depressions) the ECB and thus the EMU and the commercial banks cannot be saved. *The EMU will be forced to accept higher inflation to ease the burden on active credit policies, or it will have to adopt stricter fiscal policies* in the South, and a complete re-organization of the public sector, where necessary.

If the ECB is not reaching its limits in terms of credit expansion, it does not matter whether the euro is dissolved or not. The ECB can sustain the commercial banks that are exposed to risky or toxic debt by credit policies. But if the ECB cannot do that, then a major restructuring of the banking sector is required to diversify the risks, limit competition even more and proceed with even more 'cartelization' in Rothbard's sense. In fact, both are likely to happen, that is *both* a tighter control of ECB over commercial banks through major restructuring, *and* a credit expansion to support the new structure. This new structure can be robust to Greece's exit from the euro, that is the re-structured European banking sector will not be affected at all. The collapse of other Southern commercial banks will be a significant problem. To contain the losses of 'Northern' banks, will require significant credit expansion—bailout plans for some time. In the confines of a common currency or not, the situation is not sustainable unless unprecedented credit expansion is decided by the ECB.

For most economists, the problem is how to re-structure Southern European economies, and Greece in particular, so as to be able to generate fiscal surpluses and pay back the outstanding credit expansion (more than 120 billion euro). Apparently, the issue of fiscal surpluses is a matter of the distant future. It would be in the best interest of the 'Northern' banks to agree on ***joint ventures*** with the Greek banking sector and enterprises in the sectors of energy or oil, in order to use the proceeds for balancing their exposure to Greek public debt. In other words, a restructuring of the European banking sector is more likely (or should) take the form of *direct involvement in the emerging comparative advantages of the Greek economy.*

It is clear, from the viewpoint of economic theory that the EU would profit a great deal from free competition and generalized use of multiple, competing currencies. This would put a limit to the credit expansion policies of the ECB which endanger growth and welfare in the eurozone, but also worldwide. Agents' expectations are that the euro will depreciate for many reasons and, as a result, capital shifts in other regions of the world, implying lower productivity and competitiveness for the eurozone. The tendency will continue also in the future if the ECB insists on acting as a cartel of the European commercial banks rather than as a policy maker that should maintain monetary and financial stability, as it should the case be. But the generalized use of multiple, competing currencies presupposes the dissolution of the euro as common currency, and the removal of 'barriers to entry' from other currencies not only legally but also from artificial credit policies.

This may seem paradoxical. After all there are no 'barriers to entry' in the sense that economic agents can perform their daily transactions or agree on their contracts in any currency they choose. If there are inflationary expectations about the euro, why do not people choose the US dollar, the UK pound or another currency? The reason for the apparent paradox is that interest rates and inflation rates are kept quite low in the eurozone so there is no reason to switch to another currency for low or medium level savings. But the demand for gold has sky—rocketed after 2008, proving that a 'flight from the euro' indeed took, and is still taking, place. If major currencies move together for practical purposes, there is no reason to switch even for everyday purposes. But there is major re-structuring taking place in the industrial sectors and the consumption patterns in many European countries. There is tremendous variation in relative prices which fails to be represented in the official statistics of inflation, and interest rates are heavily regulated at will. So markets, and therefore the currency markets, are not free to clear, deciding which currency is best at least for long—term investment.

Heavy regulation is what distinguishes, at a first approximation and *grosso modo*, a monetary union like the EMU from a monetary union like the US or the UK. Different regions apparently behave differently, they are exposed to asymmetric shocks, they are widely differing in terms of comparative advantages of competitiveness, and even fiscal policies, but nobody considers them as unsuccessful in any sense. Sometimes the public debt of California, for example, is raised as an argument in favor of the EMU. Of course the Federal Reserve in the US will also bail out commercial banks and large financial institutions but there is a major difference. Monetary unions like the one in the US, presuppose that commercial banks can freely operate in any state and thus diversify risks; a feature that is absent from the EU and the EMU. The common currency is supported, and indeed it is based upon, to create easily and freely of transaction costs) savings accounts in major banks across the union. Of course all commercial banks are 'cartelized' at the top, the Federal Reserve, but cross-regional competition is higher compared to trans-national competition the European banking sector.

The re-structuring of the European banking system, which we pointed out before, will be a natural consequence, *ceteris paribus*. This 'ceteris paribus' is very difficult to sustain, since the credit expansion policies of the ECB are likely to continue no matter what the cost in terms of consumers' welfare and growth without volatile fluctuations of economic activity. But there is another element to the US banking system that makes it totally different from the European counterpart: Contagion as the result of exposure to risky debt from one bank is considerably less in the US because *US states do not issue state bonds, contrary to European states*. The ECB found itself trying to use credit expansion to contain the contagion of public debt (in terms of its consequences for the profitability and solvency of commercial banks) but other monetary unions never had to deal with problems of this sort. *In that sense, the public debt problem in a monetary union of independent states is a totally new problem* from the point of view of the central monetary authority and its credit policies.

To summarize this discussion, the explosion of public debt in a monetary union is new. The ECB tried to minimize it using artificial credit expansion in the form of bailout plan to save major commercial banks exposed to risky debt. *Whether Greece (or the South) remain in the eurozone or not, whether European major commercial banks are less exposed, and if the euro is sustainable are three different questions.*

The first issue is mostly political in nature but it can affect considerably the short—run exchange of the euro which, in the long—term will be determined by relative prices and relative productivity. The second issue (profitability of major banks) depends on credit expansion policies of the ECB no matter whether Greece stays or goes. The third question depends on how the eurozone (old or new) will fare as a well in the global economy; it is a genuinely long—term matter.

No matter whether Greece stays or goes, the main problem is *not* whether and when Greece will be able to pay back interest and capital at maturity. This will, necessarily, take time and is mostly a matter of political considerations. *The main problem is whether or not the ECB will be able to sustain its commercial banking system through bailout—credit schemes.* What is really at stake is welfare and growth for the EU. The re-structuring of Greek economy to pay for the credit expansion of the ECB—through possible future fiscal surpluses—is an issue that is unrelated to welfare and growth prospects which are hampered by the interventions of the ECB.

To emphasize the role of commercial banks in the whole process, it is perhaps instructive to consider the view of von Mises:

> The connexion between banking proper and the business of speculation and flotation is similarly loose and superficial. This is the branch of their activities on which the general economic importance of the banks nowadays depends, and by means of which on the Continent of Europe and in the United States they secured control of production, no less than of the provision of credit. It would not be easy to overestimate the influence on the organization of economic life that has been exerted by the change in the relation of the banks to industry and commerce; perhaps it would not be an exaggeration to describe it as the most important event in modern economic history. (von Mises 1953, p. 262).

The statement alone is not sufficient to provide a solid foundation for the understanding of the recent crisis in the EMU. However, along with the critical remarks of Rothbard (1983) on the role of the central bank and the credit channel, the situation becomes quite clear.

References

Hayek FA (1990) Denationalization of money, 3rd edn. The Institute for Economic Affairs, London

Kirzner (1979) Israel, perception, opportunity, and Profit. University of Chicago Press, Chicago

Rothbard M (1983) America's great depression, 5th edn. Mises Institute

von Mises L (1912) The theory of money and credit, Yale University Press, New Haven (translated 1953)

Chapter 14
The Case of Free Banking

In the Austrian school's tradition, the commercial banks should be free to issue currency, exactly as the government does since the objective is to limit the monopoly of the government or an European central bank on money. Currency competition is the way to eliminate most of these currencies in favor of a few, or even a single one, in the long, provided this currency is stable enough to accommodate the plans of private agents. A possible dissolution of the euro into its constituents need not be accompanied by issue of currency by the commercial banks, since risk—averse agents will opt for stable national currencies. Developments in the credit market might produce certain arrangements between the large commercial banks and their clients. However, the closed relations of the government and large commercial banks will, lost likely, lead to a corner solution in that respect.

The case of free banking concerns us, primarily because, bailout plans in the Eurozone have directed towards bailing out certain banks by providing "guarantees" which supposedly favor the savings in these banks. In that sense, the ECB and national governments provide "guarantees" to the commercial banks to ensure that they have the liquidity to pay back the savings in case need arises. What is the fundamental problem with the banks in this respect? It is precisely the fact that *banks are not accountable to the consumers* when, in their act as financial intermediaries, have financed investment plans that failed, or plainly they misused the funds that were made available to them. But savings, as any other investment, is to be considered as the stockholder's vested interest in the portfolio of investments that was chosen. Apparently, the saving households had no saying in the investment choices of the bank, and they must be guaranteed their capital plus interest. But this is no excuse for the current portfolio or the bank to keep going as usual. In fact *banks and financial intermediaries that failed in the course of the depression must cease to exist, if a new healthy credit and financial sector is to arise.*

As a starting condition, the savings must be guaranteed within the boundaries of the EFSF agreements. But the management of risk in the future, the primary concern of much absurdity in the so called Basel agreements, has to be properly re-allocated in the context of consumption—portfolio decisions. The Basel agreements are concerned only with banking risk, ignoring that risk is a feature of

E. G. Tsionas, *The Euro and International Financial Stability*,
Financial and Monetary Policy Studies 37, DOI: 10.1007/978-3-319-01171-4_14,

investment itself in capital markets, and the allocation of resources between consumption and savings at the household level. A situation where banks that took considerable risks and failed are bailed out, and profitable banks or other financial intermediaries continue their business as usual, is not healthy. This state of affairs gives the wrong signals to the banking sector and maximizes its attitude towards risk, instead of containing it. If a firm is bailed out unconditionally just because it is a "bank", the very notion of financial stability is empty of content. Unless the EFSF agreements focus on competition in banking, financial stability will never emerge.

The reason why banks failed is to be seen in the pre-2008 credit expansion in the EU and the US. Banks and other financial institutions transformed obligations into other portfolios (so called "toxic") that were risky but attractive—as a result—in terms of return. What made this "bubble" possible was, apparently, an increase in the price of housing relative to other investments. *This would have been impossible without the credit expansion* that distorted expectations, plans, and relative prices as the major cause of the other two. Other commercial banks, failed because they were restricted to hold equally "toxic" products, namely government bonds that were about to expire but whose repayment was difficult.

The natural question is why the banks did not get rid of the load of "toxic" government bonds earlier. Greek commercial banks did not do so for political reasons. But the European commercial banks did not foresee the situation because of the ECB's insistence on the sustainability of Greek public debt since 2008. If the ECB tells the commercial banks there is no reason to worry about, the European banks are covered. The problem was that the ECB acted as a politician and not in its capacity as a protector of financial stability. Even with half the deficit that was supposed to be true for the Greek government (close to 15 %) simple calculations would show that the debt was not sustainable and the forthcoming obligations could not be met. Moreover, there were voices in the dessert that pointed early on to non—sustainable debts in the Eurozone (Professor Michael Wickens, for example, see Polito and Wickens 2007).

The ECB, as a result, did not act so as to minimize "global systemic risk"—about which she has developed an intricate parlor—but rather as an organ of the EU Bureaucracy. The repercussions were, and will be, substantial. Since there is no guarantee that the ECB changed its role the "markets" will continue to view the ECB as the source of the problem. These "markets" are not imaginary entities or credit agencies but rather the real labor, product, and capital/investment markets in the EU. Instead of reforming the financial sector, the ECB opted for a decrease in interest rates, like any first—year economics student hoping for a "recovery of economic activity" along the lines of dated Keynesian doctrines, without addressing the source of the problem of "global systemic risk", the European commercial banks themselves.

Although it is common knowledge that the bureaucracy of the EU is more rooted in the economic system compared to other places in the world, it is less known that financial intermediation and the political system are also more confounded in the EU. Industrial and financial capital is more inseparable in the EU compared to the US, and the same is true in the vast majority of Asian countries. In part, this is largely due to the fact that the EU was formed as a *political* union of totally different economic entities. The hasty reader will have to convince herself that this was *not* the case in the US, where economic and monetary nationalism was not applied at the same grand, continental scale.

One has to admit that the bureaucracy of the EU has a relatively short history of less than half a century. It is being reshaped of course in the context of EU-27 and we are experiencing what is known as the Franco-German pact, or Franco-German axis. What matters is the implications of this plan for the European banking system and the European financial sector. In view of Basel agreements we should not expect anything more than "risk management" in the banking sector without regard for risk as a whole. Risk as a whole is totally foreign to the bureaucracy of the EU, under the assumption that all risk comes from the erroneous investment decisions of the banking sector—which is quite reasonable in view of the fact that the bureaucracy of the EU, and the ECB, rely themselves on *total control of the deposits of the European banking system and thus in control of euro money supply.*

Although Basel II outlined what was a comprehensive "credit risk" scheme for loans to consumers, *Basel II and III did nothing to delineate guidelines for the allocation of loanable funds for investment purposes.* The European banking system is free, in that sense, to take more risk in the financing of business investment, but not to consumer credit. In essence, this state of affairs implies that the European banking system is fully accommodating any expansionary or contractionary plan of the ECB at large, by placing more severe limitations of almost risk—free profits from financial intermediation to consumers. Of course, the crisis following 2008 made such profits much riskier as household incomes and wealth were reduced[1] but still the main source of risk comes from financing investment plans, not allocating credit to the consumer sector. Basel II and III (and the upcoming IV, in all likelihood) were totally indifferent to such aspects of risk, for good reason: ***Implicit control of money supply and credit***.

The regulation of commercial banks by the ECB, leaves no room for free banking in the EU. Although there is an institutional framework as well as insurance for consumer loans and other deposits, the ECB went too far in terms of regulation. Clearly, a competitive, free credit market is not compatible with banks that too many risks and were unprotected before the bailout plans, and it is well known that European banking is heavily oligopolistic. Certain mergers were also allowed by the ECB contributing to the oligopolistic structure of the credit markets. The question of the effectiveness of the bailouts and the question of competition in the European banking sector are two sides of the same coin: By bailing out the large banks, essentially, the ECB tries to maintain a questionable notion of stability in the sector, where an inter-national monopoly (the ECB) provides selective support for national bank monopolies and oligopolies. By the same token

[1] Despite this fact most loans to the consumer sector were and still are backed up by land or housing property, so risk was negligible.

one should bail out large companies using as argument the approaching lay offs. The fact that nobody considers this as a sound idea, the argument suddenly becomes reasonable when it comes to the banking sector. However, the banks that failed should be allowed to exit the market, and let the consumers decide where they should deposit their savings and, of course, under what conditions in terms of interest yields.

Here is how von Mises argues about central interventions to bail out the banks:

> In any event, the practice of intervening for the benefit of banks, rendered insolvent by the crisis, and of the customers of these banks, has resulted in suspending the market forces which could serve to prevent a return of the expansion, in the form of a new boom, and the crisis which inevitably follows. If the banks emerge from the crisis unscathed, or only slightly weakened, what remains to restrain them from embarking once more on an attempt to reduce artificially the interest rate on loans and expand circulation credit? If the crisis were ruthlessly permitted to run its course, bringing about the destruction of enterprises which were unable to meet their obligations, then all entrepreneurs—not only banks but also other businessmen—would exhibit more caution in granting and using credit in the future. Instead, public opinion approves of giving assistance in the crisis. Then, no sooner is the worst over, than the banks are spurred onto a new expansion of circulation credit. (von Mises 2006, p. 127).

Apparently the monetary and credit authorities of the EMU believe that the expansion of credit is the key to the problem of the recent great crisis. The lowering of interest rates is a policy action that comes in the worst possible time—in the middle of the depression. The depression itself is the outcome of the credit boom of the 2000s which distorted considerably all European and factor markets. It is exactly in a new artificial boom that the ECB and the Eurozone try to find out the solution of the problem. But the problem, the current depression, is entirely due to a credit expansion, in the first place. In the words of von Mises:

> The discrepancy between what the entrepreneurs do and what the unhampered market would have prescribed becomes evident in the crisis. The fact that each crisis, with its unpleasant consequences, is followed once more by a new "boom," which must eventually expend itself as another crisis, is due only to the circumstances that the ideology which dominates all influential groups—political economists, politicians, statesmen, the press and the business world—not only sanctions, but also demands, the expansion of circulation credit. (von Mises 2006, p. 128).

Apparently the banks should be wiser after the crisis and they should limit their credit by directing funds only to "relatively riskless" investment projects. But what constitutes a "relatively riskless" project cannot be decided by the bank alone. Otherwise, the banks would not have gotten into credit problems before the crisis. There is naturally a herding behavior on the part of the banks, in that they follow what other banks too, but the essence of the matter is that, profitable projects are decided by the market and its condition. With distorted product and factor markets, many projects that look profitable *ax ante*, they are likely to incur losses *ex post*.

It is true that, on paper, the EU has tried to pursue free or more open markets, remove barriers to entry (but not exit), and the European labor markets are severely regulated by the state and numerous interest groups. But even if all markets were free to perform their functions, an artificial decrease of the rate of interest would bring about a crisis. Not as severe as the current crisis but a depression, nevertheless. With markets heavily regulated at all levels, by EU law-making and national idiosyncrasies, another artificial expansion of credit or an artificial reduction in the interest rate, will be catastrophic. In a nutshell, the EU, and other has less confidence in markets than it does to its own interventions and law—making. *What is not being understood is that, the current severe crisis must be allowed to run its course, re-instate relative prices and interest rates at more reasonable values, and proceed from there onwards by allowing at the same time, free credit, factor and product markets.*

A transition to a system of free banking is, of course, quite troublesome at the moment or in the near future. Not it is to be recommended as an immediate policy measure in the midst of a depression. However, there is no other reasonable solution in the long run. Apparently free banking implies freedom from the ECB or the national central banks. This is not freedom from control and institutional measures (primarily, avoiding credit expansion without full reserves) but rather freedom from the interest rate policies of the central bank(s). Credit expansion without full reserves is, of course, the way in which banks try to maximize profits without relying on savings which, in good times, is the standard option of firms that rely on credit. But in bad times this discrepancy will bring about a collapse of the banking and business sector. A competitive banking sector with iron restrictions on credit would have made the crisis almost impossible:

> If all further expansion of fiduciary media had been forbidden in any form, that is, if the banks had been obliged to hold full reserves for both the additional notes issued and increases in customers' demand deposits subject to check or similar claim—or at least had not been permitted to increase the quantity of fiduciary media beyond a strictly limited ratio—prices would have declined sharply, especially at times when the increased demand for money surpassed the increase in its quantity. The economy would then not only have lacked the drive contributed by any "forced savings," it would also have temporarily suffered from the consequences of a rise in the monetary unit's purchasing power [i.e., falling prices]. Capital accumulation would then have been slowed down, although certainly not stopped. In any case, the economy surely would not then have experienced periods of stormy upswings followed by dramatic reversals of the upswings into crises and declines. (von Mises 2006, p. 129).

The proper policy of the ECB would have been to *increase* the rate of interest, *not* decrease it. By doing so the right signals would have been given to the business sector, and funds would be attracted from other parts of the world. Since the real reserve ratio of the commercial banks is low, an increase in interest rates would be the only meaningful solution to the problem of reserved funds. By reducing the interest rates, the problem of reserves becomes worse, prices do not go down, and there is really no "brake" in the course of the economy.

Both in Bretton Woods and in the EMU, the issues were reduced artificially to only one, that of the exchange rate, which is a significant relative price but by no means the only one, and by no means the exogenous variable that can be controlled at will to help set the economy in the right track. The issues of a new financial and credit system were set aside, and nothing new came out as a theoretical or empirical prescription. The reason is that different nations have different interests but that is only part of the explanation. For the most part, underlying the foundations of a monetary union is a banking and credit system whose workings essentially determine, in the final analysis, the propagation of cyclical fluctuations and the origin of these fluctuations.

As von Mises argued:

> In the last two generations, hardly anyone, who has given this matter some thought, can fail to know that a crisis follows a boom. Nevertheless, it would have been impossible for even the sharpest and cleverest banker to suppress in time the expansion of circulation credit. Public opinion stood in the way. (von Mises 2006, p. 131).

The reason why a crisis follows a boom is that, unless there has been considerable technological progress or innovation in processes of production or the utilization of the factors of production, any boom is only possible because of "cheap money" or artificial credit expansions without consideration of risk (which is practically impossible to calculate precisely *ex ante*). The crisis that follows is the natural result produced by market disequilibria that is the natural result of the mutual incompatibility of the expectations and plans of economic agents in the credit, banking, factor and product markets. In simple terms, credit was given to projects that failed later on. These funds could not be recovered resulting in the collapse of the financial system.

References

Polito V, Wickens M (2007) Measuring the fiscal stance, Discussion Papers 07/14, Department of Economics, University of York

Mises L (2006) The causes of economic crisis, Mises Institute

Chapter 15
The Explosion of Public Debts

The theory is precisely the same when it comes to governments that borrow from the international markets. The acquired funds could have been transferred to the private sector or the public sector for investment and consumption, or they could have been plainly wasted in one way or another. Borrowing in the form of issuing bonds is no different to plain *fiat* money creation before the time of maturing. After that time the government has to pay back a multiple of the initial amount determined by the rate of interest on its bonds. Ideally, the average, realized rate of return of investments that were financed by borrowing, when compounded, will be enough to pay back the bond holders (some of which may well be national commercial banks). If not, another cycle of issuing bonds begins to repay immediately the bond holders, and divert the remaining funds to productive investment, make it available as credit to the private or the public sector etc. As long as the average compounded domestic rate of return exceeds the average rate of servicing the debt, there is no problem, although inflationary pressures are mounting.

The problem of allocating borrowed funds to productive investment is, of course, difficult and cannot be solved but at the market level through the credit mechanism. Domestic firms who expect an average rate of return r, will always borrow in excess of own funds as long as $r > R$, where R is the nominal rate of borrowing, net of inflation. Some firms will resort to credit and others not, and of those that will do some will be successful and others not.

At first sight there is no problem with this policy that boosts investment in the interest of growth. In practice, the availability of cheaper money and the lowering of interest rates will make marginal or unprofitable investments appear profitable, and they will be undertaken, thus absorbing the new available funds. To the time of maturity, assuming firms have to repay the credit institutions at nearly the same time, some firms will have exited the industry and they will not be able to do so. The firms that did marginally better, are likely to cry out and ask for cost reductions (often in the form of wage cuts, if that is possible, or layoffs and permission to extend the maturity of their loans) and other firms will be able to pay back on time. If the lowering of interest rates and the availability of credit was taken for granted by the firms—that is, if they expected this to be a permanent

E. G. Tsionas, *The Euro and International Financial Stability*,
Financial and Monetary Policy Studies 37, DOI: 10.1007/978-3-319-01171-4_15,

reduction, it is highly likely that many "roundabout" processes were financed—projects that take time to produce and require capital stock or equipment having long life—and, therefore, by failing they account for a large part of employment, investment, wealth generation and, naturally, a larger part of the allocated funds. A simple example would be investment projects that were set up in order to create "heavy industry" but lacking the comparative advantage in the international product markets *ex post*, eventually they failed.

In such cases, the government could not commit to its obligations and either the government asks for new funds in the form of newly created bonds, or defaults. To that idyllic picture, one should add that the borrowed funds or the proceeds of international loans, are used to support the salaries of public employees, support government—owned or private business that should not close down because of their importance in terms of employment, financing a large public sector, accommodating the demands for funding private sector projects that are definitely unprofitable (but politically useful) etc. Over the course of 20 or 30 years it is evident that the accumulation of public debt is not balanced by the average return on productive projects. In fact the latter could be negative, when both the domestic return and the actual interest on public debt are considered in real terms, net of inflation.

Needless to say, the government should run a balanced budget if $r > R$, otherwise the budget and the current account should be positive. If not the accumulation of public debt is catastrophic and soon the country will find itself asking for loans or bail out plans simply to pay wage and salaries in the public sector plus pensions and of course, to finance health care and education at the very least. It is probably easy to blame the politicians, in general, for the situation, or even the political system as a whole. In Greece, Spain, and Portugal this attitude is not uncommon and Europeans are becoming increasingly upset with the German chancellor and the French prime minister.

The political system is, of course, responsible for the situation, but we must know exactly why this is so. In the period after the World War II, governments were totally devoted to the Keynesian ideas of irresponsible fiscal and monetary expansion up to late 1970s when "stagflation" appeared. Some countries in the European periphery (Greece being the leading example) continued the Keynesian practices up until, roughly, the early 1990s. It is true that the problems of inflation in the mid 1980s necessitated the adoption of certain austerity measures, but pure *fiat* money creation as well as *fiat* money creation through excess borrowing, continued. Despite inflationary expectations, the private sector was expecting "cheap money" in the long run. By late 1990s, the credit expansion was booming, and the Greek Olympic Games put much more pressure on public finances as well as on the public debt—which began skyrocketing since the early 1980s, under a socialist administration.

It is possible that a conservative administration (conservative in terms of borrowing and allocating funds to investment) would have been more successful, save for the fact that a large public sector in not easy to reduce, even gradually, when both socialist and conservative administrations have no desire to do so. All things considered, it seems quite plausible to argue that the explosion of the Greek public debt (the so called "weak link" of the Eurozone) *was entirely due to the distortion of the domestic credit market, and the subsequent distortions in all other markets, caused by fiat money creation from government's debt.*

Greece's problems would have been its own outside the Eurozone. However, in the context of a monetary union the problem is inflated because outstanding debts must be paid. The EMU decided in favor of a so called "hair cut" of 50 % of the public debt. That this decision was inadequate is revealed by the basic arithmetic of the Greek debt which is in the form of government bonds to national pension funds and to lesser extent national banks. One fundamental question is whether the government's decision to absorb the reserves of pension funds, in the form of lending, was inflationary. Under normal conditions this would not be so, because the lending would be repaid to time to maturity in full. However, this was not the case since the government did not honor its obligations, and in that respect it created fiat money and inflation from the beginning—although the effect was realized when the time to maturity came. In other words, the government inflated credit supply, albeit at an earlier date. Since the outstanding balances of major pension funds were negative even from the early 1990s, and it is certain that a huge, unproductive sector is still dominant, *we must assume that the expansionary credit policy of the Greek administrations was never reversed, and is still intact.*

The effects are still alive and well, despite the austerity measures or the formal control of the budget and economic policies of Greece by the so called "*troika*" (IMF, EU, and ECB). The austerity measures amount to an increase in tax rates (including VAT and pensioners), special taxes across the board and salary cuts in the public sector. Despite the measures, after a year and a half, government expenditure is increasing and the situation in tax revenues in devastating. We cannot deny that the forces of the Financial Police do their best to reduce tax evasion but still there are no results.

Whether Greece will honor its obligations regarding public debt is, essentially, a rhetorical question. Greek administrations cannot honor these obligations, before they begin creating public surpluses instead of public deficits. The irresponsible measures taken by the recent administrations towards increasing tax rates and applying uniform taxation to capital, like housing, must be substituted by *policies directed towards healthier conditions in the credit markets and banking*. The budget must be balanced as soon as possible, with cuts in public expenditure in the short run and recover of tax revenues in the medium run. The combination of the two conditions implies that the government must be relieved of debt obligations in the medium run, liberalize the credit and labor markets, let the product and capital markets trace out their new equilibrium, and provide a new institutional framework for its workings in terms of a new Constitution, in order to make clear the objectives and the responsibilities in the sequel.

This commitment along with backing from the EMU could provide wonders if credit and capital markets were to be liberalized. Contrary to many competing economic theories we are to place much confidence to commitment *itself*, when it is not accompanied by economic results. These results without a 100 % haircut would be totally impossible to achieve, provided the haircut would be backed by bonds issued by the ECB, with a very short time to maturity. The conversion of Greek debt to short run debt of the EU would provide Greece with the necessary foundation. Such backing would also presuppose a transfer of the management of Greece's economic affairs to the EMU.

Chapter 16
The Current Policies of the ECB

Following its announcement of lower interest rates, the ECB decided to lend 489 million euros to selected European banks at the low rate of 1 % (December 21, 2011). This amounts to an increase in money supply by a significant amount and a further lowering of interest rates, at least for certain European banks and the projects that will be financed. What will be the likely effects of this policy action? According to the analysis of the Austrian school, the effect depends on how the monetary expansion will be distributed among consumption and production and also among the various branches of production and the various branches of consumption.

Assuming the European banking system distributes the new credit to *producers*, there will be an increase in the demand for producers' goods (used as intermediates) and a rise of the relative price of producer goods relative to consumption goods. Final or nearly final consumer goods will experience the largest drop of prices, and the same will happen with producer goods that are closest to the final stage of production. The price reductions will make the late stages of production less profitable relative to the earlier stages of production, where part of the new credit funds will be transferred. In turn, the prices of products in the earlier stages will begin to increase and, in that manner, price differentials among all stages of production diminish. At the various stages of production, prices increase not only because of the general increase in the prices of producers' goods but also because price increases in a given stage, give an extra advantage to the preceding stage: Profit opportunities will make production dearer in early rather than late stages of the process. Not only that but a relative increase of the average length of production will happen, along with investment in new, longer processes that were not profitable before, when interest rates were higher or when credit was not available. Additionally, one should expect an increase of employment in the earlier stages and, in theory, an increase of the wage rate in these stages.

Of course if there are "specific goods" which can be used only in the production of a given commodity, their demand is likely to increase in the early stages (where more resources will be attracted, anyway) as well as in the new stages of production that will emerge as a result of the increase in the average length of the process. *If, instead, the demand for consumer's goods increases relative to the*

E. G. Tsionas, *The Euro and International Financial Stability*,
Financial and Monetary Policy Studies 37, DOI: 10.1007/978-3-319-01171-4_16,

demand of producers' goods, then we should exactly the opposite sequence of events—a shifting of resources to late stages of production, a shorter average period of production, and higher prices in the later stages. As Hayek has emphasized:

> But to think of interest only as a direct cost factor is to overlook its main influence on production. What is much more important is its effect on prices through its effect on demand for the intermediate products and for the factors from which they are produced. It is in consequence of these changes in demand and the changes in cost which it brings about by raising the prices of those factors which are in strong demand in early stages compared to those which are less demanded there, that the prices of the intermediate products are adjusted (Hayek 1967, p. 83).

Another way to formulate the same argument is the following. By expecting an increase in the demand for producers' (non—specific) goods, it would be more profitable to invest in the early rather than the late stages of production. The signal that the entrepreneurs have, in this respect, is precisely the fall of the prices of the consumption goods and the increase in the price of producer goods, which necessitates an increase of employment of resources produced in earlier stages. If markets operate freely, and relative prices move in this direction as an immediate result, the shifting of new credit to "more basic" or early resources will be a natural consequence along with an increase in the average length of the production process. The banks, in the hands of which, the new credit will be placed, are likely to think that early and non—specific products or resources are less risky that products that are close to being final or products that can be developed quickly. So they have an additional motive to accommodate the increased demand for output in the earlier stages (relative to the final stages). Therefore, in this case, the risk considerations of the banks, and the profit expectations of the private sector, are likely to coincide in propagating new credit through the market system.

It is not unreasonable to assume that the ECB followed the announcement of new credit by a decrease of interest rates, because the new funds need to be secured and thus do not disturb further financial stability or overall risk of the financial and banking system. It is also reasonable to assume that the new interest rate of 1 % is below its equilibrium level; otherwise there would be no need for intervention. As we saw, old and new entrepreneurs will shift their attention to more basic or earlier products that is "original" means of production or intermediate goods produced in the earlier stages, in the terminology of Austrian economics. Of course some original means that were used before will now be released or left unutilized. Prices or original or early intermediate goods will rise. For example, entrepreneurs will find it profitable to buy products that they used to manufacture themselves, from other firms at an earlier stage, or buy capital and machinery. It is in that sense that the Austrian school speaks of more "capitalistic" modes of production when it refers to the increase of the average length or the shifting or resources to earlier stages.

The critical point in this analysis is, indeed, that the shifting or resources to earlier stages will necessarily materialize in reduced supply of consumer's goods, at least after some time when inventories will be depleted. Necessarily the price of these goods will increase and there will be "*involuntary reduction of consumption*" (Hayek 1967, p. 88). Since most consumers would not be willing to change their way of living immediately, they will continue for some time to spend the same amount on consumption and, therefore, this

> will mean a new and reversed change of the proportion between the demand for consumers' goods and the demand for producers' goods in favor of the former (Hayek 1967, p. 89).

Thus, having started with a situation where the price of producers' goods increases, we now face a different situation: The price of consumer goods rises and the prices of producers' goods diminish, thus making the initial plans less profitable across the board of the production process, save (or less so) for those industries that are closer to the *final* stages of production. The market corrects itself the mistakes and the discrepancies that have taken place as a result of an artificial lowering of the interest rate below its equilibrium level, and the artificial increase in credit. *But this correction involves a new crisis* since the accumulation of capital in the earlier stages is no longer in line with consumer demand. A new shift of resourced to the later stages will become necessary sooner or later, before a new equilibrium can be attained.

The banks are unlikely to realize the movement of relative prices that has made the production of consumption goods more profitable; they will only notice it when industries involved in "longer" or "round about" methods will begin failing in their obligations, as the result of the decrease in the prices of their products. So the banks are likely to keep financing "round about" or capital—intensive ("capitalistic") products and projects based on their initial perception that such projects involve less risk. The problem is likely to be less severe if the banks provide the new credit in stages by examining closely the profitability of new projects and industries. In that case, the increased demand for consumers' goods can be accommodated by expansion of the firms (or new firms) operating near the final stages of production. However, the banks or other financial institutions do not have such a mechanism and operate based on "rules rather than discretion". In other words, they cannot anticipate or forecast accurately the risks involved in the various investment projects because they do not look at relative prices but at past performance, and in this case, past performance is the safe way to destruction.

Of course, at low interest rates of 1 %, one might think that the total amount of non—performing loans for the banks will be quite small. If the banks, for example, distribute the new credit, *uniformly* across the various stages of production, they cannot lose too much since the eventual loss from investments in longer or earlier processes will be balanced by the profits that will be created in the later or less capitalistic processes associated with the more or less final production of goods associated with consumption. The uniform allocation of credit would be advisable from the point of view of the banks, and corresponds to nothing else than diversification to minimize risk. *But from the point of view of the economy, the crisis will not be avoided. There will be destruction and deployment of capital and other intermediate resourced, including labor, from the early stages of production.*

Some non—specific resources from the earlier stages will be employed, after some time, in the later stages of production. But the specific resources will be destroyed as it happens during the course of a classical crisis.

We should not fail to mention that, in the process, inflation will settle in. This is not the consequence of the effect of credit expansion on the "general price level". It is, on the contrary, the consequence of the credit expansion and the artificially low interest rate on the prices of producers' goods *relative* to the prices of the consumers' goods, as well as the *relationships* between all these prices. From the preceding analysis that should have been made clear.

There is a naïve argument that we should consider here: When the central bank (like the ECB) provides new credit at extremely low interest rates, a boost to investment is forthcoming, and the financial system cannot be disturbed since the losses cannot be too large. According to this argument (implicit in many ECB policies) it appears that the "golden rule" has been found according to which (1) investment increases considerably, (2) credit funds are secured and as a result, (3) the puzzle of uninterrupted growth with financial stability has eventually been found. *This, in fact, provides a new standard of monetary policy by controlling both monetary expansion and interest rates.* The argument rests on the assumption that liquidity is constrained as a result of the recent crisis of 2008 and therefore, credit expansion is necessary to stimulate the economy but at interest rates which (1) are low enough to guarantee solvency of the financial system, and (2) low enough to boost investment and sustain sizeable growth for a long period of time. The argument is also supported by another mechanism: Interest rates for *new* credit are *lower* than interest rates in general.

If the mechanism can work, there is no doubt that the Eurozone will enjoy prosperity for a very long time. Additionally, the mechanism does not impose any burden at all on the public finances of any country since it can only improve the fiscal stance by the expected increase in tax revenues from increased business activity.

There is no doubt that this policy will increase "investment". To be precise it will increase the employment of non-specific and specific factors or intermediate products in the early and more "capitalistic" processes of the process of production. But, as we saw, the reverse tendency will soon begin and the prices in these processes will decrease, thus setting in motion a destruction of capital and all other resources which were employed under the initial, false expectation that the profitability of projects in these stages has increased. The profitability has, in fact, remained exactly the same, and the only thing that has changed is (1) the artificial reduction of interest rates below their equilibrium level, and (2) the artificial availability of new credit. The process of re-establishment of equilibrium in the credit market involves, quite naturally, a latent increase in interest rates. Whether this truly happens or remains latent, is immaterial because it will be re-established in the induced change of demand for consumers' goods relative to the demand for production goods, and the respective changes in relative prices.

This policy of the ECB, as a result, will have to face the fact that re-establishment of equilibrium will take the form of an economic crisis which, of course, will put an end to the ideas of sustainable growth through such practices; in fact, the policy will set in motion the mechanism for a depression. Perhaps not as great as the one of 2008 or the depression of late 2011, but *it will, certainly, create a depression instead of uninterrupted growth and prosperity.* Of course the banks that will be selected to distribute the new credit in a "healthy" way are unlikely to lose from this policy. But it is not the banking sector that will initiate the depression because of wrong decisions, as in 2008. It will be manufacturing itself - along with its effects upon the service sector. *It is certain that investment will increase for a limited period of one or two years but then the reverse motion will set in with deployment of capital* (in the "capitalistic" and round about processes) *and other resources or intermediate products, placing the economy into a new depression.*

It is highly likely that the ECB will not accept the depression as a necessary outcome of its policy as it can always attribute it to this or the other "exogenous" fact. It is possible to keep on supplying new credit at low interest rates for a period of time but, naturally, this process has a definite end either (1) before facing serious inflationary pressures or (2) because there is no need for the banking sector to distribute uniformly the new credit across the time cross-section of production processes; thus facing non-performing loans. Due to the low interest rates the second possibility is unlikely but the first is quite serious. Although the banking sector does not face serious risks, manufacturing will be diverted to unprofitable usage of credit and will be destroyed in the process of providing him with "cheap credit". In a few words, *the policy will be ineffective and will soon create a new recession.*

One reason why such policies create the opposite result relative to what is expected, should be evident: The artificial lowering of interest rates, especially for investment, diverts resources to uses that prove to be unprofitable because of the necessary adjustments in the relative prices among different producers' goods and among producers' versus consumers' goods. The other reason is less obvious but we hinted to that effect when we referred to "*involuntary reduction of consumption*" (Hayek 1967, p. 88) or "*forced saving*". This argument was central in Hayek's thought and he refined it in many instances.[1] When the increase of credit by artificial means or the monetary expansion becomes infeasible, it is necessary to rely on savings to continue the credit expansion. When the interest rate is reduced below its equilibrium level, "cheap credit" is possible only up to the point where it can be supported by additional funds from the consumers. But this is only feasible at *higher* interest rates. The eventual establishment of equilibrium in the credit market *will involve corrections where interest rates go up, not down,* so as to secure funds from consumers' savings—if inflation is a concern of economic policy. The "*involuntary reduction of consumption*" cannot go on for long periods of time, making it necessary to increase the interest rate on deposits. In turn, this

---

[1] See for example F. Hayek, "Capital and industrial fluctuations", *Econometrica*, April 1934, p. 161.

will decrease the profits of the banks that are involved in the credit expansion and, apparently, the banking sector as a whole. The adjustments of the interest rate on deposits are likely to be considerable especially in the tenuous situation of "*involuntary reduction of consumption*" or "*forced savings*".

This is where commercial banks begin to reconsider the situation, because of their reduced profits. Without regulation they are likely to keep new credit as reserves to be able to face the risks that are emerging from the restructuring of production and the resulting restructuring of relative prices. If the ECB insists on advancing these funds to the private sector for financing new investment, the effects will be the ones we described already. If not, the banking sector will appear "stable" but that, in turn, would beat the purpose of the credit expansion.

The solution to the problem is to let the credit markets operate freely, so that the equilibrium interest rate balances the needs of the consumers and the financial needs of the producers. In credit or financial markets' equilibrium, the available funds for investment, across all stages of production, are determined in total by what is available of total income after consumption and taxes. When "liquidity in the economy is low", more funds have to be attracted from consumers, and this is only possible at higher interest rates (relative to the ones prevailing). It is not the business of the government to supply more funds, either by creating new money or by diverting funds from other uses. The equilibrium in the financial markets is not independent of equilibrium in the markets for all intermediate products, from the earliest to the latest stages of production; in fact, a *general* equilibrium presupposes the necessary adjustments in all these markets towards the equilibrium. *Under the general rule that loans by commercial banks equal precisely savings minus reserves, there can be no imbalances in the real sector created by distortions in the financial markets.* Since the most profitable users will demand the loans available, the interest rate will move freely to guarantee the efficient use of funds and, in turn, the efficient use of funds will result in the best possible situation for the financial sector. When the Central Bank intervenes either with artificial credit, lower interest rates or—what is worse—with both, it effectively distorts: (1) the notion of "the most profitable users", and (2) the balance between savings and funds available for "the most profitable use". *The balance, on the one hand, as well as "the most profitable use", on the other, are to be determined by the equilibrium and the markets; they are never given in advance.*

The validity of the Austrian theory rests, essentially, upon the premise that the business cycle is, in fact, the credit cycle, or the history of credit policy in any particular period. In the following Figs. 16.1 and 16.2, we examine the (quarter–to–quarter) rate of growth of GDP and rate of growth of industrial production versus the growth rate in total business credit, for Greece.[2]

It is quite remarkable that in the midst of recession after 2008, credit expansion by over 15 % and the subsequent contraction, accounted for almost the entire

[2] The data are quarterly (2000–2011) and have been obtained from ELSTAT, the Greek Statistical Authority.

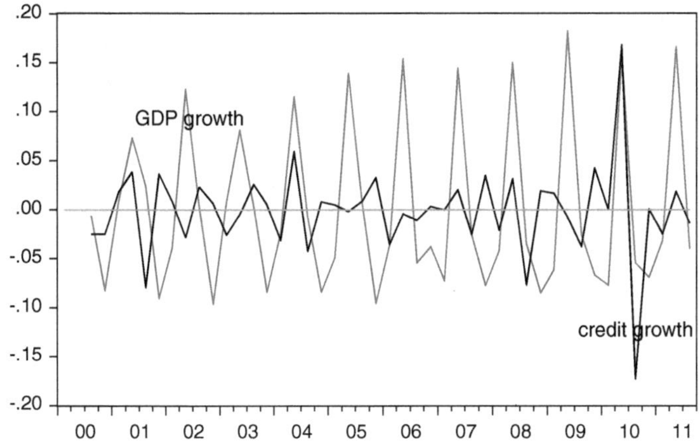

Fig. 16.1 Growth rate, GDP and credit (Greece)

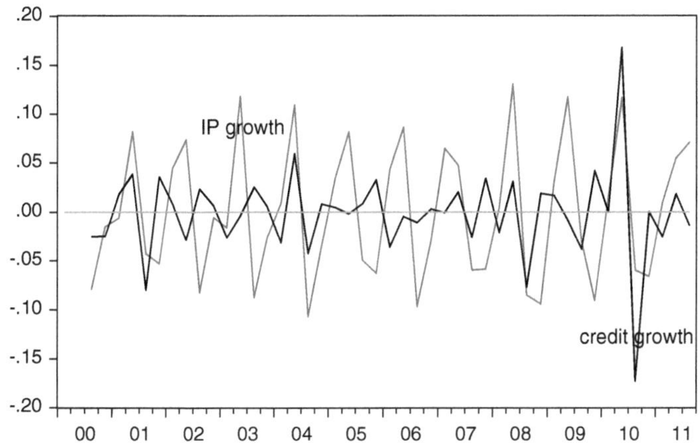

Fig. 16.2 Growth rate, industrial production and credit

fluctuation in GDP or industrial production. In the period 2000–2008, credit changes predict GDP changes after nearly two quarters but the synchronization appears greater during in the period after the 2008 crisis and, *in fact, there has a Greek crisis only during 2010 when credit boosted followed by a severe contraction, creating a drop in GDP of about* 5 % (which could have been even larger in the view of revised data).

In view of these results it is odd to expect that the recent ECB credit expansion accompanied by low interest rates will have any positive impact on European economies, other than the profitability of selected banks. In fact, it will set in motion a new business cycle instead of a recovery with multiplicative effects across the European economies.

As we remarked earlier, the real problem in the EMU is the exposure of European commercial banks to risky or 'toxic' government bonds (Greece's for example) and the extent to which the ECB will be able to provide enough credit expansion to maintain the solvency of the commercial banking system, no matter whether or not Greece and/or Southern European countries stay or go from the Eurozone. The primary objective of the ECB is the performance of the commercial banking system. As long as the outstanding obligations of Greece cannot be met, the ECB must meet these obligations in an implicit way, by loans to Greece in the form of bailout plans which are, in reality, bailout and credit expansion policies in favor of the commercial banks of France and Germany, for the most part.

What is important to understand is that even if Greece is let go, the outstanding obligations to French and German banks must be covered, and this is a problem that must be addressed by the ECB; not the performance of the euro or the Eurozone, and not by any other third party. It is also important to understand that the credit policy of the ECB in the form of bailout for Greece did not happen because the Greek government could not pay wage bills and pensions but rather because, *in excess of them* and given tax revenues and expenditures, the Greek government could not meet interest payments and capital payments forthcoming at maturity, resulting from its public debt in the hands on major French and German commercial banks.

What is, in effect, necessary, is a change of focus from the balance sheet of the commercial banks to more global concerns. Such concerns cannot be addressed in the confines of the Eurozone because the Central Bank of the Eurozone has already opted for certain decisions: *Unconditional* credit expansion to bail out *certain* banks and credit expansion to *certain* banks at low rates of 1 % as a growth—enhancing policy. Under these conditions the Eurozone is not sustainable. *The ECB's credit expansion policy is disastrous, its interest rate policy is highly biased and destabilizing (leading out of equilibrium) and overall prospects about the euro, in terms of productivity and competitiveness, are gloomy.* In international markets, sooner or later, the demand for the euro will fall leading to depreciation, calling not for "increased exports" but rather a major—restructuring of the European productive sector towards more liberalization to achieve a new constellation of relative prices in the world economy.

Chances are that the careful reader would raise the following question: How can the ECB control both credit expansion and interest rates at the same time without knocking the door of inflation? One is likely to dismiss the question based on the heavy regulation of the European economy by the bureaucracy and the ECB. But we can consider an alternative view:

> Variations in the ratio between the stock of money and the demand for money must ultimately exert an influence on the rate of interest also; but this occurs in a different way from that popularly imagined. There is no direct connexion between the rate of interest and the amount of money held by the individuals who participate in the transactions of the market; there is only an indirect connexion operating in a roundabout way through the displacements in the social distribution of income and wealth which occur as a consequence of variations in the objective exchange-value of money. (von Mises 1953, p. 346).

von Mises' view that "[*t*]*here is no direct connexion between the rate of interest and the amount of money*" is provocative in its own right since it implies that there is no "demand for money curve" in the usual sense. In fact, this "curve" if it exists, it must be a derived product of "*money held by the individuals who participate in the transactions of the market*". As a matter of fact, the policy makers can control both the interest rates and the amount of monetary or credit expansion. Theoretically, one "cannot" do that because control of one magnitude will determine endogenously the other. This conclusion from the traditional "demand for money curve" is misguided, in the sense that the curve itself is created as one proceeds:

> If the distribution of income and property is modified in such a way as to increase capacity for saving, then eventually the ratio between the value of present goods and future goods must be modified in favour of the latter. (von Mises 1953, p. 347).

From a credit expansion that favors the solvency of commercial banks exposed to risky public debt, we cannot infer much in terms of economic consequences. It is also necessary to know the details of the credit channel, that is the reconstruction of the commercial banks' portfolio in terms of financing consumer or business credit, as well as the details of business credit. Once the European banks are covered from the ECB in terms of their "exposure" to risky public debt, it is necessary what will happen afterwards, and how the commercial banks will reshape their loan decisions. Apparently, interest rates will have to be determined based on such considerations, but the important fact is that there is no pre-determined "demand for money curve"; at least not in a stable and known form that can be used for drawing useful economic inferences.

References

Hayek FA (1935/1967) Prices and production, 2nd edn. Augustus M. Kelley, New York

Mises L (1912/1953) The theory of money and credit. Yale University Press, New Haven

Chapter 17
Some Remarks on the Greek Problem

To look closely at the "Greek problem" means examining some aspects that are often taken for granted. One of them is the low productivity of the Greek economy, the absence of competitiveness, the highly regulated markets *etc*. Although a detailed examination is impossible in this essay, let us look at the average productivity of labor in *manufacturing* for three countries, Greece, Germany and Spain, in Fig. 17.1.[1]

Evidently, the performance of the Greek economy in terms of productivity has been quite remarkable since the 1980s and in 1994 it surpassed the performance of Germany (DE) and Spain (ES). In fact, this is true for most if not all sectors of the Greek economy.[2] This fact is not difficult to explain. The capital/labor ratio has increased *tremendously* in all sectors of the economy since the 1980s as shown in Fig. 17.2 for 15 sectors of the Greek economy, according to the recent ELSTAT classification.

Undoubtedly, this manifests in tremendous investments in the capital—producing or more "roundabout" processes of production that sky—rocketed after 1994 and the decisive decrease in interest rates. Considering this as a *mal* investment process, it should show itself in rates of technical change or the rate of growth of total factor productivity. As shown in Fig. 17.3, the situation for most sectors of the Greek economy is not good as technical change[3] deteriorates significantly over time in most of its sectors (2, 3, 4, 6, 9, 12, 13, 14) at least in the 1990s. These sectors are Mining, Manufacturing, Construction, Transportation and Communications, Public Administration, Education, and Health. Agriculture (1), Commerce (7), Hotels and Restaurants (8) and other public interest services (15)

---

[1] Average labor productivity is defined as Q/L where Q is a measure of real output and L is employment. All data (except Greece) come from the EUKLEMS data base. For Greece we utilize the latest available data from ELSTAT, the Greek Statistical Authority.

[2] The results are omitted to save space but are available on request.

[3] Technical progress is estimated from a translog cost function and the associated share equation of labor. Technical progress is measured using the elasticity of cost with respect to an index of technological progress (ECT), the time trend in this application. Declining or negative ECT shows improvement or presence of technical change.

E. G. Tsionas, *The Euro and International Financial Stability*,
Financial and Monetary Policy Studies 37, DOI: 10.1007/978-3-319-01171-4_17,

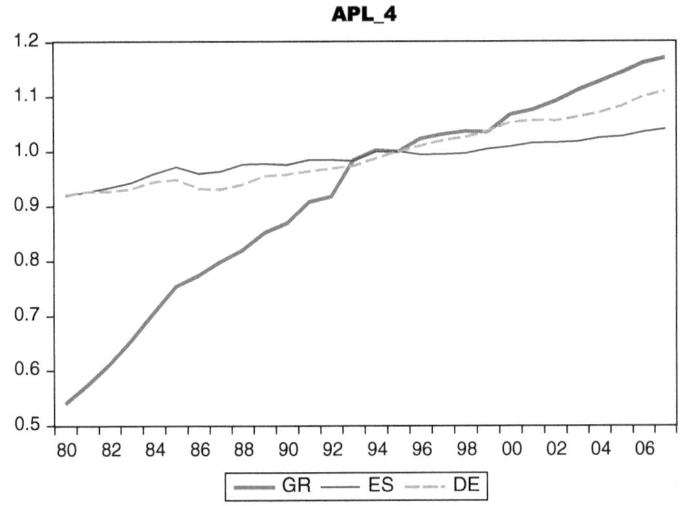

Fig. 17.1 Average productivity of labor

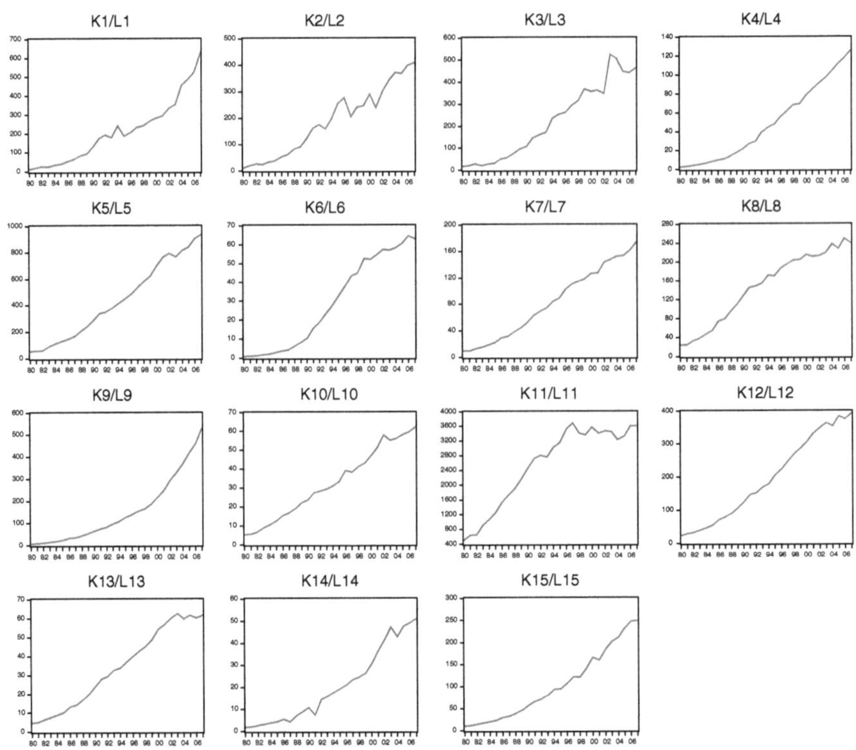

Fig. 17.2 Capital—labor ratios in Greek economy

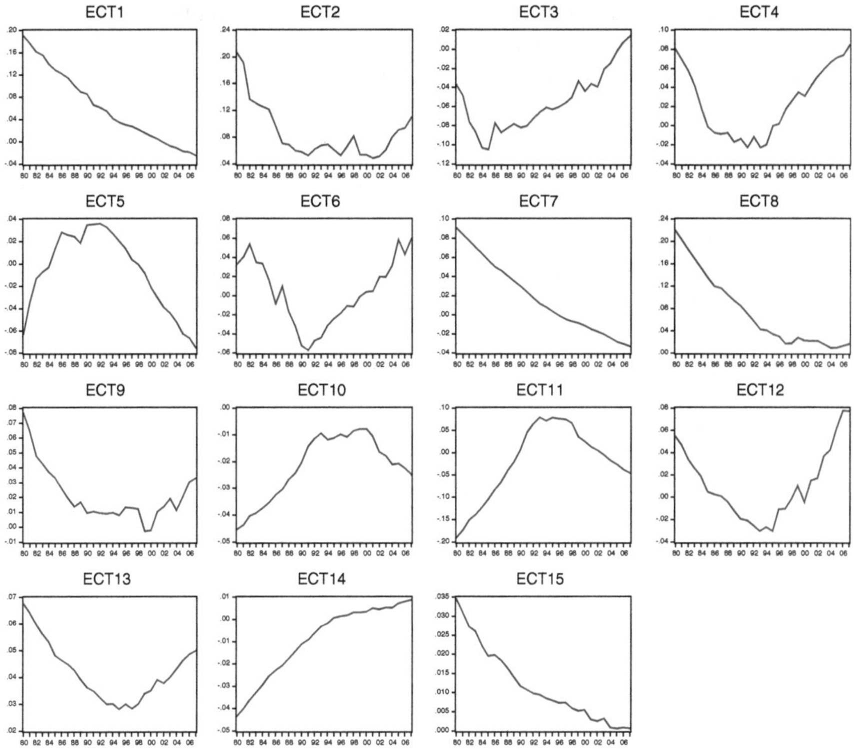

Fig. 17.3 Technical progress in the Greek economy (cost elasticity with respect to time)

show an intertemporal improvement which is expected in view of the orientation and the comparative advantages of the Greek economy.

In fact the essence of the "Greek problem" is the deterioration in "total factor productivity" in the capital—producing or "roundabout" sectors to which considerable real resources have shifted because of low real interest rates in more than 25 years and particularly after the "Stabilization Programme" in anticipation of the EMU. Manufacturing, construction, and the public sector have experienced significant drops in their "productivity" despite the fact that they appeared more capital intensive in view of their capital—labor ratio.

The "Stabilization Programme" had little to do with the free operation of Greek markets, and more with the target of joining the EMU and adopting the euro in order for Greece to become a member of the "hard core" of the EU where the decision making process takes place. There is little doubt that both Greek and European governments considered this to be a strategic objective, *on political grounds*. This, of course, is acceptable but the unintended consequences were detrimental for both Greece and the EMU.

The explosion of public debt has been an "unforeseen event", one might argue. In fact, the non—sustainability of Greek debt was evident by a simple examination of maturities and the current fiscal stance of Greece. Following the subprime crisis the new socialist Greek government announced that the deficit was 14 % of GDP instead of the previous (conservative) government's official release of 8.5 %. The conservative administration had also revised GDP estimates upwards and had indicated that the deficit might have been larger compared to the figure provided by the previous socialist administration. *Despite the fact that public finances were worse than anticipated, even to a large extent, this cannot possibly make up for the fact that upcoming mature Greek debt could not have been accommodated in full.* In that respect, the explosion of public debt has *not* been an "unforeseen event" but the fact remains that few economists, if any, warned against it before or immediately after the subprime crisis. Certainly, precautionary measures have not been taken by the ECB to address the problem instead of finding herself in the uncomfortable position to monetize the debt *to the extent that it affected the European commercial banks*.

It is flawed to think that the interventions of the ECB bailed out the whole Greek economy. The ECB simply bailed out major European commercial banks. In fact, only 30 % of the Greek public debt is foreign; owned, almost exclusively, by major European commercial banks. The remainder, 70 % of debt, is a *net burden* for the Greek economy. Although it can be negotiated this would have immediate real effects on the deterioration of Social Security and associated funds, and also on the public sector itself. Apparently, "haircuts" and ECB interventions do not do much to alleviate such problems.

In view of these difficulties, the administration imposed "austerity" measures. These include, most, extra—ordinary tax payments of all varieties (even on housing ownership and selected occupations), wage cuts in the public sector, implicit motives for early retirement etc, horizontal cuts on pensions and capital reimbursement upon retirement etc. The Greek administration surely showed no lack of imagination in devising new tax schemes, reducing incomes across the board and trying to reduce the extent of the underground economy. The argument is that austerity measures reduce "aggregate demand" and thus they reinforce the recession. The counter-argument is that public finances must be put in order, *not because of upcoming maturing debt* which is secured by the ECB as far as European commercial banks are concerned, but in order to avoid further horizontal taxation and other unpopular measures that will reduce incomes (and "aggregate demand").

So the two arguments are not so different since, at the end, they both resort to "aggregate demand" to justify their validity. The fact remains that the ECB will back maturing obligations. This provides Greek administration with some comfort in the short run—which also explains why the political game is quite active despite the seriousness of the economic situation for the nation. However, this provides no relief for the stance of Social Security or the wage bill for the public sector (which currently is almost 50 % of tax revenues). In that sense the "structural reforms" which the Greek government is called to implement in the last minute, despite the fact the government should have implemented them gradually since 1994 or 2000, cannot possibly work out. *First*, the political system is too reluctant to resort to "cold turkey" implementations of reforms that should have taken place in the past 15 years. *Second*, even if it does so, "aggregate demand" will collapse nullifying the effects from restructuring of the public sector. *Third*, the *troika* advises for wage cuts in the private sector to improve productivity and competitiveness, and this argument is used in various ways by the Greek political system, for or against.

The third argument has no validity whatsoever since it refers to the medium—or the long—run. It *may* or *may not* be true that wage cuts across the board in the private sector will improve competitiveness but this is simply irrelevant for the short run.[4] As for the first argument, whether or not the political system can or cannot implement "cold turkey 'structural reforms'", is a question outside the realm of economics. *The pragmatic issue is what happens with "aggregate demand"*. Taxes and austerity measures reduce "aggregate demand" but they *seem* likely to improve public finances. Unless tax rates are adjusted upwards, in the next period, the government is likely to end up with less fiscal revenues, if government expenditure is not reduced heavily.

There is no easy, short—run way out of this vicious circle. If consumers expect the austerity measures to last, they will consume and save less. How does this affect the relative profitability of different sectors across the time—horizon of production? *First*, the profitability of the consumers' goods sector is decreased and some investments will have to be liquidated in this sector. *Second*, marginal long—run investments or "roundabout" plans are also likely to be liquidated in the process, due to a long period of low interest rates and *mal* investment in the sectors that now exhibit technical regress, as we discussed above. This process is aggravated by the drop of demand in the final or semi—final goods sector. Effectively, the economy experiences negative shocks in employment and investment across the board, *grosso modo*. *Third*, Greek commercial banks are likely to be more prudent in their financing and will refrain from risky investments of all sorts including business financing for working capital or long—term investment.

This situation, which is really a nightmare, is not conformable with the present configuration of interest rates. Some competitive sectors will require funds at a rate much higher compared to the prevailing, while others would not be able to meet current debt obligations. Apparently, new borrowing should be directed to the competitive sectors or firms, while the second will be liquidated in the process, showing up as non—performing loans and banking risk. But it is not the business of the government or the commercial banks to figure out the "competitive" sectors or firms; this should come out as equilibrium in the credit markets. *If commercial banks act as competitive firms, without any guarantees from the government or the ECB, the desired match of banking lending one the one hand, and most profitable or competitive projects on the other, will naturally come out as an equilibrium outcome*.

[4] Apparently, wages should increase in the sectors that have competitive advantage and improve during the recession, leading the economy out of it. Pragmatically, there are many employment related and non employment related costs which hamper productivity and competitiveness and their comprehensive examination is not possible here.

The recession is bound to create new competitive advantages for specific sectors. These sectors will be in need of finance and they should be financed by rational financial intermediaries at the appropriate high interest rate—high compared to the present. As a matter of fact the interaction of the real and financial sector will produce endogenously, in equilibrium, *the* competitive and well—performing sectors and firms within them. This fundamental truth, to which few economists would object, implies (1) a relative distancing of the commercial banks from the national Central Bank or the ECB, (2) open credit markets where interest rates are determined in a competitive fashion. Once the new competitive advantages of the country have been determined in the international markets, *then and only then* the Administration can consider again the configuration of tax rates and the increase of its tax revenues *without hampering* the intertemporal allocation of resources that has emerged from the free (or relatively free) operation of credit and banking markets.

The problem of unemployment can be partially resolved by the rational reallocation of resources and credit funds to the sectors that are competitive in the international markets. The sectors and firms within these sectors are *ex ante* unknown, and can only be determined in competitive credit and banking markets. It is beyond doubt that this will necessitate a considerable increase in interest rates, if interest rates are determined freely in the relevant markets. The *overall* interest rate is immaterial and *may* or *may not* be affected. The existing credit, consisting almost solely of savings, will have to be allocated into risky projects more wisely *at much higher interest rates*. In the long—term employment and incomes will recover, along with the balance sheets of the commercial banking sector, improving public finances and putting Social Insurance on sound foundations.

Chapter 18
Can There be Stable Currencies After the Euro?

General

The ECB during 2012 set a new mode of monetary and credit policy, amounting to new credit given at low interest rates of 1 % to be propagated into the system by selected commercial banks. We have shown that, despite its prospects, this policy is futile and will, in fact, result into a new recession. If we consider this as the first in a series of last attempts to save the essential unity of the Eurozone, the question begs itself: What will happen in the future?

It is of course quite possible that the European Bureaucracy will attempt to save itself along with its monetary system. The Eurozone started out as a zone of monetary, price, and fiscal stability zone. There is, in principle, nothing wrong with that, save for the fact that aggregate statistics can never reflect the real state of the economy. The real state of the economy is always determined by the configuration of relative prices and the relations between supply and demand for different consumers' and producers' products. Despite the fact that monetary and fiscal targets provide considerable discipline they cannot control for the fact that as long as distortionary taxation is not reduced along with cuts in public expenditure there are qualitative factors at work which, unfortunately, cannot be contained within the framework of aggregate provisions for monetary, price, and fiscal stability.

The monetary and financial system of the European Bureaucracy cannot be sustained unless it becomes open and competitive, that is unless the interventions are minimized, and credit expansion is restricted to the supply of savings. But the European Bureaucracy can only survive as long as it has total control of the monetary base and the credit supply, along with its allocation and distribution through its favorite commercial banking channels. If such rights are taken away of the ECB, the markets will sooner or later (indeed, sooner rather than later) establish credit and financial market equilibria, that will prove unfavorable for the European Bureaucracy.

It is true that the Eurozone came out wounded from the 2008 crisis. Heterogeneity in the Eurozone, certainly traumatized its economy considerably, thus putting the old theory of "asymmetric shocks" in the foreground. The old theory,

E. G. Tsionas, *The Euro and International Financial Stability*,
Financial and Monetary Policy Studies 37, DOI: 10.1007/978-3-319-01171-4_18,

of course, has some validity. But *most economists tend to forget that "asymmetric shocks" can be propagated only if the Central Bank is accommodating*. The recent policy of increased credit at extremely low interest rates constitutes the definition of accommodation.

A dissolution of the Euro is likely to produce a "shock" into the international financial markets. The shock will be mostly due to the uncertainty of monetary and credit policies that will determine the international allocation of credit to the various stages of investment. Since European productivity is expected to lag behind productivity in the US, the prospects of this new allocation are not expected to be good. If the ECB were to restrain itself and rely on opening the European markets to international competition, there would be no problem, but the prospects are different. The active credit and monetary policies of the ECB signal a further deterioration of European productivity to the parts of the international entrepreneurial sector that can read the signals.

Currently, *the credit expansion at low interest rates will favor undoubtedly the more "capitalistic" or early production sectors in the EU*, although this expansion will soon revert to an overall depression. Since there is no anticipation of permanent increase in productivity relative to the US, it would be preferable to dissolve the euro into zones of credit and monetary stability: *Such zones will be decided on the grounds of restricting investment to gross savings; that is into zones determined to finance investment without inflationary or artificial interventions in the credit market*. Such zones or groups can only emerge endogenously based on the needs of financing investment, and the relative demands of producers' versus consumption goods. In principle, the Eurozone and the ECB could have taken upon themselves this responsibility but they did not do so. In fact, they could not do otherwise, since the European Bureaucracy placed political constraints upon the possible outcomes of credit and financial markets.

Since the political constraints were severe, their dissolution will result in a situation that will accord well with equilibrium in international and national credit and financial markets. From that perspective, it is hard to imagine that the effects of the "shock" into the international financial markets from the dissolution of the Eurozone, will sustain themselves into the long run. *Provided the dissolution comes with a commitment to group—specific credit and financial or monetary policies, all conditions will be in place for a new international order without unpredictable shocks*.

In fact, the dissolution of the eurozone into subsets of currencies does not involve anything more than restrictions on artificial credit expansion and interest rates, along with the usual fiscal policy restrictions. This complicates the situation regarding the allocation of resources; it does not make it simpler or more straightforward. In this sense *monetary nationalism is certain to propagate further the effects of malinvestment* and lead to a situation where the establishment of a new equilibrium will be even more difficult.

True enough, "asymmetric shocks" may hit the members of a monetary union in an asymmetric way, but we have to have the correct perspective. Exogenous shocks will necessarily hit different sectors of the same economy in an "asymmetric" way. This will always be the case since the demand for different products along the time—specific sequence of the production process may react differently to asymmetric shocks. This is precisely the reason why financial markets should be left free to operate in order to establish interest rates that will mitigate the shocks by equilibrating demand and supply in the various subsectors or regions. *Without such flexibility in the financial markets it is impossible to devise a sustainable growth policy.*

Some Important Questions

The following specific questions must be addressed.

1. Whether and how to redenominate sovereign debt in the departing nations.
2. Whether and how international contracts denominated in euros might be altered.
3. The effects on the stability of the banking system.
4. The link between exit from EMU and sovereign debt restructuring.
5. How to manage the macroeconomic effects of exit, including devaluation, inflation, confidence, and effects on debts.
6. Different timetables and approaches to transition (e.g. "surprise" redenomination versus signalled transitions).
7. How best to manage the legal and institutional implications.
8. A consideration of evidence from relevant historical examples (e.g. the end of various currency pegs and previous monetary unions).

As a result of our analysis it turns out that we can provide definitive answers to all questions. We believe that we have addressed [8] and [3] in a rigorous manner. Indeed, the theory and the historical experience show us that (1) monetary unions have failed when they departed from their "standard", and (2) the stability of the banking system is not at stake when the real sector has secured its plans in terms of financing and profitability. Departing from a "standard" always involved a credit expansion in excess of savings, no matter if they were denominated in gold (as in the past) or a relatively stable currency.

Regarding [5] we recommend monetary sub-groups that respect the policy of minimal intervention into monetary and credit markets. Regarding [6] we recommend currency and exchange rates that are as "open" as possible to reflect the current structure of production. But the fact remains that *a possible dissolution of the euro cannot lead to more stable currencies unless there is implicit market coordination.* This implies that although new currencies may be formed they will have to be pegged to some target and avoid the possibility of floating exchange rates. Otherwise, a possible dissolution will lead to disarray and a constellation of different policies that will distort the allocation of resources across time and space even further. In principle, there is no problem with a set of monetary "nationalist" policies which, however, are disciplined in terms of monetary and credit expansion and avoid devaluations of the currency or surprises in fiscal policies—including both expenditures and taxes. Such disciplined monetary "nationalist" policies are in the right direction but without coordination there is no guarantee that they will be followed over a long time horizon so, in the final analysis, they are an excuse for inflationary policies. One may argue that certain countries have managed indeed to be disciplined in the monetary and fiscal arena without being part of the Eurozone. This is certainly true but when it comes to a closer examination of these policies one has to wonder: (1) whether the time-structure of production has been unaffected by malinvestment and (2) whether the absence of freely determined interest rates is a condition that is compatible with monetary and credit stability. The emphasis on monetary "nationalist" policies ignores several facts. First, that the allocation of investment and resources does not depend on national policies alone but the configuration of policies in Europe. Second, that the emphasis on "aggregates" is neither a necessary nor a sufficient condition for dynamic equilibrium. Third, and perhaps more important, that inflation in specific prices can be significant even when "aggregate inflation" and other statistics appear to have been stabilized.

Regarding [7] we have to make sure that (a) central banks are committed to financing investment by existing savings, (b) no creation of fiat money, and securing of balanced budgets.

[1], [2] and [4] are interrelated. When members leave the Eurozone, their obligations will affect the stability of the system. It is likely that such members will be countries that are mostly involved in the later rather than the early or basic stages of production. In that sense, along with devaluation, they are likely to benefit from a dissolution of the euro, in the very short run. But in the long term they will have to face the chaotic situation created by malinvestment and the positive effects of devaluation will disappear. The argument that devaluation can sustain a permanent change in industrial structure capable of maintaining stable growth is highly misguided as it ignores the basic fact that most other relevant international prices will adjust quickly to annihilate its effects. When quantity variables cannot adjust in the short run the effects will be easily absorbed by the price mechanism.

The crucial question concerns their debts. Recently the idea of "haircut" has been advanced and implemented. The "haircut" affects the credit and loan markets and the ability of financial intermediaries to finance new investment. Even after devaluation, common sense would suggest repayment of debt in real terms or in terms of a stable currency. The "haircut" is an explicit recognition of the fact that certain countries failed to allocate the funds efficiently and this failure is subsidized by the ECB. Question [1] then has to be seen in a new light: If it were for the wrong credit and interest rate polices of the ECB, are we to redenominate the debts? The redenomination of debt and its "haircut" are equally unacceptable and unfounded—unless the resources are allocated so that real problems are alleviated. The attainment of equilibrium in the debt and bond markets requires, first of all, a stabilization of interest rates at levels where the supply and demand of funds are approximately equal. Currently, the interest rates and the government bond spreads are determined more or less by the Credit Rating Agencies, who act as market regulators but they cannot substitute the markets themselves.

Under free competition of currencies in international as well the national markets, there will be a natural tendency to accept the more stable currencies.[1] If public debt is denominated in the same units or in terms of a portfolio of stable currencies, stability of the financial system is not at stake and, at the same time, the problem of devaluation and its inflationary consequences will be mitigated. Confidence in the plans of the government will also be guaranteed since there has to be fiscal solvency when the free choice of currency will deprive the Central Bank from its monopoly over inflationary money creation.

A unilateral decision of a country to exit from the eurozone is, in principle, a dangerous undertaking. The danger is not so much for the euro itself, if the country is small, but for the country in question. The return to a national currency, controlled by the Central Bank or the government, and the control of credit, will prove detrimental. In that sense, the fiscal and monetary discipline implied by participation in the eurozone is necessary, when the institutional framework is not consistent with open markets, competition, and stable monetary and fiscal policies. This is well understood by all participants in the eurozone and there is little point in analyzing it in more detail. However, the weak euro (which is, to a large extent the result of ECB policies) could have been avoided if the dollar or the pound could have been used freely and, this in fact, what happens what the European authorities refer to "speculative games" and "speculators".

It is not possible to assume that we can predict all the details from a possible dissolution of the euro, in general, nor we are in any position to suggest "optimal" ways to dissolve the monetary Union: *Such optimal ways simply do not exist unless the new currencies are so formed as to ensure monetary and credit discipline*. This will be a process and we can only suggest the preconditions for a stable dissolution of the euro: Free competition of currencies or "pre-emptive" adoption of pegs to stable international currencies by the national Central Banks followed by complete freedom in foreign exchange markets. This is the way to avoid inflation as well as cyclical fluctuations resulting from arbitrary policies made at the highest level possible. In turn, this is the ultimate guarantee for the stability of the international financial system.

The problem of public debts is more serious and deserves more attention. Eventually, public debts can only be controlled by consolidating the budget and collecting more revenues from a successful private sector. But *a successful private sector needs, above everything else, stable monetary and credit conditions*: If they cannot be guaranteed institutionally, there can be no real success in the investment plans and the coordination of plans and expectations of economic agents. Interest rates are likely to rise in most European countries if credit markets were let to operate freely, resulting in a shortening of the average period of production and less "capitalistic" methods of production. In turn, this would set the true and stable

[1] This is a case where it should be well known that good money drives out bad money.

foundation for a subsequent restructuring of investment and production with the correct balance between short-term and long-term investment plans of the private sector. Additionally, this would be the only way for sustained growth with a particular industrial structure and the correct composition of the capital stock.

But in most European countries there is tremendous lack of competition laws and enforcement of institutions that promote competitive markets. Accompanied by labour markets operating under extremely non—competitive conditions, there is no way for movements in relative prices to coordinate correctly production and investment plans. The fact that the eurozone needed competitive conditions and free markets rather than monetary and fiscal discipline—which is also necessary-has been largely ignored by the EMU and the ECB and is the main cause of the decline in productivity and the adverse reaction to the shocks of 2008.

Besides the lack of competition in general, the monopoly of the ECB over fiat money creation, has been proved detrimental to the cause of an economic union. The ECB's claim of "monetary stability" is easy to refute once we look into the credit and financial markets, and the disequilibium in housing, automotive, or financial markets, which *manifests itself* in the explosion of public debts and the decline of investment and productivity. When markets perform well, it makes sense to have "monetary stability" in some sense, but when all markets fail to function, acting solely on the monetary front is disastrous.

Over—investment in the public sector or other industries (automotive, housing etc.) has been a feature of the European economy for far too long,[2] at least since the US expansion in early 2000s. This malinvestment more precisely, has been actively supported by the governments, while low interest rates made it cheap to accumulate large amounts of public debt or leave for the future the need for fiscal re-structuring. It is not at all surprising that the markets corrected themselves through liquidation of malinvestment in the process of economic crisis, or "speculative attacks" that raised the spreads for particular countries of the eurozone.

Contrary to popular beliefs, even by noted economists, the process of liquidation must be left uninterrupted to complete its working if we want to create the foundation for healthy economic growth in the EU. *The economic crisis is not a "disease" that can be corrected by the policies of the Central Bank but rather a natural, market process which has been set in motion by the Central Bank.* With artificially low interest rates, malinvestment is not covered by savings but by an artificial increase of credit which actually took place in the midst of the recession (for example, see Figs. 1 and 2 above). If we cannot understand the simple fact that the rate of interest must be left free to determine which investments get the priority out of total savings, but instead we insist on active credit and monetary policies, the European economy is bound to remain in recession for several years to come.

---

[2] See Bogus, 2010, p. 121.

The fact of the matter, and the answer to many questions, lies in the fact that the all—powerful ECB operates through the European commercial banks. Its credit policies can be enforced only if the banks are "healthy" and profitable, so it is natural that the stability of the banking sector is the primary concern of the ECB. The contradiction is that most people feel positive about the idea of bailing out a bank but negative about the idea of bailing out a nation. In the first case, they think that the ECB, effectively, bails out consumers' savings but in the second case they feel that they subsidize a nation for being lazy or unproductive. But, in fact, the two options are two sides of the same coin: Public debt is owned by the banks, to a large extent, so there should be no difference between the two. For example, the Greek "haircut" involved explicitly two things. First, the immediate and *explicit* bail out of banks in danger, and second, the *explicit* denial to reduce public debt holdings by insurance and pension funds. The reason is, of course, that the ECB primarily cares about the banks because it operates through them and in the particular instance a failure of a Greek bank would immediately create contagious effects in several other European banks.

Bank failures are quite reasonable in the process of economic crisis. Malinvestment by firms that failed, is investment that has been financed through the banking sector and specific banks in particular. If a firm is allowed to fail, so should a bank do. The excuse that "financial stability" is the primary concern, but employment or capital is not, cannot be sustained; for any policy maker that cares about some notion of "social welfare" it is the firms that should be bailed out first, not the banks. Through the bailout policies of the ECB, "financial stability" becomes the primary, and in fact the only concern. *The problem of avoiding unemployment or liquidation of malinvestment is treated, implicitly only* through credit expansion which is approved by the ECB and is realized by the commercial banks.

We do not argue that financial intermediation is the market's way to deal with the problem of balancing investment and savings. But free financial intermediaries cannot operate under heavily regulated markets and more often than not markets with low interest rates, nor can they operate inside a safety net that effectively destroys competition in the banking system. Wrong or risky decisions made by the commercial banks must be treated as failures and the banks in question must be liquidated. *In the long run* this is in the best interests of investors, consumers' savings, and the ECB alike; healthy and competitive financial intermediation should be the primary concern of a Central Bank. What the ECB is afraid of is, in fact, the *short run* consequences of a bank run or contagion to other commercial banks.

Contagion is highly probable when the banking sector is problematic and depends on the ECB's intervention to sustain its obligations.[3] If it is known in advance that banks will not be bailed out, consumers will be more responsive to signals from the stock market regarding the financial situation of the banks they

[3] See Segoviano and Goodhart, 2009 for measurement of contagion.

put their savings into. If a bank will be bailed out anyway, it is not possible to achieve an equilibrium in the banking sector when interest rates are regulated.

As a matter of fact, low interest rates cannot attract new savings, but they are myopically in the best interests of a bank since their cost is lowered. But then the commercial banks will depend on some sort of artificial expansion of loans, that is a credit expansion which must be approved by such a recognized authority as the ECB. An increase of interest rates, in the midst of a recession, is considered disastrous because investment and consumption will go down. The fact that savings will go up and will substitute part of the previous artificially created credit, is not considered in this naïve argument. Liquidation of malinvestment which is not aligned with savings is also not considered, believing that "investment" will increase necessarily when interest rates are lower.

Suppose interest rates are *increased* in the midst of the depression, contrary to current ECB policies. For any factor that can be used more or less freely across the various stages of production, its price will be lower and its employment will also be lower in the earlier stages. Apparently this will be in favour of the later or more or less final or close-to-final, products. The price of the factor in later stages must increase eventually. The effect on the "aggregate price level" thus, depends on how stage—specific is the factor, as well as on marginal productivities, that is the relative demand for the factor in question across the various stages of production. For example, there will be a drop in the prices of capital goods and an increase of prices of final or close-to-final products and factors. Eventually, the increased demand for goods in the later stages will also involve an increased demand for capital goods, produced at earlier stages, which it will raise their prices, making it reasonable to end up with a higher "aggregate price level", *with significant time lags*. The policy makers should not ignore these time lags when the true effect on prices is considered. Yet the effect depends heavily on the time—structure of production. If the production process has a relatively long average duration (perhaps because of low interest rates for a long time period), prices of the consumption goods will have to increase to meet current increased demand. The increased demand of factors in the early stages will increase their prices either immediately (if the process has a short average length) or after some time (if the process is more "capitalistic").

If the process has, a short average length and it is more or less easy to increase the demand of factors from the early stages, as in a service—economy, for example, the increase in prices will be felt immediately more or less. If the process is more "capitalistic" we should expect a *gradual* increase of prices, as the demand for factors of production is shifted between the different stages of production and thus, the different industries. But *in this sequence of shifts, we can say that "investment" goes up*! In the long run, investment must necessarily go up because of two reasons: (1) The increased demand for final goods necessitates an increase of investment in the relevant sectors, and (2) intermediate or capital goods will, eventually, be required in order to facilitate the increased demand in the later stages through capacity expansion, which requires investment and goods from the earlier stages of production.

There are two other elements that we must consider in this analysis. *First*, if the increase of interest rates is considered to be a permanent shift in the policies of the Central Bank, it is likely that consumers will choose to save more across all income ranges, or the income ranges that matter for the largest portion of savings. *Second*, the increase of interest rates will induce more savings but also less consumption; less, compared to entrepreneurial expectations about profit opportunities across the time—structure of production. We need not bother ourselves with the second argument because this is subsumed in the increase of prices of final products initially, relative to prices of capital goods, and the subsequent increase of the second (relative to consumer goods) as the result of a general increase in the demand for capital goods.

If the increase in interest rates is conceived to be a shift in the policy regime, and consumers indeed tend to save—and invest—more across the board, the immediate effect must be an increased demand for capital goods and the decrease in the demand for consumers' goods. The final effect will be that production in earlier stages is encouraged, so "the returns and the prices obtained for these goods in the different stages of production will be generally higher and a larger proportion of them will be used in the earlier stages of production than before" (Hayek 1967, p. 77). This will tend to counteract the concentration of the time profile of production towards the later stages (the effect of an increase in interest rates without, however, a policy shift and thus without a shift of the savings curve). In the process, certain prices will increase and others will decrease but the same scenario will take place (with the actors reversed) under a decrease of interest rates. The "balancing" of the time profile of production as the result of counteracting forces, will *increase* investment but it will result in *quite different industrial structures* or time profiles depending on whether or not an increase of interest rates has a shifting effect, through the mechanism of expectations.

If, in the sequence of events, the Central Bank decides to intervene by changing credit (with freely determined interest rates) soon the reverse motion will set in, because of freely varying prices of producer or consumer goods and the free movement of capital across industries and time profiles of production, as the result of a market determined interest rate. Thus the market corrects itself in the form of liquidating some investment and creating another, in the form of a classical business cycle.

It is easy to see that an artificial lowering of interest rates and the subsequent increased use of factors in the earlier stages of production implies necessarily imports of capital goods from the countries whose production has a longer average length or whose process is more "capitalistic" (say the "North"). The fact that this is a malinvestment on the part of the "South" will be revealed only with considerable time lags and in no way concerns the "North". Thus, *with higher interest rates the comparative advantages of the "North" seem to be hampered, and the profits of the banks are decreased in the short run*. Yet, with higher interest rates, savings will go up making it unnecessary to rely on credit expansion; a development that could make the financial sector healthier. Precisely because a Central

Bank relies on the commercial banks, a policy of higher interest rates is not followed, even if it is evident that this is closer to the global equilibrium outcome.

If we were to ask whether the ECB should be in position to decide the allocation of investment across industries and firms, most economists would immediately respond in a negative way, since they know to what extent central planning can fail. The fact that the ECB controls interest rates (the loan rate to be more precise) appears sensible to the same economists! But controlling the loan rate(s) is equivalent to choosing a particular allocation of funds across processes of production and the time—structure of production. This allocation can be efficiently determined when interest rates are freely determined but it is distorted significantly when interest rates are regulated by the Central Bank. If central planning can fail when it comes to allocating funds, it can also fail dually when it comes to determining prices or the loan rate, based on policy consideration that are orthogonal to the needs of the markets considered as a whole.

There is another question we must address. Why should the commercial banks accommodate the Central Bank, in the midst of a recession, by accepting a policy of lower loan rates? After all this will imply lower profitability in the short run. The only resolution is that the Central Bank and the commercial banks expect to invest the amount credit expansion in relatively riskless business. With a lower loan rate, more "capitalistic" or earlier projects are favoured so it is natural to expect that their profitability appears, *relative to current expectations*, to be higher. Therefore, such projects are likely to receive the lion's share from credit expansion at low interest rates. Yet, as we know, these are precisely the projects that will be liquidated in the medium run, when it turns out that their profitability was misjudged based on the artificially low interest rates. Clearly, low interest rates improve *expected* profitability across the board but relatively more for the production process that take longer, so an industrial structure is created where the average length is (artificially) higher compared to the equilibrium configuration of prices and the loan rate(s).

With a lower loan rate, the Central Bank and the commercial banks send a signal to the private sector that they want to see more "capitalistic" and longer processes in the economy. *The question is: Why should the commercial banks accommodate this policy if they cannot also lower the deposit rate*—to keep "profitability" constant. One possible answer is that through the expected raise in prices, real profits can be higher for the banks, but apparently this is not very convincing. The other answer, and indeed the only possible one, is that the Central Bank considers investment so elastic to the loan rate that bank profitability can improve through the argument that "cheap price attracts all demand". *For the argument to go through, it must necessarily be the case that all new investment attracted by low interest rates is risk—free.*

Indeed, when the loan rate is low, the financial burden of the firm is so low that it *must* be profitable. As a result, non-performing loans will be practically zero, so *fiat* money creation through new credit will succeed almost surely. Of course, the Central Bank or the commercial banks do not know that demand for their cash will come mainly from firms in the earlier stages of production. It will take a long time for such firms to realize profits, by definition. However, the profit expectations will not be realised when such firms will find out that in later stages the demand is not increased accordingly. As a result, projects that were considered to be sound and safe, are no longer so, and non-performing loans will begin mounting from the earlier stages of production. If the Central Bank renews the supply of fiat funds to the system, the same tendency will appear with some time lags but will, apparently, only make worse the economic situation.

There is a possible way out of this destructive situation for commercial banks if the Central Bank decides to increase the *deposit* rate, *ceteris paribus*. This will attract new funds from consumer savings *not* to help business but to improve the financial situation of the banks: The reasonable reaction of the Central Bank would be to bailout the commercial banks, leaving to the government such considerations as employment or investment. Another alternative would be to bailout the banks exposed to risk *explicitly*, using additional credit expansion. However, the short sighted view is likely to prevail in the sense that an increase of the deposit rate will only make the financial situation of banks worse, without attracting new funds, based on the assumption that the savings curve is *not* elastic, when the rate is *low*. An increase of the deposit rate cannot, indeed, attract new savings when consumers are worried to re-instate their previous standard of living. Yet, *if the commercial banks were left to operate on their own, without the support of the Central Bank, they could only increase the deposit rates considerably* to attract new funds and thus improve their financial position, which was put to risk by providing credit to projects that proved to be non-performing.

Clearly, some firms in the earlier stages would fail, their obligations to the commercial banks could not be met and, depending on the distribution of credit across firms, some commercial banks would fail. In fact, *the commercial banks accommodate the Central Bank in its plans only because they know that, eventually, they face no risk whatsoever, since they will be bailed out by the Central Bank*. Otherwise, there would be no reason why risky projects should be financed with a lower return (the loan rate) at the same cost (the deposit rate): The fact of the matter is that *the cost of additional funds to the commercial banks is exactly zero*. To the extent that the Central Bank does not care about unemployment (of factors of production) there is no cost to fiat money creation for the Central Bank as well. Of course, there remains the cost of inflationary pressures. But *the Central Bank can very well "hide" itself*: First, there will be significant time lags between credit expansion and the appearance of increased prices. Second, increased prices can always be attributed to exogenous or numerous other case—specific factors. Third, and more importantly, *the Central Bank can always blame the poor fiscal stance of a government that accommodates its policy*.

The last point deserves some attention. In the midst of a recession, inflation is easy to blame on a government that has public deficits. A recession made worse by the policies of low interest rates on behalf of the Central Bank, implies higher unemployment benefits and shrinkage of the tax base for the government. In fact, the national government would be exposed even if it did its best to improve the deficit, correct its institutional framework, open the markets to competition (but not the banking sector), contain public sector expenditures etc. If we suppose that the national economy is already in recession and the Central Bank decides to provide new credit at low interest rates, a policy that reinforces the depression, there is no way for the national government to improve the situation: Apparently, tax revenues will be reduced despite all efforts to reduce expenditures (in health, education, defence etc.). In fact, *the most significant mistake in the system is the monopolistic position of commercial banks that accommodate the policies of the Central Bank.*

The identification of the *most* significant mistake does not mean there are no other mistakes. A country with exploding public debt problems is a country that was allowed to borrow at (relatively) low rates without consideration for the use of funds. The government can, indeed, improve the fiscal stance and re-arrange its structure, provided there are no significant disequilibria in the markets, in general, that cannot be correct. Yet, there are disequilibria that are not only significant but quite sizeable, and cannot be corrected because they are exogenous. *These disequilibria are none other than the low interest rate and fiat credit policies of the European Central Bank.*

The fundamental precondition of an independent monetary authority, like the ECB, is to refuse fiat money creation to accommodate the fiscal needs of the national government(s). With the establishment of the eurozone this fundamental precondition has been altered in a significant way: Since the material base of the ECB consists of the commercial banks, the monetary union's objectives have been significantly altered. "Monetary stability" of the eurozone is no longer a concern and can be altered at will by the monopoly of the ECB over regulating all interest rates, as well as credit expansion. "Monetary stability", an issue questionable in itself, was translated arbitrarily to stability of the "financial system", that is the system consisting of *existing* European commercial banks. But the existing system is not open to competition, precisely because the ECB does not want to deal with the complications and uncertainties of a new system of "followers" of its credit and interest rate policies.

One may argue that the Federal Reserve System in the US or a national Central Bank in any country, operate in exactly the same way.[4] We are not to dispute this argument. Nevertheless, when one advances this argument from the national level to the level of an economic and monetary union, an obvious problem appears: Without factor mobility, especially of capital—intensive processes, and capital itself, at least to the extent observed in the US or any single country, the restructuring of industrial structures, from movements in relative processes or the loan rates, will be so slow as to render them practically useless for equalization of returns across processes, the time—profile of production and, therefore, different industries across space and time.

Based on this evidence, we have to reconsider a basic fact: *The arbitrary and unsynchronized policies of individual governments were substituted for the global,*

[4] See Bogus, 2010, Chap. VII.

arbitrary policies of the ECB. Synchronization was not achieved because different industries and nations have different time profiles in terms of the overall, global process of production. The former planning role of individual governments was given up for an "independent monetary authority", the ECB that failed miserably in this capacity. The ECB acted and still acts as a central planner, intervening without any sense of the consequences, in the European allocation of resources and future, European growth prospects. *The role of ECB as an "independent monetary authority", was self-contradicted when the ECB embarked on the ambitious, but impossible, plan to promote growth based on credit expansion at low interest rates.*

References

Hayek FA ([1935] 1967) Prices and production. 2nd edn. Augustus M. Kelley, New York

Segoviano M, Goodhart C (2009) Banking stability measures, IMF working paper 09/04. International Monetary Fund, Washington

Chapter 19
The Gold Standard and Free Banking

As Rothbard writes:

> One of the reasons for the growth and prosperity of the United States has been the fact that we have enjoyed one money throughout the large area of the country. We have had a gold or at least a single dollar standard with the entire country, and did not have to suffer the chaos of each city and county issuing its own money which would then fluctuate with respect to the moneys of all the other cities and counties. The nineteenth century saw the benefits of one money throughout the civilized world. One money facilitated freedom of trade, investment, and travel throughout that trading and monetary area, with the consequent growth of specialization and the international division of labor (Rothbard 1985, p. 51).

This is merely common sense, and it constitutes the major reason for foundation of the euro at least in nominal terms. But Rothbard continues as follows, providing more insight into the foundations of a monetary system necessary to support growth:

> It must be emphasized that gold was not selected arbitrarily by governments to be the monetary standard. Gold had developed for many centuries on the free market as the best money; as the commodity providing the most stable and desirable monetary medium. Above all, the supply and provision of gold was subject only to market forces, and not to the arbitrary printing press of government (op.cit).

In that sense it was not the dollar that was responsible for the stability of the value of money, but the *golden* dollar. Without this qualification it is impossible to understand the essentials of US growth. Under freedom of banking or under strict peg of monetary circulation to gold, business fluctuations cannot arise (since even if they are exogenous they will be propagated, and balanced out through the market system), inflation is impossible, and international balance of payments will be automatically in equilibrium. Summarizing the experience from the 19th century, Nataf (2002) writes:

> It is in this perspective that international monetary stability in the nineteenth century constituted an important factor for the development of international trade and economic progress. If not perfect, this monetary organization did not present the disadvantages engineered by fiat paper currencies: inflation and erratic fluctuations [...] Some financial centers like Paris, London, or New York, working under central banking or under the bond

E. G. Tsionas, *The Euro and International Financial Stability*,
Financial and Monetary Policy Studies 37, DOI: 10.1007/978-3-319-01171-4_19,

> deposit system, were disrupted by recurring business cycles. In contrast, Scotland and the six New England states, working under freedom of money and banking, did not engender the recurrence of booms and busts. Boston, Glasgow, or Edinburgh, benefiting from monetary competition did not generate such crises. Rather, these cities absorbed economic troubles coming from the outside with striking ease. It is thus logical to credit the classical gold standard, not with disturbances, but with stabilizing effects during its era.

This is in fact a unique historical experience where some countries operate under free currency competition, other operate under golden coinage and still some others operate under the autonomy of the central bank. Clearly, the limitation of money and credit expansion (via golden coinage or free competition of currencies) is responsible for stability even in the presence of external, "asymmetric" shocks. The market reacts automatically to such disturbances instead of propagating by accommodating them through credit expansion that changes relative prices and produces malinvestment.

Since 1944, in the Bretton Woods agreement (1944–1971), gold was reinstated as the foundation of the international monetary system and produced, indeed, great stability up to the end of 1950s. The gold standard was abandon since the US government decided not to devaluate the dollar, as it should, because of the continuing increase in the price of gold. The international system passed to fixed exchange rates, which propagated the oil price shock, and finally the gold standard was abandoned in 1976. Although gold was no longer money, its demand rose sharply, and its price went up to $800 per ounce, compared to $35 in 1968. But *this was, in effect, re-monetization of gold exactly as it happened after the sub-prime crisis of 2008*.

What was the reason for the "failure" of the gold standard? As Professor Nataf (2002) explains:

> Domestically inconvertible, the dollars served as reserves in assets of the European central banks. This new gold exchange standard carried a similar defect to the preceding one. Dollars accumulated outside the United States were in principle redeemable in gold by the Federal Reserve System. In fact, they continuously accumulated without repayment.

But this effectively destroyed the international monetary system because of non-convertibility and because in addition the US dollar should be the only major currency following the Bretton-Woods agreement. Since the gold is re-monetized through its increased demand as an alternative to money savings, there is no point in arguing that gold cannot serve as money: It is already money in practice, especially following the 2008 crisis. Summarizing the 1914–1944 period, Nataf (2002) writes:

> The gold coin standard functioned until 1914. In order to finance the war, the pound, the franc, and the mark were severed from gold. Governments suspended their convertibility. Overnight, the European monetary framework based on gold was radically transformed and pounds, francs, and marks became merely fiat paper currencies which depreciated rapidly against gold or the dollar (still a gold dollar). The metallic parities disappeared de facto and the "national currencies" began to float in a disorderly fashion. This monetary chaos lasted long after the war.

For the 19th century we know that the gold standard produced financial stability that facilitated economic growth and the development of industry, exactly as in the US, as Rothbard (1985) describes. The importance of the gold standard for the current situation in euro, derives from the variation of gold prices which are closely related to fluctuations of exchange rates for the usual economic reasons. It is, however, important to consider the importance of the gold standard in the context of a practical situation:

> Each national currency, in such a system, can fluctuate only within narrow margins called "gold points." A special edition of the Revue Economique states that from 1821 to 1869 the maximum variations of gold prices... were of 1 % for France and 0.1 % in England (Boyer-Xambeu 1994, p. 1167). If the pound sterling drops on the foreign exchange market for an amount in excess of the cost of gold transportation, there ensues a "gold drain" out of England which forces its value back to parity. Inversely, if the pound appreciates, there ensues an inflow of gold into England which forces its value back down to parity. Under the gold standard the currency exchange rates are forced, by a market mechanism, to fluctuate within such narrow margins (less than 1 percent) that one could rightly call this a "fixed exchange rate" system.
>
> The franc/dollar ratio, during the 20-year period 1979–1999, is significant in this regard. The dollar was worth between 4 and 10 french francs during that period. Major and rapid variations recurred frequently. The "stabilization" at around 6 francs was far from its supposed purchasing power parity of 6.5 francs. As an example, let us suppose a parity of 1 dollar for 5 francs under a gold standard. This means that the maximum variation would be less than 5 centimes (a dollar could not be exchanged for more than 5.05 francs or for less than 4.95 francs). With a parity of one dollar for one euro, under a gold standard, the dollar could fluctuate only within a narrow range (1.01 euro and 0.99 euro) and vice versa with the euro (Nataf 2002).

In fact the gold standard operates like a fixed exchange rate system, in the sense that gold inflows and outflows resulting from appreciation or depreciation restore the currency to its correct parity through the mechanism of markets. Of course this system is a long way from the enforced fixed or managed exchange rate systems that we have seen in the past. The question is then, why did not the ECB rely on a gold standard for the euro, given its extremely large gold reserves? Precisely because the issue was not to abolish monetary and credit expansions at the central and national levels to create conditions of monetary and financial stability, but rather, but rather to allow the ECB to centralize and self-manage money and credit.

The critical issue is the separation between politics and money. The stability of the value of money rather than artificial "price stability" is the true path to financial and monetary stability. The artificial "price stability" enforced by the ECB has done major damage to all sectors of the European economy by distorting relative prices and expectations about profitability. *The return to a form of the gold standard (following a period of parallel circulation of euro and golden coinage to determine the rate of exchange) would be the best solution for the problem of crises and business fluctuations in Europe that damage severely current and future investment.*

The problem is, of course, that the European bureaucracy cannot afford to lose control over credit and money. But as a result, the euro is not sustainable in the long run because of the different relative prices in European states and the *de facto* different value of euro in each one of them. The euro is likely to be abolished for the same reasons that the gold standard was abolished in 1971 and 1976: A series of devaluations followed by irresponsible counter attacks in the form of credit expansion or even fiat money creation, will put the European economy into an even worse recession that the one we are still experiencing since 2008. The devaluations will *de fact* dissolve the euro into two or more currencies when the situation in Southern Europe, in particular, will worsen the balance of payments and make the scarcity of monetary base even worse than today's. as Kimball (2005) writes:

> When Austrians defend the gold standard, they are really only defending the right for people to voluntarily direct their own affairs. They are merely upholding the fundamental tenants that underlie all peaceful social cooperation [...] Supporting the gold standard is supporting the veracity that voluntary exchange is beneficial to all parties involved and that coercion cannot produce a more socially beneficial arrangement. It is completely wrong to believe that the gold standard was rejected by the market or somehow failed. It did not fail. It was violently abolished by governments because it did not serve their inflationary schemes.

For example the US abandoned the gold standard in 1933 while all European countries abandoned it after 1914 and the First World War. The abandonment of the gold standard in the US had a distinctly Keynesian flavor in view of the New Deal, and followed the creation of the Federal Reserve in 1913 to allow 'cartelization' of the banking sector and allow the government to follow inflationary policies. Many economists that blame the gold standard for the Great Depression, tend to forget the monetary expansion that followed the war, and the revealed preference of the US and other European governments to adopt active fiscal and monetary policies that would have been impossible under the gold standard.

For the Austrian economics school,

> From the coin clipping of ancient kings and princes through the tidal wave of paper money inflations to the manipulative subterfuge of modern central banking, political influence or control over money and banking had brought in its train nothing but economic havoc and social conflict (Rockwell 1992, p. 44).

Of course the abolition of political authority or intervention in monetary and credit markets is the essential reason why Austrian economists prefer the gold standard. Political intervention is harmful in the sense that it generates booms that will necessarily be followed by market corrections, that is depressions. As one Austrian economist writes:

> To sum up, money production is subject to the same constraints as all other branches of production, constraints that ultimately spring from the value scales of the individual market participants, who consent or do not consent to cooperate. From this point of view, the free market production of money is inherently optimal, irrespective of the number of monies and of their relative quantities. The relevant question is therefore not: How much money should be produced? The question is: Are there any legal restrictions that hamper the competitive production of money? And as stated above, there seems to be no economic reason for the establishment or maintenance of such restrictions. Any number of monies spontaneously chosen by the market participants is, at any rate from an ex ante point of view, the optimal number, and any quantity produced of any of these monies in a free market is the optimal quantity (Hüllsmann 2003)

Although free and competitive private issue of currency is not to be adopted immediately, it points out to the basic conclusion that we have reached, namely: *If we consider the market as the ultimate test, any constellation of currencies that will arise from the dissolution of the euro is optimal provided it is the spontaneous outcome of the transactions of economic agents.* The process can, of course, be quite long and complicated but it can be simplified by the simultaneous circulation of two currencies, say euro and a new golden euro (Nataf 2002). This semi gold standard will deprive the ECB from some authority over the monetary base, and the distribution of gold versus paper euro across different members of the EMU will implicitly determine, *grosso modo*, the different currencies that can be optimally emerge, at least *ex ante*.

We do not deny that free, private, competitive production of currency *might* be a solution in the long run. An argument often raised against this conclusion is that there would be too much uncertainty resulting from the fluctuating exchange rates between the different currencies. As Hüllsmann (2003) explains:

> While this observation is correct, it does not lend itself to the conclusion that a homogenization of the monetary system would be beneficial. The point is that any differences between products, firms, places, and times are sources of uncertainty. If such differences subsist on a free market, then we have good reason to assume that the package greater-heterogeneity-plus-uncertainty ranks higher on individual value scales than a reduction of uncertainty by greater homogeneity. We have already pointed out that, on an unhampered market, everyone may attempt to establish a homogeneous paper money. If he cannot bring the other market participants to accept his product, we may conclude that the citizens prefer the greater variety, and the greater uncertainty, of a heterogeneous monetary system to the increased certainty under a unified system (op. cit.).

It is for precisely this reason that parallel circulation of euro and another currency should be allowed for some time until a fixed exchange rate can be defined. Of course, if we opt for a "Northern" and a "Southern" euro, and allow two Central Banks, the "Southern" euro will deteriorate rapidly, since everyone will expect inflationary policies from the "Southern" Central Bank. *The solution is either to allow a return to previous national currency systems plus the circulation of the euro, or the simultaneous circulation of a paper and golden euro—under the condition of immediate, unconditional convertibility, and no taxes on gold.* Apparently, this ties the hands of the ECB but its unconditional freedom is precisely what generated the depression following the sub-prime crisis of 2008. If the ECB did not engage in active policies to "stabilize" the euro the consequences of the crisis would have been absorbed by the system much more easily and swiftly.[1]

As we have seen previously, the Greek government not only expanded its credit in the midst of the recession (2010) by a huge amount but it also sell a large amount of gold from the reserves of the Bank of Greece to the ECB. Perhaps the two events are correlated but the issue cannot be researched easily due to

[1] Sargent and Wallace (1975) argue that monetary policy shocks cannot be considered exogenous and constitute "probably an important reason that the hyperinflation developed" (p. 350).

confidentiality. Effectively, therefore, credit expansion is possible inside the EMU. The fact that most credit is allocated to *mal*investment (large welfare sector and also interest payments to European banks) is responsible for the poor performance of the Greek economy during the four years since the sum-prime crisis. The correlation of credit and the negative performance in terms of industrial performance and GDP, as we saw, is the main witness in this case. What brought Greece, as well as other Southern European economies, in this state of distress is lucidly explained by Hüllsmann (2003):

> To sum up, increases in the supply of any money are not liable to be more harmful, per se, than a decreasing or stable money supply. The traditional focus of monetary economists on changes of quantifiable aggregates such as the money supply proves to be very inappropriate in this case, as in many other cases. The negative consequences that are commonly associated with inflation—in particular, the waste of resources due to adjustment problems—do not primarily spring from increases of the quantity of money, but from the lack of currency competition. And as we have seen, the very existence of a (government-protected) paper money entails problems that are unknown on a free market. Alas, for the same reason it is comparatively easy to handle these problems, at any rate from a purely technical point of view. All that is necessary is to abolish the monopoly privileges of the paper money producers, who would then quickly be driven out of business.

Not surprisingly, in periods of high inflation the government tends to restrict the purchase of foreign exchange to "protect" the national currency, and even today Central Banks across Europe restrict the buying and selling of gold. *Of course the ECB does not want to drive itself out of business, and this fact we really consider to be the true tragedy of the euro.*

To free banking, as well as to free competitive currency we must add a caveat. There has to be an institutional framework that can support it besides the fact that it is best from the point of view of the markets. There is a unique free banking experience in Sweden (1830–1903). As Lakomaa (2007) argues:

> Evidence has been presented, supporting the hypothesis that the system's longevity, in spite of opposition in Parliament, was due to the king being a staunch supporter of free banking. Not until the king changed his mind could a central bank monopoly be formed [...] When the system finally was abolished and replaced with a modern central bank, it was a consequence of a general change in political sentiment. The time of laissez faire was over and politicians were now in favor of pursuing an active monetary policy.

Therefore, despite more than 70 years of positive experience with *free* banking, *without* a Central Bank, all essentially rested upon the king's decision, and when politicians decided that *laissez faire* was *passé*, the system was changed. This should make us aware of the fact that *"political sentiment" plays a central role and many times, in fact more often than not, it may be unfavorable to the market or efficient outcomes*. In fact, the US adopted the Federal Reserve ten years late, but one can safely assume that the "political sentiment" was synchronized: As a causal effect of this "political sentiment", we should not forget, in general, the formation of "independent" central banks that "ended" the hyperinflations (Sargent 1986, pp. 99–100).

A reasonable question is why the UK escaped much of the recent crisis emanating from the eurozone. Goodhart (2011) provides his own explanation:

> In our opinion, much of the perceived 'safe haven' status of the UK during the recent financial crisis has been due to investor confidence in a combination of the country's fiscal and monetary policies. The risk is that, thinking in terms of the simplistic Uncovered Interest Rate Parity model, *foreign investors may begin to demand higher interest rates to compensate for fears of further sterling depreciation.* We have already seen a sharp decline in net gilt purchases by foreigners in the last couple of months (they turned net sellers in August). These data can often be quite volatile, so one should not read too much into it just yet, but it certainly suggests to us that policy-makers should proceed with caution. (emphasis added).

It is precisely that this combination of fiscal and monetary policies that is endangered by the Bank of England's "Quantitative Easing", meaning the injection of £75 millions following another similar policy in 2009. Of course there is always the danger mentioned by Goodhart (in terms of higher interest rates to compensate for a risk of devaluation) but the key implication is not so much inflation resulting from the monetary injection but rather the *real effects*. The monetary injection *cannot be neutral and its effects depend on where in the system the money is injected*, as well as on the configuration of lending and borrowing rates. For example the spreads on business loans relative to bank rates tend to become lower after 2009 in the UK (Fig. 4 in Goodhart 2011). A possible increase following the increase of bank costs would direct investment closer to the consumption goods sector, and endanger some long-term investments. Of course, "*policy-makers should proceed with caution*" as Goodhart suggests, although it is quite uncertain what precisely is meant by that.

Of course, interest rates cannot rise simply because foreign investors may demand a risk premium in case the sterling devaluates. If "*policy-makers proceed with caution*" they should, in fact, concern themselves with the real effects that are associated with an increase of interest rates, not simply the capital flows to which Goodhart placed unnecessary emphasis. Besides the foreign investors there is domestic investment in the UK which should, apparently, be at the center of attention of policy makers. From that perspective, the fact that interest rates are too low and an increase can only bring positive effects in the re-allocation of investment and resources is totally ignored in such aggregate analyses which focus entirely on capital flows that can affect the value of the currency from day to day. The stability of the currency depends on its underlying micro-economic fundamentals whose configuration produces the capital flows which are taken as exogenously given in such analyses.

References

Boyer-Xambeu M-T, Ghislain D, Lucien G (1994) Regimes monetaires, points d'or et serpent bimetallique" de 1770 μa 1870". Revue Economique 45(5):1139–1174
Goodhart C, Ashworth J (2011) The Bank of England's second round of quantitative easing may do little to improve economic confidence or to encourage bank lending, and may even lead to more upward pressures on inflation British Politics and Policy at LSE (14 Oct 2011) Blog entry
Hüllsmann JG (2003) Optimal Monetary Policy. Q J Austrian Econ 6(4):37–60
Kimball J (2005) The Gold Standard in Contemporary Economic Principles Textbooks: A Survey. Q J Austrian Econ 8(3):59–80
Lakomaa E (2007) Free banking in Sweden1830-1903: Experience and debate. Q J Austrian Econ 10(2): 25–44
Nataf P (2002) Before and After the Euro: Strategies for Sound Money in the 21st Century. Quart J Austrian Econ 5(4):21–30
Rothbard M (1985) The Case for a genuine gold dollar. In: Rockwell LH (ed) The Gold Standard: An Austrian Perspective. MA: D.C. Heath, Lexington, pp 1–17
Rockwell LH (1992) The Gold Standard: Perspectives in the Austrian School. MA: D.C. Heath, Lexington
Sargent T, Wallace N (1975) Rational expectations, the optimal monetary policy instrument and the optimal money supply rule. J Political Econ 83(2):241–254
Sargent TJ (1986) Rational expectations and inflation, Harper and Row

Chapter 20
An Unexpected Supporter of the Gold Standard

A monetary Union is not good by itself unless it rests on real economic foundations. *A good monetary Union, in turn, is a Union that protects the stability of the value of money.* Without going into unnecessary investigations regarding the "value of money", suffices to say that the—often overlooked-flight from the euro and the sky—rocketing gold prices are not unrelated to the policies of the ECB that reduced considerably the value of the euro through its monetary and credit policies. Of course lower productivity in the EU compared to the US is often blamed but this cannot be the whole story. In fact, the lower European productivity can be *explained* by the *mal*investents following the credit policies of the ECB.

A monetary Union cannot protect the value of its money unless it pegs the currency on something tangible that emerges from the international market as a good substitute for money, for example silver, gold, aluminum or oil. The markets show a distinct preference for gold, therefore pegging the currency to gold is the best that the Central Bank can do for immediate recovery from the depression and restoration of the prospects of growth. An unexpected advice on the gold standard comes from L. Trotsky:

> Your almighty dollar will play a principal part in making your new soviet system work. It is a great mistake to try to mix a "planned economy" with a "managed currency." Your money must act as regulator with which to measure the success or failure of your planning. Your "radical" professors are dead wrong in their devotion to "managed money." It is an academic idea that could easily wreck your entire system of distribution and production. That is the great lesson to be derived from the Soviet Union, where bitter necessity has been converted into official virtue in the monetary realm. There the lack of a stable gold ruble is one of the main causes of our many economic troubles and catastrophes. It is impossible to regulate wages, prices and quality of goods without a firm monetary system. An unstable ruble in a Soviet system is like having variable molds in a conveyor-belt factory. It won't work. Only when socialism succeeds in substituting administrative control for money will it be possible to abandon a stable gold currency. Then money will become ordinary paper slips, like trolley or theater tickets. As socialism advances, these slips will also disappear, and control over individual consumption—whether by money or administration—will no longer be necessary when there is more than enough of everything for everybody!.

E. G. Tsionas, *The Euro and International Financial Stability*,
Financial and Monetary Policy Studies 37, DOI: 10.1007/978-3-319-01171-4_20,

When there will be *more than enough for everybody* in socialism, is another story, yet Trotsky is very explicit about several things. First, the absence of a gold standard in the Soviet Union does not permit a firm basis for calculation and central planning—which of course was impossible for many other reasons as we know from the Mises-Hayek-Lange debate. Second, *to regulate wages, prices and quality of goods without a firm monetary system* is impossible according to Trotsky because a sound monetary system is needed. This is important because Trotsky was one of the first advocates (if not *the* advocate) of New Economic Policy (NEP) even during 1920. Therefore, not only a price system and relatively free markets are necessary, but also a sound financial system based on the gold standard, or the gold ruble. Trotsky understands that managing money supply *is an academic idea that could easily wreck your entire system of distribution and production.*

Trotsky, surprisingly, understood that the powerful dollar *must act as regulator with which to measure the success or failure of your planning*, and he sees the golden standard as the necessary rule by which to build the monetary system (for socialist planning, of course). Trotsky wrote these lines in 1934, about a year ago the gold standard was abandoned in the US, and he suggested the gold standard rule for an indefinite period of time—that is until communism, so practically forever.

With free markets there is, of course no reason why a currency should be used as a "measure of success" for an economy. But there is truth in the proposition in the sense that only stability of the monetary system will guarantee the best performance in a system of free markets. On another occasion, Trotsky writes:

> From a technically fiscal point of view, the ruble can still less lay claim to superiority. With a gold reserve of over a billion, about 8 billions of bank notes are in circulation in the country. The coverage, therefore, amounts to only 12.5 %. The gold in the State Bank is still considerably more in the nature of an inviolate reserve for the purposes of war, than the basis of a currency. Theoretically, to be sure, it is not impossible that at a higher stage of development the Soviets will resort to a gold currency, in order to make domestic economic plans precise and simplify economic relations with foreign countries. Thus, before giving up the ghost, the currency might once more flare up with the gleam of pure gold. But this in any case is not a problem of the immediate future.

Therefore, Trotsky admits that the gold standard can simplify the economic relations (of the plan) and in that way facilitate socialist economic planning. Admittedly he shows more realism than Lange in the Mises-Hayek-Lange debate, where Lange practically ignores money. But Trotsky was a leading member of the government of the Soviets in two difficult periods ("war communism" and NEP) so he knows better than that. It seems that Trotsky here wants to simplify merely the "economic relations with foreign countries" (in which a stable currency is needed) *but also* to make domestic plans "more precise": This cannot mean anything else but a contraction of bank notes closer to the gold reserves of the Central Bank.

Trotsky continues as follows:

> In the period to come, there can be no talk of going over to the gold standard. Insofar, however, as the government, by increasing the gold reserve, is trying to raise the percentage even of a purely theoretical coverage; insofar as the limits of banknote emission are objectively determined and not dependent upon the will of the bureaucracy, to that extent the Soviet ruble may achieve at least a relative stability. That alone would be of enormous benefit. With a firm rejection of inflation in the future, the currency, although deprived of the advantage of the gold standard, could indubitably help to cure the many deep wounds inflicted upon the economy by the bureaucratic subjectivism of the preceding years.

Here, Trotsky reverts to an intermediate position. It is not necessary for the Soviets to adopt the gold standard (although, [*t*]*heoretically, to be sure, it is not impossible that at a higher stage of development the Soviets will resort to a gold currency*). However, the ruble must not be under the direct control of the "bureaucracy"[1] and *the Soviet ruble may achieve at least a relative stability* provided gold reserves are increased and "*the limits of banknote emission are objectively determined and not dependent upon the will of the bureaucracy*".

For all it matters, even Trotsky in the 1930s understood a fundamental truth that was foreign to policy makers of the New Deal in the US or Europe: Absence of fluctuations, growth and international trade are nearly impossible without the gold standard or at least—in his "intermediate" position—without a convergence of bank notes in circulation to the amount of gold reserves. It seems that Trotsky's observations went unnoticed in the "Socialist Calculation Debate", perhaps because Trotsky in the 1930s and up until to his death (1940) was a marginal figure in the world politics of USSR and the communist movement.

[1] By the term "bureaucracy", Trotsky invariably refers to the ruling clique formed and imposed by Stalin and the Communist Party upon the people.

Chapter 21
Fundamental Problems of the Eurozone

We maintain that it cannot but be the case that there is low inflation in the EMU; actual inflation is hidden below the statistics and the sizeable movements in relative prices which as a result of the credit and monetary expansions, set in motion sizeable reallocations of investment as well as new investment which is, in fact, *mal*investent. The flight from euro is documented in the recent increases of gold's prices, so we hardly need any evidence in addition to that. But the flight from euro can result only as the result of depreciation relative to the US dollar *and* the associated inflation in the eurozone. However,

> the flight from money sets in as a reaction to a previous inflation. It does not drop out of the clouds as an entirely uncaused plague, but is the natural consequence of a previous regime of more or less extended inflation. It follows that the conventional bias against it gets things exactly upside down. The truth is that the flight from money is a great force of liberty. It destroys the institutional embodiments of inflation: fractional reserve banking and paper money. It stops inflation and thereby puts an end to the rechanneling of income in favor of the happy few with good connections to the politico-monetary establishment, and to the detriment of the politically unconnected rest of society. This consideration alone would be reason enough to welcome it.

If there were no inflationary pressures in the eurozone,[1] or no inflationary expectations why should the flight from euro happen? We do not take it for granted that the entire increased demand for gold was from the Eurozone, and not from the US, but it is obvious that the international monetary and exchange—rate system is *not* at rest; the primary cause of this unrest can be none other than the "public debt problems" of the EU, its was of handling them, the high probability of contagion from "public debt problems" in Greece, Ireland, Portugal, Italy and Spain, and the reaction of the ECB.

We have shown that the "public debt problems" reduce to the ECB's purposeful objective to maintain the stance of large commercial European banks –an objective that cannot be justified on any grounds. The European banks are precisely "*the happy few with good connections to the politico-monetary*

[1] For a documented flight from the Deutschemark during the hyperinflation see Sargent (1986, pp. 83-84).

E. G. Tsionas, *The Euro and International Financial Stability*,
Financial and Monetary Policy Studies 37, DOI: 10.1007/978-3-319-01171-4_21,

establishment" in this instance. But this does not prevent us from seeing the truth: The ECB and its tremendous credit expansions created a latent inflation problem in the eurozone. The sub-prime crisis propagated explosively the problems that resulted from such policies. Instead of reverting to stable money, the ECB continues its "price stability" policies which are totally wrong in view of the *mal*investments that have been created as the result of its past and current policies.

The "public debt problems" of Greece or other Southern European countries are a convenient scapegoat. The maturity of large capital payments (and payment of interest, more accurately) for these countries, *allowed the ECB to misrepresent the fundamental problem*, which is none other but an arbitrary currency (the euro) wishing to compete the US dollar based on arguments that, more or less, remind us of the classic arguments in favor of "protection of national currency".

Although the ECB can misrepresent the fundamental problem, it cannot avoid flight from the euro, depreciation, and increasing gold prices. *In so far as the ECB assumed the role of a Central Planner*, it better follow Trotsky's advice:

> In the period to come, there can be no talk of going over to the gold standard. Insofar, however, as the [European Central Bank], by increasing the gold reserve, is trying to raise the percentage even of a purely theoretical coverage; insofar as the limits of banknote emission are objectively determined and not dependent upon the will of the bureaucracy, to that extent the [Euro] may achieve at least a relative stability (words in brackets have been substituted from L. Trotsky.

In recent, serious academic research, it is certainly surprising that we find some distinctly Austrian themes that underlie the analysis in this essay:

> Financial systems are inherently fragile because of the very function which makes them valuable: liquidity transformation. Thus regulatory reforms, as urgent and desirable as they are, will definitely strengthen the financial system and decrease the risk of liquidity crises, but they will never eliminate it. This leaves monetary policy with a very important task. In a framework that recognizes the interactions between monetary policy and liquidity transformation 'optimal' monetary policy would consist of a modified Taylor rule in which the real rate rejects the possibility of liquidity crises and recognizes the possibility that liquidity transformation gets subsidized. Failure to recognize this point risks leading the economy into a low interest rate trap: low interest rates induce too much risk taking and increase the probability of crises. These crises, in turn, require low interest rates to maintain the financial system alive. Raising rates becomes extremely difficult in a severely weakened financial system, so monetary authorities remain stuck in a low interest rates trap. This seems a reasonable description of the situation we have experienced throughout the past decade (Giavazzi and Giovannini 2010).

The puzzle put forward by Giavazzi and Giovannini is, indeed, a very real one. From the Austrian perspective, low interest rates support investment plans that are "round about" or more "capitalistic" and thus they are associated with greater risk in terms of their profitability. But from the current point of view, even lower interest rates are "required to boost investment" and put the economy and the financial system out of their troubles. This is, indeed, "*a reasonable description of the situation we have experienced throughout the past decade*", and the "low interest rate trap" has been known for decades, ever since von Mises and Hayek, in fact.

As Giavazzi and Giovannini mention: "*Raising rates becomes extremely difficult in a severely weakened financial system, so monetary authorities remain stuck in a low interest rates trap*". What they forget is that interest rates are prices which can and should be set by the markets; there is no need for a monetary authority to place itself in a situation where it "gets stuck". If interest rates are artificially low, because of monetary and credit policies, thinking in terms of aggregates, like aggregate investment and the "weakness" of the financial system, is of no use. Interest rates must go up to favour investments later in the time—profile of production, thus beginning a process of "healthier" investment. The re-allocation of investment from early to later or close—to—final product processes, represents the correct re-direction of investment. The short run effect on aggregate investment can be negative but in the short run the economy would have moved into the right direction, increasing the demand for capital.

In fact, Giavazzi and Giovannini (2010) conclude that it is worth.

> investigating whether different monetary policy rules (across time or countries) are correlated with differences in the duration of investment: in particular the share of residential investment in total investment or in GDP (for an attempt see Dew-Becker 2009)—the idea being that a monetary policy that subsidizes liquidity transformation might be associated with a longer duration of investment and a higher share of residential investment.

Construction and residential investment are important key sectors particularly in Greece and Southern Europe. In fact, monetary policies targeted toward sectors "*with differences in the duration of investment*" form the foundation of an Austrian analysis. Of course, Austrian economics raises serious doubts about the efficiency of such policies: Instead of *targeting* certain sectors, the task should be left to the markets through freely varying interest rates. In fact, an insight from Austrian analysis is that the likely raise in interest rates will favour more the consumers' sectors rather than the more "round about" sectors. The raise in interest rates will also attract savings (despite the drop in consumption) that can support the financing of *sound* investment plans, as opposed to artificially round about plans of high risk, that become dominant under a policy of low interest rates. The low interest rate trap is, in fact, an artificial outcome resulting from the ECB's policies of low inflation, and 'solvency' of the commercial banking sector, in totally artificial terms. The rate of interest should be left to determine *freely* the intertemporal allocation of resources as well as the reallocation of existing and allocation of new investment into new productive activities that can increase the demand for capital and thus "total investment".

To learn from history, in terms of the systemic risk and the spillover effects, we should examine the bank panic of 1907 in the US, a well known event. During the crisis the US capital markets were open and relatively liquid; in addition, the spillover effects were minimal. As argued by Rodgers and Wilson:

> The lack of spillover and systemic failure was due to (1) contractual arrangements in the securities markets that allowed coupon and dividend payments to occur despite the suspension of such payments through the banking system, and (2) the integration of the U.S. securities markets with major European securities markets that fostered gold flows into the

U.S. as U.S. asset prices became appealing to global investors. The securities market arbitrage examined in this study was an important aspect of the international gold standard that has not been examined by previous studies of this historic period.

In that way the gold standard acted as a natural mechanism to absorb the risks and minimize the destructive spillover effects from a national crisis to the international markets. Continuing on their analysis they make the following important observations:

> First, the payment system for bond and stock payments generally occurred outside of the banking system, and thus investors could continue to receive payments even when bank deposit convertibility was suspended. Second, due to the gold clauses that occurred in most bond indentures, coupon and principal payments were stipulated in gold, which helped to integrate these securities into the international markets. Third, most corporate bonds were in bearer form, allowing securities to readily move between securities markets, both domestically and internationally. Fourth, many American bond issues were jointly traded in New York and in Europe, allowing an active arbitrage to develop between these markets.

Based on these observations we can understand better why the subprime crisis had such a large impact on the international economy, and particularly the euro and the explosion of public debts. Market restrictions that prevent arbitrage lead to large spillover effects, increase of systemic risks, and rapid devaluation of certain European government securities. Since gold backing was and still is absent, gold prices went sky—rocketing leading effectively to *monetization of gold*. It is also important that in 1907, "*the payment system for bond and stock payments generally occurred outside of the banking system, and thus investors could continue to receive payments even when bank deposit convertibility was suspended*". But the banking system in Europe is the only way to arrange payments for bonds and securities which are arranged centrally by the ECB. *The centralization of the financial system and the critical role of the ECB are thus found to be of central importance for the increase of systemic risk and the spillover effects to the international securities markets.*

It is important to understand in this respect that the negative effects from the subprime crisis were magnified by the restrictions placed on the functioning of financial markets. This magnification showed materially not only on the monetization of gold but also on the explosion of public debts. The ECB has announced that it would continue to accept Greek bonds even if they were "junk", that is below the BBB rating to which the ECB resorted from its initial assessment of A-rating. The "missing gold flow" from Greece was in fact present when the Central Bank of Greece sold a large amount of gold to the ECB, justifying the view that an effective "gold standard" cannot but always be the case, even in a latent and managed form.

Without the simultaneous trading of "toxic" securities in international markets, the ECB's willingness to protect unconditionally Greek bonds, and the absence of arbitrage which took the form of an effective "Eurobond", the spillover effects developed rapidly in Portugal, Ireland and Italy. An outflow of gold should have taken place from Europe into the US (say) which is absent and de-stabilized the financial system. The idea that agreements like the Basel agreement can ever stabilize centrally and in a managed way the European financial system is impossible if not self—contradicting. The correct way to solve the problem would have been a mechanism that can act automatically to minimize risks and restore the functioning of arbitrage. *A convenient and practical way to risk—management at the global level is, in fact, the return to some form of the gold standard as soon as possible, and the simultaneous trading of securities in international markets.*

In an empirical study of bubbles and their dating in the US economy, Phillips and Yu conclude that:

> Our estimates suggest that bubbles emerged in the housing market before the subprime crisis and collapsed with the subprime crisis. The bubble then migrated from the housing market to selected commodity markets and the bond market after the crisis erupted into the public arena. All these bubbles collapsed as the financial crisis impacted real economic activity.

Then the US economy recovered quickly, a fact that is not the case in Europe. The "bubble" is still not over in terms of spreads and the migration or spillover from one market to another is still running its effects. The apparent explanation is that the European economy is, in fact, a set of segmented markets and segmented bond markets, and the central role of the ECB propagates disequilibria and spillover effects in and from these markets. *The common currency does much to amplify these effects, so in that sense the Euro is not sustainable, and the ECB is acting in the wrong way to maintain its stability.*

Using estimates of joint probability density functions, Segoviano and Goodhart manage to quantify jointly systemic risk, and contagion risks. Their analysis of major US banks revealed the following:

> U.S. banks are highly interconnected, with distress in one bank associated with high probability of distress elsewhere [...] Distress dependence across banks rises during times of crisis, indicating that systemic risks [...] Risks vary by the business line of the banks [...] Links across major U.S. banks have increased greatly. [...]. On average, if any of the US banks fell into distress, the average probability of the other banks being distressed increased from 27 percent on July 1, 2007 to 41 percent on September 12, 2008 [...] On September 12, [...] we estimated the probability that one or more banks in the system would become distressed, given that Lehman became distressed. This reached 97 percent.

Although this is a reduced form analysis without explicit consideration of the behaviour of bank investments and the profitability of projects funded it is useful to show that there is "interconnectedness" in the banking sector. Of course the conclusion is quite obvious, not because it follows from a "too big to fail argument" but rather because commercial banks usually engage in investment allocations that are too dissimilar and, in addition, they rely on one another to propagate credit expansion through the banking multiplier. Thus, measurement without theory, although somewhat useful, it does not throw light on the real underlying factors in "interconnectedness". The interconnectedness of the banking system relies on (1) similarities in investment decisions, (2) the working of the banking multiplier that we examine in later chapters, and (3) "conjectural variations" that result from the monopolistically competitive structure of the industry. Yet there is a sense in which calculation of distress probabilities (marginal or conditional) is orthogonal to the problem at hand: If the banks did not propagate the credit shock through the multiplier and, at the same time, did not engage in "safe" long-term and capital-intensive projects there would be no reason to be in distress and therefore distress probabilities reflect rather artificial "common trends" in bank profitability resulting from the fact that they are inclined to behave in the same way after a credit shock, rather than anything else.

Reference

Giavazzi F, Giovannini L (2010) The low interest rate trap,http://www.voxeu.org/article/low-interest-rate-trap

Chapter 22
Stability and the Eurozone

The euro's most significant advantage, from the Austrian point of view, is the enforcement of stability in exchange rates and the discipline that it imposes on governments that have the motives to be fiscally and monetary irresponsible. The point has been emphasized by de Soto (2012, "An Austrian defense of the Euro", Ludwig von Mises Institute). In the words of von Mises:

> The gold standard makes the determination of money's purchasing power independent of the changing ambitions and doctrines of political parties and pressure groups. This is not a defect of the gold standard, it is its main excellence. (Mises 1966)

Hayek defended the gold standard precisely on the grounds of fiscal responsibility and its incompatibility with policy-induced inflation which distorts relative prices and provides the wrong signals to economic agents:

> It is, I believe, undeniable that the demand for flexible rates of exchange originated wholly from countries such as Great Britain, some of whose economists wanted a wider margin for inflationary expansion (called "full employment policy"). They later received support, unfortunately, from other economists who were not inspired by the desire for inflation, but who seem to have overlooked the strongest argument in favor of fixed rates of exchange, that they constitute the practically irreplaceable curb we need to compel the politicians, and the monetary authorities responsible to them, to maintain a stable currency [...] The maintenance of the value of money and the avoidance of inflation constantly demand from the politician highly unpopular measures. Only by showing that government is compelled to take these measures can the politician justify them to people adversely affected. So long as the preservation of the external value of the national currency is regarded as an indisputable necessity, as it is with fixed exchange rates, politicians can resist the constant demands for cheaper credits, for avoidance of a rise in interest rates, for more expenditure on "public works," and so on. With fixed exchange rates, a fall in the foreign value of the currency, or an outflow of gold or foreign exchange reserves acts as a signal requiring prompt government action. With flexible exchange rates, the effect of an increase in the quantity of money on the internal price level is much too slow to be generally apparent or to be charged to those ultimately responsible for it. Moreover, the inflation of prices is usually preceded by a welcome increase in employment; it may therefore even be welcomed because its harmful effects are not visible until later [...] *I do not believe we shall regain a system of international stability without returning to a system of fixed exchange rates, which imposes on the national central banks the restraint essential for successfully resisting the pressure of the advocates of inflation in their countries—usually including ministers of finance.*

E. G. Tsionas, *The Euro and International Financial Stability*,
Financial and Monetary Policy Studies 37, DOI: 10.1007/978-3-319-01171-4_22,

(emphasis added, Hayek 1979 [1975], Lecture given February 8, 1975 and entitled, "Inflation, the Misdirection of Labor, and Unemployment" at the Academia Nazionale dei Lincei in Rome in celebration of the 100th anniversary of Luigi Einaudi's birth.)

There are many points worth emphasizing in this analysis. *First*, it is clear that "full employment" or expansionary policies are largely responsible or in the background of a system of flexible exchange rates. *Second*, it is the "cheap credit" that the government wants to provide by abandoning fixed exchange rates. *Third*, a system of restraining the central banks is necessary for a successful implementation of flexible exchange rates.

As Hayek says in the passage quote above: "With fixed exchange rates, a fall in the foreign value of the currency, or an outflow of gold or foreign exchange reserves acts as a signal requiring prompt government action. *With flexible exchange rates, the effect of an increase in the quantity of money on the internal price level is much too slow to be generally apparent or to be charged to those ultimately responsible for it.*" This is precisely because the effect of an increase in the quantity of money is not mechanical or automatic but it affects the price level through a subtle way by changing relative prices and affecting the distribution of investment among activities and time horizons. But with fixed exchange rates one source of uncertainty is eliminated, and this is the uncertainty in *international* relative prices which are as relevant to the problem as they are domestic relative prices. There is not only a domestic distribution of investment over time and productive activities but also a distribution at the global level that has to be taken into account. To control this distribution is much too complicated under flexible exchange rates as the problem depends on the decisions of many governments and the preferences of unpredictable political parties at the international level. A system of fixed exchange rates "*reserves acts as a signal requiring prompt government action*": It is as though the government (credibly) committed itself to the stability of the currency and thus, fiscal or monetary irresponsibility and arbitrariness is eliminated.

It is, of course, undeniable that the Euro provided precisely a *framework* for stability in the European Union. As de Soto (2012) wrote:

> In fact, during the years prior to the crisis, all of these countries, except Greece, easily observed the 3 % deficit limits, and some, like Spain and Ireland, even closed their public accounts with large surpluses. Hence, though the heart of the European Union was kept out of the American process of irrational exuberance, the process was repeated with intense virulence in the European periphery countries, and no one, or very few people, correctly diagnosed the grave danger in what was happening. If academics and political authorities from both the affected countries and the ECB, instead of using macroeconomic and monetarist analytical tools imported from the Anglo-Saxon world, had used those of the Austrian business-cycle theory—which after all is a product of the most genuine continental economic thought—they would have managed to detect in time the largely artificial nature of the prosperity of those years, the unsustainability of many of the investments (especially with respect to real estate development) that were being launched due to the great easing of credit, and in short, that the surprising influx of rising public revenue would be of very short duration. *Still, fortunately, though in the most recent cycle the ECB has fallen short of the standards European citizens had a right to expect, and we*

could even call its policy a "grave tragedy," the logic of the euro as a single currency has prevailed, thus clearly exposing the errors committed and obliging everyone to return to the path of control and austerity (emphasis added).

The artificial prosperity that preceded the sub-prime crisis of 2008 was due to the ease of credit, artificially created in Europe and the US. De Soto (2012) rightly points out that austerity is nothing but the necessary reversion to a normal equilibrium of European economies and *particularly in those that have borrowed heavily* to sustain their policies. Although the heart of the European Union has been "kept out of the American process of irrational exuberance" the situation was different in the South. With fixed exchange rates, that is common currency, the shocks that are necessary to bring back these economies to equilibrium now become part of the Eurozone as a whole, not only the specific countries themselves. Depending on the relative size of these economies, and most importantly the precise quantitative linkages in terms of imports and exports, austerity measures and re-alignment of economic policies is an issue that must be addressed on the Eurozone level because it is a global problem.

But this analysis reveals that it is not only budget deficits that determine the problem. It is, most importantly, the "cheap credit" that prevailed before the crisis—and indeed it was the main determinant of the crisis. Although it is more difficult to increase money supply in the Eurozone, compared to the United States or the United Kingdom—and thus a major source of instability is eliminated, there are certainly other ways to act that are against monetary stability. De Soto (2012) rightly argues:

> In contrast with the situation of the dollar and the pound, in the euro area, fortunately, money cannot so easily be injected into the economy, nor can budget recklessness be indefinitely maintained with such impunity. *At least in theory, the ECB lacks authority to monetize the European public debt*, and though it has accepted it as collateral for its huge loans to the banking system, and beginning in the summer of 2010 even sporadically made direct purchases of the bonds of the most threatened periphery countries (Greece, Portugal, Ireland, Italy, and Spain), there is certainly a *fundamental economic difference* between the behavior of the United States and United Kingdom, and the policy continental Europe is following: while monetary aggression and budget recklessness are deliberately, unabashedly, and without reservation undertaken in the Anglo-Saxon world, *in Europe such policies are carried out reluctantly, and in many cases after numerous, consecutive and endless "summits."* They are the result of lengthy and difficult negotiations between many parties, negotiations in which countries with very different interests must reach an agreement. (emphasis added).

In that way the question of monetary ease is transformed to a political problem which does not seem to have a straightforward solution, as de Soto rightly argues. In that sense it is certainly correct that the Euro provided the necessary *framework* for monetary stability. But this is only a general framework whose precise details and specifications have yet to be explored and quantitatively determined. It is certainly more difficult for the ECB to inject new money into the economy but *it is not so difficult to resort to credit ease and cheap credit* through the manipulation of interest rates or programs based on preferential treatment of particular types of investment. The "bailing out" of commercial banks shows plainly that the ECB acts to protect its own interests, to a large extent independently of stability as a general goal. Commercial banks that have failed by exposing themselves recklessly to risk should have been allowed to go out of business as in the case of every other private enterprise. But commercial banks constitute the foundation of the ECB at the national level so implementation of its policies requires a stable banking system: A stable banking system is not a necessary nor a sufficient condition for monetary stability to the same extent that a "stable" private sector where unprofitable investments are not allowed to be liquidated is not a necessary nor a sufficient condition for stability of the economic system. Stability cannot mean a static world where nothing ever changes—in fact, stability and reversion to equilibrium requires extensive re-allocation of investment following a crisis. The same is true for the banking sector: *Financial and monetary stability does not necessarily mean stability and absence of change in the commercial banking system—in fact it requires extensive restructuring of the banking sector* to revert back to a healthy and sustainable equilibrium where "calculated risk" prevails in the financing of investment.

When we say that the Euro provided the *framework* for financial and monetary stability, we mean that certain variables have yet to be specified precisely. Although fiscal consolidation is not a problem, there are mainly two other variables that have to be accounted for. The first is the fact that an economic problem is transformed to a political issue, precisely as de Soto (2012) analyzed. The second is the fact that economic policy in the Eurozone is to a large extent left to the ECB and the banking sector. There is a false sense of financial stability that is adopted when it is understood as maintaining artificially the profitability of commercial banks that are allowed to make their own private decisions regarding the relationship between risk and return. It is not of importance the private decisions of banks are wrong or right, appropriate or inappropriate—this has to be verified *ex post* in equilibrium. What is of immense importance is that *competition in the banking system is incompatible with the notions of "financial stability" adopted by the ECB*. It is as if free entry and exit apply to the whole economic system *except* the banking sector.

Without competition in financial intermediation, it becomes impossible to maintain financial stability—understood in this sense: Optimality requires financing those investment projects that provide the best risk-return profile among the many that compete for funds. If banks know that they will be bailed out, at least to some extent, they do not have the motive to find these projects and restrain credit to those that are compatible with growth in equilibrium. Nor does the investment sector has any motive for self-selection in the competition for credit, thus distorting the balance between own funds and borrowed funds. Effectively if the banking sector does not have tight budget constraints, as any other firm does, it is impossible to reach an efficient equilibrium for the economy as a whole. *It is precisely for this reason that Austrian economists have argued in favor of 100 % collateral in bank credit*. As long as this measure does not apply effectively the financial intermediation does not face any binding constraints, and it is free to repeat the same mistakes. In different terms, *the re-structuring of the banking sector requires a new institutional framework for the operation of financial institutions in the Eurozone*. This is part of the precise specification of variables that, as we have argued, are necessary for specifying further the *framework* of monetary and financial stability which was created by the common currency.

The purpose of a new institutional framework is not to limit the risk undertaken by financial institutions—that is to tell them what *not* to do. This is impossible without *some* form of central planning, against which it is unnecessary to argue here. Private decisions should be protected and promoted. But such decisions should be made rationally as in the case of other private agents like households and firms, and banks can be no exception. Objectives, budget constraints and free markets, are, effectively, all that is needed, *in the absence of externalities*, to secure smooth functioning of credit channels and decisions in the real sector. Currently, budget constraints and free markets are not allowed fully in the Eurozone and this is precisely where the attention of policy-makers should be directed. Evidently, the necessity of Central Banking rests upon the premise that commercial banks are not restricted tightly in terms of their reserve funding for financing investments. With a binding 100 % reserve requirement the role of the Central Bank becomes superfluous because it cannot influence the economy anymore. *This leads to the question why a Central Bank is needed at all when a competitive system of private banks can do as well*—indeed, considerably better, without the need for information required at the central level to coordinate the activities of all financial institutions. It is precisely the fact that the Central Bank cannot be really independent that makes it necessary as an economic organ.

Of course the ECB is the cornerstone of the Euro so it is natural to ask whether we recommend its "abolition". That measure is too radical and, in fact, the *opening of European banking system to competition can do approximately as well.* The ECB should *institutionally advise* the adoption of 100 % reserve requirements and make any necessary adjustments where this is possible. Opening to competition means that banks should be left free to compete on the European level and, apparently, with non-European banks as well. Access to credit should be possible for any firm or private agent independently of the national boundaries, without restrictions. Regulation should be restricted to re-structuring of the institutional framework along the lines of reserves requirement.

We mentioned previously that smooth functioning of the financial intermediation system requires another condition, namely absence of externalities. The absence of tight, binding budget constraints certainly operates and yields the same results that an externality would do—if there are no markers to internalize the effects from the non-binding constraints. But *there are other, significant externalities in the financial intermediation system.* Current financial policies and institutional frameworks act as externalities spilling-over the cost of private banking to the whole society. No "systemic risk" can possibly arise from a competitively operating banking system that cannot have the back up of a Central Bank as lender of last resort. In that sense "systemic risk" is uncertainty created by an exogenous factor, like a negative shock to investment, which is however, maintained and propagated through the preferential treatment of financial institutions in terms of their budget constraint. There is no reason for a financial institution to collapse if prudency prevails and borrowed funds are always backed up fully. It is, of course, possible for a financial institution to fail because of its losses due to misalignment with marker signals or erroneous decisions but so it is possible for any other private firm. In fact, there is no way to maintain financial stability without competition in the banking system—and this is precisely what is prevented by the existing institutional framework upon which the ECB operates. A monopoly of power has been assigned without due consideration of the specification of the institutional framework in terms of how the financial institutions under its control are operating. It is one thing to emphasize "systemic risk" due to the collapse of a financial institution, and it is quite a different thing for a financial institution to have losses and willingly go out of business. There is nothing wrong with the second: After considering the cost of deposits and operating expenses, if the financial institution cannot cover them fully in the long-run it necessarily will go out of business *without any other cost to depositors and without any other social costs*. If the financial institution is not allowed to "speculate" and cannot lend more than it can fully cover, competition will have a tendency to establish equilibrium where the configuration of prevailing interest rates reflects demand and supply in the market of funds, along with equilibrium in all other markets.

If the externality is allowed institutional and legal form there is always the possibility of "systemic risk" which is, in reality, the internalization of private losses of financial institutions not by new markets but by the society as a whole. In fact the internalization of the externality can be provided by financial markets if they are allowed to operate freely and competition prevails, or at least there is a tendency for competition forces to operate. *Internalization can be always provided by a private system of insurance like the FDIC* to which the banks could resort if they do not wish to impose tight budget constraints and, as in the case of insurance companies, the institution would rely on direct funding by the commercial banks. The problem is that, with insurance, private banks will always have the motive to exhaust their wedge between lending and borrowing and thus distort competitive interest rates. The transmission of this decision to investment will distort all other relative prices and will act as a monetary shock in the economy. It is important to understand that this is permanent shock which is amplified when other negative real shocks hit the economy. It is this amplification which creates "systemic risk" but is, in reality, the transmission of a monetary shock through the various sectors of the economy. In this sense *any "insurance" fund is motivation for exposure to uncalculated risk and risky use of deposited funds*. It provides a false sense of security without avoiding "systemic risk" and at the same time it creates another problem: The role of the insurance fund will always provide motivation for its transformation to a central or federal authority that will be assigned the role of managing credit. In effect, competitive banking will always sort out the problem and, in equilibrium, only healthy and sound financial institutions will prevail, enforcing financial stability. Any other central management authority will be, in fact, a recipe for instability and "systemic risk".

Without a significant increase in the reserve ratio it is impossible to think that the Eurozone will recover from its problems. It is true that the Eurozone inherited the large exposure of private banks to the public debt accumulated by their governments, during a long period of time. The ECB was supposed to act independently of the government and refuse to monetize the debt—which, in fact, did to some measure but of course not entirely. The debt crisis was thought to be a burden which was inherited from the past and the banks should be bailed out to be given a chance in the new environment that was emerging with the management of the debt crisis and the enforcement of fiscal discipline in the European South. However, the issue is more complicated. Indeed, there was a large exposure of private banks to public debt but at the same time we have to reconcile with the sub-prime crisis, and the housing bubble in the U.S. It cannot only be the public debt that it is responsible for this chain of events. Indeed, there has been an expansion of credit all the way up to 2007 and even during the sub-prime crisis and immediately afterwards. Credit expansion, spread over two decades, has created the ideal conditions for the emergence of a classical crisis in the sense of Hayek and von Mises: A lot of investment was no longer profitable and had to be liquidated with cataclysmic effects for the banking sector and the accommodation of payments for the public debt.

The increase of unemployment and the devastation of real economy that we see in the European South is the result of forces that were operating long before the sub-prime crisis and, in fact, lead to it, with unsurpassed consistency and accuracy that could have been possible only by the analyses of the Austrian school. It was a crisis in the "real sector" of the economy although this did not become apparent before 2010. Most economists were caught unaware although the evidence of credit expansion, unsurpassed in history, was in front of them. It is still not clear to most economists what the main determinants of the crisis were and how the financial sector in Europe along with the currency was found before the cliff of destruction. Therefore, it is still not clear whether the "hair cut" of public debts, the austerity measures enforced and the "bailing out" of the commercial banking sector will manage to put the European South back in line, and rescue the Euro from its potential destruction.

To most casual observers it should be clear that, apart from austerity, most other policy measures aim at "stabilizing" the financial system, reducing "systemic risk" etc. Austerity, on the other hand, seems to contribute to the deterioration of tax revenues and, at best, it generates a marginal situation in budget deficits. This is not to say that austerity measures were unnecessary—quite the contrary. The debt problem made fiscal solvency far more difficult and the situation was not sustainable. Theoretically, austerity measures can resolve quickly fiscal stance *but they did not*. Instead they led to an immediate deterioration of growth and employment and, practically, confined the tax base considerably. Although it is quite possible that these measures will yield results in the near future, there is no denial that the measures were taken with considerable delay and, when they were finally taken, were not seem to be very effective: The reason is that *despite the generous "haircuts" of public debt and the bailing out of commercial banks, liquidation of investment is a process of adjustment that requires quite a long time.* During this process, the deterioration of the tax base and the re-adjustments in labor and capital markets, necessarily create a recession which is compatible with the re-alignment of supply and demand in all sectors of the economy. In this process the sectors that react first are the ones with lower capital intensity and the chain of events is transmitted to the capital and equipment sectors. Without devaluation being an option under common currency, the real effects are magnified without the option of absorbing part of them by the general price level—although relative prices change a great deal. The shift of investment across sectors can be massive as the accumulation of credit over the years was driven into unprofitable projects whose sustainability was possible only by low interest rates and cheap credit.

It is important that a recession would happen even in the absence of the austerity measures because there is no other way to reinstate equilibrium in the economy. The austerity measures, of course, have nothing to do with preventing the depression—that is clear to everybody. The seemingly counterproductive measures are necessary in order to move towards stance in the fiscal sector, as in all other sectors of the economy. The argument that these policy measures deepen the recession is irrelevant, as it is equivalent to saying that the re-alignment and re-structuring of investment in equipment deepens the recession and affects the whole economy. Of course it affects the whole economy and that is precisely the point in any general equilibrium analysis, viz. that partial adjustments are impossible and a general attainment of a new equilibrium is necessary. After years of government's intervention into the economy, of all forms and magnitudes, *the argument against austerity measures is an argument that treats preferentially the public sector* and, essentially, wants to socialize the losses from the economic activity of the government and the state. The fact that so far the austerity has not even touched upon public education, health, transportation etc., is of no concern to those who argue in favor of the return to Keynesian welfare state and "protection" of the poor and the strata of the population that were hit the hardest by the recession. Without a tax base these arguments are, of course, irrelevant, especially when there is extensive tax evasion and an excessively large public sector that adjusts quite slowly, if at all, to the signals provided by the recession.

There is also the common belief among many that it is the absence of European *political* integration which is responsible for the devastation of the economic situation in the South. This belief ignores the fact that the adjustment towards a new equilibrium is not a political process or a "bail-out" plan but a real process that must be left intact to reinstate the equilibrium in labor, capital, and product markets. Political arguments are largely irrelevant as the options that are open to governments are quite clear: Drastic reduction of budget deficits, competitive conditions in financial intermediation, increase of the tax base, and facilitation of firms and households to repay their debts. The general plan is in no way incompatible with re-structuring of the tax system and the public sector—in fact, such changes are absolutely necessary. This is only common sense. What is not common sense, and must be emphasized, is that the recession is the result of a prolonged, massive misalignment of investment that has to take place. The question is what can be done to protect the majority of the population from the results of the recession.

It is not to be denied that the tax system in the European South is sub-optimal or "unjust". But what is a better tax system? Consistent with the idea that the recession requires adjustments in all sectors of the economy, the tax system should, first of all, yield the necessary revenues to finance a public sector that is as small as possible. The priorities must be put under scrutiny, not without the participation of the voters of course. Productive activities that contribute to growth and employment should be taxed less precisely because they contain the conditions which are necessary for a solid tax base. Therefore *the matter of taxation is not so much an issue of incomes but an issue of productivity*. Without commitment, with the backing of the European Union, that the tax system will not change in the near future another layer of uncertainty is added which makes the recession even worse. So long as there is extensive corruption and evasion a decrease of the tax rates, and VAT in particular, is impossible. How to reduce corruption is an issue of much wider importance and involves many other sociological parameters, which involve as part of the general re-adjustment processes, the *adjustment of the political system itself*. It turns out that the role of European institutions should be strengthened when it comes to the wider political re-alignments that will have to take place in the aftermath of the recession. Perhaps such political re-alignments have to take place during the recession as they can enforce a more general change of tastes and attitudes on the political and social level. Apart from that, it is of immediate priority to remove all frictions from the markets and the capital market in particular. The public's agony over the future prospects of the economy, that is the agony over the prospects of economic growth, can be answered only through *more competitive markets, less regulation, and healthier as well solid and sustainable foundations for the financial intermediation sector*.

What is not understood well is that the bailing out of the European South economies is almost impossible without *corrections of the misalignments on the European level*. This is because of the misconception that the recession is entirely due to historically accumulated public debt—which is to confuse the cause and effects. Public debt was, indeed, unsustainable, but it was in tight bondage with the credit expansion that led to the present crisis. Moreover, the re-structuring that takes place during a recession cannot be confined within the national boundaries to the extent that factors of production are mobile. There is a productive re-alignment on the European level, and also at the global, international level and concerns the division of resources among Europe and other countries that compete in the world economic arena. The interaction is complicated by the fact that, internationally, Europe operates under flexible exchange rates but the common currency is, undoubtedly, a source of stability and a foundational issue when it comes to the international competitiveness of Europe.

As we have remarked, when different economies operate with a common currency the price system cannot absorb the effects of real shocks so they are amplified through the process of adjustment that takes place in the economy. This is unavoidable to the extent that even in a single country, regional responses to shocks are different as the process of re-structuring of the distribution of resources takes place in time and space. It is incorrect to argue that the common currency is proper only for countries which are homogenous or similar—the absurdity of the argument becomes apparent after considering the large regional differences in Germany, France, the United Kingdom or the United States. The issue is to promote the mobility of productive factors at the European level and create the institutional framework that will facilitate their competitive distribution across time *and* space. Comparative advantages are critical and their importance will be enhanced by the functioning of competition and the markets. Therefore, the question is not about homogeneity of the different countries but, most importantly, the distribution of resources on the European level. Without institutional mobility of factors and more solid financial institutions, it is hard to see how Europe and the Eurozone in particular could possibly sustain long-term growth that is shared by all—to varying degrees, of course.

From a certain point of view, the European bureaucracy guarantees that one-sided attempts to deviate from fiscal and monetary consolidation become impossible or at least, difficult. This is certainly true but it is of critical importance to ask whether the European bureaucracy is headed towards coherent governance or leans instead towards fragmentation and attainment of a balance of forces through negotiations and summits. The principle of coherent governance requires that national governments or national bureaucracies share the same common goals and interests and they have the same motivation to act according to the fundamental principles of competition and free markets. *The question is just how much can we trust the workings of the European bureaucracy in terms of monetary and financial stability*? Nothing has prevented the ECB from lowering interest rates in the midst of the recession—thus adopting a misguided policy which has important consequences for the recession itself. To trust a slowly-moving and clumsy Bureaucracy with so much fragmentation and nationalism is, indeed, a quite optimistic view for the stability of the euro. To the extent that it is a central authority, the ECB and the European bureaucracy can and will adopt wrong and disastrous economic policies if they are left unwarned.

The bureaucracy has its own limitations when it comes to measures of economic policy. It is not an accident that the disagreements between Germany and France tend to revive all the old arguments against Keynesian policies. There will, of course, emerge a balance of forces after many iterations of the negotiation-renegotiation cycle but is unclear in whose interests will the final balance be. There are differing views about financial and monetary stability, and the main argument is whether the European South, Greece in particular, will manage to implement the austerity measures without leading the economy and society into collapse.

References

de Soto J (2012) An Austrian defense of the euro, Mises Institute
von Mises L (1966) Human action: a treatise on economics, 3rd rev. edn. Henry Regnery, Chicago, p 474
Hayek FA (1979) Unemployment and monetary policy: government as generator of the "business cycle". Cato Institute, San Francisco, pp 9–10

Chapter 23
Conditions for Genuine Financial and Monetary Stability

To the extent that there is a European bureaucracy the question is whether there is a need to move further to coherent governance or stay within the present, fragmented system. Coherent governance requires a notion of common political and economic interests whose objective foundation already exists but has not found yet a concrete, material form. Conditions for financial stability exceed the national boundaries and cannot be treated properly within them. Even small steps *cannot* be taken towards more stable financial sector by the member-states themselves and solely at the national level. For example, national banks that impose willingly upon themselves a 100 % reserve requirement will have to face the competition from their foreign counterparts. If the latter expand their credit to the private sector domestic banks will have to face loss of market power and customers that will be followed from a short-term deterioration of their profitability if the projects financed by the foreign banks, or the banks that did not adopt the reserve requirement, turn out to be profitable on the average. Imposing a reserve requirement is not unlike systematically distorting relative prices, and especially the wedge between loan and deposit rates. Commercial banks are, in general, willing to sacrifice some cost savings or some profitability to maintain dominant position in the market by exploiting a "lender's advantage" which drives loan rates below deposit rates for certain projects or during certain time periods. *This systematic distortion and manipulation of relative prices by the banks is a major source of instability.*

This systematic distortion can be avoided by encouraging more competition in the banking and financial sector and thus, letting the financial markets determine the equilibrium rates of interest. But it may also be that the wedge is negative, on the average or for particular projects or during some time period, as the result of adjustments in the private sector and liquidation of certain unprofitable investment. In that sense, the wedge or premium can be negative as the result of reallocation of investment that takes place during the crisis—which has a negative effect on *ex post* bank profitability. This will reflect only the fact that the commercial banks have engaged into financing *ex post* unprofitable projects that were thought to be profitable *ex ante* given the artificially low interest rates that prevail in the economy due to other reasons. That is, given the configuration of interest rates,

E. G. Tsionas, *The Euro and International Financial Stability*,
Financial and Monetary Policy Studies 37, DOI: 10.1007/978-3-319-01171-4_23,

realized returns on loans may be lower than deposit rates due to the deterioration in profitability of the more capital-intensive projects that turned out unsustainable. There will still be a negative premium between the loan and deposit rates *ex post*, although and despite the fact that loan rates could be at their *ex ante* common value across the financial sector. The critical point is that the general configuration of interest rates, determined largely by the ECB, is not sustainable since at low interest rates the commercial banks find it profitable to finance investments that will turn out unprofitable when it will be realized that the *ex ante* and ex post rates of return do not coincide. The natural course is for commercial banks to suffer deterioration in profits and make the necessary adjustments in their portfolio. The liquidation of real investment will necessitate some losses for the financial sector but this is a source of stability: Reinstatement of a new, general equilibrium of the economy is impossible without *either freely determined interest rates or perfect mobility in the financial sector.*

None of the two conditions are presently satisfied in the Eurozone. Interest rates are kept artificially low fearing a deepening of the recession and commercial banks are treated preferentially without imposing binding budget constraints upon them. *These major distortions account for a large part, if not the entire part, of fiscal consolidation problems in the South.* This is because the process of overall economic adjustment is significantly delayed by the imposition of constraints upon solvency in the financial intermediation sector which is not allowed to clear. The control of interest rates does not provide the correct signals for a recovery of investment by the private sector while at the same time this policy does not secure medium-term or long-term bank profitability—that would allow a considerable decrease in the funds required for bailing them out. Fiscal consolidation is not only an institutional matter or a matter or corrupted and incompetent governments. This is, certainly, part of the problem but it in no way the entire problem: Without proper re-distribution of resources at the microeconomic level, that is without re-direction of investment to projects and time horizons that are *truly* profitable, there is no way for decreasing unemployment and shifting employment across the sectors of the economy to result in restoration of a new equilibrium where expected and actual rates of return are approximately equal. In turn this contributes to further reductions in the tax base and a desperate government that mindlessly act as a tax collector, without regard for the impact on the distribution of resources.

The real effects from the re-distribution of resources do not seem to be well recognized by policy makers who still think in macroeconomic terms, hoping that recovery and growth can only come from a net increase in aggregate investment. However, even lower aggregate investment can produce positive effects after interest rates and, therefore, relative prices for products and factors of production, are allowed to vary freely. The re-distribution of resources and re-alignment of investment projects with new interest rates will drive resources to the more profitable uses and these will be, given the current conditions, *precisely less capital-intensive and more labor-intensive*. Stimulating the demand is not only impossible; it is actually a bad idea when there are extensive distortions in relative prices. The general level of prices will increase and unemployment can also increase without paying due attention to what constitutes the fundamental problem—and this is none other than financial markets not allowed to operate in a competitive fashion.

Therefore, it is a *prerequisite* of financial and monetary stability that adjustments in the economy are allowed to take place, during a recession, that will reinstate a new equilibrium. Putting it in such general terms no one will raise an objection to be certain. However, the implications are far reaching. Will interest rates be allowed to move freely in the Eurozone? Alternatively, will commercial banks be left on their own to make decisions and suffer the cost of their choices? Additionally, are output markets operating under competitive conditions? Are the markets for factors of production operating competitively so as to allow frictionless mobility across markets and possible uses?

Coherent governance means that there is similar institutional framework in the Eurozone. Although the institutional framework that resulted from the Treaties and the ECB is there, what is missing is a common will for letting the financial markets operate in a competitive framework. It is thought that "freedom" in financial markets is irresponsible and this is what caused the recession, the housing bubble, the sub-prime crisis etc. In reality, cheap credit is what made long-term investment like construction and housing look *ex ante* profitable only to realize that the actual, *ex post* rates of return bared no resemblance to loan rates. If financial markets were truly free to operate then they would reinstate *immediately* a new equilibrium at higher loan rates which by itself alone would provide the right signals to the private sector that further engagement in capital-intensive investment has reached its limit. On the contrary what has happened is that credit was kept artificially low encouraging *speculation*, as capital-intensive investment takes some time to reach completion. If relative prices are not allowed to absorb the shocks then only the real, quantity variables can adjust and eventually, a large part of unprofitable investment will be liquidated. Speculation could have been prevented—although it is simply a rational phenomenon created and propagated by cheap credit—provided markets, including financial markets, would have been allowed to clear.

As a result a defense of the Euro upon the conditions of stability that it generates, cannot rely on the long and tedious process of discussions and negotiations in the European Council. This process did not prevent the recession or the crisis and, of course, it could not have been otherwise. A defense of the Euro must rely upon conditions for financial and monetary stability. Although monetary stability is, at present, guaranteed, *the question of financial stability raises the issues of competition and a new structure of the European banking system*. As a matter of fact, coherent governance, in the present conditions, requires less bureaucracy and simplification of the decision processes, rather than retaining the existing schemes. This will facilitate a global re-structuring of markets on the European level which can come out only as the result of more structured governance with the authority to act, together with the European Central Bank, to promote conditions for market clearing and tendency towards equilibrium. Since the issue is related to structural reforms only re-structuring of governance can overcome the problems and frictions created by the fragmentation and idiosyncrasies of the country-members.

More structured, coherent governance is able to allow *fuller merging of financial and productive or investment capital* through the competitive functioning of *financial* markets. Banking and its operations are dominated by the need to guarantee smooth performance of the *financial* system which, in turn, regulates performance in the product and factors' markets.

Chapter 24
International Financial Stability

With competitive banking and/or freely moving interest rates in Europe, what would happen if elsewhere in the world, there was monetary or credit expansion and competition from foreign banks and financial institutions? If foreign governments (say the United States) continue to expand their deficits and/or the money base, a classical recession will take place to correct the misallocations of investment with its subsequent effects in factor and product markets. The recession would certainly affect European exports to the United States but it would promote them in countries that used to import from the United States. With no pressures upon the Euro coming from fragile financial markets, the appreciation of the dollar would only make the recession worse in the United States. Further credit expansion in the United States to sustain bank profitability would recycle the recessionary effects—without clearing in American financial markets where interest rates are not allowed to change. Higher exports from Europe, and the signals from the appreciation of the dollar, will shift investment to Europe to those sectors that benefit directly from the exports and, subsequently at the margin, in sectors that benefit indirectly through the impact of the exporting on all other sectors. One would, clearly, observe a growing and prospering Europe and a recession in the United States. Without freely functioning and competitive financial markets, in the sense we described above, it would be impossible to re-shuffle investment in the United States among those sectors that are equally profitable *ex post* and *ex ante* given the configuration of interest rates. Without a change in interest rates it is impossible to realize material gains from the welfare-improving re-distribution of resources that will increase employment, output and tax revenues at the same time. As long as the Federal Reserve accommodates the deficits of the government it is impossible to remove the burden from relative prices and let it fall on the shoulders of the real economy—which is, in reality, what is needed during a recession.

Much of the "co-movement" in output fluctuations is due to sustained distortions in interest rates and other relative prices. If these were to be eliminated, under international resource mobility, there would be little reason to have the amplified fluctuations and deep recessions with short recovery periods that we see after the 1970s. There are, of course, non-traded goods and their complications; however, the point is that a stable Euro is a source for global financial stability, as long as

E. G. Tsionas, *The Euro and International Financial Stability*,
Financial and Monetary Policy Studies 37, DOI: 10.1007/978-3-319-01171-4_24,

this is understood in the proper sense: Not in the sense that nothing ever changes in the Eurozone and thus there is no "uncertainty" which complicates private decisions but rather *in the sense that banking and financial markets operate in a stable manner*. A stable manner is one which allows for adjustments and re-alignments of interest rates with the actual constellation of the distribution of resources and the agreement between *ex post* and *ex ante* rates of return. In a similar way, a freely floating dollar along with mishandling of credit and interest rates in the United States is a source of global instability. A recession in the United States will be transmitted elsewhere through transactions in products and factors and will affect the global distribution of resources. In that case there would be a layer of uncertainty generated by the policies of the Federal Reserve and the federal government. However, the effects of the recession will be mitigated in countries that have stable currency and fully competitive financial markets, whereas in the United States the depth of the recession will be significant. Immediate adjustments of interest rates in Europe would absorb the larger part of the fluctuation and would successfully prevent engagement in unprofitable investment that would, otherwise, take place in view of distorted American interest rates.

Letting aside the obvious fact that investors prefer to engage in activities under stable conditions, artificially low American rates cannot attract investment without, eventually, generating a rational "bubble" that will seriously affect the American financial system and, through it, the entire real economy. The question is not one of more investment or less investment in Europe compare to the United States, but rather investment in Europe which keep the financial sector solid and healthy; this can, in turn, be the case only if there are no distortions in interest rates so that re-structuring and re-distribution are allowed to take place. A solid and healthy financial sector means less variable profitability, a target that can only be achieved with freely floating interest rates.

Unless it is fully realized that at the heart of the current recession and the subsequent economic problems, lie the systematic and persistent distortions in financial *markets*, and without removing them is impossible to maintain *stability of the real economy*, one cannot hope to comprehend that, in turn, the elimination of distortions in *financial* markets eliminates distortions in all relative prices, under competitive conditions. In that way the prerequisite for stabilized growth in the real economy is *financial* stability, that is free and competitive financial markets. On the global level there is not much one can do to guarantee financial stability. In fact this is impossible if interest rates are floating in Europe but they are predetermined in the United States. This does not imply that a *more* stable Euro does not become a *source* for global financial stability—quite the contrary. However, it is only a source, implying that there are also other sources, like government decisions about spending and interest rates elsewhere in the world, which contribute to *higher instability*. Higher instability is, eventually, more significant for the United States rather than Europe although there are real effects in both continents. In the final analysis, the question boils down to the international distribution of resources which is determined by their relative prices (relative to one another and across continents) to which interest rates play a fundamental role of immense importance. *Global financial stability requires globally flexible interest rates and competitive banking* which limits the interventions of the Central Banks. At the same time it creates the conditions for efficient tax systems and higher tax revenues by enlarging, through growth, the tax base, thus providing less motivation for spending by federal authorities. In turn, this requires coherent and restructured global governance in coordination with the central banks. Naturally, *more financial stability requires more flexible interest rates and more competitive banking*, although "more", at the global level, cannot always and necessarily imply "sufficiently high".

More coherent governance will have, undoubtedly, to consider economic growth and prosperity for the system as a whole. Regional differences cannot be avoided but that is irrelevant since regional differentials are at the core of a proper distribution of resources. There is a large potential of growth and welfare from redistribution of resources among uses, products, markets, and continents. Once this potential is exhausted, through the operation of free financial markets, and the global system operates under stable conditions, the issue of economic growth becomes trivial: Entrepreneurship and inventiveness are unlimited and so is the potential for long-term economic growth.

Part of coherent governance is the realization of the fact that governance and political affairs have very little to do with the actual working of the economic system. Governance sets the institutional framework and the rules of the game, it encourages the creation of markets where it is most difficult to emerge but, otherwise, and in other respects, the interference with "aggregate demand" and distortionary taxation—or even worse the direct change of relative prices, has very little to recommend itself as "economic policy". Indeed, what is very little understood is that *the policy of Central Banks to set directly interest rates is the most pathological case of imposing price controls*, whose damaging role is explained in all introductory economics textbooks. Similarly, expansionary policies inspired by the Keynesian focus on "aggregate demand" may increase employment and output temporarily but, at the microeconomic level, the forces that are at work, tend to increase unemployment in the long-run through the misdirection of resources. This effect can be even short-term if investment does not change and labor is misdirected to the various sectors of the economy through the effect on interest rates. When interest rates are controlled and, as a result, financial markets are not allowed to clear, the effect on unemployment will be even higher. *At the heart of unemployment lies a misdirection of production or resources* that leads to:

> existence of discrepancies between the distribution of the demand among the different goods and services and the allocation of labor and other resources among the production of those outputs (Hayek 1979, 25).

At the heart of financial instability also lies a misdirection of resources which changes the distribution of global demand and globally available resources in international production. It is not trivial to correct misdirection and distortions to achieve a new, efficient global equilibrium. The distributions of demand and resources can be coordinated only on the basis of the constellation of relative prices of which the most important is the rate of interest. Without prices it is impossible to reduce the discrepancies between the distribution of the demand and the allocation of labor and other resources, in Hayek's terms. But this is precisely what the central banks have been doing for years.

Another major source of global financial instability is the constellation of different economic policies that are followed in terms of tax rates (particularly on investment and capital) and government spending. A tax increase to accommodate more government spending is not unlike a monetary stimulus which changes the distributions of resources through the interest rates (or directly if interest rates are controlled) and can have negative long-run effects on both output and employment. *This policy leaves the deficit unchanged yet it has tremendous real effects*, which shows that budget deficits *per se* have nothing to do with the problem. The crux of the matter is that changes in the constellation of tax rates misdirect investment and change the distribution of consumption while at the same time expansionary policies (even if they do not change the deficit) change further the distribution of demand irrespectively of the distribution of resources that are used in production. These policies have predominantly national effects but they tend to be transmitted globally and affect the global distribution of demand and the global distribution of resources. Complications in the system of tax and interest rates, internationally, tend to make these discrepancies persistent and lie at the heart of the global nature of recessions (but the national character of recoveries, for the most part) and in that sense they constitute a major contribution to financial instability.

Rothhard in "America's Great Depression" (p. 21) argues as follows about the role of the government:

> Reducing its tax-spending level will automatically shift the societal saving-investment–consumption ratio in favor of saving and investment, thus greatly lowering the time required for returning to a prosperous economy. Reducing taxes that bear most heavily on savings and investment will further lower social time preferences. Furthermore, depression is a time of economic strain. Any reduction of taxes, or of any regulations interfering with the free market, will stimulate healthy economic activity; any increase in taxes or other intervention will depress the economy further.

Notably this policy recommendation is in direct contradiction with austerity measures which tend to increase taxation indiscriminately without, at the same time, taking any measures "or of any regulations interfering with the free market". In order to understand the recommendation we have to qualify it further in its true meaning: It is not the size of debt or deficit which affects the recession so much but, on the contrary, it is, first, the re-alignment of the distribution of resources and demand, and, second, the size of the government, which is measured hypothetically by the level of spending but more precisely by the actual significance of its economic interventions. While true that the decrease of taxes will stimulate economic activity, it is equally true that the decrease of taxes has, mainly, an effect on the distribution of demand which is further misaligned relative to the distribution of capital and labor. Although a short-term recovery is made possible by the decrease of taxes, in general, and even by the decrease of taxes "that bear most heavily on savings and investment" how does that help the re-alignment of the distributions of demand and labor to reduce unemployment and increase output in the longer run? This is simply not possible. The argument that fiscal consolidation has nothing to do with the problem tends to forget that fiscal discipline cannot result from uniform decreases of spending but from decreases of spending in those areas of government involvement that are the most significant *both quantitatively and qualitatively*. Fiscal consolidation does not act only to balance the budget but also to restore a new equilibrium where the government is, loosely speaking, "smaller". Unfortunately it does not have a tendency to minimize the number of important, distortionary decisions of the government, *at least for the most part*, but it does help in a precise sense: It allows the shifting of resources to the private sector which, *hopefully*, will be allocated in the correct way, so as to reduce the magnitude of misdirections and misallocations produced by the distortions in the price system.

Do we have reasons to believe that this "crowding out" in favor of the private sector will, *hopefully*, be allocated correctly? There are, indeed, tendencies in the economic system and the markets that justify this viewpoint. During the recession the *expectations* of entrepreneurs about profitability and rates of return have to revise downwards even if the real after-tax interest rates are unchanged. The cost of borrowing, in effect, is higher, because it is augmented by the lower probability of profitable capital-intensive projects which shift the resources to labor-intensive processes whose return can be acquired more quickly. In turn there is a natural tendency to increase output and employment in those sectors that are less capitalistic and which will tend to come out first from the recessionary state. Our analysis is not unlike the so-called "regime uncertainty":

> It is time for economists and historians to take seriously the hypothesis that the New Deal prolonged the Great Depression by creating an extraordinarily high degree of regime uncertainty in the minds of investors. Of course, scholars have had their reasons for not taking the idea seriously. For a long time, historians have viewed the statements of contemporary businesspeople about "lack of business confidence" as little more than routine grumbling—sure, sure, what else would one expect Republican tycoons to have said? Historians generally report such statements as if they were either attempts to sway public opinion or unreflective whining. Since World War II, economists, with only a few exceptions, have overlooked regime uncertainty as a cause of the Great Duration for other reasons, such as the availability of standard macroeconomic models whose variables do not include the degree of regime uncertainty and, even if one wanted to incorporate it into an existing model, the absence of any conventional quantitative index of such uncertainty. Somewhat inexplicably, most economists regard evidence about expectations drawn from public opinion surveys as scientifically contemptible. Moreover, economists crave general models, equally applicable to all times and places, and so they resist explanations that emphasize the unique aspects of a specific episode such as the Great Depression (Higgs 1997).

In this sense, "regime uncertainty" results from expansionary policies or similar policies whose end effect is the misalignment of the distribution of demand and resources. In the case of the European Union for example, even during and after, M1 continues to *expand*, although in Greece it does not do so but effective interest rates in Greece continue to *decline*. This is, clearly, not a wise policy and certainly not a policy that contributed to international financial stability or stability of the euro. The aspect of expectations is of immense importance and it is quite evident that expectations adjust quickly over the business cycle. Moreover, these expectations are fundamentally based on expectations about rates of return which are formed based on expectations of demand, among other things. During a recession these expectations are revised and there starts a re-shifting of demand even in the absence of policy changes in interest rates, *ceteris paribus*. The main problem is that the *ceteris paribus* condition is often violated and policy measures are taken in the direction of demand-based stimuli, artificial control of prices, subsidies to investment etc. which prolong the recession instead of aiding recovery.

Taking again Greece as the example, there is some recovery of exports after 2011 due to the artificial stimulus in the Eurozone and the artificially low interest rates. This cannot last in the longer term and it is not sustainable, as evidenced from the further deterioration of investment and capacity utilization which follows a downward turn since 2007. As Hayek emphasized:

> We must certainly expect recovery to come from a *revival of investment*. Neither subsidization of investment nor artificially low interest rates is likely to achieve this position. And least of all is the desirable (i.e. stable) form of investment to be brought about by stimulating consumer demand (Hayek 1979, p. 42, emphasis added).

The great insight of Hayek was his rejection of macro-economic stimulus as a source of recovery and growth and his insistence that only the recovery of investment and capacity utilization are effective it what concerns the process off ending the recession. His other insight was that investment cannot recover from artificial means but only after minimizing government's involvement so that free markets and the price mechanism will be able to shift investment and create new capital in accordance with the actual distribution of demand and resources. This form of recovery of investment is (1) the micro-economic process of re-shifting demand, and (2) the efficient operation of financial and capital markets which reinstate a clear picture of actual and realized rates of return, on the average.

In the Hayekian and Rothbardian approach we must also examine its symmetric opposite, viz. that *a reduction of tax and expenditure can, actually, have a positive effect on output and employment*. A simultaneous cut of taxes and expenditure, which is disproportionately in favor of cutting expenditures and, therefore, reduces the budget deficit, will re-shift resources in favor of private investment. The measure can be accompanied by, at least a temporary, constraint on commercial banks to adopt a 100 % reserve requirement, a refusal to finance short-term obligations and operating expenses of private firms and, to some measure, a more extended liberalization of the functioning of the financial intermediation system. There, of course, remains the problem of financing interest payments of the accumulated public debt. To a certain extent the generous haircut along an extension of the period for the accommodation of short-term financing of debt would provide the necessary time for the recovery of investment after balancing the budget to considerably lower levels of both spending and taxes—with a faster rate of decrease for the first.

We must emphasize that accommodation of the short-term obligations arising from interest payments cannot be analyzed in isolation from other economic problems. Sustainable financing (accommodation) requires an economy that shows signs of recovery and this can only be achieved through the recovery of investment *and also* recovery of the rates of utilization which have fallen dramatically during the recession in Greece. Prices and costs have decreased considerably, although not to the full extent possible, and signs of recovery are clear in the exporting sectors. A further reduction of taxes and expenditures would promote this tendency even further, and would set the stage for re-shifting and increase of the level of investment. With very low loan rates and a prolonged period of cheap credit, *expected* rates of returns in *certain* sectors have fallen dramatically so investment will be re-allocated and/or increased in sectors that are more profitable during the recession, given the existing economic conditions. *There is no other way, simply, to expect recovery from "growth-oriented" policies of a different form.*

Given the current conditions in terms of economic policy and the "regime of uncertainty" it is, admittedly, quite difficult for the private sector to determine exactly where exactly obtain higher rates of return can be obtained. This enhances the motivation to engage in speculative or non-productive activities—although at the same time it is likely to enable also further engagement in innovative activities which reduce considerably the costs of production and are, naturally, consistent with the sectoral distribution of demand. But the fact of the matter is that *the uncertainty surrounding the rates of returns is, for the most part, created by the economic policy regime itself.* Will the program of reducing the size of the public sector succeed? Will taxes eventually be reduced? Current prospects about both these problems are not good. It is quite possible that the budget will, eventually, balance but there remains the problem of financing the debt and the problem of low incomes—which is really a problem of a tremendous misalignment in the distributions of demand and resources. *The increase of incomes can only be sustained by the recovery of investment* which, in turn, depends on cutting taxes and expenditures—assuming financing the debt will not be much of a problem. But the recovery of investment depends also on different interest rates which can only be, actually, determined through the functioning of financial markets. To the extent that this policy measure will not be undertaken by the ECB, even to a small degree, we cannot hope for a short-term recovery.

We have argued that although the Rothbardian argument is correct, it depends essentially on the "right" or approximately market-clearing interest rates. Without this requirement the reduction in the size of government *will have only a relative and limited tendency* to put the economy out of the recession. It depends crucially on the micro-economic adjustments that will take place—adjustment that will re-shift resources from existing to other uses. In turn this depends entirely upon the *expectations* of the private sector about rates of return in different uses. So, in fact, without an *increase in interest rates*, coming endogenously from the free operation of financial markets, this series of operations and causes-effects becomes rather difficult to achieve.

Of course the "*relative and limited tendency*" of reductions in taxes and expenditures to drive the economy out of the recession is a quantitative issue. We do not mean to imply that it is necessarily small but only that the effect depends on expected rates of return, that is it on relatives prices that are already out of equilibrium *to large extent* and therefore do not yield the right signals to the private sector. The classical analysis applies under the simplifying assumption that prices are free to vary in the relevant markets—an assumption which is violated when interest rates are not allowed to clear the financial markets. Now, under significant distortions it is, of course, true that the Rothbardian argument applies but the private sector cannot accurately predict the profitability of investment at different time horizons and sectors of the economy and, therefore, that the adjustment process following a reduction in taxes and expenditures will yield *some* increase in output and employment. The *extent* of the increase is, however, *quite uncertain* and may range from zero to quantitatively significant depending on the particular configuration of the distortions. This is why Rothbard accompanied his proposal by liberalization of markets: Without a price mechanism that works the effects will be *uncertain* and they will be *maximal* under full flexibility of prices and particularly—according to our analysis— under flexibility in interest rates.

It seems relevant that flexibility financial markets along with the restraint of the central bank to engage in monetary expansions (which is more of an issue in the United States rather than, currently at least, in Europe) is closely related to coherent governance. Once it is realized that flexible interest rates absorb automatically "speculative attacks" or rational "bubbles" the central control of interest rates becomes unnecessary, and the only issues remaining are those related to monetary or fiscal expansions which are, fundamentally, *political issues*. We have tried to argue convincingly and beyond reasonable doubt, that monetary and fiscal stimuli generate a business cycle which can only be corrected when competitive markets exists and the price mechanism is allowed to operate to clear the markets. Moreover, reductions in taxes and expenditures—which effectively reduce the "size of government" generate positive output and employment effects when the government sector is "large" essentially due to the "crowding out" in favor of the private sector and the reinstatement of equilibrium in investment along with the reinstatement of equilibrium between the distribution of demand and the distribution resources—which is altered by a fiscal stimulus or tax increases. But if reinstating flexibility in financial markets boils down to a political matter, then it must be clear that political governance must be re-structured to assign some decisions to markets themselves, under the supervisory and institutional control of the Central Bank, the ECB in our case. What remains as a responsibility for the re-structured political governance authority is the institutional framework as well as the *design of new institutions* to ensure flexibly working markets.

The re-structured coherent governance becomes a priority for the European Union and the Eurozone. The quantitatively and qualitatively important distortions, particularly those in the financial markets, must be removed to ensure the furthering of the role of the Euro in international stability. The field of action of the new coherent governance is quite extensive. It ranges from the design of new institutions and introduction of regulatory reforms to ensure competitiveness and anti-cartel law-making and enforcement, to the gradual abolition of restrictions in the functioning of the markets for capital and other resources, and the financial markets in particular. It includes the gradual harmonization of law-making on functioning of financial institutions and commercial banks in the Eurozone, the gradual increase in reserve requirements, and the enhancement of competition in commercial banking and other institutions of financial intermediation. Moreover, it includes gradual enforcement of reductions in taxes and expenditures in the member-countries to ensure not only fiscal consolidation but, at the same time, smaller government sectors, a fact that becomes, under the existing conditions, a prerequisite for the recovery and further increase of investment—and therefore, output, employment and welfare.

Part of coherent global governance in the European Union will *not* have to be the settlement of issues relating to public debt. The short-term financing of public debt will automatically be settled once the European economies are back on track in the aftermath of the recession when, necessarily, as the result of policy measures that we discussed, investment will have recovered and distortions will have been eliminated. The correspondence of the distribution of resources to the actual distribution of demand will generate a process of adjustment—over time, regions, sectors and counties—that will re-allocate the resources, and investment in particular, to maximize output and employment in the new equilibrium.

A well-known issue that is involved in global governance is the harmonization of tax rates in the European Union. This is only part of the problem. It does avoid "tax competition" in the sense that resources will have no longer a motive to shift among countries that are similar in other respects but the crux of the matter is that countries are not, and cannot, be similar in other respects. The real problem is to remove all distortions in the distributions of resources that are created, first, by the existence of *national* distortions, and second, the *different* quantitative and qualitative nature of these distortions, *among countries*. Countries are moreover different in terms of size of government, different taxation systems, different levels and composition of government expenditures, etc. Proceeding in a gradual manner, it makes sense for global governance first to eliminate distortions at the national level and then proceed to harmonize the different fiscal or governance systems. The elimination of distortions and frictions in financial markets, which we have argued is of immense importance, requires coordinated efforts, along with the ECB, and in a most natural sense, along with regulatory authorities elsewhere in the world, particularly the United States. In this respect, *the natural first step would be the establishment of a system of fixed exchange rate between the Dollar and the Euro, and possibly the Pound and the Yen.*

This step involves, of course, quite a few side issues, many of which are political in character and it is likely to emerge only after the successful implementation of coherent governance on the European level. The most important reform that we propose here is a system of variable interest rates which guarantees financial stability along with a commitment to a healthier and more solid banking system based upon the gradual increase of reserve requirements. The next most important reform is a wider fiscal consolidation based upon similarly sized government sectors, ideally minimal, operating of course under the principle of balanced budgets. This particular reform is likely to involve the harmonization of operation of several publicly provided services, as for example in health, transportation and education, on the European level—since coherent governance is, by its very nature, a global matter.

We have remarked many times that was is essential in coherent governance is, perhaps above everything else, financial markets are competitive and they are allowed to clear at freely determined nominal interest rates. With regulated financial markets, and dominant themes such as those of hostile "speculators" or cursed "bubbles" in the agenda of governance or regulation, it is impossible to overcome the hurdles created by institutional deficiencies and institutionally induced distortions in the economy. Freely, competitive interest rates are essential in a new scheme or paradigm of governance in order, precisely, to guarantee the stability and the solid foundation of this new paradigm: This is none other than *growth* which can be induced by investment. Investment growth, in turn, depends critically on interest rates and the ability of capital markets to clear. The point is put into simple terms by Garrison (1996):

> Mainstream macroeconomics bypasses all issues involving intertemporal capital structure by positing a simple inverse relationship between aggregate (net) investment and the interest rate. The investment aggregate is typically taken to be interest-inelastic in the context of short-run macroeconomic theory and policy prescription and interest-elastic in the context of long-run growth. Further, the very simplicity of this formulation suggests that *expectations—which are formulated in the light of current and anticipated policy prescriptions—can make or break policy effectiveness.* The Austrian theory recognizes that whatever the interest elasticity of the conventionally defined investment aggregate, *the impact of interest-rate movements on the structure of capital is crucial to the maintenance of intertemporal equilibrium. Changes within the capital structure may be significant even when the change in net investment is not.* And those *structural* changes *can be equilibrating or dis-equilibrating* depending on whether they are savings-induced or credit-induced, or—more generally—depending on whether they are *preference-induced or policy-induced.* Further, *the very complexity of the interplay between preferences and policy within a multistage intertemporal capital structure suggests that market participants cannot fully sort out and hedge against the effects of policy on product and factor prices*" (Garrison 1996).

This passage describes very precisely the nature of effects that we have in mind when we suggest liberalization in capital and financial markets—apparently the two markets are closely related through borrowing. Indeed, expectations can make or break effective economic policies, as we remarked above and, more precisely, it is the whole distribution of expectations that should be brought together with the distribution of demand and resources to determine the final fundamental tendency towards a new equilibrium—which is always a "disequilibrating" force relative to the current configuration of decisions of private agents and the distribution of supply.

References

Garrison RW (1996) The Austrian theory: a summary. In: Ebeling RM (ed) The Austrian Theory of the Trade Cycle. Ludwig von Mises Institute (emphasis added)
Hayek FA (1979) Toward a Free Market Monetary System. J. of Libertarian Studies. 3(1):1–8
Higgs R (1997) Regime uncertainty: why the great depression lasted so long and why prosperity resumed after the war. Independent Rev 1(4):561–590

Chapter 25
On Monetary Policies

Von Mises has insisted that money is not a creation of the Law or a simple medium of exchange but rather a commodity itself whose value has to be determined, along with the prices of all other commodities, in the general equilibrium of an unhampered, competitive economy. As he wrote:

> Production goods derive their value from that of their products. Not so money; for *no increase in the welfare of the members of a society can result from the availability of an additional quantity of money*. The laws which govern the value of money are different from those which govern the value of production goods and from those which govern the value of consumption goods (L. von Mises, Theory of Money and Credit, p. 86, emphasis added).

Clearly, money is a special commodity for "*no increase in the welfare of the members of a society can result from the availability of an additional quantity of money*". This is indeed what distinguishes money from other consumption or producer's goods and what sets it apart as a special kind of its own. What von Mises had in mind is, essentially, that changes in the quantity of money induce losses for some private agents and gains for some others so: (1) it is impossible to theorize in advance about the final quantitative effect, and (2) if we reduce the quantitative effect to welfare measurement it is impossible to make a statement because welfare comparisons are impossible in the subjective theory of value of the Austrian School.

> The increase in the quantity of money does not mean an increase of income for all individuals. On the contrary, those sections of the community that are the last to be reached by the additional quantity of money have their incomes reduced, as a consequence of the decrease in the value of money called forth by the increase in its quantity; this will be referred to later (*TM&C*, p. 139).

Therefore, a monetary expansion or contraction has real effects and is, therefore, non-neutral, in that it affects different economic agents in a different way, a fact that is systematically forgotten by the Monetary School. The demand of agents whose the monetary increase reaches first, increases, and the prices of products for which they demand more will rise.

E. G. Tsionas, *The Euro and International Financial Stability*,
Financial and Monetary Policy Studies 37, DOI: 10.1007/978-3-319-01171-4_25,

> But this rise of prices will by no means be restricted to the market for those goods that are desired by those who originally have the new money at their disposal. In addition, those who have brought these goods to market will have their incomes and their proportionate stocks of money increased and, in their turn, will be in a position to demand more intensively the goods they want, so that these goods will also rise in price. Thus *the increase of prices continues, having a diminishing effect, until all commodities, some to a greater and some to a lesser extent, are reached by it* (op. cit.).

The effect on all prices will, in general, be *differential* as the result of a monetary expansion. However, the increase of prices means profits for certain groups and losses for other groups of private agents like, for example, the final consumers who are not engaged into producing anything. Until the wages, finally, raise there will be a period during which the consumers will be worse off and the duration of this period depends in the velocity of circulation and the time it takes for a monetary injection to reach the state where increased demand for labor is required and, therefore, wages will have to increase in the short-run. But even with higher wages it is not certain that consumers will be better off in the future, since this depends entirely on the relationship between wages and the prices of the basket of goods that they used to buy.

> [B]ut *it will no longer be possible for them to secure profits that will compensate them for the losses they have suffered.* That is to say, they will not be able to use their increased receipts to purchase commodities at prices corresponding to the old level of the value of money; for the increase of prices will already have gone through the whole community. Thus *the losses suffered by the [consumers] at the time when they still sold their products at the old low prices but had to pay for the products of others at the new and higher prices remain uncompensated.* It is these losses of the groups that are the last to be reached by the variation in the value of money which ultimately constitute the source of the profits made by the mine owners and the groups most closely connected with them (pp. 208–209, emphasis added).

Therefore, the monetary expansion with its differential impact on demand and prices, generates a re-distribution of incomes in favor of those groups of agents that receive the money first and against those that are towards the end of the chain of the monetary transmission. There is no way to compensate the consumers for the losses that they suffered when, in the period during which wages have not yet increased, they had to pay for the increased prices of consumption goods. Since no new value has been or can be created by the monetary injection losses and profits have to be the same, on the aggregate, so the loss of one group is the source of profit for another—the one closer to the chain of monetary injection. Therefore, *although there are important real effects there can be no real aggregate effect*, in the sense that the final effect of the monetary expansion or contraction is nothing else but a re-distribution of incomes rather than a net increase or decrease of aggregate income. There is, of course, no way to measure the final effect on aggregate welfare as there is no such thing as aggregate welfare and it is impossible to Pareto-rank the individual welfare changes that have taken place.

Unless we have reason to believe that this re-distribution of incomes is desirable, in some sense, there is no way to justify the monetary expansion which benefits some groups of agents at the expense of others. The essence of the

Misesian argument is dynamic in nature and it is impossible to comprehend in static terms or in terms of comparative statics. From the point of view of comparative statics, we have an increase or a shock in the incomes of the group that is closer to the beginning of the chain of the monetary injection. This will have to result in higher prices and higher demand for all goods as well as, *finally*, higher incomes for all groups. The comparative static analysis, of course, misses the entire transition period during which new incomes are generated and others are, *immediately or almost immediately*, lost. Since no wealth has been really generated the initial increase of incomes has to be balanced by the losses of incomes in the *transition* period to the *final* equilibrium. Therefore, there can be no *net* increase in employment or outputs when the full chain of events has been completed and incomes have been balanced one against the other. In this sense there can be no "magical" way to stimulate the economy through a monetary injection and the only aggregate effect will, ultimately, be a re-distribution of demand and incomes at the expense, of course, of changes in prices.

It is precisely the fluctuations in the value of money and, therefore, the fluctuation of prices and the induced monetary and financial instability, which lay at the heart of Austrian arguments against policy-induced changes in the money supply. This instability has important real effects, and, as we have seen, these are, precisely, the re-distribution effects. Since consumers are never at the benefitting end of the transmission chain or the transmission mechanism, *a monetary expansion implies net losses for the consumers*, which aggregated through the time required for the mechanism to complete its effects upon all or most prices, can be significant.

Since the exact configuration of demand and supply for all goods and services is unknown to the government, or any other agent, it is impossible to determine the precise quantitative effects of the monetary expansion in advance. In Mises words:

> All monetary policies encounter the difficulty that the effects of any measures taken in order to influence the fluctuations of the objective exchange value of money can neither be foreseen in advance, nor their nature and magnitude be determined *even after* they have already occurred (pp. 238–39, emphasis added).

Notice that it is difficult to determine such effects, *even after* the effects of the monetary expansion have been completed. This is because, first of all, it is impossible to measure the effect on all individual incomes and, second, because actual economies do not operate under the textbook *ceteris paribus* assumption. However, it is not essential to know precisely these effects in order to decide definitely against changes in money supply. The Austrian School's analysis shows, beyond any doubt, that there can be no aggregate effect but there are important, real, re-distributional effects resulting from monetary expansions or contractions. For von Mises it was quite important to leave the markets determine the value of money and, therefore, limit the power of government or other authorities to change the supply of money. It was only after his analysis that it was realized that the supply of money is neither lower nor higher than the actual quantity needed to complete all transactions that *can* be completed *given* the amount of resources and private decisions. For quite some time, economists think that there is "too little" money and, therefore, a monetary expansion during a period of recession, can have positive effects, at least in the *short-run*. In the long-run the only effect can be on higher prices and there seems to be very little disagreement on this.

Where can positive short-run effects, from a monetary expansion, come from? Apparently, from the re-distributional effects and the positive effects on incomes of those private agents which are closer to the beginning of the chain of the monetary transmission mechanism. To this extent *the effects depend entirely upon what the commercial banks do with the increased supply of money*. The banking sector, of course, behaves differently during a recession or an expansion. It will act so as to maximize expected profits, and from that point onwards, the chain of events is outside the control of the Central Bank or the Federal Reserve. Who gets the money first in the form of loans particularly during a recession, is determined by what uses of funds are less risky and may, potentially, yield higher expected returns for the commercial banks. These are likely to be consumers or firms which have managed to maintain credibility and profitability during the recession, although the outcome can still be risky and commercial banks may find themselves, finally, making losses. In the mean-time it is likely, but not entirely certain, that the new injections will be used by consumers or firms who wish to benefit from cheap credit and do not want to finance their activities using their own funds. Most likely these agents will want to finance short-term obligations or operating costs and use their own funds in other activities, savings perhaps, which can earn them higher return compared to the low loan rates. Since they are faced with decreased demand for their products these successful business firms will not undertake investment before they obtain the right positive signals from the demand side nor will they expand capacity utilization under the existing conditions. Therefore, most likely, the new funds will be used to finance activities which were normally financed by own funds and the own funds can simply be put into savings accounts—thus returning back to the commercial banks. In this case, which is quite plausible, *the monetary expansion will terminate at this stage without ever reaching the consumers and without even going further beyond the successful firms to the rest of the economy*! The commercial banks will find themselves making losses due to the difference between loan and deposit rates and these losses will be the profits of the successful private agents—provided, of course, that they continue to be successful. The Central Bank will see that there are no aggregate effects and the recession continues to be as worse as before. Other than an unnecessary subsidy or gift to successful business there will be no other effects and, in fact, the new injections will never reach the marginal firms that could use the new funds to maintain profitability—artificially and temporarily, of course. There will simply no way for the new funds to reach agents in distress, as the Central Bank may wish, because this is in direct contrast to the profit maximizing behavior of the commercial banks, and there is no other way through which new money can be injected into the economy. We will not even have re-distributional effects *in this case* and money will be completely neutral, unable to drive the economy out of the recession.

As de Soto (2009) points out, excess capacity in many sectors,

> but especially in those furthest from consumption, such as high technology, construction, and capital goods industries in general) in no way constitutes proof of oversaving and insufficient consumption. Quite the opposite is true: it is a *symptom* of the fact that we cannot completely use fixed capital produced in error, because the immediate demand for consumer goods and services is so urgent that we cannot allow ourselves the luxury of producing the complementary capital goods nor the working capital necessary to take advantage of such idle capacity. In short the crisis is provoked by a relative excess of consumption, i.e., a relative shortage of saving, which does not permit the completion of the processes initiated, nor the production of the complementary capital goods or working capital necessary to maintain the ongoing investment processes and to employ the capital goods which, for whatever reason, entrepreneurs were able to finish during the expansion process (de Soto, p. 416).

Money neutrality, *in this case*, which does *not* hold in general, is driven by the fact that, during a deep recession, commercial banks have no interest to finance indiscriminately and firms do not have any incentive to expand when they can simply substitute one source of funding operating costs (own funds) by another (borrowed funds from the monetary injection). *However, money will not be neutral in another very important sense—namely that it creates financial instability.* Even if all firms which are financed by the commercial banks turn out to be successful, indeed, banks will be making a loss due to the difference between the (already low) loan rate and the higher deposit rate. If, in addition, a fraction of these firms turn out to be unprofitable and unable to repay loans in the short-term, or if such firms did indeed expand and increased their demand for factors produced by other firms, along the chain of monetary injection, which turn out insolvent, then, in fact, the increase of money supply will depress further the economy. *Notably, commercial banks will have to face losses both in the beginning and in end of the monetary transmission mechanism.* In the beginning of the chain, because of fund substitution by some firms. In the end because any possible expansion of real activity will turn out to be incompatible with demand. In the latter cases the firms who borrowed the new funds will not be able to repay or sustain their debt.

Therefore, there is a very precise sense in which the monetary expansion leads directly to financial instability. Since the prospects of demand do not look any better, firms have no incentive to actually invest any funds that they can borrow cheaply. However, banks will be making losses under these conditions, and these losses are the profits of successful firms that can substitute funds. In this case the so-called "lender's advantage" is a major source of financial instability. Notably, financial instability or instability in general does not result from policy uncertainty—although, finally, this is the major reason—or general uncertainty which shows up in the fluctuation of prices, which may or may not change, interestingly enough. Instability results, immediately, from the insolvency of the banking sector that is created, and sustained, by the monetary expansion.

The increased profitability of the successful firms may result in their setting *lower prices*, particularly if they want to increase their market power. They will be able to use, at least part of their fund substitution gains, to create an edge for themselves and attract more demand. Whether this actually happens or not it is impossible to tell in advance or even after the events have taken place. But if it happens, so that there are some real effects, we know that there will be no aggregate effect and only the Misesian re-distribution effects will take place. In this analysis *it is not impossible that the monetary expansion ends up having a negative effect on prices*. In fact, it is quite likely, if we take into account that firms will have found a mechanism through which they can actually lower their prices without losing, but instead, gaining even with a mild or no increase at all in demand. If their demand actually rises quite a bit, they have more reasons to do so. However, there is no way for the commercial banks to profit from this situation. There is yet the possibility that the banks do absolutely nothing with the new funds resulting from monetary expansion. Indeed, if banks are already in distress they have the motive to simply keep the funds to sustain solvency without engaging into any new lending. *In that case the monetary expansion will have no effects at all.*

Since it is impossible to defend monetary changes on the grounds of common interest—since there are only re-distributions involved—it turns out that monetary policy should not be part of coherent governance. Monetary policy acts in the same manner as tax policy does, when tax rates are reduced for certain groups and reduced for others, in a preferential way. It is not unlike reducing taxes for those who are closer to the beginning of the chain and increasing them for those at the end point. The difference is that taxation has aggregate as well as re-distribution effects, unlike monetary policy. *It is also impossible to defend active monetary policy and financial stability along with price stability at the same time*. In general terms, monetary policy induces changes in relative prices and the aggregate price. It also induces changes in the profitability of commercial banks. It induces re-distributions and the combined effect is impossible to quantify, before or even after, the events have taken place. However the financial instability effects are known to exist and they are known, theoretically, to be important. *In effect, the monetary authority undermines its own ground, by undermining the profitability and solvency of the commercial banks*. This effect is not widely known and is likely to mislead the government into thinking or hoping that changes in money supply can stimulate the economy and—even more remote from actual reality—that it can drive an economy out of a recession. It all depends on what banks and firms will do *in the given social, economic and historical circumstances* and different agents may react differently compared to others, depending on their expectations about rates of return resulting from different decisions. As von Mises wrote:

> The biggest variations in the value of money that we have experienced during the last century have originated not in the circumstances of gold production, but in the policies of governments and banks-of-issue. *Dependence of the value of money on the production of gold does at least mean its independence of the politics of the hour.* The dissociation of the currencies from a definitive and unchangeable gold parity has made the value of money a plaything of politics (pp. 17–18).

The true meaning of the Misesian approach to money is that a standard must be found that makes possible the dependence of monetary policy on the politics of the hour. During a long, historical process the operation of unhampered markets have established gold and silver as money. Fiat money is what makes possible for the government to increase or decrease the supply of money and this is, precisely, what must be avoided by all means possible. This standard need not, of course, be the gold standard but any standard that makes it harder for the "politics of the hour" to intervene in the monetary affairs. *Any credible commitment, which can, however, be backed up only by coherent governance, to maintain the money supply reasonably or predictably changing, would be enough.*

This is, in fact, the true Austrian School's defense of the Euro. Precisely, that it created a zone of potential fiscal and monetary stability. We should not, of course, mistake monetary stability with an everlasting unchanged money supply; money supply can and should change in response to productivity and growth but it is the task of the market to perform this operation through its slow and forecastable changes in the value of money. The market is not short of ways to create money, when and where need arises. von Mises' contribution can be best understood once we realize that he treated money as a special commodity, but a commodity nonetheless. Its price should be determined by the market, that is supply and demand, without the need for a government or central authority to step in and assume the role of the regulator: That would make as much sense as regulating the quantity of any other commodity by claiming that is there too much or too little of it in the economy. If it makes little sense to do so for any commodity it makes no sense at all for money itself.

This should not mean to imply that there is a notion of absolute stability that can be, metaphysically, attached to money or prices. Even financial stability cannot mean everlasting absence of change:

> Abandoning the pursuit of the chimera of a money of unchanging purchasing power calls for neither resignation nor disregard of the social consequences of changes in monetary value. The necessary conclusion from this discussion is that *the stability of the purchasing power of the monetary unit presumes stability of all exchange relationships and, therefore, the absolute abandonment of the market economy* (von Mises 1978).

Therefore, monetary and financial stability cannot be taken to mean stable prices in the sense of unchanging prices. In fact, it is precisely price changes those that are able to guarantee the smooth functioning of a market economy. On the contrary, monetary and financial stability should be taken to mean the following: Money supply is not changed in unpredictable ways and financial markets, along with the market for money, are allowed to clear. *The central objective is smooth functioning of the markers, not any metaphysical or empiricist notion of never-changing or policy-induced-changing in the fundamental quantities of the markets.* As von Mises explained:

> The first aim of monetary policy must be to prevent governments from embarking on inflation and from creating conditions which encourage credit expansion on the part of banks. But this program is very different from the confused and self-contradictory program of stabilizing purchasing power (von Mises, *Human Action*, p. 225).

To have *stable* currency in the sense of *unchanging* purchasing power is, therefore, impossible. The value of money *must* change as a response to the changes of supply and demand, as in the case of any other commodity. A currency is stable only in the proper sense, namely that the price of money is indeed allowed to change according to market forces, that is the result of changes in the supply and demand of money which reflect and summarize all changes in the supply and demand of all other commodities. *A sound monetary policy is one that prevents governments from inflationary actions and banks from credit expansion.* Von Mises was clear about this and his statement is in complete accord with the rest of the conclusions of the Austrian School. It is a misguided conclusion to state that the Austrian defense of the Euro rests upon its stability understood in the sense of a "gold standard" behind the Euro.

If that was all, then *there would be nothing to defend* as expansive monetary policy and bank credit expansion have been quite frequent in the Eurozone. The Austrian defense of the Euro must, therefore, rest and find a solid foundation only upon the possibility that, in the Eurozone, conditions for making such tendencies more difficult have been existing so far or can exist in the future. The (relative) refusal of the ECB to monetize the debt provides one reason and, therefore, one line of defense for the Euro. The second line of defense is, clearly, fiscal consolidation which, however, has to be augmented by coherent governance in the sense of reducing and re-structuring government sectors across the Eurozone. The third line of defense, which is presently not solid, is the possibility that on the level of the Eurozone it *will* become easier to abandon inflationary policies and credit expansion either by the ECB or the commercial banks. The possibility *is* there because it *might* be easier, at the central level, to get at the *root* of inflationary pressures and, at the same time, limit the extent of fractional banking. The root of inflationary pressures lies, of course, in changes in the monetary base in the broad sense—that is, inclusive of credit.

The root of inflationary pressures does not lie in monitoring the consumer price index or similar aggregates which are uninformative about the structural changes in the micro-economic level. This has nothing to do with the actual purchasing power of money. *What has, in reality, to be monitored is policy actions and policy decisions regarding money and credit.* Therefore, the defense of the Euro is, for the most part, a defense of relative *ability* to abstain from inflationary policies and credit expansion which, however, did take place in the past and are likely to take place in the future. It is, however, important to emphasize that it is one thing to follow inflationary policies and credit expansion at the national level, without coordination and regard to what other national governments are doing, and a quite different thing to do so in a coordinated manner. Of course, a common currency is impossible without fiscal restrictions on all and particularly without common monetary policy. Monetary coordination is, for the most part, a recipe for coordinated monetary and credit expansions similar to those we have seen in the Eurozone or those in the United States after the Roosevelt administration. A central authority cannot resist the temptation to expand in order to have a stronger grip over the economy. Despite the fact that the European bureaucracy can make decisions only through a long and pain-staking process of summits and negotiations this did not prevent it from expanding money and credit during the recession or lowering interest rates through the ECB.

What is, however, of some importance is that it is possible to arrange the monetary injection so that it is spread preferentially in certain banks and certain countries. This is possible in the Eurozone but it would have been impossible without monetary coordination. Of course we cannot hope to have *aggregate* real effects from this injection but it is likely that there will be *temporary, short-run effects* where it is desired: The temporary boom following the injection will be followed by a recession, however, and it is quite uncertain, especially during a recession, that the banks will be able to transfer the money where the Central Bank intended it to go—as, usually, under the expansionist illusion, there are no such intentions in the first place. Thus, although the monetary authority does create a business cycle there remains a probability, however small, that the effects of a temporary boom can be realized in certain countries or regions. Within these countries or regions there stills remains the question of *how exactly* the monetary expansion will be realized, that is *which groups of private agents* are closer to the regional or national chain of events that will unfold and start from the commercial banks of that country or region.

It remains, however, the possibility of re-distributing income among the member states depending on whether the chain of monetary transmission starts, indeed, with transferring the new funds to the commercial banks of specific countries that may be of "interest". It is entirely unclear whether this policy makes any sense instead of a specific regional policy or direct bail outs of the commercial banks, from the point of view of the *actual* effects of the monetary expansion. But it shows that even a uniform or proportional transfer of the new funds to all commercial banks in the Eurozone, will result in a re-distribution of income between the member states. During a recession even if the recipients of the new funds are the commercial banks in the most depressed countries, it is unlikely that these commercial banks will ever release the funds instead of keeping them to sustain solvency and, of course, market power. Any positive but, again, temporary, effect will have to come through the rise of prices of exported goods and the short-term relative improvement in the profits of the exporting sector. However, even this effect will soon be annihilated through the classical, Misesian re-distribution mechanism resulting from the monetary expansion. It relies on the assumption that the prices of these goods have been depressed quite a bit so that the exported goods have become competitive in the Eurozone or the European Union as whole, so that their demand can increase. But the gain of the exporters not only comes at the expense of importers and consumers elsewhere but also in the confines of the same country: If the exported goods are traded in the domestic market as well, the domestic consumers will also bear the cost of this increase of profits from the exporting sector and, at the same time, prices will begin to rise domestically hampering overall competitiveness—understood in the sense of competitiveness for other goods. Not only the domestic consumers will have to suffer more but even the most basic requirement—the fact that prices must fall during a recession—will not be met. *In fact this is precisely what the statistical data show us: A remarkable inertia in price decreases in those* countries of the European South that have been affected the most by the recession.

What is there to defend about the Euro, then? Precisely the fact that the concentration of power in terms of monetary policy makes it easier to reform monetary and financial affairs through new, re-structured coherent governance. It is fundamentally easier to change things in a common currency area rather than in each individual country. Without coordinated action the income re-distributions resulting from monetary expansions at the national level, are impossible to foretell in a quantitative sense. This is not less so in a common currency area but, at least, it is easier to limit collectively, through credible commitment of a single body, the actions of that body. This is not to ask for unwarranted belief in the omnipotence of the European Commission but rather a belief that any action that has to be undertaken is, fundamentally, easier to be taken at the highest level possible rather than at the level of the member-state governments.

It is important to emphasize that coherent governance does not mean concentration of all decision-making power to the European Commission; it does not mean that the central authority can possibly know more the distribution of demand and resources compared to individual private agents. This can, simply, not be the case. However, what is implied, indeed by coherent governance is that sustaining a commitment for competitive markets and stable financial markets—in the precise sense we have defined—is easier within the Eurozone than otherwise. The commitment *can* be credible and this *can* be done in the context of the common-currency-area but not otherwise. The prerequisite is the functioning of competitive markets and a commitment for non-inflationary policies on the part of the ECB; that is, policies that not result in manipulation of the supply of money and manipulation of government expenditure and distortionary taxation.

References

de Soto JH (2009) Money, bank credit, and economic cycles, 2nd edn. Mises Institute, Alabama
von Mises L (1978) On the manipulation of money and credit, p 107

Chapter 26
A New Fiscal Policy?

We have argued that fiscal consolidation is the necessary first step towards what is really required for sound economic systems; namely, a general reduction in the size of taxes and expenditures. This, again, is easier to do at the global rather than the national level. Fiscal reduction, as part of coherent governance, should be accompanied by (1) limiting fractional banking, (2) liberalizing the financial markets with special attention to freely determined interest rates, and (3) removing the hurdles and obstacles to mobility of resources in the Eurozone. This fiscal reduction can, of course, be designed as a gradual process whose details, however, have to be delineated so that the private sector can adjust as best as possible to predictable changes.

Part of the problem is alleviating the burden from distortionary taxation and constructing equivalent tax schemes at a smaller scale, since we will have to reduce considerably government expenditure. The balanced reduction will make it possible to reduce effectively most indirect taxes considerably and re-design the system of income taxes that can support the new, lower, government expenditure. Economists tend to think in general and broad categories such as wages, profits etc., and think also that progressive taxation is desirable on the grounds of "social justice". Moreover, they tend to formalize tax schemes in terms of so-called "optimal taxation" where a "social welfare function" is maximized subject to all resource constraints and the requirement of a balanced budget. For the Austrian School there is no such thing as a social welfare function, and "all resource constraints" cannot be simply considered as a given in any problem or treatment. In that sense "optimal taxation" is a myth that persists despite the Austrian School's theorem on the impossibility of socialism. What is even worse is the misperception that if firms maximize profits, it doesn't matter in terms of their decisions whether the tax rate on profits is five or ninety-five percent! Moreover, to make things worse, in the optimal taxation problem, profits have to be zero by decreasing returns to scale so it does not matter whether a tax is imposed on profits or not. Profits can also matter under non-competitive market structures. Surprisingly, there is also a positive result, in the sense that the "optimal" tax rates on stocks, like the capital stock, should be zero.

E. G. Tsionas, *The Euro and International Financial Stability*,
Financial and Monetary Policy Studies 37, DOI: 10.1007/978-3-319-01171-4_26,

Despite what the objectives of a firm are, it cannot be true that the tax rate on profits does not matter in terms of the factor and product decisions. The misconception arises from several other misconceptions. First, the fact that profits can be clearly defined and delineated and this can be done in the same way for all firms. Second, that firms actually maximize profits instead of *seeking* new profits. Third, tax policy studies usually ignore the problems of the multi-faceted uncertainty which is inherently present in the production and decision-making processes of the firm.

In the words of Kirzner:

> Let us not forget that the market process has the function of alerting market participants to opportunities which nobody has expected. To initiate governmental policies to grapple with externalities is, in effect, to pretend knowledge which no one can, in principle, honestly claim to possess (Kirzner 2000, p. 82).

And elsewhere:

> This entrepreneurial alertness is crucial to the market process. Disequilibrium represents a situation of widespread market ignorance. This ignorance is responsible for the emergence of profitable opportunities. Entrepreneurial alertness exploits these opportunities when others pass them by. G. L. S. Shackle and Lachmann emphasized the unpredictability of human knowledge, and indeed we do not clearly understand how entrepreneurs get their flashes of superior foresight. We cannot explain how some men discover what is around the corner before others do. We may certainly explain—on entirely Robbinsian lines—how men explore for oil by carefully weighing alternative ways of spending a limited amount of search resources, but we cannot explain how a prescient entrepreneur realizes before others that a search for oil may be rewarding. As an empirical matter, however, opportunities do tend to be perceived and exploited. And it is on this observed tendency that our belief in a determinate market process is founded (Kirzner 1976; Dolan 1976).

The idea of a *market process* distinct from equilibrium and *alertness* as the key element of entrepreneurship are ideas that help us to explore further, and indeed define, price adjustment in competitive markets in terms of these ideas. Price adjustments provide the signals to private agents about the existence of new opportunities; the configuration of prices out of equilibrium is, in fact, a mechanism of discovery, a terrain where knowledge is exercised and such prices are, in fact, formed, based on a series of transactions which incorporate knowledge in the face of uncertainty as well as the formation of such knowledge. It is in this sense that "the market process has the function of alerting market participants to opportunities which nobody has expected". Profits cannot be treated as something given to be maximized, but rather, as something uncertain that results from the discovery of a new opportunity. This discovery not only determines prices and, on the whole, the price mechanism itself, but also the price mechanism determines where one should look for new opportunities and new uses. Profits are not simply uncertain or random variables but the embodiment of uncertainty and the reward for exercise of purposeful action which is, finally, embodied in the formation of knowledge. It is not a reward for uncertainty per se because uncertainty does not exist before the objects of uncertainty are delineated and specified—which is also part of the problem that the price mechanism effectively resolves. It is, rather, reward for coping with uncertainty successfully in discovering opportunities and thus advancing knowledge in the broad sense of the word.

The view of the economy that advances by progressing from one steady-state to another is a useful theoretical abstraction—of limited value to be certain, but an abstraction nonetheless. When applied to the design of economic policies it is particularly ill-suited to its purpose because it assumes that knowledge and discovery proceed from one state of affairs to another and at each state no one has any motivation to discover anything new as all opportunities ceases to exist. The process is, in fact, inherently dynamic in nature and it is, precisely, the constellation of out-of-equilibrium relative prices that determines, in fact, the configuration of actions of agents that results in changes of these relative prices as the outcome of reaping the benefits that, potentially, arise from opportunities: Such opportunities are determined, in a complicated way, by the knowledge that is embodied in the price mechanism itself and make it, in a precise sense, a *process*.

Effectively, changing arbitrarily the constellation of out-of-equilibrium relative prices is equivalent to changing the body of discovery and knowledge that can result from human actions. Changing one price relative to the others is a policy decision that not only changes the distribution of resources but rather a policy decision that directs attention to quite different opportunities whose nature and final outcome cannot be predicted in advance.

We find it rather surprising that, theoretically speaking, it is not widely understood that *even when the tax rate applied to all factors and products is the same, then the situation is inherently distortionary*. Effectively, this is the same as a tax rate on profits. However, under uncertainty, it is clear that the decisions of the firm will be different because choices are made subjectively and any "real" or inflation-adjusted variables rely on something uncertain itself, the precise configuration of all relevant nominal prices. Even if prices were known in advance—that is, if we take the outcome of the analysis to be considered as a given datum—there would be no room left for such a thing as non-distortionary taxation. Subjectivity and uncertainty—even when confined to its simplest form of random fluctuations in the output of the firm due to weather—result in a situation which is completely different compared to a world where everything is known in advance. This, of course, shows plainly that knowledge and discovery can be meaningfully exist only under conditions of "uncertainty"—since if everything was certain and thus known there would be no room for the role of knowledge, a trivial fact. A uniform value-added-tax, say, in this case, would produce distortions because *ex ante* and *ex post* decisions, in the form of supply curves, would not coincide: The firm can decide *ex ante* but the outcomes of the decision are only realized *ex post*, that is after key uncertain elements of the problem have been resolved, for example, the weather is known and production results in specific outcomes. If the firm knew the weather in advance then it would have made a different decision. Although this seems irrelevant to the problem at first sight, quite the contrary is true and any neutrality of taxation disappears. This is because the subjective value of wealth changes under conditions of uncertainty and the discrepancy between *ex ante* and *ex post* decisions effectively means that the problem of the firm becomes "distorted" in the first place. *Relative prices acquire a different meaning under conditions of uncertainty* as they reflect not marginal productivity but rather a "distorted" notion of marginal productivity that has to be weighted by the marginal utility of wealth or profit. Marginal productivity is still of importance to the problem at hand but it only one component; the other component being subjectively defined marginal utility which is, in quite a number of ways, a nebulous concept for economic analysis, and a complicated "object" to deal with.

If all taxation is distortionary to minimize distortion is to seek the Holy Grail. Distortions do not materialize until all relevant decisions have been made and the market mechanism has determined relative prices. The object to minimize is not known before the minimization is itself performed and the concept of minimal distortion loses its meaning. The problem becomes quite different, namely to devise a system of tax rates which is known in advance and hampers the discovery procedure involved in competition as little as possible. The matter is quite complicated and cannot be analyzed without reference to the particular social and historical conditions that prevail. Kirzner's observation that "opportunities do tend to be perceived and exploited [a]nd it is on this observed tendency that our belief in a determinate market process is founded", seems to provide an empirical foundation upon which to stand and examine in more detail the effect of alternative tax structures. But the conditions under which opportunities were discovered under a given system cannot be replicated under another and, most obviously, welfare comparisons cannot be meaningfully performed. Cross-country comparisons are also hampered by the fact that institutions and cultures differ to a great extent.

Kirzner's observation is based on empirical grounds but this does not mean that it can be used or exploited, in a certain way, to tell in advance what a particular determinate market process would be *other* than the fact that it is *determinate*. It is the result of rational human action but it is not the outcome of any specific design—at least not one whose consequences were fully known to someone before its implementation. Kirzner's observation may seem puzzling to the empiricist, particularly if he is trained in the "repeated sampling" school of Statistics. Since no replications of the market process are available, how can it be "on empirical grounds" that we know opportunities are found and exploited? It is precisely by their *results*, which are empirical facts—open to interpretation but facts nonetheless.

Rothbard made the point that there is much discussion about the kinds of taxes that can be imposed rather than on the total amount of taxation which is taken as given. He described this fundamental mistake as follows:

> It is particularly odd that economists who proudly refer to themselves as advocates of the free market have in recent years led the way in this mistaken path. It was allegedly free-market economists for example who pioneered in and propagandized for the alleged Tax Reform Act of 1986. This massive change was supposed to bring us "simplification" of our income taxes. The result, of course, was so simple that even the IRS, let alone the fleet of tax lawyers and tax accountants, has had great difficulty in understanding the new dispensation. Peculiarly, moreover, in all the maneuverings that led to the Tax Reform Act, the standard held up by these economists, a standard apparently so self-evident as to

> need no justification, was that the sum of tax changes be "revenue neutral." But *they never told us what is so great about revenue neutrality. And of course, by cleaving to such a standard, the crucial question of total revenue was deliberately precluded from the discussion* (Rothbard 1994, emphasis added).

Of course the idea that all taxation is distortionary, because it diverts resources from the market to the government, is well known in the Austrian School. Von Mises for example wrote:

> The changing economy is entirely different from this imaginary construction of an evenly rotating economy with income equality. Continuous change and the inequality of wealth and income are essential and necessary features of the changing market economy, the only real and working system of the market economy. In the frame of such a system no tax can be neutral. The very idea of a neutral tax is as unrealizable as that of neutral money. But, of course, the reasons for this inescapable non-neutrality are different in the case of taxes from what they are in the case of money (Human Action, chap. XXVII, part 6, 5).

The reason is explained immediately after:

> A head tax that taxes every citizen equally and uniformly without any regard to the size of his income and wealth, falls more heavily upon those with more moderate means than upon those with more ample means. It restricts the production of the articles consumed by the masses more sharply than that of the articles mainly consumed by the wealthier citizens. On the other hand, it tends to curtail saving and capital accumulation less than a more burdensome taxation of the wealthier citizens does. It does not slow down the tendency toward a drop in the marginal productivity of capital goods as against the marginal productivity of labor to the same extent as does taxation discriminating against those with higher income and wealth, and consequently it does not to the same extent retard the tendency toward a rise in wage rates (Human Action, chap. XXVII, part 6, 6).

To von Mises the distortionary effect from a head tax operates through the redistribution effects that it has and the operation of marginal productivities relative to wages. We tend to believe that this one aspect of the problem and there is another, namely that in the general case, production and marginal productivities cannot be taken in isolation from individual, subjective preferences that complicate the problem considerably. Von Mises is right, however, that the effects from a head tax are less severe, in terms of their effects on savings, investment and wages, compared to progressive taxation. As a practical recommendation, given that all taxation is distortionary, von Mises argues as follows:

> Taxation is a matter of the market economy. It is one of the characteristic features of the market economy that the government does not interfere with the market phenomena and that its technical apparatus is so small that its maintenance absorbs only a *modest fraction of the total sum of the individual citizens' incomes*. Then taxes are an appropriate vehicle for providing the funds needed by the government. They are appropriate because they are *low and do not perceptibly disarrange production and consumption. If taxes grow beyond a moderate limit, they cease to be taxes and turn into devices for the destruction of the market economy* (Human Action, chap. XXVII, part 6, 15, emphasis added).

Hayek has also followed these general lines of thought. Regarding the effect on savings he wrote:

> Closely connected with this problem is the effect of progressive taxation on an aspect of capital formation which is different from that already discussed, namely, the place of formation. It is one of the advantages of a competitive system that successful new ventures are likely for a short time to bring very large profits and that thus the capital needed for development will be formed by the persons who have the best opportunity of using it. The large gains of the successful innovator meant in the past that, having shown the capacity for profitably employing capital in new ventures, he would soon be able to back his judgment with larger means. Much of the individual formation of new capital, since it is offset by capital losses of others, should be realistically seen as part of a continuous process of redistribution of capital among the entrepreneurs. The taxation of such profits, at more or less confiscatory rates, amounts to a heavy tax on that turnover of capital which is part of the driving force of a progressive society (Hayek 1960).

This turnover of capital constitutes, indeed, the main vehicle for implementing coordination of capital and investment decisions, and the operation of capital and financial markets along with the notion of financial stability. Taxes will hamper the ability to produce knowledge and, therefore, help a market economy to drive itself to increased prosperity, understood in the common sense of the word. Hayek's innovative idea was that: "Much of the individual formation of new capital, since it is offset by capital losses of others, should be realistically seen as part of a continuous process of redistribution of capital". Taxing successful individual formation of new capital would make as much sense as subsidizing those that were making losses. Apparently, this cannot be growth-enhancing particularly during a recession. Hayek expanded on the idea to conclude that, at the same time, it leads to hampering of competition, which was truly a remarkably contribution:

> The most serious consequence, however, of the discouragement of individual capital formation where there are temporary opportunities for large profits is the restriction of competition. *The system tends generally to favor corporate as against individual saving* and particularly to strengthen the position of the established corporations against newcomers. It thus *assists to create quasi- monopolistic situations*. Because taxes today absorb the greater part of the newcomer's "excessive" profits, he cannot, as has been well said, "accumulate capital"; he cannot expand his own business; he will never become big business and a match for the vested interests. The old firms do not need to fear his competition: they are sheltered by the tax collector. They may with impunity indulge in routine, they may defy the wishes of the public and become conservative. It is true, the income tax prevents them, too, from accumulating new capital. *But what is more important for them is that it prevents the dangerous newcomer from accumulating any capital. They are virtually privileged by the tax system. In this sense progressive taxation checks economic progress and makes for rigidity* (op. cit., emphasis added).

On the practical side, Hayek as von Mises take government expenditure as given as ask what is the "best" amount of taxation. As Hayek wrote:

> What is needed is a principle that will limit the maximum rate of direct taxation in some relation to the total burden of taxation. The most reasonable rule of the kind would seem to be one that fixed the maximum admissible (marginal) rate of direct taxation at that percentage of the total national income which the government takes in taxation. *This would mean that if the government took* 25 % *of the national income,* 25 % *would also be the maximum rate of direct taxation of any part of individual incomes*. If a national emergency made it necessary to raise this proportion, the maximum admissible rate would be raised to the same figure; and it would be correspondingly reduced when the over-all

> tax burden was reduced. This would still leave taxation somewhat progressive, since those paying the maximum rate on their incomes would also pay some indirect taxes which could bring their total proportional burden above the national average. *Adherence to this principle would have the salutary consequence that every budget would have to be prefaced by an estimate of the share of national income which the government proposed to take as taxes.* This percentage would provide the standard rate of direct taxation of incomes which, for the lower incomes, would be reduced in proportion as they were taxed indirectly. The net result would be a slight over-all progression in which, however, the marginal rate of taxation of the largest incomes could never exceed the rate at which incomes were taxed on the average by more than the amount of indirect taxation (op. cit., emphasis added).

The insight of the Austrian School is that what really matters if the total tax burden including personal income taxes as well as indirect taxes which is different for different private economic agents when they engage in consumption and, therefore, the total burden of different income groups—however unsatisfactory this benchmark will be—should be controlled by providing first an estimate of the government's share in national income—despite the fact that this, as an aggregate measure, is not very informative about what the government actually does although it does provide a first approximation and a very rough guide. The argument is not really over whether a flat rate is better or worse than progressive taxation—all taxation is to be avoided to the extent possible and this extent is determined by the requirement of as small a state possible, qualitatively and quantitatively. It is clear that the flat rate is, for example worse than progressive taxation *if* total tax revenues are allowed to be *higher* under the flat tax rate. And Rothbard continues:

> Hence, the seemingly common-sense view that a retail sales tax will readily be shifted forward to the consumer is totally incorrect. In contrast, the initial impact of the tax will be on the net incomes of retail firms. Their severe losses will lead to a rapid downward shift in demand curves, *backward* to land and labor, i.e., to wage rates and ground rents. Hence, instead of the retail sales tax being quickly and painlessly shifted forward, it will, in a longer run, be painfully shifted backward to the incomes of labor and landowners. Once again, an alleged tax on *consumption*, has been transmuted by the processes of the market into a tax on *incomes* (op. cit.).

This important argument is, often, forgotten in theory and practice and this is used to justify a sales tax on the grounds of "simplicity". If we take, however, into account corruption and the inability of small firms to manipulate the law and escape the tax, then it becomes clear that, besides its negative impact on labor and other factors of production, *the sales tax will also hamper competition*. Another *important* aspect of taxation is often forgotten, namely that there are cases, *particularly during periods of recession where the effect of taxes is entirely asymmetric*. During a recession the typical firm finds itself with increased stocks of unsold commodities. Its first reaction would be to reduce hours of work, and thus employment, since the lower demand can be accommodated with the existing stock. *An increase in taxes* will induce the firm to cut further on employment and capacity utilization, as in Rothbard's argument. But a *decrease of taxes* will not motivate the firm to increase capacity utilization, production or employment! The firm can use these savings in a variety of ways but unless, if and when the demand recovers and the stocks of unsold commodities begin to diminish, there will be no reason for the firm to start spending on increased employment or expanding on capacity utilization. This, of course, is under the assumption that the tax burden is not too severe as to drive the firm out of business because operating expenses cannot be covered in the short-run.

A particular problem with Hayek's setting of a tax rates at most equal to the government's share in "national income" is the conceptual difficulty with justifying this share in purely subjective terms. Leaving the problem aside—at it cannot find a plausible solution in the not too distant future—is that what actually matters is not the share of government in general but its share in productive activities that succeed in terms of productivity and are weighted by their efficiency compared to the efficiency of the private sector. This share would, necessarily, be much smaller compared to the actual share of government expenditure in GDP as not government expenditure is productive and the efficiency/productivity of the productive activities has to be determined. Hayek's suggestion is meaningful once the government sector has been minimized or, at least, it has been drastically reduced to what the majority of voters consider as "acceptable". There are still problems with Buchanan's voluntary taxation concept, which is of related interest in this case, but we cannot dwell on the relevant issues here.

Part of the problem with minimizing government expenditure is that certain activities should be left for the private sector and, for certain groups, this is like giving away certain "fundamental citizen right" to the private sector. Indeed, the issue is more complicated that it seems at first sight. The reduction of the public sector and its "crowding-out" in favor of the private sector, should be performed under a well-understood and clearly delineated framework whose purposes would be: First, the encouragement of competition in the provision of relevant services and, second, prices that do not exceed actual or shadow prices currently charged or implied by the state running these services. The role of coherent governance in this process is that costs can actually be reduced if there are significant economies of scale, a fact that can be exploited only on the European level as a whole—that is, as part of global economic policies in the Eurozone and the European Union. From that point of view, privatizations and reductions of the level of government expenditures and taxes are *easier to implement jointly and globally*.

We believe it is quite important to understand fully the asymmetric nature of taxation—the fact that increases or decreases of tax burden do not work in the same way. Increases in marginal tax rates induce negative growth but decreases do not, in the short-run, during a recessionary period. During a period of growth the effect is likely to be more symmetric because of the absence of the "buffer stock" role of unsold inventories of the firms. During a recession, the tax cut operates more like a direct subsidy to the firm's income rather than as a motive to increase capacity given the unfavorable expectations of the firms regarding the demand. Superficially, this would seem to suggest that there should be no way of the recession by cutting tax rates. This view would be erroneous because it ignores the other determinants that enter into the problem. *A tax cut simultaneously with a decrease in expenditures would free up resources that could be used elsewhere and more profitably in the economy*. The essential feature of this policy is that the re-distribution of resources that is induced, in favor of investment, is accompanied by lower tax burden which re-enforces the investment effect in those sectors whose overall expected profitability has increased, in the recessionary period. The cut in expenditure makes it possible to reduce the tax burden despite the fact that tax rates are lower and "overall" economic activity is depressed. It is true that the effect may be smaller, in terms of increased capacity utilization, for the firms whose demand expectations are gloomy, but this is not so in the sectors whose expected profitability is rising, despite the recession.

A particularly relevant example is offered by Canada. By the mid-90s the Canadian government ran deficits for almost twenty years and one-third of tax revenues was absorbed by interest payments to accommodate the public debt with a debt-to-GDP ratio of about 78 %.

> Yet the Canadians swiftly solved the crisis with serious reforms. In just two years, from 1995 to 1997, total federal government spending fell by more than seven percent, while the budget deficit of $32 billion (four percent of GDP) was transformed into a $2.5 billion surplus. *There were also tax increases, but the ratio of spending cuts to tax increases was about five to one*. Canada's federal government ran 11 consecutive budget surpluses, causing the debt-to-GDP ratio to plummet from 78 % in 1996 to 39 % in 2007. *In the decade after reform, Canada out-performed all the other G7 nations on economic growth, investment, and job creation*. According to International Monetary Fund data, from 1996 to 2005, Canada's average growth of real GDP was 3.3 %, with the United States the runner up with 3.2 % average growth, and the G7 excluding Canada averaging only 2.1 % growth. *Even in the short-term, Canada's dramatic spending cuts (and moderate tax increases) in the mid-1990s had only mild side effects, causing only a temporary uptick in the unemployment rate* (Murphy 2013 emphasis added).

What is important in the Canadian experience is that there were tax increases but "*the ratio of spending cuts to tax increases was about five to one*". In an "overall" sense the effective tax burden was clearly lower. Since the "overall" or aggregate effect is not particularly interesting, we must conclude that drastic cuts in government expenditure, during a recession, are, in fact, the only way to accommodate public debt while at the same time they can stimulate the economy. The stimulus takes place at the micro-economic level and the re-direction of resources to the private sector: *Even in the face of increased tax rates*, some sectors will have positive expectations about their demand because *their tax burden is expected to be lower*. It would be quite interesting to look at the sectors of the economy that were responsible for job creation and/or increased capacity utilization. As with the case of a monetary or credit stimulus, the configuration and timing of job creation depends on where the fiscal cut and the subsequent re-direction of resources takes place, and affects the private sector. Suppose, for example, the government decides to sell some of its rights in the construction business and this is taken by the private business. The private enterprise will invest, first, in construction projects that have the utmost priority, which will be revealed by those willing to pay for such services. The discovery of such opportunities is facilitated by the fact that, now, the private construction company can figure out such opportunities, even during the recession, because there will always be a demand for such services, even after the demand shock from expenditure cuts has been realized: Some constructions will, undoubtedly, now be of less priority in terms of time preference of the private sector who has a demand for these services, but others will keep to be profitable in the (new) margin. The discovery of these projects is out of reach for the government sector but not so for the private sector who has all the motivation to find profitable projects in the midst of the recession. Job recovery, in turn, will start precisely from there and will be transmitted, slowly perhaps, to the rest of the economy. The fiscal consolidation that has taken place is, in the aggregate sense, a negative shock. But from the point of view of reinstating a more rational configuration of the resources that corresponds to the actual distribution of demand *at the micro-economic level, fiscal consolidation acts as a positive shock for specific enterprises and specific sectors of the economy.*

There will, of course, be private enterprises that experience the consolidation as a direct negative shock. What types of enterprises will they be? First, private constructors who have contracts with the government and, in all likelihood, they reaped benefits in terms of preferential relationships and significant cost increases. Second, firms whose demand prospects now look gloomier because they are affected by the loss of incomes of consumers who work for the government or who were affected first from the fiscal cuts. There will be negative effects, to be certain. But to generalize this to the economy as a whole is a tremendous fallacy of composition. *To ignore the important re-distribution that will take place is to miss the whole sequence of actual effects that will take place, during the course of time, in the various sectors of the economy.*

References

Dolan EG (1976) The foundations of modern Austrian economics

Hayek FA (1960) Constitution of liberty. University of Chicago Press, pp 306–323

Kirzner Israel M (2000) The Limits of the Market: the Real and the Imagined. In: Kirzner IM (ed) The driving force of the market: essays in Austrian economics. Routhledge, London, pp 77–87

Kirzner I (1976) Equilibrium versus market process

Murphy RP (2013) What economic research says about fiscal austerity and higher tax rates. In: Library of Economics and Liberty. von Mises Institute

Rothbard MN (1994) The consumption tax: a critique—review of Austrian economics 7(2):75–90

Chapter 27
The "Price Puzzle"

We have chosen construction as an example, deliberately, because this sector is usually the first to be hit by the recession and also because of the price bubble that has created an immense stock of unsold houses and apartments in the United States and Europe. We see, all over Europe and particularly in its South, an impressive fact: Although prices adjust, they do so sluggishly and, of course, construction, has not recovered. Despite the large income shocks prices of certain consumption goods have not decreased considerably, and unemployment has increased. In Greece, price adjustments took considerably more time relative to the rest of Europe and, at the same time, they have not adjusted as much.

It certainly seems as if economists have abandoned their whole arsenal of tools to explain this "price puzzle". They attributed it to the large fraction of black economy and tax evasion, to "institutional factors"—which does not really mean anything, the cost of energy and oil in particular, etc. All these factors are, certainly, at work, and create a constellation of conditions which create an environment in which we have to explain the price adjustments but they are not, by themselves the explanatory factors. There has been a lot of re-structuring taking place in terms of business failures particularly in the service sector which is, by far, the largest in all European economies and across the world. This re-structuring has been quite extensive but it is not unseen that new businesses have appeared in the place of old ones—not one for one, of course. Demand has been the subject of large negative income shocks. At the same time, in the supply side, at any given price producers are willing to produces less which accounts for a shift of supply curves *upwards*. The equilibrium effect is a large quantity adjustment downwards while at the same time prices decrease only mildly—more so if the supply shocks are, as they were, large. *This is, in fact, what we actually observe: Big quantity effects in terms of business failure, and/or increased capacity without large price drops*. Taking into account the demand-driven effects, price drops would have to be much more extensive but these effects are offset by the gloomy expectations of business' which tend to move supply curves *upwards*.

The "price puzzle" in Greece, according to which prices appear to be far more sluggish relative to the rest of the Eurozone, is, in fact, a perfect textbook example: *Since the demand and supply effects were more extensive in Greece relative to the*

E. G. Tsionas, *The Euro and International Financial Stability*,
Financial and Monetary Policy Studies 37, DOI: 10.1007/978-3-319-01171-4_27,

rest of Eurozone, this is precisely why prices behaved sluggishly. What most economists seem to think is that supply curves either did not shift at all or that they are totally irresponsive to prices, when, in fact, quite the opposite is true. In the construction sector the application of the basic principles is most instructive: Prices have adjusted a little but the quantity effect has been tremendous, as a large part of housing capital is left to depreciate. There is simply nothing else to expect in the context of free markets. As a matter of facts, *if demand remains unchanged, we should even see price increases.* With further changes in the supply side the quantity effects will be larger and prices cannot fall. This is not due to oligopolistic structures and price agreements or tax evasion etc. These phenomena are certainly parts of the environment but even in their absence, standard economic theory would encounter no problems explaining the adjustments of the market: *Considering simultaneously demand and supply, would show why we should expect quantity adjustments with sluggishly-appearing prices. This is an equilibrium phenomenon*, not a phenomenon that we can attribute to institutional factors *per se*, or a general attitude of producers to maintain sluggishness.

Chapter 28
Re-Distributional Effects of Austerity Measures

We have argued that a reduction in government expenditure will result in re-distributional effects arising from the re-shifting of resources from the public to the private sector. Since new funds are now available for savings the effect is likely to be felt, first of all, in the profitability of the banking sector and its overall stability. This is important because it is a common misconception that financial stability is endangered during a recessionary period *if* the government does not act in an expansionary manner. In fact, quite the opposite is true. First of all, the commercial banks are not forced to buy government debt and create an artificial credit expansion whose final effects will be quite the opposite from what the government intended. Second, financial stability is maintained in the short-run by the transformation of expenditure cuts to savings. Third, *if* we have a reduction of public debt it is hard to see how overall financial stability is hampered by the austerity measures. The question is whether we will have, indeed, a reduction of public debt. Accommodation of interest payments would seem impossible in the short-run unless the measures are accompanied by a re-structuring of the tax system which yields higher tax revenues.

In fact quite the opposite is true. Since the government has reduced expenditures it can now accommodate interest payments easily without imposing higher tax rates across the board or by re-shifting tax rates and/or tax burdens. In fact, tax burden can remain the same—although, historically, expenditure cuts have been accompanied by tax increases but with a ratio of cuts to taxes that is in favor of the former. However, this seems to contradict our argument that expenditure cuts have been transformed into savings. For example, the construction company which was operated by the government is not on its own and has been bought by private agents. The government has cut its expenditures (in the form of wages, losses incurred, cost of materials etc.) which can be used to accommodate debt payments. But at the same time consumption has been reduced by the private agents who bought the construction company from the state in order to complete this transaction. The effect is a net increase of savings. The effect can take place in the course of time since, during a recession, it would be hard to cut back on consumption but the important element of the effect is that *it relies on expectations of*

E. G. Tsionas, *The Euro and International Financial Stability*,
Financial and Monetary Policy Studies 37, DOI: 10.1007/978-3-319-01171-4_28,

the private sector about the government's credible commitment to cut expenditures and privatize to a large extent.

If the domestic sector cannot perform these transactions there is always the possibility to do the privatizations in the international markets. This is immaterial for our argument. What seems to be important is that the proceeds from the privatization *can* be transferred to the commercial banks *along with liberalization of the domestic credit and financial markets*. This would ensure that the proceeds will end up in the most profitable uses—a fact that would necessitate higher loan rates. If the government uses directly the proceeds to finance its interest payments, the effect would be felt as direct increase in private investment rather than as direct increase of net savings—which is, however, immaterial even if loan rates are not adjusted and financial liberalization does not take place. The effects would be more pronounced with the financial liberalization but they do take place regardless.

What lies at the heart of our arguments is not the fact that expenditure cuts have aggregate effects—which they do—but the fact that the aggregate effects are formed from micro-economic effects. Austerity measures have negative demand side effects but at the same time they re-distribute resources and open up new opportunities for the private sector. If not anything else the direct transfer of a public enterprise to the private sector, makes its operation more efficient and profitable. This effect cannot be ignored and focus entirely on the demand effect or the fact that unemployment will have to increase in the short-run. The direct transfer—an extreme case, of course—will permit the government to use the funds that it was sacrificing in other purposes and, at the same time, resources would be employed more efficiently. If we add to this argument the net-savings-effect it is beyond any doubt that *austerity measures help create new wealth through the re-shifting of resources.*

How would a Keynesian expansion work during the recession? Demand would increase, provided the expansion is in the form of income transfers or tax cuts to the consumers. Consumers would like to revert back to their old standard of living and would start buying more goods. Keynesians think that this will foster growth, forgetting that the increased demand can be accommodated easily by the massive inventories of business', which have cut back on employment and capacity utilization. All that will happen is a decrease of inventories without new production. However that is not the end of the story as much depends on expectations of consumers and producers about the nature of the policy shock. If tax cuts to the consumers are temporary they will prefer to save more for the future. Inventories will decrease but not as much as when consumers spend their entire new net income. The firms also know that since the tax cut is temporary it does not make sense to engage in new investment. If the tax cut is credibly known to rest forever, consumers need not save more (or as much) and can spend safely thus reducing business inventories. When inventories have decreased considerably the firms can begin to increase capacity utilization and employment. The fiscal shock will be felt first in the consumption non-durables sector and afterwards it can transmit through the rest of the economy.

There are, however, quite a few problems with this Keynesian approach. Prices will, at first, remain the same as inventories are reduced, and consumers are better off as they have increased income. The inventories that are, actually, reduced are in the consumption sector which is towards the end-point of the time-structure of capital. In the course of time, prices of these goods will have to increase as inventories cannot accommodate the increased demand *before* firms begin to increase employment and capacity utilization. As they begin to do so, prices will increase even more, gradually. Consumers will find themselves less able to maintain their standard of living and will start re-allocating their income to products whose prices have not increased at all or as much. Whether or not the new demand hits the consumer's durable goods sector is quite uncertain as it depends on the magnitude of the tax cuts. If the tax cuts are mild, it is most likely that the effects will be contained with the consumer's non-durable goods sector, and that existing inventories will be sufficient to accommodate increased demand. If some expansion takes place it will also be contained within this sector, with some employment effects which are also likely to be mild. In this case, the tax cut to the consumers works like the tax cut to business' during the recession. It cannot generate new employment unless it is credibly expected to be permanent.

Before the inventories are exhausted price begin to rise as the policy measure is known to be permanent or at least likely to be sustained for a number of years. As producers in the non-durables sector begin to see their demand rise and engage in new investment, prices also increase. This provides signals that profitability in the non-durables sector has increased. Time-consuming projects begin to look less profitable now and resources will have to shift to the non-durables sector to accommodate the increased demand. This shifting is constrained by the fact that some increase of the capital stock used in the non-durables sector is necessary, which will be provided first by the less-durable but time-consuming sectors. The shifting of resources will, of course, take some time if it ever reaches the capital goods sector. Therefore, the expansion is limited to the non-durables sector. However, the increase of wages will be felt across the economy as employment increases in that sector making capital-intensive projects look even less profitable and causing a *depression of investment*. The non-durables sector will have to invest at increasing cost and, if it ever does so, it will have to pay higher interest rates and prices will have to increase either to accommodate the higher cost of capital or make up for the fact that capacity and production cannot increase any longer. Firms in the capital sector have no incentive to increase production and increase prices instead which accounts for the higher cost of capital in the non-durables sector. The depression of investment has made it impossible to engage in new projects and this cannot change momentarily. Demand for capital from the non-durables sector will have to be sustained high for new projects to emerge. However, this demand is limited by the increased cost of capital and the associated increase of prices of consumption goods.

Sooner or later the consumers will find that the tax cuts resulted, finally, in less income in real terms, that is in terms of the prices of goods that they actually buy. Some firms will see that their inventories begin rising while others will find that they are not profitable anymore despite the fact that the tax cut is permanent. *Consumers will change their decisions* and turn their attention to goods whose prices have increased less or not at all, setting in motion the same chain of events in other sub-sectors of the non-durables sector or in other sectors altogether, that is different goods. Therefore what the tax cut sets in motion, is a re-shifting of the resources without creating significant long-term effects, while at the same time it depresses further investment by decreasing artificially investment in the capital-intensive sectors.

The standard argument is that the tax cut has not been large enough—or perhaps other counter-effects took place. In the words of Paul Krugman:

> If temporary fiscal stimulus does not jolt the economy out of its doldrums on a sustained basis, however, then a recovery strategy based on fiscal expansion would have to continue the stimulus over an extended period of time. The question then becomes how much stimulus is needed, for how long—and whether the consequences of that stimulus for government debt are acceptable.[1]

That is, indeed, precisely the question. If positive effects are to be felt in the economy these have to arise from new investment and increased production in the capital-intensive sector. The stimulus would have to be so large as to shift considerably demand and supply curves not only in the non-durables sector but, in turn, to sectors that are far more remover in the time-sequence of capital. As long as inventories can accommodate the new demand from the fiscal stimulus, it is quite improbable if not impossible, for the fiscal stimulus to get an economy out of the recession. The deterioration of tax revenues would have to be so large that it makes it would make it impossible to sustain the level of public debt. But even in that case the massive fiscal stimulus would create an artificial re-configuration of relative prices and set in motion a business cycle that would, eventually, result in massive destruction of capital not only in the capital-intensive sector but even more so in the non-durable consumption goods, due to the artificially high cost of capital that it would create.

Therefore, it turns out that, in fact, austerity measures help to correct misdirections of resources and misallocations that have been accumulating for years due to an expanding public sector. We have remarked, also, that it would much easier to cut down on public expenditures and the size of public sector at the highest level; that is through coherent governance for the European Union. In the European Union, although fiscal consolidation has been achieved to a great extent, with remarkable results, the coordinated reduction of taxes and public expenditures has yet to come. At the country level there are significant political pressures and resistances that hamper the ability to provide a rational, perhaps gradual, reduction of the extent of involvement of government in the economy. At the European level this would have been easier to implement in the form of institutional reforms whose purpose is to correct the misallocations of resources and

[1] (Krugman, Paul. (1998) "It's Baaack! Japan's Slump and the Return of the Liquidity Trap", in: http://web.mit.edu/krugman/www/bpea_jp.pdf).

make them correspond more closely to the actual distribution of demand. The distortions in capital and financial markets have been, of course, persisting for years and have shaped up a particular economic environment. It is clear that this economic environment is not friendly to growth or to extensive investment and capital formation that would help drive European economies out of the recession.

All distortions cannot be corrected at once. There has to be, in practice, a gradual process of adjustment in the markets and the public sector itself. *What is of immense importance for coherent governance is to commit credibly on an agenda for reforms and their sequence in time* so that expectations of the private sector can be revised accordingly and maximize the potential benefits. Financial liberalization and commitments to restore equilibria in financial markets, is an important first step. The banking sector should work under a tighter fractional reserves system. The commitment to reinstate financial equilibrium includes a commitment of monetary and financial stability where credit expansion is to be lowered significantly, particularly in recessionary periods or when the economy starts showing signs of depression. Across the European Union, a new programme of fiscal consolidation is needed with government expenditures and taxes significantly reduced in the medium-term—although lowering tax rates may be impossible for fiscal solvency to achieve in the European South, at least in the short-run. Restoration of equilibria with lower expenditures and taxes is the essential step towards setting the necessary prerequisites for a recovery of investment in the capital-intensive sector. The shifting of resources that will follow, will occur in time as well as in specific sectors of the economy (depending on the time-structure of capital) and space.

The recovery of investment will have to take place in a new configuration of regional and national patterns starting from sectors in countries whose expected relative profitability, relative to the rest of the European Union, begin to rise more steeply. This depends, initially, on the extent of *relative* decreases of the tax burden which, naturally, has to occur in countries that were above the average in terms of tax burden and size of the public sector. A simplification of the European tax system, along with gradual reduction tax *rates* across the board, would help immensely this process of re-allocating investment. In the long-term this is the only way for sustainable growth, higher wages and standard of living, as well as the re-structuring of the financial system along the lines of financial stability. Our defense for the Euro rests, precisely, on these grounds: The soundness of the Euro depends on extending further the policies that were adopted in the Treaty of Maastricht in the directions of: (1) reduction of public sectors and tax burdens, (2) liberalization of financial markets and structural changes in commercial banking, and (3) institutional frameworks that guarantee the working of competition. The role of the Euro in international financial stability rests, precisely, upon this configuration of policies that will foster investment growth in the Eurozone and will, as a result, act as a source of growth for the international economy.

Reference

Krugman P, Dominquez K, Rogoff K (1998) It Baaack: Japan's slump and the return of the liquidity trap, Brookings papers on economic activity 2:137–205

Chapter 29
Further Remarks on International Financial Stability

International financial stability depends on flows of funds that exploit arbitrage opportunities in international markets, in the form of various financial products, some of which are considered "toxic" or harmful to the economy. The fact is that without certain of these products, like futures which rely on future expectations about profitability, the economic crisis would have been far more devastating in terms of destruction of existing capital. The reason is that their trading acts as a buffer stock against large quantity adjustments that would have otherwise to take place. The quantity adjustments would have to be even larger without a price mechanism for national public debts in the international markets. The price of debt, or the interest on new government issues, reflects an overall assessment of the profitability of *uses* of the new bonds and, in that way, they reflect in an overall sense, the opportunity cost of capital in financing national investment.

The "debt crisis" is, in effect, a mechanism that reflects the extent of distortions under the given economic, historical and social circumstances. Relative to interest rates in the economy, the wedge relative to the average interest rate on public debt, at a given time period, reflects not only the true opportunity cost of capital; but also an accurate approximation to the potential, expected profitability by shifting resources from the public to the private sector, through the operation of markets. Therefore, it also reflects the expected benefit from the adjustments that will have to take place so that a new equilibrium is restored with a lower public sector, *ceteris paribus*. If a given level of public debt is unsustainable, according to the markets' assessments, an arbitrage opportunity emerges, in the sense that if the state wants to sustain the debt and accommodate successfully interest payments, then interest rates will have to raise in order to compensate for the fact that there are more profitable uses for the funds that will be directed to the financing of debt. The dual situation is that an opportunity has emerged where it is a profitable use of funds to "gamble" on the level of debt through the bond markets. Given the probability of insolvency—which can be assessed by the markets—higher interest rates (1) reflect compensation for risk but, perhaps more importantly, (2) they also reflect, at the same time, *first*, the fact that the system is stable in the time horizon determined by the structure of the government bonds (otherwise successful repayment would have been impossible) and *second*, they reflect the cost of funds

E. G. Tsionas, *The Euro and International Financial Stability*,
Financial and Monetary Policy Studies 37, DOI: 10.1007/978-3-319-01171-4_29,

that would have to be withdrawn from the private sector, put to productive use and yield positive profits in the same time horizon. In effect, the "debt crisis" reflects a new configuration of relative prices which create arbitrage opportunities in international markets due to the fact that solvency in a particular country requires a re-shifting of funds and resources, on the international level. "Speculation" in this context is simply a reflection of the undeniable fact that such resources *cannot* move in the short-term to accommodate production, *given* the time-structure of capital and the configuration of national resources; therefore, an immediate increase in the price of these resources will occur in view of the sudden increase in demand. If production did not take time and the same was true for capital re-distribution and new resources, we would observe massive quantity adjustments in the capital markets as well as in markets for other factors of production.

Given the conditions we have specified above, a rise in interest rates for government bonds, *ceteris paribus* again, reflects an *upper bound* on the rise of the price of capital and resources that is required to compensate for the fact that national resources cannot adjust immediately to engage in profitable production; for foreign-based resources that would have even more difficult. But, *in turn, this means that the configuration of national interest rates does not correspond, approximately, to the configuration of the time-structure of capital.* The reason is that given the arbitrage opportunity, resources and funds should divert from domestic production to "speculative" activities and accommodation of government's debt through purchases of bonds. This is severely hampered by the fact that all production is putty-clay but this does not preclude new investors from engaging into savings through financing the debt rather than investing in production. In terms of two-year government bonds, say, projects that would require two years *or more* to complete and generate profits, appear less profitable given the overall prospects and expectations about demand and profits. A "flight to speculation" should be expected, unless the cost of capital is higher, as it should, to offset the arbitrage opportunities. In that case international investors should be less motivated to engage in purchasing government bonds rather than buying stocks of companies whose profitability would be at least as much over the two-year time horizon.

During a depression, the overall terrain in the stock market is not smooth; there is a lot of volatility and expected returns are much lower compared to the international average, particularly in a country with important structural problems and significantly or massively negative growth rates. Expectations about profitability of projects over most time horizons are gloomy since the demand has been subject to large negative shocks and is not expected to recover significantly in the medium-term. As the natural tendency is for capital to move towards less capital-intensive processes with almost immediate return, a depression of investment takes place along with shifting of resources to the less capital-intensive or less capitalistic modes of production. But this tendency is hampered by the large inventories of firms already in these sectors and the fact that expected profitability is not particularly high. The drop of prices in these sectors provides a signal to the firms in more capital-intensive processes that profit opportunities are not likely to arise from the sectors that are closer to consumption in the time-structure of capital. Firms across the time-distribution of capital would find it more profitable to liquidate their inventories and engage in savings through the purchasing of government bonds; apparently, this is hampered by the net losses of these firms and the fact that liquidation of inventories is not possible, at cost prices, since prices do not adjust but very sluggishly as the result of the simultaneous shifts of the supply and demand curves—the "price puzzle" that we explained above. The fact that domestic funds cannot be generated to accommodate public debt through liquidation of investment, the only solution is for *international* funds to shift in the country at higher interest rates compared to loan and deposit rates but also the *maximum possible* rate of return not only in the domestic economy but on the global level. It is in this sense that we characterized before the necessary increase in domestic prices of resources as an upper bound.

This "liquidity trap" at almost zero loan rates is generated by the depression of demand which is the result of business cycle set in motion by the credit expansion at these low rates. Business closures, high and persistent unemployment, along with insufficient savings to, possibly, redirect to purchasing government debt, requires a shifting of funds from international markets, at higher interest rates. The question is whether this is a rational shifting of resources. From the point of view of private agents this is certainly the case. But *the fundamental issue is that the public sector could have been reduced significantly* and set in motion a recovery process for the domestic private sector. In view of the Canadian experience, even with higher tax rates during the recession, but a significant increase in the ratio of expenditure cuts to tax burden, two years at most would be required to generate fiscal surpluses and a recovery of growth—albeit at the cost of higher unemployment in the short-run. This could accommodate public debt and interest payments more easily with less reliance on new debt at higher interest rates.

The interesting question concerns the effects of the higher interest rates on debt on the economy, during a severe recession. There is, of course, little sense in trying to offset the "speculative attacks" through repurchasing of debt by the European Central Bank. This simply diverts attention from international markets to the Treasury of the European Central Bank without other, significant, effects. The fact that the "speculative attack" could have been avoided, in the first place, by a "cold turkey"-like policy of reducing deficits and restoring fiscal consolidation does not concern as much as it should the public authorities—perhaps based on the unfounded concern that this will deepen the recession. Suppose, then, that *short-term* obligations of the government are financed through issuing of new bonds and this process continues until interest rates have gone so high that it is impossible, in the future, to accommodate the situation, even with surpluses in the budget excluding interest payments.

"Speculation" on the debt of the country in question, results in diversion of international resources—perhaps also resources from the European Central Bank—that could have been used elsewhere and foster investment. The accommodation of lending would go up to the point where expected profitability from investment is equal to the average rate of interest that would have to paid, effectively, over a given time horizon that is at least equal to the time horizon of new investment, and the associated diversion of resources. Clearly, the accommodation of the *short-run* obligations of the national government, in the absence of significant reductions in expenditure, is not a profitable use of resources although it yields significantly higher interest rates for the "bail-out" authority or international investors. This does not mean that these resources could have been employed profitably elsewhere at loan rates that should have been significantly higher to offset the policy-related distortions of the preceding credit expansion—reflecting the fact that the opportunity cost of capital is now significantly higher due to scarcity.

What the "bail-out" authority does is purchasing new government debt, possibly at low interest rates, thus distorting even further international financial equilibrium but at the same time the government has the incentive to borrow even more, at higher interest rates, from the international markets, since it has the backing of the European Central Bank—until, of course, government bonds are traded in international markets. During this process, savings and existing investment look entirely pointless and uncertainty is generated ex post: If the crisis could have been foreseen the funds between savings and investment just before the crisis could have been invested in public debt, instead. At low loan rates this would have been impossible to predict by the private sector or even the experts in the field—despite the fact that economists of the Austrian School have been warning about the detrimental effects of the low rates and artificially cheap credit for almost eight decades. If credit and financial markets were let free to operate under competitive conditions, interest rates would change to accommodate demand for new capital in the new, most profitable uses of the resources: Starting from the non-durables sector and working back through the entire time-distribution of capital. The argument that demand is insufficient, as the Keynesians argue, is irrelevant since profitable opportunities can be found and generated from scratch if the constellation of interest rates is allowed to be determined anew, freely, and reflect the *distribution* of existing demand among the various sectors of the economy.

Since capital and funding is scarce and financial markets are allowed to clear, there would be influx of foreign capital to the extent that new interest rates reflect the average rate on debt. At such high interest rates mergers and acquisitions are likely to occur which would provide for more efficient operation and returns to scale from firms operating on the international level. Firms near the left tail of the time-distribution of capital (durable consumer goods, say) see their profit opportunities increasing due to higher prices of capital and interest rates, they are likely to expand capacity after inventories have been exhausted due to the increased demand from firms in the middle of the time-distribution. Profits begin to rise but not employment since there is considerable stock of inventories. Increased profitability, whose signal is provided by rising prices for capital goods, allows for a positive revision of expectations and entry is likely to arise despite the fact that the capital goods sector is still liquidating inventories at higher prices and thus higher profits. The general signal is that the capital goods sector is recovering. *What is the source of this recovery? It is the fact that, for a certain extended period of time, the relative prices of these goods in the international market, have been depressed so much that exports begin to raise as new orders arrive.* Although domestic demand has been depressed considerably, supply curves for capital goods cannot shift, *for a certain extended period of time,* which roughly coincides with the recession. During that time a competitive advantage has been created for the capital goods sector which will show up in international markets. Indeed, during the current recession what we observe in the European South is, precisely, the recovery of exports of those goods whose prices have been suppressed the most due to the nature of the process of production, and the extent of relative shifts in supply and demand curves.

Firms toward the end of the time-distribution of capital (non-durable consumer goods, say) do not see their prices decreasing as much and the sector adjusts, in the main, through large quantitative effects rather than changes in relative prices. The sector will recover only after employment has increased in the left tail and the middle of the time-distribution of capital or, at any rate, in those sectors which have recovered through exports in the international scene. *A second effect comes through the decrease of costs in the less capital-intensive sector* which is generated by the severely depressed prices of their inputs from the more capital-intensive sectors or the sector that require more time to complete productive operations. Profitability will also recover in these sectors but capacity utilization will not, of course, begin to increase unless there is reduction in existing stock of inventories through the increased demand that will be generated from new employment in the sectors whose prices have been depressed the most.

In fact, the higher interest rates on public debt provide an *indirect* signal to the international markets that savings and investment have been depressed so much in the domestic economy, that a significant drop of prices for certain goods is *forthcoming*. These goods will gain a competitive edge on in the international level that will be realized only when their relative prices compared to similar goods produced elsewhere, have been depressed considerably. This is the moment where exports begin to increase and re-distribution of resources begins to take place in the international markets. The real signal is, of course, provided by the drop in prices, not by the increase of interest rates on public debt. Since resources are not perfectly mobile the forthcoming decrease of prices begins with the increase of interest rates on debt to reflect, in a distortionary manner given inefficiencies in financial markets, the forthcoming wedge between loan rates and prices of capital goods. With competitive markets interest rates would have to have been higher, and closer to what can be expected from opportunity costs arising from liquidating present stocks versus investing in purchase of government for the same time horizon. But this tendency cannot, in fact, be realized automatically. While prices of capital goods have been reduced significantly due to the policy-induced, artificial abundance of capital that cannot realize profitability, the restoration of equilibrium requires higher interest rates and thus higher prices of capital goods. This will have to come about only eventually, that is over the course of time, and can come through two ways: First, the increased competitiveness of these goods internationally and, second, through the decreased cost of capital in the less capital-intensive sector.

Superficially, "financial instability" has been created by the "debt crisis" but this is only the final effect of a long chain of events that started with distortions in the configuration of relative prices for investment goods due to cheap credit. Unless credit becomes more expensive and some part of capital is destroyed or, eventually, be exported, there is no way for the free market to restore the distortions that were created from the credit and monetary policies. The real source of financial instability lies, precisely, at these distortions and not the natural reaction of international markets, which is, certainly, to "speculate" on the debt. This "speculation" reflects another important aspect of the problem, namely that domestic resources have not been distributed optimally between the domestic public and private sectors, giving rise to deficit problems and problems in accommodating public debt. "Investments" of the public sector—short-term obligations, in reality, to cover excessive operating costs—have turned out unprofitable. Since the financing of the losses cannot come from the revenue side, for various reasons related to depressed demand and high tax rates, and the state is sluggish in implementing structural reforms to cut down on expenditure the only way for adjustment is to pay higher prices on foreign "resources" to accommodate public "production". Since domestic investment and savings have been depressed considerably, the domestic sector—including commercial banks—cannot finance these activities.

The question is what is wrong with the European Central Bank's intervention to "bail out" commercial banks in distress, because of the increase in non-performing-loans and the depression of savings, or the European Central Bank's intervention to, implicitly or explicitly, accommodate the public debt and re-purchase government securities in open market. We have commented extensively on then inappropriateness of preferential treatment for commercial banks and limiting competition and healthy entrepreneurship in the financial intermediation sector. This is one aspect of the problem. The other important aspect is that, by accommodating the debt and also engaging in "hair-cuts" or extensions of the horizon for re-payment, the European Central Bank sustains the conditions which were created by the wrong allocation of resources and does not let interest rates move freely to restore equilibrium. The concern is, of course, that if commercial banks are left without help and the government is unable to repay short-term obligations it will, eventually, go bankrupt leading to a considerable depreciation and "flight from the Euro".

This is, of course, entirely correct and it makes it appear as though a single country with its bad decisions on deficits and debts has put the Euro into grave danger. To considerable extent other commercial banks in Europe will be affected because of "spillover effects" and their exposure to the problematic country's debt. This tends to ignore, of course, the responsibility of the European Central Bank which permitted an enormous expansion of credit and the subsequent over-investment in sectors that were unprofitable, in reality. One can blame it, equally "convincing" on the United States and the "housing bubble", the "sub-prime crisis" etc. In reality, there has been a concerted expansion of credit in both continents whose effects are, precisely, the terms in quotes.

Agreements to apply "hair-cuts", especially with Private Sector Involvement are not, of course, bad per se. This merely reflects that part of public debt cannot be accommodated and investors have to come in terms with the European Central Bank to sacrifice *some* of their arbitrage profits. Even with generous "hair-cuts" this is a mutually beneficial transaction. *If* that was all, and the national government was committed to *reduce* expenditures and raise *new* taxes, there would be no problem. However, if the government increases tax burdens without cutting on government expenditure consistently and in a committed way, that is through structural reforms, the deficit will not allow financing of short-term obligations *including* interest payments. The question is why interest payments should be included in this calculation: Because they add to the "bail-out" funds of European commercial banks which hold the "black sheep's" government bonds. *It is thus, an implicit way to "bail-out" in addition to the funds that have been directly provided* without concern for future profitability and stance of many European commercial banks. But it is also a measure to implement structural reforms more rapidly instead of engaging in political discussions about suspension of interest payments for a certain period, further "hair-cuts" which would endanger the stance of private sector, extensions of the time horizon, etc. These political discussions are always troublesome, they take a lot of time and, at the end, it is not certain whether they help the problematic country or merely give her an excuse for procrastination and delay to implement the necessary reforms.

If an extension was provided in the first place and the exposed banks were allowed to fail or engage in mergers and acquisitions, the financial system would have to be liberalized to restore equilibrium at higher interest rates. The concern that this will result in a European recession is, of course, totally unfounded, given the correct re-allocation of resources that would take place. This, naturally, would take time but it is unavoidable and its effects, as we have shown, have to be positive. *The European Central Bank by using massive resources to "restore financial stability", effectively shifted resources to the commercial banks* thus enlarging its own size which is not very different from expanding, instead of restricting, not only money and credit but *also the size of the public sector* in the wide sense of supervision by the European Central Bank and the European Commission. The commission of resources to "bail-outs" has to be taken out of the private sector which would use the funds in the most profitable and efficient uses. The suggestion that banks can do the same through financial intermediation is misguided because of the tight control on interest rates and the lack of motivation for commercial banks to change their behavior in terms of financing projects and processes that are, indeed, profitable, at the *market* rates.

Therefore, the European Central Bank not only *increased financial instability*, understood in the correct sense—since the root causes have not been eliminated—but also showed no commitment to restore competition in the financial intermediation sector. With tight controls, *"speculative attacks" could only increase* to realize arbitrage profits from artificially low real rates and increasing average real interest on national public debts. *This is precisely what has been observed during and immediately after the "bail-out" plans.*

These plans are, in fact, an open acceptance of the fact that savings and investment have collapsed in quite a few European countries, not only those in the European South. Instead of a fiscal stimulus or concerted reduction in government expenditures (with mild increases in taxes, where possible and applicable) *the European authorities decided that it is much better to create an artificial monetary stimulus, that is active monetary policy* not only indirectly through the "bail-out" plans but directly as well, as evidenced by increases of base money.

Let us suppose that it is only indirectly that the European Central Bank engages in the stimulus. To prove that it a stimulus, indeed, we have only to consider that it comes about through a reduction of reserves held by the European Central Bank which are diverted to other uses in the economy. Of course, a classical monetary expansion would decrease the real rate. Let us examine more closely the particular nature of this expansion. Its characteristic is that the new funds are diverted to the commercial banks as in the case of any other monetary expansion. The fact that the *justification* is bailing out the commercial banks does not qualify it as any different compared to other monetary expansions of the past. The element that is qualitatively different, in this instance, is related to the nature of expectations of the commercial banks and how their supply curves respond to the situation that has taken shape during the recessionary period. The immediate effects of the recession show up in a shift of the demand for loans to the left, which depresses both real rates and the equilibrium amount of loans. At these low real rates, very few banks would be solvent, but the financing of their operating expenses is covered by the bail out plans of the European Central Bank. These commercial banks can continue their operations but they have (1) to restructure their investment portfolios, and (2) make arrangements so that at least part of their non-performing loans will be paid back. If their expectations about profitable investments are revised downwards, in the new equilibrium of financial markets, we should observe a period where loans are depressed and real rates increase. Since interest rates are set by the European Central Bank the extent of this correction would not be as large as we would expect in equilibrium, under the operation of free markets. With constant interest rates we would expect a gradual decrease in loans that would be *less* than the quantity actually required and resulting from (1) a movement along the existing supply curves for loans and equilibrium relative to the new demand, and (2) a movement along the new demand curve showing a reduction in quantity and increase in interest rates to reach the new equilibrium at the preset interest rates. The mechanism at work is one of *accommodating expectations*, where the supply curves move to the extent necessary to accommodate the demand for loans at the existing interest rates. But if the commercial banks are not willing to follow this policy and their supply curves move to the left, the equilibrium would involve much higher interest rates and a reduction of loans. This would exercise pressures on the European Central Bank to increase its interest rates, an event that is highly unlikely. Under these conditions, it is clear that banks portfolios would have to be re-structured so that relatively safer investments are financed through higher interest rates—a fact consistent with the general scarcity of capital in the economy. With fixed interest rates the quantity effect will be much larger and the result will be general excess demand for loans. *Relative to the past the essential difference is that banking expectations have to be revised from accommodating to rational.* The only way, in practice, to reduce the excess demand is that the private sector revises its expectations further so that, at any level of interest rate, a smaller quantity of loans is demand so that the demand curve moves further to the left. It would, then, be possible, that credit further decreases and interest rates are *lowered.*

The main result from the revision of expectations is that interest rates would have to move up and then down as the result of the "flight" from the cheap credit policies of the past. Liberalization in the financial intermediation sector would bring about the necessary changes with the minimal adjustments and clear signals coming from the *increasing* interest rates. The fluctuation in exchange rates would cause an additional misallocation of resources whose effects would be felt both in the real sector as well as in banking. The revision of expectations in the private sector regarding the demand for loans can be expected to take place fairly quickly, so the excess demand will be lower even with artificially low interest rates. If the banking sector over-reacts in terms of risk aversion this would cause an even higher increase of interest rates. The problem is not that the behavior of the financial sector does not accord well with the distribution of resources and demand in the economy—in fact it does. *The real problem is that this behavior of the financial sector cannot accommodate the European Central Bank's intention to keep interest rates at low levels.* The bail out plans that were used to support the policy of low interest rates results in unintended consequences, which materialize concretely in the re-structuring of portfolios in the financial sector, in favor of much less credit provided at significantly higher interest rates. The past policy of concerted increase of cheap credit is now transformed to a banking-based policy of safer investments at much higher interest rates—a policy that is quite sound since there are safe investments with high return which cannot, however, be financed given the general lack of funds and the existence of excess demand in the market of loanable funds.

The notion of financial stability sometimes employed in the literature is contrary to fundamental principles; for example, sometimes, financial stability is related to average return-on-assets (ROA) in relation to its volatility, measured by the standard deviation. But return-on-assets or profitability, and its volatility, are directly related to the risk-return-based decisions of commercial banks, as in the case of any other firm. If profitability is stabilized, as the result of the intervention of Central Bank, effectively competition is severely hampered and financial markets are *regulated—not stabilized*—to prevent entry and exit from the industry. This gives rise to an important aspect of the problem: If commercial banks, unlike any other firm in the economy, are directly subsidized to maintain profitability or operating costs, *what motivation is there for them to change their risk-return profiles and significantly alter their decisions as the result of the global crisis?* In fact, the accommodation of the European Central Bank's policy requires, precisely, that no such changes should be made. In effect, supply curves would not change and the result would be even lower interest rates that would exercise "pressure" upon the Central Bank's policy to reduce them further.

Much of the dynamics during the transition period to a new equilibrium, under these conditions, depends on the decisions of commercial banks. It is a possibility that commercial banks will act as expected from rationally private agents and reduce substantially their loans at much higher interest rates. From that point of view, one has to wonder about the significance of the European Central Bank's policy of maintaining low base rates. Given fixed interest rates, the cheap-credit-policy required a massive shift of banking sector's supply curve to the right. With the depression of demand, maintaining the low rates and solvency of banks at such low interest rates, requires a shift of supply curves to the left; however, *relative* to expectations and supply curves before the crisis, the supply curves remain yet to the right: *Relative* to the situation before the crisis, loans are *somewhat* reduced and interest rates remain *considerably lower*. However, relative to the actual equilibrium that should occur, credit is still higher and interest rates lower—although the wedge is reduced relative to the pre-crisis situation. Even this conclusion is conservative, in the sense that banking expectations have been adjusted to their pre-crisis levels: In fact they should adjust far more to account for the worst conditions of the economy. Relative to the equilibrium generated by the gloomier expectations, the situation after the bail outs is this: *Credit is still maintained at high levels and the wedge between existing and equilibrium rates is still very large*. In this sense, the banking sector, acting rationally, sustains the conditions that set in motion the business cycle and the severe depression. *It seems as if the European Central Bank wishes to revise expectations of the financial intermediation sector relative to those that emerged from the cheap-credit-policy, but not relative to the pre-crisis situation.* This is impossible and irrational, and the inherent tendencies to increase market rates, resulting from banking sector's expectation, cannot be reversed or changed directly by the European Central Bank. Implicitly, the European Central Bank seems to think that since commercial banks will always backed up there is no reason to revise their expectations *relative to pre-crisis*; but this is impossible and cannot happen if commercial banks are acting rationally.

The notion of financial stability that results from competitive equilibrium is, in fact, quite different. It is incomprehensible to think that failed banks or firms should be subsidized in the short-term or even in the long-term to maintain and sustain an ill-defined and ill-understood "institutional framework" of operation for the European Central Bank which, in effect, determines the mode of operation of financial markets. Instead, the notion of financial stability that results from competitive equilibrium is that the distribution of financial resources and the distribution of resources corresponding to the distribution of demand across the various sectors of the economy should be in close correspondence. It is well known, from the analyses of the Austrian School, that changes in interest rates under competitive conditions reflect the scarcity of capital in its various uses and the price mechanism in this case, that is the operation of financial markets, helps to re-allocate capital and other resources among the most profitable uses, that is the uses that exhibit the highest demand for capital.

What if there are external or exogenous shocks? Most shocks arise from policy in the form of fiscal or monetary expansions and contractions. Without such policy effect, what remains is the genuine uncertainty inherent in all modes of production. However, this uncertainty has been already accounted for, in the determination of the constellation of expected, real interest rates that prevail in the markets. In that sense it is not possible to have external or exogenous shocks that will have any effects which have not already been taken into account in the formation of *equilibrium* prices. The transition to equilibrium will, of course, require sector-specific and resource-specific adjustments which are reflected, directly, in the formation of out-of-equilibrium prices.

"Exogenous shocks" can still be generated if there are free markets operating in one part of the world and active Keynesian policies in another. This will generate a global re-distribution of resources that will be reflected, first of all and almost immediately, in asset prices and futures prices. What is seen as "speculation" by many is nothing but the free market's tendency to exploit arbitrage conditions, wherever they exist, and the market's *immediate* response to the fact that resources cannot be re-directed momentarily or without costs. The fact that policy-induced shocks will change the distribution of capital and resources on a global scale is unavoidable. The question is whether there is a mechanism to absorb the shock. Although the shock cannot be absorbed in the economy where the policy changes have been implemented, by any other means than large quantitative adjustments; in the free market zones of the world the shock will be absorbed first by price adjustments and the quantitative adjustments will, necessarily be smaller. The shock will generate a business cycle in the form of re-distribution of resources on the global scale, but the recession (resulting from fiscal or monetary and credit expansion) will, *eventually*, be worse in the country where the shock originated.

The argument is not unlike the Austrian School's analysis regarding the effects of expansion on the time-structure of production. Production has to be understood in the global sense expanding the stages and types of the time-structure. The precise sequencing of the effects from the shock depends on the types of projects that commercial banks will finance first from the new funds arising from the monetary expansion. The results of the fiscal shock depend on where consumers spend their new income. We have analyzed such effects in detail, in previous chapters of this study. Here, we will focus more on how the expansionary shock affects financial stability in the broad sense. As we have pointed out, the effects will be felt first on asset prices. One line of argument is as follows:

> [B]ank credit creation begins with decreases in non-borrowed reserves that then work through to increases in business and/or consumer lending [..and] once such lending exceeds what can be readily absorbed by or used for GDP transactions, the excess spills over into incremental demand for shares and/or other leverageable financial assets, including real estate and commodities (Vogel, Harold L. 2010. *Financial Market Bubbles and Crashes*. New York: Cambridge University Press. p. 224).

However, it may be more sensible to argue that increases in asset prices will, to large extent, *precede* the real adjustments that will take place in the form of increased investment in specific sectors of the economy, as sector-specific (not "aggregate demand") begins to increase. Precisely because resources cannot be transferred instantly across the time-distribution of production, prices will increase and that will also result in an increase of asset prices in the sectors whose demand increases more steeply. The increase of asset prices implies that money can be made easily in the stock market and this will re-inforce the funding possibilities for firms that face increased demand. Gradually, asset prices increase across the board, *preceding* the sequence of events in the time-distribution of capital and production. One reason is the fact that new orders precede by far the actual implementation of production and the necessary re-distribution of production. There are several effects at work that we should analyze.

1. Firms that borrow late from the banking sector find it easier to borrow through the stock market since there is a general tendency for price increases and, therefore, increases in asset prices, across the entire sector whose demand has increased. In turn this leads to increases of asset prices across the board and less reliance on loanable funds from the banking sector especially for firms that are further removed, in the temporal distribution, from where the shock originated.
2. The banking sector will find it easier to direct the new funds to firms that are not listed in the stock market and cannot exploit the tendency of asset prices of rise. Therefore, it is more likely that loanable funds will be directed to less capital-intensive firms.
3. Since marginal rates of substitution between present and future consumption are not changed, subjective valuations about the rate of interest also do not change. However, the general tendency of making "easy money" in the asset markets results both in higher incomes for stock-holding consumers and also increased demand for stocks, which reinforces the tendency of increasing asset prices.
4. As futures prices increase, despite the fact that no "fundamentals" have changed, "speculation" increases and a rational bubble is set in motion which, superficially, seems to favor speculative activities and arbitrage rather than "real" production—forgetting, of course the fact that re-distribution of resources and actual production take time.

The combination of these effects shows us, that it is not only the time-distribution that is upset from the expansion. It is also the case that *the actual and expected distributions do not correspond to each other*, because of the changes in *relative* prices in asset prices, including futures which reflect subjective valuations of the actual time-distribution. Following the fact that production takes time adjustment of the two distributions also takes time, but in the meantime "financial speculation" emerges to capitalize early on the future profits of the firms whose prospects look better as the result of the expansion. When the effects are completed, firms that are less capital-intensive will find that their demand has decreased as many consumers are engaged in making "easy money". This, in fact, sets in motion a working-back through the time-distribution of production revising sector-specific prices and the distribution of sector-specific demand. As some consumers capitalize early on their profits and spend on consumption there is, of course, another positive effect. However, as it becomes increasingly difficult to exploit arbitrage opportunities as financial markets are clearing.

As the capital-intensive firms are finalizing their investment projects, they will observe that there is, actually, less demand for capital across the time-distribution, as the effects from the expansion and the increase in asset prices are beginning to exhaust across the economy. The over-supply of capital and the associated depression of prices will set in motion a chain of decreasing asset prices which is likely to result in a stock market crash—the market's way of establishing that projects initially thought to be profitable are, actually, not. The consumers that invested in their shares and did not capitalize early will, now, face considerable losses which will depress further their demand for most commodities, making the capital-intensive firms and, in turn, most other firms, appear less profitable. The collapse of asset prices precedes the actual collapse of investment and the liquidation of firms that cannot cover operating expenses. The positive consumption effects of decreasing prices, that is the re-configuration and adjustment of relative prices, will of course exist, but they are not likely to be as large as the wealth effects from the collapse of asset prices.

The net result will be losses of consumers and liquidation of investment, along with an increase in non-performing loans for the banking sector which is reinforced by the wealth effects in the non-durables consumer goods sector and the loss in incomes that results, *eventually*, from *any* expansion. The collapse of asset prices re-configures the actual and expected time-distributions of resources along with the re-allocation of capital and resources that makes closer the correspondence between the distribution of demand and the actual time-distribution of production. *This is, in fact, not an evil phenomenon resulting from "speculation" but rather an equilibrium tendency of competitive markets.* Not competitive financial markets exclusively, but all markets as a whole in general competitive equilibrium.

It becomes evident from this analysis why the burst of rational bubbles or collapses of the stock market precede the recession and the crisis, along with their natural outcomes of liquidation of certain investments and the re-configuration of investment resources in the national and global level. The depression makes it clear that capital is scarcer and, therefore, following the liquidation of capital-intensive firms, *there should be an increase in interest rates, accompanied by a mild increase of the risk-free rate*. The second tendency is due to the increased demand of safer investments or savings by the consumers who experienced positive wealth effects by capitalizing early in the stock market. As the vast majority of consumers experience negative wealth effects the pressure on the risk-free rate to rise will be much lower: In general, this is precisely what we observe, namely low or negative equity premia and higher risk-free rates, particularly during a recession. This implies, among other things, that the positive wealth effects of "smart" consumers or experienced investors are likely to be somewhat significant.

The tendency will be for the commercial banking sector to suffer even more from the non-performance loans and the deterioration of revenues under an increase of deposit rates or the reduction in savings to accommodate the given (perhaps moderate or mild) increased demand for safer investments. But this reveals the real sources of financial instability: Re-shifting of funds across the globe and the different equity and futures markets reflect the effects from the expansionary policy which has changed the correspondence between actual and expected distributions of production relative to the distribution of consumption. It is not the movement of financial funds that *causes* the instability—which is, in reality, nothing but price adjustments for resources that cannot change or move instantaneously—but it rather a reflection and a flawless prediction of what will actual happen in the real sector, that is a massive re-distribution of capital, investment and resources. It is important to understand that without "speculation" in equity or futures markets, along with so-called "toxic products"—which simply depend on complicated agreements about the future re-allocations of resources that will take place—the magnitude of quantitative adjustments (in terms of investment liquidation and negative wealth effects for the consumers) would have to be even large. The change of relative prices in these financial markets absorbs the larger impact of exogenous policy-oriented shocks, although of course actual liquidation of resources has to take place, as rationally expected from the markets.

Regulating financial flows across the globe, that is regulating "financial instability" would then seem to rest upon the following assumption: Since financial flows are rational and predict flawlessly what will happen in terms of re-distribution of resources, why not tax or regulate these flows since the quantitative adjustments will take place anyway? The argument rests entirely upon equilibrium or steady-state considerations—which is quite surprising in view of the fact that favors regulation. During the transition period, that is out of equilibrium, transactions will have to take place, despite what neoclassical economic theory assumes by placing an "*arbitreur*" on the top of all this. The plain truth is that, out of equilibrium, engaging in financial speculation and "easy money" is much more preferable compared to engaging in investment and production; but the point is that the private sector cannot know this in advance. It is only through relative prices that this can become known. "Speculation" merely reflects this fact, in a precise sense, but this can be known only in equilibrium which no one knows in advance or can predict. What private agents can predict or expect is short-term opportunities which are generated by the *change in relative prices* of real and financial products, before any resources can actually move.

Private agents do not, and cannot, see in the changes of the constellation of relative prices what will happen in terms of re-allocation of resources (a simple application of the Misesian theorem on the impossibility of central planning) and they do not even care. What they do care about is how to make profits based on the short-term, that is out of equilibrium, changes in relative prices. A subset of private agents, firms, especially in the capital-intensive sector, invest because they see their prices going up and their inventories reducing. The increase of their asset prices makes it easier for them to invest through equity rather than debt. If the Central Bank were to regulate international financial flows or even stock markets for that purpose, these firms would have to resort to debt, making the collapse of the banking sector even more severe. In that sense, free operations of all financial markets makes for a more widespread allocation of losses across the economy thus, directly and most efficiently, allocating risk and enhancing financial stability to the extent possible—that is, in view of the fact that some instability is unavoidable due to the intervention of fiscal or monetary authorities in the economy.

Taxing international flows of financial capital would, effectively, distort relative prices and would place a larger part of the burden on the domestic economy. At the same time it, first, would distribute *more* burden on consumers and firms and, second, would re-allocate the *relative* burden depending on how the relative prices change as a result of taxing international flows of financial capital. The flows that cannot be performed because they are no longer profitable in the margin, because of taxation, would have to take place in the domestic economy thus leading necessarily and beyond any doubt to even larger quantitative adjustments in the real sector—adjustments that will, of course, be distributed differently among the various sectors, depending on the time-structure of production. In turn this would mean more, not less, financial instability in the domestic economy but globally as well, as some domestic financial capital would "flight" into other uses that are not subject to taxation. If this not possible then, merely, the quantity adjustments will be more massive.

All standard arguments not based on this analysis miss the entire point of the price mechanism on a global scale and, therefore, the fact that *international flows of financial capital are not "simply speculative" but are, in fact, closely related to real flows,* viz. *the re-distribution of resources that has to take place resulting from policy-induced interventions in the economy*. Financial instability cannot be analyzed in isolation from instability in the real sector—yet the latter is nothing but a complex of rational responses to increases in prices of certain goods (and distortion of their structure, that is changes in relative prices) as the outcome of expansionary policies by a certain government or many governments that act in a concerted manner. In the "housing price bubble" most economists cursed and blamed it on the "bad markets" or the "inefficient markets" and the "toxic" financial products that emerged endogenously from the situation. However, they could not explain how this affected the entire economy—through the massive changes in relative prices, the liquidation of several housing projects and the *re-allocation* of resources to other, relatively profitable uses. The government thought that it would be a good idea to expand the deficit or engage in further monetary injections, thus upsetting even more the distribution of resources and offsetting all tendencies for restoring a new equilibrium.

These policy shocks are transmitted from, say, the United States to the rest of the world where other, similar, policy distortions exist and thus there are multiple shocks that have to be propagated and, in that way, change further the distribution of resources through further and more significant changes in relative prices of resources. In this sense, financial instability reflecting and affecting at the same time, the change of decisions that has to take place in view of the changes in relative prices, is a complex configuration of decisions and re-configurations that *has* to take place in view of the complexity of the constellation of policy decisions that operate simultaneously, through different time horizons, in the world economy. The complex pattern of financial flows that emerges as a response may result in a global crash—or at least what is commonly known as "instability". However, the reason would not be "inefficient markets" but rather the arbitrage opportunities that are generated, precisely, from the artificial changes in the world distribution of resources and the associated changes in prices. Unless this is widely understood, it is impossible to understand that it is hopeless to regulate financial flows while at the same time keeping intact the real, quantitative effects that arise from the policy itself. It would have been equally sensible to regulate the movement of real resources and, in fact, it would make no difference.

Chapter 30
The Accommodation of Public Debt by Commercial Banks

A significant aspect of the bail-out programs was that banks were forced to buy government bonds of European countries in distress (particularly Spain and Portugal) so that interest rates on debt could be contained and the governments would find it easier to repay. This expansion of debt or accommodation, of course, acted as a catalyst and, in effect, it was equivalent to a "European bond" backed by the European Central Bank—an idea that was resisted forcefully, in this form, by Germany. But the effect was the same, on the main. The accommodation of debt and the artificial reduction of interest rates were not in line with the changes that were taking place in the European economies for years, following the significant credit expansion. If it were not for the significant increase of institutional uncertainty generated by the policies that were shaping up in the European Union—given that nothing of this magnitude has been allowed by the Treaty of Maastricht or Basel I—the signals that were given to the private sector, amounted to the fact that "speculation" with the public debt was more profitable compared to fostering transactions in stock markets or real investment.

An increase of rates associated with public debt at various horizons signals that it is, *presently*, more difficult to sustain interest payments, *ceteris paribus*. If properly discounted for risk and default, the increase of this "risk-free" rate would require a shift of resources from consumption and stock markets, along with a decrease of asset prices, in response to higher real rates on debt. In principle, this would ensure a private sector participation in the "accommodation" of public debt. This, however, is not the kind of accommodation that was needed by the governments since, in fact, by "accommodation" they mean short-term financing at *lower* rates. The funds that could not be attracted from the private agents should become available through the banks which, in turn, would be provided the funds directly by the European Central Banks and a policy of "reverberation", viz. involvement of foreign agents to reduce the tax burdens on the domestic economy along with generous "hair-cuts" of the debt which fall on the shoulders of the bond holders.

It is, in fact, quite remarkable that, for many decades "risk-free" rates were quite large and equity premia quite were low or even negative. In retrospection, and contrary to the prediction of neoclassical models, this is consistent with the

E. G. Tsionas, *The Euro and International Financial Stability*,
Financial and Monetary Policy Studies 37, DOI: 10.1007/978-3-319-01171-4_30,

view that the markets took account of the possibility of default or, what is the same thing, the fact that stock market crashes are quite probable, as the result of the shifting of resources from consumption and stock markets that would be required to sustain public debts. The cause, rather than being "exogenous shocks" in production, would be a policy-induced non-sustainability of the debt and, eventually, the possibility of running Ponzi schemes. Apart from this with the transformation of the commercial banking sector into holders of national European debts at low rates, the European Central Bank sacrificed its independent role against the governments and involved itself into the politics of public debt. As in the 1980s, when the other major debt crisis emerged in Latin America, the European commercial banks were required to hold large amounts of debt at low rates, despite the negative experience of Dexia, a Franco-Belgian banking consortium, which was particularly exposed to the Greek debt. The Spanish Bankia was even nationalized to prevent collapse as it was exposed to defaulted mortgage agreements.

The difference relative to the Latin America debt crisis of the 1980s is that "hair-cuts" accompanied by austerity measures finally seemed to succeed to contain the national debt crises and avoid further spillover effects. The European "rescue program" was much larger, and despite the fund that it involved the International Monetary Fund, not only resulted in forcing the commercial banks to buy national debts at lower rates to avoid "speculation" resulting from massive selling of national bonds in distress, but after four years (in 2012–2013) it does not seem to provide an adequate solution to the problem. Although the Latin American debt crisis ended in almost two years, the Eurozone crisis is taking much longer. Why is that? As an experienced diplomat argued:

> The European Central Bank sometimes looked like an intermediary between the governments and the banks. But at first it acted as an advocate for the banks, while protecting its independence from the governments. As lender of last resort to the private banking system, the ECB intervened to support the banks, especially with its three-year loan programme. The ECB refused to act as lender of last resort for the governments until September 2012, when it agreed to buy euro-zone sovereign debt without limit, on condition the governments concerned adopted strict reforms (Bayne 2012).

However, this argument forgets that commercial banks were rescued only in order to be able to buy government debt later on. The idea behind the conception of the European Central Bank was, precisely, that it would never act as lender of last resort for the governments; otherwise the policy frameworks of the past of high borrowing and inflation along with monetization of debt etc. could never be overcome. At the same time, austerity measures in Greece, Portugal and Spain, and even in Ireland, were taken with considerable delay. The discussions over the efficiency of these measures took quite some time and generated considerable popular resistance that, eventually, made the implementation of structural reforms a difficult and painful political process that, along its way, widened the scope for anti-democratic speculation by certain extremes.

Unfortunately, the scope for dramatic reductions in the size of the public sector along with tax cuts was not realized widely. In Ireland it was even suggested to abandon the low-business-tax regime which was responsible for the country's tremendous growth over several years. Fortunately, this suggestion faced considerable resistance. Fearing the short-term depression effects of cutting public expenditure, many Southern European governments resisted austerity measures—that would be accompanied by direct short-term financing of the public debt. Arguments have been advanced that the social order would be disrupted and democracy itself was in danger if further austerity measures were taken during a deep recession. Bayne (2012) explained the situation lucidly and calmly:

> With neither IMF, commission nor ECB acting as an intermediary that could reconcile economics and politics, the euro-zone's discussions often became acrimonious. When the crisis first broke, the attitude to Greece was threatening, rather than helpful or even dispassionate. German public opinion attacked the Greeks as feckless; Greek opinion saw the Germans as bullies. Political frictions with Germany made it much harder to gain political support in Greece for painful economic measures (Bayne 2012).

The German press gave, in fact, the excuse that the Greek governments needed to delay or postpone the necessary structural reforms that were built over the course of almost three decades. The Germans seemed to think that such political pressure would contain the Greek problem to strictly Greek reforms when, in fact, that was impossible because of the "contagion" of the Greek crisis to the rest of the Eurozone. The emergence of crisis in Spain, Portugal, Ireland and Italy proved that the problem had deeper roots, in the accumulation of large debts in the past, despite fiscal consolidation in the sense of the Treaty of Maastricht. Fiscal consolidation itself proved to rest on a shallow foundation because, precisely, it did not (and, perhaps, could not) allow for concerted reductions in public sectors across Europe along with, the once celebrated, target of reducing "tax competition" through tax harmonization. The political and social conditions for such measures were not mature in the 2000s for such structural reforms but with the advent of the credit expansion the large distortions that were introduced in (the time-distribution of) production began to explode leading to the present crisis.

Bayne (2012) and many others, particularly the French and governments in Southern Europe, blame it on the lack of political unification of Europe. As Bayne (2012) in his insightful article:

> Throughout the euro-zone, electorates were suffering from the impact of the recession. They had not been prepared for the need to rescue other euro-zone countries. There was therefore strong resistance—notably in Germany, but also in Netherlands, Finland and Slovakia—to spending scarce resources on their less prudent partners. Rather than explaining that this was the only way to save the euro-zone, governments gave way before public opinion. They tried to limit the domestic cost of the rescues, both by an ineffective search for external financing and by insisting on corrective measures of increasing austerity by the vulnerable members.

The lack of common political objectives and the immaturity of public opinion are thus held responsible for the "fact" that directly helping the governments in distress would have been "the only way to save the euro-zone". Since imposition of increasing austerity in the vulnerable countries and "ineffective search for external financing" would have to fail before they were even introduced, the governments should show some solidarity in helping one another in sustaining their huge shares in national production. On the contrary:

> In the 1980s the participants were able to reconcile the severe domestic pressures with their international objectives. The US Administration won over congress through the skilful use of 'reverberation'. The euro-zone was not successful in this respect, neither in the vulnerable countries nor in those that expected to finance the rescues. External and domestic pressures were not reconciled, but were visibly in conflict (Bayne 2012).

It is undoubted that what we have called—although in a very different sense from that of Bayne's (2012)—"coherent governance" does not yet exist in the European Union. Yet this does not explain why the massive rescue packages did not manage to solve the problems. Let us remind the reader what was precisely involved. In March 2012, a treaty introducing "fiscal discipline" on new grounds, confirmed the new ESM, whose funds were amounted at €500 billion. The euro-zone contributed an additional €150 billion and the IMF contributed another $430 billion. The second Greek rescue package, involved €145 billion. Most bond-holders accepted a debt swap, involving a haircut of over 50 %, which reduced outstanding Greek debt by €100 billion. For example, four Spanish banks received €36.97 billion in European aid. Of this, € 17.96 billion went to Bankia, which holds 10 percent of Spanish savings deposits, while €5.43 billion were disbursed to Novagalicia, €9.08 billion to Catalunya Caixa and €4.5 billion to Banco de Valencia. A further EUR 2.5 billion was paid to Spain's state-backed "bad bank" set up to bear losses, estimated at up to €60 billion, following the collapse of the country's property market. The UK's estimated package should reach €0.9 trillion in order to restore confidence in the banking system. In Denmark, 13 of the country's 140 banks were bailed out by the Central Bank or acquired by their competitors. *The volume of the rescue package is estimated to be €593.9 billion.* European Union governments approved about €311.4 billion for capital injections, €2.92 trillion for bank liability guarantees, €33 billion for relief of impaired assets and €505.6 billion for liquidity and bank funding support, *a total of €3.77 trillion.*[1]

This massive package, of which €311.4 billion were devoted to pure capital injections, should set in motion an expansionary effect whose magnitude would have no precedent in economic history. Yet if that massive package, of which a significant part is implicitly devoted to rescuing governments in distress or show signs of temporary recovery, then something fundamentally wrong exists in the very structure of the economies of the European Union. *First*, part of the massive package is used to accommodate non-productive needs of governments in distress which, in view of the absence of coherent governance—in the precise sense that we defined it in this study—in the European Union, are unwilling to reduce drastically expenditures and taxes. *Second*, as the result of the package we are likely to see a further credit expansion that will worsen the heavily distorted resource allocation in the European Union starting from the economies of the

---

[1] I am indebted to my co-author Professor Roman Matousek of the University of Sussex for updating and providing these data.

Eurozone. *Third*, as part of the package, financial stability is further endangered by making European commercial banks effective bond-holders under guidelines from Basel III which have very little, if anything to do, with "rational risk-return" decisions and behavior. *Effective monetization and accommodation of public debt by the European Central Bank is, certainly, forthcoming*. This will transform the European Central Bank to its American equivalent with all the disastrous consequences that this action will bring in the future of credit and monetary policy.

Bayne (2012) in his interesting and insightful study put economic diplomacy, by professional zeal perhaps, at a position which is not deserved by the actual process of the European and global crisis and their true causes and effects. Political negotiations and the search for a "neutral institution" that could supervise the various agreements—despite the fact that a "neutral institution" cannot actually exist—have their limits which are determined by the economic environment and the cumulated effects of policy measures that have taken place in the past. The International Monetary Fund could play the role of such a "neutral institution" but the effects of its policies are not neutral at all. The International Monetary Fund accommodates the interests of United States' economic policies and, despite the fact, that it can supervise effectively negotiations and political discussions or economic diplomacy will act, I fact, quite inefficiently when it comes to coherent governance on a global scale. The International Monetary Fund can deal effectively with negotiations when the partner is a single country but not when the partner is a monetary union consisting of some major economies whose effect in the global economy is non-negligible. This is the major reason why the Latin American crisis of the 1980s was successfully resolved. As Bayne (2012) argued the International Monetary Fund managed to reduce the negotiations to a country-level avoiding a collective negotiation with the debtors as a whole. In the latter case one or two countries could upset the process by raising objections that would be shared by other countries leading to a dead alley. In effect the Latin American crisis was contained and resolved by hair-cuts and successful imposition of austerity measures.

The very same measures were considerably delayed in the Eurozone crisis. Although the role of European Central Bank as a "buffer zone" was assumed and attracted considerable interest from the markets and the private sector, eventually it was the European Central Bank who assumed the main burden in re-shifting resources to accommodate national public debts, capital injections, bank liability guarantees, relief of impaired assets, liquidity and bank funding support etc.

What was considered by some to be an Austrian School's support of the Euro, namely the time-consuming process of negotiations in the European Commission, *proved to be a main source of sustaining the crisis* and, afterwards, enabling agreement over implementing the wrong decisions—most importantly the monetization of debt through buying of distressed bonds in the open market to reduce interest rates. Generous haircuts or even rescheduling of the debt would have been consistent with the market's reaction since in fact debt-holders would be willing to sell distressed bonds below nominal prices to minimize losses. Of course they would also be willing to accept extensions of the time horizons for eventual delayed repayment of part of reduced capital. Part of the problem was that such policies were delayed considerably for more than two years, effectively supporting explosion of debts and contagion. Possibly, a "careful calculation" of debt holdings by European commercial banks would have shown precisely which banks were in distress by holding Greek debt or unsustainable national of other countries. This would provide measures of exposure for countries that would be in distress, like Spain, Portugal and Ireland and, in turn, Italy and other major economies.

The reason why such "careful calculations" could not have been possible in the first place is that the market's reactions *could not have been predicted and, therefore, could not have been performed*. Such "careful calculations" require general equilibrium calculations that cannot possibly be performed by monetary authorities and central banks. This is, in its essence, another application of the Misesian Theorem on the impossibility of central planning. But let us consider in detail the precise consequences of the market's responses which have not been considered, in detail so far.

Reference

Bayne N (2012) The economic diplomacy of sovereign debt crises: Latin America and the eurozone compared. Int J Diplomacy Econ 1(1):4–18

Chapter 31
The Consequence of the Market's Responses

The selling of bonds from countries in distress, like Greece, put a strain on Greek resources to accommodate these transactions. The lower demand for Greek debt should *decrease* rates *and* the number of outstanding bonds. Since net supply decreased, there should be a net increase in rates and a further reduction in outstanding bonds. What happened then was further selling of bonds by the European Central Bank which *would* lower the bond rates if it were not for the fact that their demand was increased by the commercial banks: Eventually this restored, approximately, the previous equilibrium at almost the same bond rates! Clearly this policy did not help the payment of short-term obligations, which is why the European Central Bank resorted to the policy of "hair-cut" inspired by the Latin American debt crisis of the 1980s.

But there was a significant difference in that the commercial banks, in that case, were *not* forced to accommodate further the holding of government bonds. The demand curves were not forced to move artificially (to the right) and the healthy response of the market, in the form of higher rates, was not offset by an artificial further reduction. In fact, the result of this policy was *not* to reduce the quantity of bonds in equilibrium but restore them to their previous level. If we account for interest it is not clear at all that the amount of debt outstanding would be reduced, so a "hair-cut" was necessary.

What was the mistake in that case? *First*, the fact that the European Central Bank restored artificially the demand for Greek debt through its control on the commercial banks. The banks could sustain the exposure to the Greek debt if it were not for the fact that their financial stance deteriorated as the result of non-performing loans that exploded after the credit expansion of the 1990s and the 2000s. *Second*, the Greek debt crisis could have been arranged in a different way by bilateral agreements between the (central) Bank of Greece and its debt-holders as it happened in the 1930s. This arrangement was pretty much along the Latin American arrangements of the 1980s. It could have been argued, as it was indeed the case, that the Greek debt problem had nothing to do with the European Union or the stability of the Euro and it was confined to Greece itself. Naturally, this could have prevented the Dexia problem and timely negotiations would have facilitated a rescheduling of Greek debt, a hair-cut and, of course, it would have

E. G. Tsionas, *The Euro and International Financial Stability*,
Financial and Monetary Policy Studies 37, DOI: 10.1007/978-3-319-01171-4_31,

made the implementation of structural reforms easier *provided* it was accompanied by a concerted decrease of public expenditures in the European South to prevent similar problems. On the contrary, arbitrary arguments have been advanced that 150 or 120 % of debt-to-GDP ratios would be "sustainable". These arguments would fly in the face of negative growth rates in Greece and other countries that could not sustain even ratios around 80 or 50 %. Arguments prevailed that debt could be sustained without massive reductions in expenditure and structural reforms by focusing on the "recessionary" effects that this would have, ignoring the fact that over-investment and destruction of capital along with deterioration of demand were coming from the previous credit expansion. These arguments ignored historical experience, for example the Canadian policy that has managed to reduce deficits and debt while, at the same time, turning the recession to growth and deficits to surpluses.

It was considered automatically correct and self-evident that national debt problems, accumulated from the past but also aggravated by large primary deficits, indicated and were intimately connected to the stability of the Euro. It was considered self-evident that the European Central Bank or the European Commission should be actively involved in a problem which was, to a large extent, *strictly national* and should be arranged by the Greek government and the Bank of Greece on the one hand, and the European commercial banks along with the major holders of Greek debt including of course the European Central Bank *as a debt-holder*, *not* as a policy maker in the Eurozone. There are, naturally, several ways that could have been used to prevent the European Central Bank from engaging directly into the negotiations if that was considered a negative signal for the markets.

Tax burdens imposed on European citizens to support the arrangement of Greek debt would have been totally unnecessary. In fact, the entire tax burden and the resources of the European Central Bank were shifted to rescue the European banks from their careless decisions that resulted from the credit expansion, *not* from their exposure to Greek debt—an exposure that could have been rectified easily through other means. Two almost unrelated issues, the Greek debt and the collapse of European banking were arbitrarily combined to one to provide a justification for the European Central Bank's intervention to stimulate further the European economy through active monetary policy, maintain the stance and solvency of European banking and at the same time, as an excuse, to project this entire intervention into the *mostly* circumstantial fiscal problems of Greece that lead to problems in accommodating debt interest payments. The problem were *mostly* circumstantial because they were *not entirely* due to fiscal irresponsibility but also the wider credit expansion at low rates—the policy of "cheap credit"—that was prevalent in the entire Eurozone for almost two decades. How can one seriously entertain the possibility that *a total of* €3.77 *trillion* was shifted from the European Central Bank to commercial banks just to prevent the "contagion" from Greek debt? Even the "Greek rescue package" was mostly diverted to the commercial banking sector in the form of guarantees and to maintain their solvency and profitability.

If the policy of "cheap credit" was not adopted in the first place, across the Eurozone but also the whole of the European Union and the United States, the financial intermediation sector would not face the massive losses that it faces now. Rescuing and bailing out from the European Central Bank would not have been necessary. Yet this massive rescue package is "interpreted" as "contagion", "Greek crisis" etc., instead of examining more precisely the real causes and the underlying micro-economic structural changes that have taken place well before, and of course after 2007 and 2008. The fact that these structural changes should eventually materialize in large primary deficits and inability to sustain the debts of European public sectors, escapes the attention of standard economic analyses which tend to focus on anything but the responsibilities of the European Central Bank in terms of its own credit and monetary policies over the course of years that followed the conception of the Euro. Such policies had a *distinctively Keynesian flavor*: Fiscal consolidation that, however, allowed massive public sectors, monetary expansion through credit ease but also expansion of monetary base, low interest rates, and classical monetization of debt by the central bank. Rational bubbles, stock market crashes and debt crises that have occurred historically as the result of such policies, were largely ignored and, which is far worse, are still systematically ignored by technicians and policy makers.

Placing the burden of debts on the shoulders of commercial banks is a policy that has proved to be disastrous *in the given economic conditions*. The financial intermediation sector, in the midst of the worst recession after 1929, has also to deal with non-performing "risk-free" debt on top of its problems in managing problems related to non-performing loans that resulted from its mostly rational decisions which were formed in an environment of "cheap credit" and artificially low loan rates. It is, of course, true that the adjustment to a new equilibrium, resulting from liberalizing financial markets and reducing public sectors, will have some negative effects but there is simply no other way if massive adjustment is to be made and restore growth and investment in the medium-term. Undoubtedly, this will necessitate and require a re-examination of the role of the European Central Bank and coherent governance in the European Union to facilitate such adjustments on a global scale—where it is easier to introduce and implement vast structural reforms which are needed, contrary to popular opinion and the opinion of national governments who insist on fiscal consolidation independently of the size of public expenditures and tax revenues.

Chapter 32
Is Eurozone Effectively a Socialist Commonwealth?

According to certain assessments the European Union and the common currency do not reflect the Christian-Democratic vision of their founding fathers and the Treaty of Rome, but rather a socialist vision for the creation of a mega-state.

> The agenda of the socialist vision is to grant ever more power to the central state, i.e., to Brussels. The socialist vision for Europe is the ideal of the political class, the bureaucrats, the interest groups, the privileged, and the subsidized sectors who want to create a powerful central state for their own enrichment. Adherents to this view present a European state as a necessity, and consider it only a question of time. Along the socialist path, the European central state would one day become so powerful that the sovereign states would become subservient to it (We can already see first indicators of such subservience in the case of Greece and Ireland. Both countries behave like protectorates of Brussels, who tells the governments how to handle their deficits) (Bagus 2012, p. 4).

According to Bagus (2012) Germany had to agree on the common currency and give up the Deutschemark as the price to pay for the reunification—a plan whose inception had taken place in Paris. Germany's insistence of fiscal and monetary stability and its unwillingness to subsidize the Southern European government deficits can be traced back to the (more or less) stable and non-accommodating policies that the Bundesbank has adopted in the past.

> The institutional setup of the EMU has been an economic disaster. The Euro is a political project; political interests have brought the European currency forwards on its grievous way and have been clashing over it as a result. And economic arguments launched to disguise the true agenda behind the Euro have failed to convince the general population of its advantages. The Euro has succeeded in serving as a vehicle for centralization in Europe and for the French government's goal of establishing a European Empire under its control—curbing the influence of the German state. Monetary policy was the political means toward political union. Proponents of a socialist Europe saw the Euro as their trump against the defence of a classical liberal Europe that had been expanding in power and influence ever since the Berlin Wall came down. The single currency was seen as a step toward political integration and centralization. The logic of interventions propelled the Eurosystem toward a political unification under a central state in Brussels. As national states are abolished, the market place of Europe becomes a new Soviet Union (Bagus 2012, p. 161).

E. G. Tsionas, *The Euro and International Financial Stability*,
Financial and Monetary Policy Studies 37, DOI: 10.1007/978-3-319-01171-4_32,

Bagus may be true on the historical process that led to the European Union and the common currency, and he may even be true when it comes to what the French and German ruling classes wanted to do on the European level. But the whole point is that with a unified Europe it becomes *easier*, *not* more difficult, to restore the workings of competition and free markets. This is because the ruling classes (Hoppe 1990) despite their close association with the State, have no independent interests and no independent social roots from the free markers themselves. The enforcement of competition and the anti-monopoly legislation works in the favor of a political and economic unification that undermines the influence of the State and the bureaucracy. The bureaucracy cannot do otherwise but enhance the role of competition. Monetary policy is, indeed, a problem but it not more or less so when compared with credit and monetary policies of other central banks in individual countries.

> The Euro is not a failure because participating countries have different structures, but rather because it allows for redistribution in favor of countries whose banking systems and governments inflate the money supply faster than others. By deficit spending and printing government bonds, governments can indirectly create money. Government bonds are bought by the banking system. The ECB accepts the bonds as collateral for new loans. Governments convert bonds into new money. Countries that have higher deficits than others can maintain trade deficits and buy goods from exporting states with more balanced budgets. The process resembles a tragedy of the commons. A country benefits from the redistribution process if it inflates faster than other countries do, i.e., if it has higher deficits than others. The incentives create a race to the printing press. The SGP [Stability and Growth Pact] has been found impotent to completely eliminate this race; the Euro system tends toward self explosion (Bagus 2012, p. 163).

However, the same can happen in the context of federal States or in the context of local administrations that consistently ran highest deficits compared to others. The arguments of Bagus rest entirely on two assumptions: (1) That there is no fiscal consolidation, and (2) that the size of the public sector will remain large under all circumstances. Although fiscal discipline has been eased in the European Union, at the same time we see that the austerity measures imposed on the problematic countries, favor a reduction of the public sector. *We should have no doubt that the recent massive "rescue" program of commercial banks will necessitate discussions in the European Union about the reduction of government spending* and—possibly—the reduction of taxation and the tax burden. Even if the tax burden remains unchanged, the change of the ratio of spending cuts to taxes will foster the prospects for growth and the recovery of investment.

The chain of events set in motion by increases in *relative* deficits across countries in the monetary Union, *is entirely due to low interest rates and cheap credit.* Countries, say like Greece, that wish to maintain higher deficits and a high standard of living which is maintained by issuing government bonds, could not do that at higher interest rates who would, eventually, through a long chain of causes and effects, increase the price of imports and annihilate any distortions in the distribution of European resources that made possible and advantageous the relative increase of deficits (beyond the nominal targets set by the Treaty of Maastricht).

If the policy of low rates and "cheap credit" is abolished the interpretation of what happens in the Eurozone as "tragedy of the commons" loses its hermeneutical power. Indeed, as Bogus mentions:

Before the introduction of the Euro, these countries [Greece etc.] devalued their currencies from time to time in order to regain competitiveness. Now they do not need to devalue because *government spending takes care of the resulting problems*. Overconsumption spurred by reduced interest rates and nominal wage increases pushed for by labor unions increase the competitive disadvantage. *The system ran into trouble when the financial crisis accelerated deficit spending. The resulting sovereign debt crisis in Europe brings with it a centralization of power.* The European Commission assumes more control over government spending and the ECB assumes powers such as the purchase of government bonds (Bagus 2012, pp. 163–164, emphasis added).

There are several things that we must qualify in this analysis. First, it is not entirely true that "*government spending takes care of the resulting problems*". This can be done only to a limited extent, given the restrictions put by the Treaty of Maastricht. It is true that "creative statistics" masked a true deficit of 13 % to a "mere" 6 % but running a deficit, even with "creative statistics", is simply not possible indefinitely. Second, it is not true that "*the system ran into trouble when the financial crisis accelerated deficit spending*". The causes of the crisis were entirely different, as we have argued in detail. The system really ran into trouble when commercial banks found their profitability deteriorating and their solvency impossible to maintain, due to the fact that investments they had financed began to liquidate: That was the result of the fact that the distribution of consumption has not changed as much as to justify the distribution of capital and other resources that were justified by artificially low interest rates. Third, the assessment that "*the resulting sovereign debt crisis in Europe brings with it a centralization of power*" is refuted by the intensification of political disagreements over the process of "bailing out" governments—which, incidentally, was not the real issue. The real issue was bailing out commercial banks. We agree that the process of liquidation in the financial intermediation sector should have been left to complete its working and a new banking sector should emerge. However, the "centralization of power" that, supposedly, took place was nothing else but the intensification of bureaucratic process, through which the European Union works anyway. It is true enough that different measures should have been taken to prevent the most damaging elements of the recession—measures that would, necessarily, work in the direction of reducing the distortions in the allocation of resources. But the same is true for any government, in any national state, that finds itself in the midst of a recession. Governments are attracted to the idea that they "should do something" because they are still captive in the Keynesian tradition of their advisers and, of course, because they are under the pressure of the electorate. We do not have the evidence to support the idea that the European Commission is now more powerful as it was before the Euro simply because the financial crisis somehow made it necessary to "centralize power" even more.

> Moreover, the default of a country would probably affect negatively the domestic banking system and have a domino effect on banks all over Europe, including Germany. The connectivity of the international financial system might lead to the collapse of German banks, close allies of the German ruling class, and strong supporters of a single currency. A bankruptcy in form of hyper inflation would equally negatively affect international trade and the financial system. Sovereign bankruptcies could take governments down with them (Bagus 2012, p. 72).

We have shown that this argument, although obviously true superficially is, in fact, incorrect. It tends to blend together two, almost unrelated, issues: The debt crisis of the European South on the one hand, and the liquidation of projects that were financed extensively by European commercial banks as the result of "cheap credit" policies and artificially low interest rates. The sovereign debt crisis should not, normally, be part of the European Commission's concerns, and it could have been settled on the basis of bilateral negotiations between Greece and its debtors. In this process a "hair-cut" along with rescheduling of the debt would emerge as the natural solution. *The fact that the Southern European sovereign debt became an Eurozone problem was an arbitrary decision* and it does not follow at all from the underlying economic logic of the problem. The collapse of the banking sector required trillions of funds and it was massive relative to the financial requirements of covering short-run operating expenses of the Greek government. What was done with sovereign debts was no different compared to the bailing out of commercial banks except that the latter required massive funding and massive transfer of resources.

We believe that the whole process of merging the two problems into one was a fundamental mistake that sent the wrong message to the markets. The debt problem could have been settled in a different way, as the Latin American experience shows along, of course, with the Greek experience in its past debt crises during the 19th and 20th centuries—in particular the crisis of the 1930s which was settled smoothly and efficiently. *However, what the markets feared what no so much the sovereign debt crises but the collapse of the financial system.* That was the primary, if not the only factor that would set in motion a destabilization and a "flight from the Euro". The "contagion" effects from a settlement of Greece's debt could have been contained but the massive transfer of resources to the European banking sector proves, in retrospect, that this was a problem of quite different magnitude. Relative to the credit-induced malinvestment that caused the collapse of the European financial intermediation system, the debt crisis was, by far, an episode of smaller significance.

What is of more interest is the fact that the massive transfer of resources to bail out the commercial banking sector will, undoubtedly, necessitate smaller public sectors in the European Union. This may be a difficult process (see for example Bagus 2012, pp. 44–45) but it is easier to achieve at the central level rather than in each individual country separately. This may difficult to understand by those who seem to think that central political power is necessarily based on large public sectors. Instead, *central political power can be exercised in many other ways even when the level of taxation and public expenditure is at a "minimum"*. The design of institutional frameworks is an equally important factor in the increase of the power of the State whose *direct* command over economic resources is, otherwise, at a "minimum". In this sense the power of the State is a qualitative, not a quantitative issue.

Reducing the tragedy of the Euro to a "tragedy of the commons" is an oversimplification. Even the "tragedy of the commons" interpretation, however, loses its explanatory power *if* the European Central Bank was credibly committed to credit and monetary stability with market-determined interest rates, or at least, interest rates that would move in directions conformable with the existence of distortions in resource allocation. It is not possible, in economic terms, to reduce further, in methodological terms, the expansionary policies of the European Central Bank to a "tragedy of the commons". An expansionary policy is a standard Keynesian-based intervention designed to drive the economy out of a recession or set in motion a supposedly new path of growth. The "tragedy of the commons" refers to incentives by individual countries, in a monetary Union, to increase spending at the expense of others. But what is the "common" that individual countries can take advantage of? Supposedly, the common currency. What would be the mechanism?

> German exporters benefited from an inflationary Euro in a dual way. Other Eurozone countries could no longer devalue their currency to gain competitiveness. In fact, currency crises and sudden devaluations had endangered German exporters. A currency crisis also put the common market in jeopardy. With a single currency, devaluation would no longer be possible. Italian Prime Minister Roman[o] Prodi employed this argument to convince German politicians to allow a debt-ridden Italy to join the monetary union: support our membership and we'll buy your exports. In addition, budget and trade deficits of Southern countries made the Euro consistently weaker than the Deutschmark would have been. *Higher German exports were compensated for by trade deficits of uncompetitive member states. As a consequence, German exporters had an advantage over countries outside the Eurozone*. Increases in productivity would not translate into appreciations of the currency, at least not when compared to the Deutschmark (Bagus 2012, p. 70, emphasis added and footnote 31 removed).

The argument forgets that aggregates like "devaluation" or "productivity" have little to do with the problem. Even under a common currency, prices do not adjust instantly or not at all because of many factors. Prices of the same commodities should have been higher in the Southern countries compared to Germany, a fact that *would generate a tendency* to produce them in the South rather than in Germany. That is, of course, not true for the commodities in which German industry has a clear comparative advantage, anyway, but nevertheless it does set in motion a re-distribution of resources for a vast majority of commodities in the list comprising the accounting sheets of the balance of payments. The South would gain comparative advantages. The budget and trade deficits would not have possible, in the first place, without the credit expansion policies of the European Central Bank. One can interpret this in two ways. First, in purely political terms, by arguing that debts and trade deficits were generated to buy the German exports. Second, in purely economic terms, by arguing that the "cheap credit" policy of the

European Central Bank was, in fact, a misguided application of the (Keynesian) idea that low interest rates promote investment and growth.

The purely political argument ignores the fact that (even under "cheap credit") the private sector will certainly import German cars but cannot be forced to import equipment unless it is competitive relative to the United States or the United Kingdom, or possibly other countries. Without a misallocation of resources, caused by low rates, which begins a process of malinvestment in the German industry, and more specifically in the capital-intensive sector, this advantage cannot be gained. If that is what Bagus terms "inflationary euro" it is indeed correct but the mechanism is through the working of the interest rate, not the abstract and aggregate notions of "competitiveness" and "productivity". Indeed, artificially low interest rates induce an increase of investment in the capital-intensive sectors and countries of a monetary union, or the entire world or a given set of countries, for that matter. The secondary effect of Germans facing higher prices for the commodities they import from the South, seems to be of no interest in the analysis, despite the fact that it is clearly important. *In the absence of a sustained credit expansion the effects from trade surpluses of Germany at the expense of trade deficits of the South would tend to disappear.* Productivity relative to the Mark or the Euro has nothing to do with the problem. The essence of the international transmission mechanism, with common currency or not, is that any credit-induced malinvestment in the capital-intensive sector will, eventually, bring about an increase of prices across the board but with significant changes in the structure of relative prices. The eventual increase of prices in the consumer-goods sector and the depression of demand will work backwards to the capital-intensive sector in Germany and create liquidation of investment and recession. The chain of events will work also forwards through second-order, third-order effects etc., until a new equilibrium is restored.

If the crisis has proved anything, this is precisely the fact that debt-based financing of imports from Germany will set in motion a crisis, a business cycle with catastrophic effects on the real sector. One can blame it on debt crisis, the "tragedy of the commons" with the South taking advantage of the rest etc., but the fact of the matter is that none of this would have happened, at least not to the extent we observe, if the European Central Bank did not embark on "cheap credit". From what we know, Germany did not object to this policy but only to a peripheral coincidence: the explosion of public debt in the South. This explosion is of course related to the credit expansion, in that the liquidation of investment in the South produced a deterioration of tax revenues. With public expenditures being excessively large this meant that accommodation of interest payments became impossible. If one were to blame the austerity measures for the liquidation taking place in the consumer-goods sector then, effectively, one would have to ignore the entire sequence of liquidation at the micro-economic level which works forward and backward in the time-distribution of production.

> But why would Germany take on the role of guarantor? Introducing the Euro and implicitly guaranteeing for the debts of the other nations came along with direct and

> indirect transfers of the Eurosystem. Bankruptcy of the European states, which would have had adverse effects on the German ruling class, could be averted, at least for some time. *A collapse of one or several countries would lead to recession.* Due to the international division of labor in Europe, a recession would hit big exporters and established companies even in Germany. Tax revenues would fall and the support of the population would be reduced (Bagus 2012, pp. 71–72, emphasis added and footnote 33 removed).

However, the Eurozone was already in a recession. It is also hard to see how "tax revenues would fall and [therefore] the support of the population would be reduced" unless, of course, higher taxes would have been imposed. The recession would force German exporters to reduce prices aiding in the recovery of the South and *reducing the distortions that exist in the system*. Germany did not seem to have any problem when it came to the massive bail-out program of the banking sector. She did not seem to voice an opinion in favor of restoring a healthier and more solid financial system and an *increase* of interest rates that would help, to a certain extent, the more rational distribution of resources across the European Union. She did not even suggest a bilateral settlement on the debt thus avoiding making it a European problem—when, in fact, it was not. The argument that this would affect the Euro—more than it already did after so many erroneous interventions—is not a matter that should be settled on the table of summits and political discussions, but rather an issue for the markets to resolve and decide.

To the arguments that the markets would have reacted negatively, we have to point out that the matter is far more complicated. Monetary and credit stability are the primary factors which can affect the stability of the Euro. Bilateral agreements would have stabilized the Euro far earlier than it actually happened because they work quickly relative to the transfer of resources that bailed out the European commercial banks. *The stability of the Euro, now, rests on the market's assessment of whether these banks have indeed succeeded to continue operation in the short-run.* We now have to wait and see how the credit expansion—the bailout programme—will affect solvency in the banking sector and whether the working of the financial intermediation sector has, indeed, improved. The bailout programme set in motion a chain of events whose unfolding will take considerable time and has upset international financial markets considerably. The effects have not worked out fully, by no means. The spreading of the vast financial resources that were shifted to rescue the profitability of banks will have now to work through all sectors in the European economy and set in motion a new cycle of recession and malinvestment.

In contrast, the bailout programme of countries in distress has more straightforward consequences. Although not entirely true that this process has no real effects, the effects are several orders of magnitude smaller compared to the banking bailout programme. The effects are aggravated by the distortions already in place, in the sense that some part of the bailout is absorbed by large and inefficient public sectors that resort to higher taxation rather than cutting expenditures. However, we should not forget that haircuts have taken place, which is an equilibrium market-based phenomenon which alleviates considerably the debt problems. The austerity that was induced is the correct policy *if* followed by large-scale structural reforms to reduce the overall size of the government.

Short-term movements in the exchange rate of the Euro reflect the simultaneous working of many factors that should be accounted for. If the European bureaucracy, willingly, internalized the debt problem of the South when, in fact, it could have been settled by other means, it is quite reasonable that the markets will react and the Euro will devaluate relative to other major currencies. If the European Central Bank reacts aggressively, matters can only become worse. In fact, this will offset the positive but temporary effects that will result from the increase of European exports. It will be then the "responsibility" of other Central Banks to intervene and "correct" their exchange rates. The much feared "flight from the Euro" will soon be reversed when it is realized that the European industry is recovering. What could have been confined in the boundaries of Europe has now been transmitted to the whole world and some may, uncritically, think that international financial stability is threatened. *The only thing that threatens permanently international financial stability is the fact that there are systematic interventions in the supply and demand for currency.* These interventions ignore the fact that they cannot but work at the micro-economic level by distorting the distribution of production and resources. They do create real effects but they also create arbitrage opportunities in terms of induced flows of financial capital which precede the flow of physical capital which cannot take place instantly but only through the course of time. The much feared increase of interest rates which—according to textbooks—would reduce investment has an entirely different effect when there are significant distortions. It would result in a net influx of financial capital and a flourishing of the stock market that would *increase*, not decrease, investment in *certain* industries.

With many distortions in place the working of this mechanism becomes extremely unpredictable so the corrections of distortions by the operation of free markets and the elimination of monetary interventions become of immense importance. A commitment to low inflation, in practice, does not have any value if it is not accompanied by more competitive conditions and the liberalization in banking and financial markets. By the textbook interpretation the commitment to low interest rates should have been a recipe for raging inflation but this symmetrical argument seems to be ignored conveniently by those who think that higher interest rates would cause a recession! There is no way out of this vicious circle unless interest rates are let free to be determined *in the whole constellation of markets* that simultaneously enter into their determination through the working of supply and demand.

As Bagus (2012) writes:

> Even though we have not seen a pure tragedy of the commons in the Eurosystem, we have come close. With the current crisis, we are actually getting closer due to the ECB's direct buying of government bonds: the ECB announced the direct purchase of the bonds in May of 2010 to save the Euro project (Bagus 2012, p. 107, footnote 23 eliminated).

In fact, to proceed as if the "tragedy of the commons" were correct, one would have to ignore that the larger part of the unsustainable debt has been *historically* accumulated. To ask for settlements and provisions to be made in advance of the adoption of Euro, one would have to have the European governments listing all the possible causes of disruption and "failures" of the Euro, and eliminate them by means of legislation. That would, of course, be a real tragedy.

Despite the "tragedy of commons" interpretation and the political interpretation of the Euro that has been provided by Bagus (2012), and despite the view that Euro could be defended on the grounds of the inefficient European bureaucratic process that must precede every decision, the defense of the Euro must rest, as we have analyzed, on entirely different grounds. Undoubtedly, the way to the Euro has been a political process and many of the views taken up in Bagus (2012) could be true. The mere fact, however, that there has been almost fifteen years between the fall of the Berlin Wall and the adoption of the Euro, makes one wonder how can it be that the German unification was a price to be paid for the common currency—which, by the way, could have been to the best interests of the German ruling class as Bagus (2012) pointed out.

> [T]he tragedy of the commons comes into play. The effects of reckless Greek fiscal behavior could partly be externalized to other members of the EMU as the ECB accepted Greek government bonds as collateral for their lending operations. European banks would buy Greek government bonds (always paying a premium in comparison with German bonds) and use these bonds to receive a loan from the ECB at a lower interest rate (at one percent interest in a highly profitable deal). Banks bought the Greek bonds because they knew that the ECB would accept these bonds as collateral for new loans. There was a demand for these Greek bonds because the interest rate paid to the ECB was lower than the interest the banks received from the Greek government. Without the acceptance of Greek bonds by the ECB as collateral for its loans, Greece would have had to pay much higher interest rates. In fact, the Greek government has been bailed out or supported by the rest of the EMU in a tragedy of the commons for a long time (Bagus 2012, p. 111).

Now, incidentally, this line of argument can be used to show that the debt crisis has nothing, or very little, to do with the disruption of the financial system that followed the sub-prime crisis. Therefore, a "profitable deal" (the speculation on debt by the European commercial banks) could have been used to make up for the losses due to malinvestment and the increase of non-performing loans. In this argument it, correctly, the European Central Bank that is blamed for everything. But what would have been, precisely, the second best? Bilateral settlements and rescheduling of the Southern debts with the intermediation of a "neutral institution" as in the Latin American debt crisis. However, the same effect could have been achieved, mainly for political reasons, by the supervision of the European Central Bank.

The "tragedy of the commons" is far too simple to be used as an actual explanation. To solve the classical "tragedy of the commons" we need the allocation of property rights. In the context of a monetary union there are no property rights to allocate since they have been given up in favor of the common currency except the *historically* accumulated debts which could have been accommodated if it were not for fiscally reckless behavior. However, this is not the whole story. The credit ease which boosted consumption in the South, along with malinvestment, should have resulted in higher tax revenues through direct and indirect taxes. But in fact tax revenues deteriorated—presumably due to corruption, tax evasion, etc. *This was, actually, not only the result of primary deficits but also, and more importantly, the result of liquidation of investment and employment* that was artificially generated by the credit expansion. The subsequent collapse of consumption was the result of the liquidation and the re-allocation of resources that took place, and it was *followed* by the austerity measures to service the debt. We emphasized, again and again, that blending together the two, largely distinct, problems of debt and "financial instability", is erroneous and cannot result in a proper explanation of the crisis.

Sovereign debt whose interest payments are imposed on others via "free riding" or "tragedy of the commons" would have been, indeed, inadmissible and even morally incorrect. But in reality the bailout financing schemes facilitated the short-run operating expenses of the Southern governments; there was, in no way, a direct repayment scheme involved; and, finally, the funds were *loans* that should be accommodated in the future. To bring in the notion of the "tragedy of the commons" here involves a fallacy, in that we have to ignore the effects of the credit expansion which were manifested precisely where the Austrian School's analysis predicts them to manifest; the less capital-intensive sectors of the South. Without the credit expansion the debt problems could not have possibly manifest at the *precise* moment when the sum-prime crisis occurred. This must indicate something but this is *not* lower tax revenues due to eroding demand from an "exogenous shock". It is the accumulation of non-performing loans by the banking sector, the *adjustment of the distribution of production* that has to take place as an effect of the credit expansion, and the *adjustment of the distribution of demand* that must result from the re-allocation of employment and investment across the Southern economic sectors, and the European Union as a whole.

A unified Europe was the vision of many in the aftermath of the cataclysmic Second World War. Trade agreements, the European Union and, finally, the adoption of the Euro, mark a long process of the eventual political unification of Europe. There is nothing wrong with this vision at all—or at least it is a political matter that should be left to the peoples of Europe to decide for themselves. That this process of unification necessarily leads to Socialism is, at best, an option that exists today all over the world—if by Socialism we mean, of course, more power for the State instead of the markets. Although it is easy for a central authority to make the wrong decisions it is equally easy to make the correct decisions. It is of critical importance that by reducing its intervention the State does not, in the present social, economic and historical circumstances undermine its own foundation. In fact it enhances its authority because there are other ways to increase its authority even when the public sector is considerably reduced.

It is, therefore, not inconceivable that the State will actually decrease considerably public expenditures and taxes—and, in fact, that is what it should do. However, the road to serfdom is not exclusively, through the economy in this era.

The road to serfdom should be fought by political means and in the political arena, along of course with the drastic reduction of the role of government in economic affairs. This includes central banking, which is a classical prescription of the Austrian School. What is the "second best" if central banking cannot be abolished altogether? The minimal involvement in the supply of money and in the determination of the rate of interest. The argument against the Euro seems to be that it is better to have a constellation of national decisions and national distortions—that operate unpredictably on the global level—rather than have a single monetary union and a Commission where such decisions are made.

The argument would have some merit under a system of competitively operating currencies but, in practice, it is well known that every national government would find it advantageous to follow inflationary policies, devaluations etc. Devaluation becomes impossible under a common currency and this is not ignored by the opponents of the Euro. What they seem to suggest is that there is still room for national manipulation of the common currency through deficits and debt. This is, indeed, correct but it is highly unlikely that the Eurozone will not revise the Treaty of Maastricht accordingly. Moreover, it is hard to see why national governments will not agree on a concerted decrease of expenditures and taxes to restore a more correct distribution of resources. This is particularly true when it will become evident that the massive banking bailout programme will need other conditions to work properly. These conditions lead, precisely, to more competitive banking and less involvement of the European Central Bank in the monetary, credit and financial affairs.

If the reduction of public sectors is, indeed, an honorable cause and a reasonable policy recommendation then it follows that this can be performed in a concerted manner, *on the European level*, rather than on the national level. What might seem like a road to serfdom can be the road to liberty and enhancement of democratic processes. It is, of course, difficult, but it is equally difficult to adopt any of the sound prescriptions of the Austrian School on the *national* level. It takes time and it is a process whose correctness has to be tested in the light of facts rather than an issue to be settled by theoretical argument and academic discussion.

References

Bagus P (2012) The tragedy of the Euro. Mises institute, Auburn
Hoppe H-H (1990) Marxist and Austrian class analysis. J Libertarian Stud 9(2):79–93

Chapter 33
Banking Efficiency

Without the European Central Bank's ability to divert massive resources to banking and produce a tremendous distortion, in addition to the one that led to it through maintaining artificially low interest rates, there would be little reason to worry about stability in the banking and financial intermediation sectors. Let us first examine the mechanism by which the banking sector responded to the chain of events that unfolded in the aftermath of the sub-prime crisis. The increase in non-performing loans caused for additional measures taken by the measures to maintain their solvency and profitability. The first such measure can be found in cost-savings which operates through two channels, namely technical efficiency and allocative efficiency.

Technical efficiency is the capacity to produce more with the given inputs, *ceteris paribus*. Allocative efficiency is the capacity to re-allocate resources in a bank or across the banking sector so that relative prices better reflect the opportunity costs of the inputs. We can assume that inputs involve capital, labor and deposits while outputs various kinds of loans, for example indexed by the time-distribution of the uses of capital from more time-consuming and capital-intensive to less time-consuming and less capital-intensive uses. In its operation, any bank faces more constraints than those of the technology; in a given institutional environment these constraints relate inputs, outputs and relative prices in complicated ways. In effect, each bank faces different relative prices of inputs compared to the observed configuration and uses these "shadow" or effective relative prices to make its decisions.

Under cost minimization the configuration of loans can be taken as given. During a crisis and a given amount of losses resulting from this configuration, cost savings can be realized by increasing technical efficiency, allocative efficiency or both. Increasing technical efficiency means a reduction of inputs to achieve the same configuration of outputs that results in net savings. In normal times it is possible for a bank to forego these savings in exchange for a dominant position in the market, known as the Quiet Life Hypothesis. If all banks operate strategically in this way then artificial barriers to entry are created and market power can be secured and it changes in relative terms inside the banking industry.

E. G. Tsionas, *The Euro and International Financial Stability*,
Financial and Monetary Policy Studies 37, DOI: 10.1007/978-3-319-01171-4_33,

Increasing allocative efficiency to yield cost-savings is possible but more involved. First, it can be done via re-allocations of the inputs of production across the financial intermediation sector that results in changes of relative prices through the shifts of the demand curves for these inputs. Second, it can be affected by a change in relative price of deposits relative to effective loan rates—that is the rates of return on the various kinds of loans *ex post*, after non-performing loans have been identified as such. Therefore, it is easier to capitalize on cost-savings via technical rather than allocative inefficiency. This will induce a change in overall market power as well as in relative dominant positions in the banking industry. The result on allocative inefficiency can take some time to complete since it requires a re-distribution of resources, for example deposits, across the banking sector. Once it is completed further cost-savings can be realized to produce a "buffer stock" against the effect of non-performing loans and the deterioration in profitability.

Artificially low loan rates, which were created by the "cheap credit" or "easy money" policies of the European Central Bank have resulted in a systematic distortion of relative prices. When some of the projects that were financed by the banking sector failed to be profitable, since the distribution of demand has not changed considerably, effective loan rates were systematically lower to what has been expected. In the short-run this should result in lower allocative efficiency but higher technical efficiency if banks resort to cost-savings from the "fat" that they use to maintain dominant position—technical efficiency that is. The sub-prime crisis showed that these cost-savings were not enough and a bailout programme has been used by the European Central Bank amounting to almost 3.77 trillion euro. The programme rescued the profitability of the commercial banking sector. What were the implications? We can only theorize about the relevant issues as follows.

(1) The bailout programme should provide less motivation for banks to increase technical efficiency and direct cost-savings. However, for some banks, technical efficiency should have increased before the introduction of the bailouts. Therefore, in the short-run, technical efficiency should increase at least for some banks. In the long-run if technical efficiency increases, it means that commercial banks try to use systematically their cost-savings to improve their financial position. If not, it means that they rely more on the bailouts and the "stable" environment that it creates to regain market power by *decreasing* technical efficiency in the "steady-state".
(2) Since the distortion in effective loan rates relative to deposit rates is persistent, and is maintained by the low interest rate policy of the European Central Bank, short-run allocative efficiency is *likely* to increase as cost-savings are urgently sought. It *may* deteriorate in the long-run as these savings are not necessary anymore in view of the backing provided by the European Central Bank. In that case, the re-allocation of resources does not result in an efficient outcome, relative to the present situation.

The short-run increase of allocative efficiency *may* obtain through the higher loan rates that can be secured, *effectively*, by the intervention of the European Central Bank and the capitalization of returns on projects that were actually successful. The possibility depends on the past investment decisions of the banks and the risk-return configuration or profiles for different banks.

In the banking literature the relationship between competition, market power and efficiency (technical, in all cases examined) is quite ambiguous. Three competing hypotheses are: The Quiet Life Hypothesis, the Market Structure Hypothesis and the Information Generation Hypothesis. According to the Quiet Life Hypothesis, bank's market power determines efficiency (Berger and Hannan 1998; Maudos and Fernández de Guevara 2007). Banks that possess market power may forego some of their monopoly rents in return for inefficiencies, i.e. a "quiet life". This leads to higher concentration, and thus to higher profits of incumbents. Hence, bank efficiency determines market structure. In contrast, the Market Structure Hypothesis posits a reverse causality: The most efficient banks acquire market shares (Demsetz 1973; Peltzman 1977). This leads to higher concentration, and thus to higher profits of incumbents. Hence, bank efficiency determines market structure.

Marquez (2002) showed that more competition among banks can lead to lower efficiency. This Information Generating Hypothesis depends on the function of banks to minimize adverse borrower selection due to superior information generating capabilities relative to other intermediaries:

> If competition increases, larger numbers of smaller banks, with lower knowledge of the market as a whole compared to larger banks, have worse abilities to screen borrowing firms. Likewise, if customers can switch increasingly easy due to lower costs, crucial information gathering capabilities of banks erode. Both effects imply inefficiencies for banks due to a higher likelihood of adverse selection of low quality borrowers (Bosma et al. 2012).

For a given level of competition, technical efficiency and market power seem to be intimately related. Causality and correlation between the two will determine whether the Quiet Life or the Market Structure hypothesis is more plausible. However, in the "steady state" it is quite likely that technical inefficiency will persist. According to the Market Structure Hypothesis it is conceivable that by increasing technical efficiency beyond a certain level cannot increase dominant position significantly. According to the Quiet Life Hypothesis, banks may look for a "quiet life" (cost inefficiency) since increasing and monitoring cost efficiency is costly, and requires resources. The price of "quiet life" comes at foregone revenues and marker power. Indeed, Hughes et al. (2003), suggest banks possessing market power might forego some of their profits dimension to pursue or accommodate alternative objectives. Clearly, the Quiet Life Hypothesis can be rejected if one finds increasing margins between price and marginal costs when cost and profit efficiency increases.

Since there is non-trivial technical inefficiency in the "steady state", some of the cost-savings can be recovered during the recession when profitability is eroded.

Therefore, in the short-run banks are likely to become more technically efficient unless they can rely on other means to recover. In the long-run there may be a tendency to revert back to old levels of technical inefficiency; unless their efforts to improve technical efficiency take time and the use of real resources: In that case it will not be possible to improve technical efficiency in the short-run but only in the long run. This would imply that less "quiet life" should be accepted in the long-run as projected from the current evidence, *ceteris paribus*.

It is also conceivable that allocative efficiency improves in the short-run (if effective loan rates are increased due to the bailouts and the particular investment decisions of certain banks in the past). This will make available another source of funding in the short-run to cope with the adverse effects of the financial crisis. However, what happens in the long-run is a different issue. If indeed it was for the investment decisions of certain banks in the past we would expect that allocative efficiency increases in the long-run but if was due to the bailouts, long-run efficiency should deteriorate, *ceteris paribus*.

Certainly, a bailout programme is *expected* to increase cost efficiency in the short-run and in the long-run, otherwise it is pointless. If that is, indeed, the case we should also expect less competition due to mergers and acquisitions and the Market Structure Hypothesis. But then the banks would be motivated to revert back to "quiet life" and technical efficiency could decrease. This presupposes that profitability of banks has recovered and they operate in a more or less safer and sounder economic environment. According to the Information Generating Hypothesis, we should also expect better monitoring and more rational decision making on the part of the banks which would result in higher cost efficiency. The combined effect is, of course, unclear in (what might be called) the long-run level of technical efficiency.

The other source of complication, besides the above argument which is really a combination of all three hypotheses, comes from the channel through which cost-savings can be recovered; that is through technical efficiency, allocative efficiency, or both. Improvements in technical efficiency seem to require some time as they call for monitoring and re-allocation of resources. Allocative efficiency, on the other hand, operates swiftly through the change of relative prices and it reflects, more or less, directly on cost efficiency. Increasing distortions in relative prices will yield reductions in allocative efficiency. The relative prices of interest, under the assumption of cost minimization, are deposit rates and the price of capital, along with the prices of other variable inputs. If deposit rates are effectively higher during the depression, this creates a persistent distortion which will increase allocative efficiency in the short-run because it brings interest rates closer to equilibrium.

At the same time we may have the opposite effect if effective deposit rates adjust downwards. In fact since deposit rates do not reflect the price of risk they can adjust downwards, in the effective sense, when it is not likely that savings can obtain a higher rate of return in Europe. There, may, of course be a "flight from deposits" from the countries in distress in banks of other countries. Since deposit rates adjust in a direction opposite to that of equilibrium a distortion with negative effects on allocative efficiency in created which is, however, to be contrasted with a reduction of costs since deposits are treated as inputs. In that case the final effect is ambiguous.

On the profit side, all effects from cost that we have described remain intact. There are additional considerations in this case; namely that effective loan rates have been adjusted in the course of the depression that has caused the liquidation and non-performance of certain investments that were financed by the commercial banking sector. Of course some projects may have been quite successful and so certain banks may find themselves in a less distressed situation. But for the most part effective loan rates would have to be lower, at least on the average. There are now less profits to be sacrificed in return for a "quiet life"—a consideration that *may* reflect on higher technical efficiency along with a reconfiguration of the optimal portfolios. The bailout programme, in essence, distorts the constellations of relative loan rates by increasing them across the board—a distortion that will reflect positively on profit efficiency. But at the same time it adjusts effective deposit rates downwards if these rates did not change due to other reasons. Although there is a tendency for interest rates to increase, this is offset, partially at least, by the rates on the deposit side. Through time, the commercial banks might be able to recover part or the entire capital that they provided to the private sector thus reinforcing tendency for loan interest rates to increase and improve allocative efficiency on the profit side.

However, much depends on the future decisions of the banks. In turn, this also depends on the financing needs of the specific sectors of the economy that are driven first out of the recession. These sectors can only be in the consumer-goods sector with low capital intensity since the policy of low interest rates has liquidated a large part of the capital stock in the capital-intensive sectors. Accounting for risk and expectations of the commercial banks, these sectors will have to borrow at higher, effective, interest rates increasing their costs and the prices. Some self-selection will also take place as firms realize that any possible increase of demand in still fragile and they do not wish to finance operating expenses entirely through borrowed funds. The extent of borrowing and the effective increase of rates will depend on the extent of increases in demand and commodity prices in the less capital-intensive sector. However, the working back of this effect in the time-distribution of capital will be extremely fragile and limited in view of the experience of the recession. As the banking sector begins to charge higher interest rates the "working-back" effect will become quite limited and it likely that the consumer-goods sector will remain to support the commercial banks.

The strong recovery of demand that would reinstate the equilibrium in the economy *depends entirely on changes in the distribution of incomes and demand.* This change will induce, subsequently, a conformable change in the distribution of capital and production that will take considerable time to complete. If demand continues to decline for some time, its redistribution towards the less capital-intensive consumer-goods sectors cannot result in price decreases; the cost of working capital in these industries becomes now higher, due to the developments and adjustments in the banking sector but can be sustained by the increased profitability.

Therefore, for quite some time, the commercial banks will have to depend on the consumer-goods sector but also on the exporting sectors which gain a competitive advantage due to the significant depression of prices in the domestic market. An "exports led" growth is quite fragile as well. Although certain firms and sectors gained a competitive advantage this will disappear, if productivity remains unchanged, when they will have to increase prices due to lack of capacity. Of course they can expand, and the banks may even find it worthwhile to finance their expansion, but without a permanent increase in productivity, expansion of capacity by itself cannot maintain the relative, temporary gain of position in the international markets—unless, of course, there are massive returns to scale.

We have mentioned that the main function of the bailout is to increase artificially the loan rates (or the "return-on-assets"). On the other hand, we may consider, instead, that it lowers operating expenses through a temporary change in the input prices. Apparently this will not be sufficient for the recovery of profitability in the immediate future and such banks need to engage in mergers and acquisitions or simply leave the market, unless these banks continue to be part of a rescue programme. For the banking sector as a whole, the question becomes whether the temporary increase of their *effective* output prices (which are effective loan rates) can improve, indeed, financial stability. This intervention is artificial, in the sense that losses are covered and loan rates on profitable investments become higher. Actual interest rates on existing loans do not adjust and instead interest revenue is re-calculated on a smaller amount of outstanding loans. It is not even certain that performing loans will continue to be so in the future and, of course, it is highly uncertain what is the proportion of non-performing loans that will, actually, perform and what extent. However, it is clear that if profitability of investments does not vary greatly then the bailout programme would have succeeded in maintaining higher effective rates of return. Clearly, *allocative efficiency should fluctuate more than technical efficiency*, apart from secondary effects arising from the monitoring and reclaim of non-performing loans through special arrangements.

It is also clear, however, that the continuation of a bailout programme and the "supervision of financial stability" come at an increasing cost for society. If a firm that makes losses is subsidized in the form of insurance for the part of output that does not perform, *the insurance risk premium should increase* and, as long as demand remains fragile, it must be reflected on the price. If not, then the amount has to be subtracted from total demand which will be re-distributed throughout the economy. Evidently, this will more than offset the temporary positive effects on output and employment from malinvestment that took place but is now liquidating. But in the bailout programme there is no such thing as insurance risk premium to make up for the losses of the past: Since prices cannot adjust to reflect higher risk the effect will be mostly quantitative. In turn this cannot but affect the marginally profitable investments thus threatening further stability via the fluctuations of allocative efficiency which are now affected by both price and quantity effects. *This cycle is likely to yield a stable "steady state" at which, however, allocative and probably technical efficiency as well, will be lower.*

Since the bailout programme is, essentially, a direct intervention in the price mechanism for market clearing in the financial sector, it will create distortions and disequilibria that are hard to correct. Despite the fact that effective loan rates are higher, it would not be rational for a bank (a) to maintain the same rates for marginally profitable investments, and (b) charge the same rate to loans for a similar firm in the same sector. In the latter case such investments would not be financed at all. In the first case, closer monitoring would be required to figure out the real "margin" which is, however, impossible to calculate *ex ante*. The standard argument is that expected profitability and its variance are what matters but during the recession the deviation between risk-adjusted expected returns and actual returns can be substantial—implying that it is no comfort to have "rational" decision making that results in actual losses. What is needed is an increase of loan rates across the board *even for outstanding loans*. In a sense this is a shifting of the burden to good investment, unless we keep in mind that almost ideal investments of the past now turned out to be just good (or even non-performing for that matter). Since an outright violation of the terms of contracts is not conceivable, loans that are considered marginal should be sold to other banks that are willing to take the risk or have better "information gathering" and monitoring capabilities. This would create a secondary market in which such loans could be traded individually or as part of a portfolio. Relative to closing down, this would be a second best for banks that cannot operate after the initial bailout programme. The concern is, of course, that an initial bailout programme can be followed by a second, which would set in motion further re-distributions of resources not only in banking but in the economy as a whole.

At any rate, competition must be restored in the financial intermediation sector if what is sought is truly financial stability. Since the bailouts are likely, as we have analyzed, to result in lower overall cost efficiency for the commercial banks, their temporary short-run effects will yield long-run losses for the banks and the society as a whole. The quest for free banking is afoot!

The previous analysis rests on the assumption that commercial banking operates along the conventional or neoclassical financial-intermediation paradigm. In fact this is a distorted view of how banks actually operate:

> As Mises correctly indicates, as long as confidence in the bank is preserved, the bank will be able to continue using the majority of deposited funds, and customers will remain unaware that the bank lacks the necessary liquidity to meet all of its commitments. It is as if the bank had found a permanent source of financing in the creation of new money, a source it will continue to tap as long as the public retains its faith in the bank's ability to fulfill its commitments. In fact, as long as these circumstances last, the bank will even be able to use its newly created liquidity for covering its own expenses or for any other purpose besides granting loans. In short, the ability to create money *ex nihilo* generates wealth the banker can easily appropriate, provided customers do not doubt his good conduct. The generation of this wealth is detrimental to many third parties, each of whom suffers a share of the damage caused by the banker's activities. It is impossible to identify these individuals, and they are unlikely to recognize the harm they suffer or to discover the identity of the perpetrator (de Soto 2009, p. 191).

The process becomes most evident if we consider merely the fact that checking accounts can expand considerably *ex nihilo* resulting in non-performing loans during the downturn of the business cycle. The key element is that, for the banking sector as a whole, although effectively new money is created, this does not correspond to savings. The allocative efficiency issue becomes much more important in this respect and it is related directly to a disagreement between savings and investment which results in considerable differences between the distribution of consumption and the distribution of resources among the different uses. The ability of banks to "create deposits" in this manner depends crucially on their attraction of new customers (which explains why negative margins can persist) but also on the proportion of loans granted which, on average, remain unused by borrowers at any given time (which de Soto calls k). With a negative premium between deposit and loan rates the bank can only make profits in the sense that funds plus interest remain in the bank and are not immediately on demand by the depositors. This "inertia" of the savers generates a temporary source of funds that can be used at will, in normal times. Of course, during a depression, a bank run can occur and, in this case, the Central Bank comes at the rescue of the commercial banks.

This "banking multiplier", originally due to Alfred Marshall, is the true generating mechanism of bank profits and shows that profits do not arise from financial intermediation but, in truth, from the savings motive of the public and the associated "inertia"—which is further reinforced by the various charges associated with early withdrawal of funds and other transaction costs imposed by the banks. It is easy to see that, even with a negative "financial intermediation" premium, the banks can generate profits even if a large portion of funds plus deposits is withdrawn. It is perfectly possible for a bank to make an 8 % profit with a margin of *minus* 3 % if 90 % of funds are withdrawn per period.[1]

Although the principle of the banking multiplier is no secret, it is not widely understood either. One neoclassical explanation of the negative premium is the Lender's Advantage which, however, ignores the fact that in the upswing of the business cycle the banks care less about monitoring the quality of investments that they finance. The large inefficiencies found in the banking sector which can range from 20 to 40 % (e.g. Berger et al. 1993) show precisely, if they are not artifacts and counterfactual, that banks indeed engage in a "Quiet Life" attitude without much concern about how deposits are transformed to good loans since, *what matters most, is not the quality of investment but rather the "inertia" of the public* which can be enforced by various ways, the least important of which is hardly the Central Bank's guarantee of savings funds.

[1] Indeed, suppose that a bank has deposits in the amount of €2,000 of which 30 % or €600 have to be retained. If the bank lends the remaining €1,400 at 7 % at the end of the period the bank has €2,098 and has to pay €2,200 if the deposit rate is 10 %. After 90 % is withdrawn the bank has to pay back €1,980 which yields of profit of 2,098–1,980 = €118 which represents a profit rate of 8.42 % over loans and 5.9 % over the original amount of deposits.

References

Berger AL, Hannan T (1998). The efficiency cost of market power in the banking industry: A test of the "quite life" and related hypothesis. Rev Econ Stat 80:454–465.

Berger AN, William H, Stephen T (1993) The efficiency of financial institutions: a review and preview of research past, present, and future. J Bank Finance 17:221–249

Bosma J, Koetter M, Wedow M (2012) Credit risk connectivity in the financial industry and stabilization effects of government bailouts. Discussion Papers 16/2012, Deutsche Bundesbank, Research Centre

Demsetz H (1973) Industry structure, market rivalry and public policy. J Law Econ 16:1–9

Hughes JP, Lang WW, Mester LJ, Moon C-G, Pagano MS (2003) Do bankers sacrifice values to build empires? Managerial incentives, industry consolidation, and financial performance. J Bank Finance 27:417–447

Marquez R (2002) Competition, adverse selection, and information dispersion in the banking industry. Rev Financial Stud 15:901–926

Maudos J, Fernández de Guevara J (2007) The cost of market power in banking: Social welfare loss vs. cost inefficiency. J Bank Finance 31:2103–2135

Peltzman S (1977) The gains and losses from industrial concentration. J Law Econ 20:229–263

de Soto JH (2009) Money, bank credit, and economic cycles, 2nd edn. Mises Institute, Auburn

Chapter 34
Banking and Regulation

As de Soto wrote:

> It is not possible to theorize a priori about the future evolution of money. Our theoretical analysis must be limited to the observation that money is an institution which emerges spontaneously, like law, language, and other legal and economic institutions which involve an enormous volume of information and appear in an evolutionary manner throughout a very prolonged period of time in which many generations of human beings participate. Moreover, as with language, certain institutions which in the social process of trial and error best fulfill their function tend to predominate. Trial alone, throughout the spontaneous, evolutionary market process, can lead to the predominance of those institutions most conducive to social cooperation, without the possession by any one person or group of the intelligence and information necessary to create these types of institutions *ex novo* (de Soto 2009, p. 737).

The same is true for banking, credit, financial intermediation and, indeed, most human institutions. It is likely that, in the absence of frictions, certain types of mutual funds will emerge which will, in part, replace traditional commercial banking (de Soto 2009, pp. 774–775). Commercial banking, by itself, is not likely to embark on a route of 100-percent reserve requirements or more thoughtful decisions, as long as there is the backing of a Central Bank. From that point of view, the existence of an all-powerful Central Bank is a fundamental friction. Abuse of power, in the form of more or less arbitrary credit expansions and low interest rates, becomes always possible. Since the Central Bank is not accountable and is prone to collusion with the government and accommodation of its policies, we must either abolish the Central Bank or determine a more detailed framework of operation which reinforces accountability and responsibility—if we wish to be practical.

The *modus operandi* of the Central Bank should be revised in accordance with coherent governance, decentralization of most of its authorities, and enforcement of competition in the financial intermediation sector. The supervisory role of the Central Bank must be put in the context of ensuring 100-percent or nearly 100-percent reserve requirements by the commercial banks. The essential elements of 100-percent reserve are two: *First*, banks should hold an amount of cash equal to

E. G. Tsionas, *The Euro and International Financial Stability*,
Financial and Monetary Policy Studies 37, DOI: 10.1007/978-3-319-01171-4_34,

the total value of deposits, checking accounts and bills in circulation. *Second*, the sum of the bills in circulation, together with the amount corresponding to deposits and checking accounts, cannot exceed the total of the cash reserves held by all banks at any given moment (de Soto 2009, p. 741). The requirements imply jointly that money in the wide sense cannot exceed the amount of money-in-circulation (including checks) and the amount of credit. Therefore, at any given moments, credit expansion is not possible beyond what is justified by the increase of savings.

The complication arising from central banking is that:

> [I]f the central bank continues to be responsible for the issuance of purely fiduciary money, there will never be any guarantee that this institution, via open-market operations on the stock exchange, could not temporarily and artificially reduce interest rates and inject capital markets with artificial liquidity which, in the end, would exert exactly the same discoordinating effects on the productive structure as credit expansion initiated by private banks without the backing of real savings (de Soto 2009, p. 747).

In that way, it would appear conceivable that the Central Bank *could* be limited in terms of its open-market operations. In the context of coherent governance this cannot be guaranteed, except on legal and political grounds, and new legal and institutional framework that would prevent the Central Bank from engaging in such operations which affect directly the interest rates. However, it cannot also be guaranteed that commercial banks will observe the law in term of 100-percent reserves. This becomes the responsibility of the Central Bank which, in turn, *must* enforce the rule. Clearly, the Central Bank *could* violate the rule so that it could engage in the *equivalent* of open-market operations. The argument that in the long-run institutions that disobey the law will have to go bankrupt is, of course, less comfort and so is the fact that commercial banks must be monitored in order to have an incentive to follow the law.

The argument that the fractional-reserve system has led, historically and in essence, to the necessity of a Central Bank is beyond doubt. First, in the form of a "clearing house" for commercial banks, and second as a lender of last resort (e.g. Goodhart 1990, pp. 85–103). Although the idea of a "clearing house" would work against a specific bank that would try to increase credit beyond its savings, if *all* banks engaged in the same operation, the idea would fail. Therefore, it must be left to the Central Bank to legalize transactions that would be, otherwise, inconceivable in a market economy. But if the argument is correct in its entirety and without any qualifications then it would follow that without a Central Bank a system of 100-percent requirements would follow. The argument is certainly correct after a period of adjustment is allowed for, during which the public can figure out which banks are credible and which are not. Thus, the abolition of the Central Bank must follow a similar historical path to re-establish the commercial banking system from scratch.

There is little disagreement that a system where a 100-percent reserves requirement and a Central Bank coexist, produces less distortion. As de Soto points out, however:

> Nevertheless we cannot conclude that all discoordination generated by the central bank would disappear, since the mere existence of the central bank and its reliance on systematic coercion (the imposition of legal-tender regulations and a set monetary policy) would still have a damaging effect on the processes of social coordination (de Soto 2009, p. 662).

That is, of course, true unless the Central Bank can be made accountable not to engage in open-market operations or expand and decrease credit artificially in the interests of "economic policy". A Central Bank along with a fractional reserve system will have to produce significant distortions in relative prices without being able to restore the correspondence between the distribution of consumption and the distribution of capital and production. This is an implication of the classical Misesian Theorem on the impossibility of central planning. But even in a 100-percent reserve requirement system the Central Bank or some other authority are required to supervise the commercial banks and examine whether they conform to the rule. *This is, unfortunately, equally impossible by the same theorem.* It is certainly true that:

> [E]ven if the central bank did not compound its errors through a fractional-reserve banking system, it would still face the constant risk of succumbing to pressure from politicians and lobbyists eager to take advantage of the central bank's power in order to accomplish the political goals deemed most appropriate at any particular moment (de Soto 2009, p. 663).

If there exists a political framework in which the Central Bank could not easily succumb to pressure, then there would be no problem. The question then becomes one of political accountability of the Central Bank given that a legal system is in place to forbid monetary expansions or contractions and open-market operations that affect the rate of interest. In this framework, if the Central Bank can, indeed, supervise effectively the commercial banks not to expand credit beyond savings and observe the 100-percent requirement, then the problem would be solved. However, *it is impossible for a Central Bank to supervise all banks and accounts at each and every moment*. This central planning task would be impossible to perform even for a relatively small country with a less well—developed banking sector along with the other financial intermediaries that act in the same role. Therefore, these tasks have to be left to the market:

"Thus it is *conceivable* that in a free-banking system, isolated attempts to expand bank credit would be curbed *relatively* quickly and spontaneously by customers' vigilance toward banks' operations and solvency, the constant reassessment of the trust placed in banks, and, *more than anything, the effect of interbank clearing houses*. In fact any isolated bank expanding its credit *faster than the sector average* or issuing notes *more rapidly than most* would see the volume of its reserves drop quickly, *due to interbank clearing mechanisms*, and the banker would be forced to halt expansion to avoid a suspension of payments, and eventually, failure" (de Soto 2009, p. 665, emphasis added).

Of course, the free-banking system is qualified and its defense rests not only on the "constant reassessment of the trust placed in banks" by the consumers but by the bank clearing house as well. If all banks engaged in expansion no one bank would deviate from the "average" yet inflation would result with all the well-known adverse effects on the distribution of resources. Similarly, it is not practical to introduce a system of privately issued fiat money on the grounds that "constant reassessment of the trust" by the public and the market would, *eventually*, select the best types of money. Apparently there has been, historically, no point in Central Banking without relying on commercial banks to artificially deviate from 100-percent rules and the opposite: Banks are willing to cooperate with a Central Bank or "clearing house" that is willing to ignore the deviations. And it is, precisely, these deviations that are found to be "profitable" to accommodate on the aggregate level by the Central Bank.

The constant reassessment of risk in "risk-free" deposits by the consumers would add an unnecessary element of cost in transactions and it is an idea that can hardly be accepted. The idea of an independent Central Bank which is, however, accountable to the public seems to be well associated with a 100-percent reserves requirement even under a gold standard. It does not mean that the Central Bank or any other institution can supervise commercial banks at each and every moment or even at a fixed date once per year. There are many motives to deviate from the rule or engage in a cartel which acts in a more or less orchestrated way. It is then the responsibility of the Central Bank to intervene and supervise the normal functioning of the system. This cannot be done unless the Central Bank and other political authorities realize that it is not desirable, eventually, to engage in artificial monetary or fiscal policies. If the system of a legally bound Central Bank can operate for a certain time it can create the historical conditions under which free markets in financial intermediation can operate easily and efficiently. It is not impossible for gold to emerge as a monetary standard once again to ensure easily calculable and easily predictable purchasing power of money. It is also not impossible for other artificial standards to emerge if we allow for a whole historical period during which the public will get accustomed to the new standard. However, it is inconceivable for any system to work or emerge unless the government and the political authorities are educated in the idea that systematic interventions in the economy create distortions which, eventually, turn out to have worse consequences compared to the problem they wish to treat.

To the extent that a banking "clearing house" is another cartel or, merely, an authority that cannot effectively engage in all detailed calculations and verifications that are required to establish the solvency of the commercial banking sector in a system operating under 100-percent reserve requirements, it is quite regrettable that it cannot work. It requires a long historical period to unfold and develop, it requires supervision, considerable calculations and controls, it requires considerable enforcement and, finally, it does require a Central Bank if it is to be reliable and acquire the confidence of the public, contrary to the arguments of the strict adherents of abolishing the Central Bank. However, the Central Bank we have in mind here is not quite the Central Bank with all its power and control over the money supply. Indeed, in a system operating under 100-percent reserve requirements, *the responsibility of the Central Bank is to enforce a legal and institutional framework and commit legally to what amounts to a gold standard.*

The purpose of the system is to reduce the operations of the Central Bank to the level that citizens with average education and familiarity with business transactions and operations, can understand and, in effect, supervise as members of a Monetary Committee that could be selected as jury duty is assigned in every-day life. We can see no other way in the vicious circle generated by 100-percent reserve banking and the need for a "clearing house" and, at its first stages, even implementing this practice is not without some obvious problems but at the end, a society has to rely on its citizens to perform their duties. As von Mises put it:

"Everyone carries a part of society on his shoulders; no one is relieved of his share of responsibility by others. And no one can find a safe way out for himself if society is sweeping towards destruction. Therefore everyone, in his own interests, must thrust himself vigorously into the intellectual battle. None can stand aside with unconcern; the interests of everyone hang on the result. Whether he chooses or not, every man is drawn into the great historical struggle, the decisive battle into which our epoch has plunged us" (von Mises 1951).

References

de Soto JH (2009) Money, bank credit, and economic cycles, 2nd, edn. Mises Institute, Auburn
Goodhart C (1990) The evolution of central banks, 2nd ed. MIT Press, Cambridge
von Mises L (1951) Socialism. Yale University Press, New Haven, p. 515

Chapter 35
Policy and Institutional Change in Southern Europe

Voices are mounting in the South of Europe that servicing the public debt is unsustainable and to avoid the "counter-productive" austerity measures it is necessary to have another generous haircut accompanied with rescheduling of interest payments. The concern of the ECB and the IMF is that extensions of this sort implied by rescheduling will be used exclusively to avoid cutting expenditures and sustaining various inefficiencies in the public sector and, primarily, in rationalizing the tax revenue collection system. The concern of Southern governments and Greece in particular, is that the austerity measures reinforce the deep recession (of the order of negative 7–5 % growth rates according to various forecasts).

The concern of governments can be addressed by cutting on tax revenues, not increasing them in a mindless manner. According to some, tax revenues that cannot be collected currently amount to almost €14 billion euro and this does not include tax evasion but only outstanding taxes. Cutting tax revenues is, for the most part, effective in reversing the depression in one or 2 years, but this clearly has as precondition the increase of efficiency in tax collection and a re-structuring of the Revenue Service: An immediate policy measure in this direction can be the re-allocation of resources and the reduction in bureaucracy. One example is that a sizeable part of civil servants in the Revenue Service are employed in transactions with the public—transactions which can, however, be performed through the commercial banks.

To offset the adverse effects of tax evasion and impose taxes that are, for the most part, flat is an overall sensible policy to the extent that tax evasion cannot be addressed directly and efficiently in the short-run. There is no question that it must be reduced in the medium-term and that this reduction requires a complete re-structuring of the Revenue Service and the public sector. But we must not forget that tax evasion is an equilibrium phenomenon that depends on the effectiveness and probability of exercising controls and cross-checking which, in turn, cannot be accomplished by the public sectors as they are now structured.

Common sense suggests that fewer taxes are easier to collect while excessively high taxes cannot be collected at all given the worsening conditions of households and small business. This, in turn, provides the reason for the dramatic situation in revenue collection which is reinforced further by the excessive expenditures of the

E. G. Tsionas, *The Euro and International Financial Stability*,
Financial and Monetary Policy Studies 37, DOI: 10.1007/978-3-319-01171-4_35,

public sector. The cross-checking of incomes and expenditures of the private sector, at the end, cannot be effected by the state, in view of the Misesian Theorem on the impossibility of central planning. It is a task that could be left to the private sector and accountants that would be responsible for complete the tax forms. This would be one way of internalizing an externality that is induced by the inefficiency of the public sector at large and the Revenue Service in particular: The transfer of property rights from the state to the private sector—rights that can be traded, of course—and the creation of markets to eliminate the larger part of the externality.

The elimination of corruption is a noble task—so noble as democracy itself. However, in the absence of incentives, markets and property rights, so many externalities prevail that, effectively, offset any *purely political* means to eliminate corruption, in its most general sense. We have hinted previously that if citizens are allowed to perform their jury duty in important penal trials, there should in principle be no problem in also serving in important public positions for short periods of time, randomly selected from among the general population and with a reasonable but not excessive remuneration, equal perhaps to average wage rates in the economy. If they are fully accountable and there is no immunity when it comes to violations of the legislature and the code for ethical and lawful performance, then this would be *a natural way to allocate property rights in the exercise of public functions*. These functions can be, initially, restricted to control of expenditures in the various divisions of the public sector without the authority to increase taxes but solely with the authority to reduce public expenditures and increase operative efficiency.

The involvement of the Central Bank in accommodating "cheap credit" or "expensive credit" should be reduced since the adverse effects of this policy intensified, if they were not responsible, for the "secondary" phenomena of the depression and the explosion of public debt. Credit has been misallocated to the various sectors of the economy through the misdirection of resources that was caused by artificially low interest rates. Low interest rates should, "in principle", reinforce growth but between the two there is, in fact, no "aggregate" relation. Growth comes from specific industries and specific sectors and low interest rates distorts the contribution of these sectors to aggregate production resulting in malinvestment which, at first, looks as if there is considerable accumulation of capital only to find that the larger part of the new and existing investment is liquidated through the process of quantitative adjustments that will have to take place over the business cycle that will be created. The important issue cannot be whether we need low or high interest rates but at what level of interest rates the distribution of consumption and production coincide or, in other words, what level of interest rates distributes *existing* savings to activities that are in demand for real resources. This is a purely micro-economic issue to which no "aggregate" answer is appropriate or desirable.

Even with interest rates that equate aggregate investment and savings, other distortions may result in malinvestment and misdirection of productive resources. Differential taxation and a large public sector are the two primary distortions of this kind. The ability of the banking sector to create artificial "deposits" or, in effect, new money, is another major distortion that has to be taken care of legally and through re-structured national Central Banks accountable to a new European Central Bank that would operate truly on the grounds of monetary and credit stability, financial liberalization and political accountability based on a new European constitution or Chart. Coherent global governance at the level of the European Union would be the natural political and institutional framework that would enforce re-structuring of this magnitude.

If the whole discussion about austerity and debt is reduced to an antagonism between France and Germany, we are likely to miss the most important points of the EMU and the adoption of common currency, along with most other European institutions. True enough that the institutional framework, as now exists, is bureaucratic and inefficient and some even blame the Euro for the sufferings of the South. These tend to forget the fact that the expansionary policy of the European Central Bank, in terms of cheap and easy credit, nearly destroyed the weakest parts of the Union who could not recover easily through exports via the process known as "internal devaluation". Although there is a common currency it does not mean that relative prices of goods, services or resources have been equated throughout the European Union. Relative prices cannot be the same even in regions of a single country like the UK or Spain and Greece and regional comparative advantages are the engine of optimal re-allocations of resources that lie that the very heart of "aggregate growth", if there is such a thing at all. Instead of blaming the disastrous policy of artificially low interest rates, most economists tend to blame a variety of things that have nothing to do with the crisis: They blame the Euro itself, the fact that active fiscal policy should have been followed, the fact that increasing taxes constitute a "crazy policy" in the midst of a recession (which, however, pushed tax revenues down the cliff), the fact that low productivity in the South is an everlasting and God-given phenomenon, the fact that even lower interest rates must be imposed, the fact that the European Central Bank and the IMF acted as "imperialists" by imposing severe and cruel austerity measures and national independence has been lost by transforming Greece and other countries to "protectorates" etc.

Many other economists, more in line with the reality of economic affairs in Greece, blame it on the fact that there is no healthy entrepreneurship or the idea that there is not even a serious "ruling class"—a "bourgeoisie" so to speak. The ruling class, in the Austrian School's terms, consists of a group of agents in close association with the State, which derives its rents from the power of the State and the public sector itself (Hoppe 1990)—politicians, bureaucrats, contractors, capitalists who derive their business from the State etc. If we equate "bourgeoisie" to entrepreneurship it is clear that only a part of entrepreneurship is part of the ruling class and the remaining is what one might call "healthy entrepreneurship". In countries with large public sectors (most western countries, indeed) the ruling class is expected to be quite sizeable then its connections with the State operate in a feedback-like way. The ruling class derives rents or even contracts and business from the government and the opposite. Healthy entrepreneurship or "bourgeoisie" is, in effect, limited and can flourish only if the space left for its activities is considerable and can find a domestic or international market. In countries with a thin industrial structure—as the result of comparative advantage but of misdirection of resources as well—the "bourgeoisie" cannot be expected to form a significant part of ownership which engages in productive activities. In effect it has to engage in non-productive activities or become dependent on the ruling class in one way or the other, or become dependent on foreign "bourgeoisie" (*or* ruling classes) and assume a secondary role: The Greek "bourgeoisie" has been blamed for this supposed role for decades.

It is not the place here to engage in a full sociological analysis. It is worth mentioning, however, that the concept of social class is not well defined and well delineated even in Marx's writings. What Marx refers to as "class" interchangeably means class (in the usual Marxian sense that the term is used in *class struggle*, for example), group, stratum, people who exercise power in general, etc. The end of the third volume of *Capital* (Marx 1959, pp. 862–863) has been left unfinished when it began to deal with the concept of class. Ollman, interestingly, mentions:

> It is our view that the same analysis could be made of Marx's other key concepts—"class struggle," "value," "surplus value," "freedom," "labor power," "alienation," etc. Like "class," each expresses an aspect of the social reality Marx believes he uncovered, and like "class," the full meaning Marx attaches to these concepts can only be deciphered by examining how he actually uses them in his writings. All of them are equally unavailable to those who would use them to express non-Marxist views.

The proper use of the term "ruling class" in Hoppe (1990) explains two phenomena: First, why the State is, indeed, a powerful organ in the hands of the ruling class and the other way around, and second, why the uncoordinated activity of capitalists in the market cannot lead, logically, to the acting of them as a consortium of common interests, that suddenly confronts the working classes in the process of a "class struggle". The ruling class and the stratum of capitalists are two different things that emerged quite naturally from the French revolution and the industrial revolution—which gave rise to a new civil state and entrepreneurship simultaneously.

If it were not for the State, the ruling classes of the South would not exist, for practical purposes and a stratum of entrepreneurship would emerge based on comparative advantages and the domestic as well as the global constellation of relative prices. Entrepreneurship would act in a Hayek-Kirzner like manner to exploit all comparative advantages and maximize productive opportunities and, along with them, maximize "aggregate growth" or "welfare".

As entrepreneurship emerges endogenously from an institutional framework which, to different extents, allows or demotivates the formation of a powerful ruling class, in the same way this shapes up the State, the government and, therefore, the *potential for "political leadership"*. Without an extensive stratum of entrepreneurs and motives for creative entrepreneurship that constitutes the foundation for investment and growth, the ground of the ruling class is not solid: A private sector which, for the most part, derives its rents and business from the State, is detrimental to growth since it does not care about discovering new opportunities and, naturally, constitutes the large part of tax evasion and corruption. Capable political leadership cannot exist with a strong ruling class, in a small country. In vast nations with considerable resources and military power, effective leadership becomes less of a problem although it continues to hamper the potential for growth and rational investment.

In smaller countries the situation is likely to be different. The historical emergence of a powerful State makes inevitable the formation of a ruling class and a tight bondage between the State and all private—but not necessarily entrepreneurial activity. Price and tax distortions are introduced to give rise to a peculiar "socialist" formation in which economic activity is not directly commanded by the State but it is delegated to the "chosen few" which constitute the ruling class. The distortions hamper entrepreneurial activity and the potential for a strong orientation towards the comparative advantages and, of course, the new comparative advantages that emerge continually in the process of the international change in relative prices and taxation—often as a result of foreign states' intervention through money, credit and fiscal policies. The survival of the ruling class depends on the activities that the State often dictates when its power has exceeded certain limits. But the survival of Kirznerian entrepreneurship is severely and immensely hampered. The further expansion of the State and the ruling class does not put into political offices those that can enhance efficiency and growth prospects but those who represent the interests of the ruling class and its political representation in the State's bureaucracy.

This is a deformed or degenerated capitalism, where ownership is private but distortions from the ruling class are so severe that the social formation operates in such a way that produces economic results that are closer to socialism rather than capitalism. The introduction of change and the hope for a new political leadership of "capable" or "visionary" personalities becomes impossible because such leadership us endogenous; it is the product of the conditions of operation of the social and economic formation. Just like Kirznerian entrepreneurs who rely on price signals to process the collective knowledge that is materialized into them, no sensible persons can see any positive signals to engage into politics—which means nothing but the despotic rule of the bureaucracy of the ruling class over the people and the State. This State, therefore, has an incentive mechanism in place, which helps to regenerate and reproduce itself for extended periods of time.

Economic sectors that actually flourish–because there is entrepreneurship—are the exporting sectors, sectors like shipping, which rely exclusively on foreign demand or sectors that are internationally competitive because of their innovative applications of new technology and/or knowledge. In the domestic market the distribution of resources has been distorted and degenerated so much that such sectors cannot possibly survive in the national boundaries which have been conquered by the bureaucracy and the ruling strata. New leadership cannot emerge because entrepreneurship is limited and limited entrepreneurship leaves open ground for the reinforcement of the political bureaucracy. Out of this vicious circle there is no way unless, as the result of an external shock, economic and political "institutions" change so that the government loses its grip over the economy and along with it, the ability of the ruling clique to use the State to run its economic activities.

The notion that countries like Greece became "protectorates" as the result of imposition of austerity measures and controlling the budget have only one interpretation: That the ruling class is beginning to lose its grip over the economy and new strata of entrepreneurship are likely to emerge—strata that will challenge the monopoly of economic and political power by the various departments of the State-dependent "private agents".

We have placed the term "institutions" in quotes for the following reason: Discussions about the necessity of institutional change abound but actual changes are scarce and most economists or commentators do not specify exactly when they refer to "institutional change". *We believe that a necessary and sufficient condition for "institutional change"—whatever it means—is the drastic reduction in the size of government in both expenditures and taxes.* The institutions that need to change are precisely the complex sets of relationships that have been formed historically between the State and the ruling class—the strata of businessmen and bureaucrats that are closely associated with the State and their activity depends almost entirely, implicitly or explicitly, upon the State, not excluding, of course, the media and many other monopolies or oligopolies in the various walks of the public life.

To the extent that a new, progressive political and social leadership cannot emerge endogenously in the domestic market, as long as the public sector continues to be large, not only quantitatively but also in the qualitative sense, the only possibility is to reduce the public sector, precisely as the ECB, the EU and the IMF do right now [2013]. The very fact that the existing political bureaucracy has been left to negotiate with these institutions is detrimental to the interests of the market economy in Greece. However, there was no other possibility or choice, although the apparent alternative would be a council of citizens and entrepreneurs that would act in the interests of the market economy. Severely distorted by the historically underperforming economy, the degenerated political institutions, dominated by the ruling class, were not ready and had, objectively speaking, no capacity to negotiate. By a curious property of degenerate institutions that makes them vulnerable to external pressure, many policies were adopted in the right direction, although most of them were adopted in rhetoric and not in actual practice or deeds.

But the important question is this: Let us agree that we need drastic cuts in expenditures, taxes and the qualitative as well quantitative command of the government over the economy. How can such changes, including privatization and liberalization of the financial system, be enforced? To the extent that the ruling elite will not allow simultaneously liberalization and reductions of the public sector, the changes that will actually take place are likely to be a mockery, where parts of the State are transferred to the ruling class. Since this class has proved its incapacity in terms of entrepreneurship it would be impossible to imagine that such changes are actual structural or institutional. Unless competition is enforced and liberalization of markets takes place—to remove price controls or other rigidities that generate rents—an institutional change that matters is not possible. The actual hurdle in implementing reforms is not so much the public but the ruling class and the bureaucracy. The stratum of "vested interests" will exercise all its power to change the economic structure and take away its privileges, unless the size of the government is reduced above and beyond its will.

The stratum of "vested interests" or "interest" and "pressure groups" and the political leadership are in close interconnection so that it has become impossible to separate one from the other. For this, we have to conclude that unless the State is deprived of its extensive role in the economy and society, new progressive political leadership is not likely to emerge. Even if it does its chances of success are slim because even it has the correct political programme, the public will not welcome its suggestions and proposals, since it has been educated in the statist philosophy for decades. In this sense, agreeing that political leadership is lacking is essentially agreeing to the statement that Statism has been so pervasive that political and economic recovery have become exceedingly difficult by the means of the country alone. There remains, of course, the potential of "enforcing" institutional change from abroad and the intervention of IMF, EU and ECB is such an example.

The problem is that these institutions cannot enforce institutional and structural changes because they have no interest in doing so. Their objective is to secure increased tax revenues and expenditure cuts enough to accommodate interest payments on the public debt. These can be extensive, of course, but as we observe there is large likelihood that the burden will be distributed uniformly across the population rather than disproportionately against the interests of the ruling elite. This is precisely why the austerity measures have been so severe, endangering social cohesion and even the rule of law. The supervision by the IMF, the EU and the ECB has a meaning when measures are taken and results are observed. When the State itself retreats in face of making even the slightest changes this supervision cannot be of much help. *The problem in turn, is for the most part, political* and has grown up together with the increase of public debt and the enhancement of the State over a whole historical period. The roots of the problem are in the factors that led to the increase of the role of the State, some of which are now obsolete in Southern Europe, along with the increasing influence of the socialist and Keynesian ideas after the War.

Nevertheless, we should not underestimate the power of institutional change—not at the national but at the European level. True independence of the European Central Bank along with financial liberalization, abstention from changes in interest rates, and a drastic reduction in taxes and expenditures by the European governments constitute the "wind of change" that can enforce institutional change in the South. In this sense it not a national but an European problem and without a global solution with the European Union, the political vicious circles that have formed over a whole historical period cannot be broken effectively. It is a process which, for lack of a better name, we have called Coherent Governance. From our analysis it turned out that liberalization and competition in the financial intermediation system, along with a 100-percent reserve requirements rule, not only are easier to implement at the European level but it is precisely in this case that they become more effective. They will yield a re-allocation of resources and production of immense importance across national boundaries in the continent, a result that will generate new comparative advantages and Kirznerian opportunities more in line with the constellation of international relative prices.

References

Hoppe H-H (1990) Marxist and Austrian class analysis. J Libertarian Stud 9(2):79–93
Marx K (1959) Capital: a critique of political economy. 3rd, Moscow

Chapter 36
Was the Euro a Bad or a Good Idea?

Common sense suggests that transactions and contracts are denominated in terms of currencies that tend to be stable and under conditions of relative stability, such contracts tend to account rationally for the inherent uncertainty in exchange rates. The discussion about "exogenous shocks" was found to be largely irrelevant to our discussion and uncertainty, for the most part, is not due and does not come from "exogenous" factors to the economy as a whole but rather from policy uncertainty. Confidence to a currency means confidence to the event that a stable configuration of fiscal and monetary policies will persist in the future without drastic changes beyond any expectation. If such changes occur there will be price and quantity effects in all markets along with a revision of plans for future investment and the re-allocation of financial portfolios. The opponents of the Euro tend to focus too much on appearances instead of analyzing the issues in depth. They argue that because the European South ran large public deficits at a specific time period the whole experiment of the common currency is at stake and then they argue about optimal currency areas, "asymmetric shocks" and various other matters that are only peripheral if not totally misguided and unfounded.

The Issue of Deficits

Based on the principle that the public sector should be minimal we should conclude that government expenditures and taxes should be minimal as well. Given this fundamental principle it is inconceivable that the government should not obey an inter-temporal budget constraint. Since the debt obligations are clearly delineated and they are well known in advance it becomes equally inconceivable that the large Greek debt payments due 2008 and 2009 could not have been made irrespective of the precise level or percentage of budget deficit. Measures should have been taken in advance to ensure that Greece at first, followed by Ireland, Portugal and Spain, should be able to repay their obligations by satisfying their inter-temporal budget constraints. The explosion of debt could have been predicted in advance—a fact that is of practical value only for the future—and more rigorous

E. G. Tsionas, *The Euro and International Financial Stability*,
Financial and Monetary Policy Studies 37, DOI: 10.1007/978-3-319-01171-4_36,

policies should have been adopted instead of the standard 3 % rule for deficit-to-GDP rule. The standard rule is bound to be inadequate in a dynamic perspective when large debt payments are forthcoming. In other words complete fiscal consolidation is impossible unless we take into account revenues and expenses (of all types) over a time horizon. That was the whole issue with "debt explosion": The inadequate consolidation of the fiscal affairs at the national level which, eventually, became a European problem.

The idea that the European South can sustain large public deficits at the expense of other members of the monetary union—giving rise to a "tragedy of the commons" or an inherently "weak euro" because of lack of constraints or discipline—is an idea that flies in the face of the evidence. Although deviations from the 3 % rule were observed, in fact, *any* amount of deficit would be incompatible with the inter-temporal budget constraints. The evidence is not the deficits themselves, but rather the fact that deficits of one party are gains for another. Since wealth cannot be created by artificial means what takes place is a redistribution within the confines of the monetary union where some parties are temporarily better off compared to others. However, the same mechanism works at the regional level of the same national economy. Some local administrations can run deficits but this is not possible for all administrations at the same time, especially when debt payments are outstanding or forthcoming from one to the others.

Fiscal consolidation and smooth functioning of the economy requires that inter-temporal or dynamic budget constraints are satisfied. This, in turn, requires, an inter-temporal reallocation of spending and tax revenues that is consistent with solvency at a given time horizon which is determined by the most significant debt obligations. If the inter-temporal reallocation of spending and revenues is not possible because of rigidities inherent in the operation of the public sector, the simple observance of rigid rules like the 3 % canon is of little importance. It would have been, of course, the duty of the fiscal and monetary authorities of the European Union to ensure that such complete fiscal consolidation was in effect. The fact that it did not happen leads us to the conclusion that considerations of accommodating capital or interest payments in the South, were not of much concern when the fiscal consolidation plans were designed or afterwards. In other words, fiscal consolidation did not properly account for future capital payments on the public debt.

"Bailouts" of Southern Economies and "Financial Stability"

"Bailing out" plans for national economies were, in effect, the price that had to be paid for the improper treatment of inter-temporal budget constraints. If one, however, compares the cost of direct assistance to the total bailout for the commercial banking sector, then one realizes that the concern was rather "financial stability".

To the extent that the commercial banking sector had to be rescued on both sides of the Atlantic surely means something. From the mechanical point of view it was the spillover effects of the sub-prime crisis that had to be dealt with in order to prevent a collapse of the international financial system.

In reality, the policy of cheap credit had reached its limits and its quantitative effects had begun to spread over the economy and, therefore, the commercial banking sector as well. The confounding of the two problems, that is the problem of public debts and the problem of the crisis induced by historically low interest rates, had distracted many commentators and economists from the fact that the international system was trying to reach a new equilibrium and liquidate all types of investment that were no longer profitable. This had nothing to do with the euro, the dollar or the sterling. On the contrary, a global process of adjustment was taking place as the result of the fundamental distortions in relative prices, the associated malinvestment, and the subsequent problems in the banking sector. At the same time large outstanding debt payments had to be made and this problem has been aggravated by the absence of inter-temporal fiscal consolidation in Europe. In this chain of events it is rather easy to confound causes and effects, but one thing should remain clear: The fact that in the absence of credit market distortions in the first place, international financial stability would not be at stake.

Asymmetric Shocks

The fact that "shocks" have to have an asymmetric effect upon regions of a natural economy because of the differential change in relative prices is well understood. By the same token shocks have to work asymmetrically in any monetary union. If a natural disaster occurs which destroys part of the capital stock, its relative scarcity will affect different regions or countries in a different way depending on their demand for capital and, more precisely, for their demand for different types of capital. Relative prices of capital will re-adjust in the short-run to figure out where capital of a specific type becomes scarcer. Through the change in the structure of relative prices, priorities can be given and through the sequencing of priorities a different allocation of capital emerges which cannot affect all sectors and all regions in the same way, precisely because their demand for capital is not the same or because, in other words, the distribution of capital is not uniform.

To eliminate asymmetric shocks is to eliminate differences in the demand and supply which is inconceivable. In this sense a monetary union of states where shocks act symmetrically is a complete illusion. In Mundell's sense, factor mobility and free markets will re-establish a new configuration of the distribution of resources arising from an unforeseen shock. Since factors are not completely mobile by their nature the adjustment should take place mostly in terms of prices. If prices are rigid then the effects will have to be mostly quantitative and the adverse effects of the shocks will be asymmetric but, what is more important, they will also be more dramatic in terms of liquidation of investment, production and increase of unemployment. What is *not* true in the aftermath of the shock is that different fiscal and monetary policies are called for and, therefore, that a dissolution of the monetary union is optimal. Inn fact, strengthening the monetary union and adopting common policies is called for to a degree even stronger than before.

This is because if markets are, indeed, free the effect of the shock will be absorbed by the price system. This increases, in the short-run, the cost of the less capitalistic sectors leading to price increases of their products but at the same time this generates signals to the capitalistic sector that the demand for capital has increased. Because the effects of the shock have been absorbed by prices the quantitative effects will be milder and temporary. By engaging in active monetary or fiscal policy that distorts artificially interest rates and thus the relative profitability of investment of different types, the quantity effects will be magnified and will be propagated through the system, aggravating the real effects of the shock. With the passage of time it is not clear anymore, to a casual observer, which part of the recession is due to the original shock and which part is policy-induced. For what it matters, a casual observer or a commentator can blame it entirely upon the shock or, most importantly, to any event that followed the shock or happened to coincide with the shock such as, for example, a local authority running a large deficit.

Differential Inflation Rates

Although the rate of inflation of a basket of goods can be monitored to harmonize the procedure of dealing with inflation, absolute and relative prices are not and cannot be the same in a monetary union as they cannot be the same in a system of regions. To the extent that demand and supply conditions are different so will be absolute and relative prices. Irrelevant arguments concerning arbitrage do not apply most of the time as there are many other arbitrage opportunities that can be carried out easily. If that were not the case there would be no need for the price system.

The paradox of monitoring aggregate statistics such as the rate of inflation or the debt-to-GDP ratio is that the authorities do not have an intrinsic interest in them; they only use them as a barometer to test whether their fiscal or monetary and credit interventions have gone beyond what is "acceptable". In the case of the Eurozone the notion of "acceptability" is clearly delineated and defined. The notion of fiscal consolidation was put into the test, and failed, through the inappropriate use or more precisely the ignorance of what is the inter temporal budget constraint. Surprisingly, after the sub-prime crisis, the only variable of the system that was not affected much was the inflation rate. Clearly this barometer failed precisely because the effects materialized into changes in relative prices, absolute prices, and quantities without affecting the "aggregate price level" at all. If there is high inflation there is a clear indication that government policies have gone too far but with low inflation, and without monitoring other statistics, it is impossible to tell whether such policies are acceptable or not. Low deficits that do not account for large upcoming debt payments fall into the same type of "aggregate statistics".

Even economists are accustomed to the idea that tradable commodities should have the same price across the world; even if they are in no demand or if their demand is very low compared to domestic demand in other parts of the world or within the confines of a monetary union. The mere fact that the demand of the same commodity can be different in different parts of a monetary union is of no significance to them. In turn the fact that a commodity is cheaper in a part of the monetary union compared to the domestic market is taken as evidence that prices are too high domestically and, therefore that there are presumably cartels, oligopolies or other distortions of competition. There may be, of course, certain distortions of competitive conditions in the domestic market but, in the final analysis, demand curves determine price-marginal cost margins and not the opposite. Even if absolute prices of the same commodity can differ because of national differences in tastes and demand, aggregate price levels are not informative about differences in individual prices and, therefore, the possibility arises that inflation rates may vary widely even within the confines of a monetary union.

Inflation rates can differ because of wide fluctuations in supply and demand even when "aggregate" demand remains unchanged. In particular, following the liquidation of investment after an interest rate shock worked its first pass through the economic system, if consumers are more constrained because they cannot lend as easily as before, their budgets have to be allocated among the different commodities using different priorities. The prices of some goods will increase and the prices of goods whose demand was sustained mainly because of the credit ease will have to be reduced or even collapse. There is no tendency for all prices to go down, let aside the hypothesis that they would have to become lower by the same rate. New comparative advantages emerge not only at the national level but also internationally and a re-allocation of resources within the monetary union occurs. If the credit ease is sustained, through a variety of means, this re-allocation is distorted and a clear pattern of profitable opportunities cannot emerge from the clouds of the recession.

The mere fact that the monetary authority needs a few barometers to test that it has not gone too far in terms of an expansionary policy does not, of course, qualify inflation as one of them. High inflation would, clearly, offer such an indication but even with low inflation an unprecedented recession can emerge without the monetary authority being able to tell in advance. The authority can monitor individual prices or an index of materials and intermediate commodities if a more objective measure is sought. But the fact of the matter remains that engaging into fiscal or monetary expansion is by itself a quite accurate indicator of the extent of damage in incomes and wealth that will, eventually, follow.

Restoration of Competitiveness

The argument that if Greece, for example, leaves the Eurozone the devaluation of its new national currency will restore competitiveness immediately is used frequently in public discussions. Some argue that structural reforms and austerity measures to restore growth take too long and, therefore, they are not part of a method of choice. How this policy would relieve the debt burden is entirely unclear if we take into account that nominal obligations will sky rocket, albeit some positive effects from increase of exports.

> Of course, the process would be traumatic—and not just for Greece. The most significant problem would be capital losses for core Eurozone financial institutions. Overnight, the foreign euro liabilities of Greece's government, banks, and companies would surge. Yet these problems can be overcome. Argentina did so in 2001, when it "pesofied" its dollar debts. The United States did something similar in 1933, when it depreciated the dollar by 69 % and abandoned the gold standard. A similar "drachmatization" of euro debts would be necessary and unavoidable (Roubini 2012).

The policy recommendation seems to be that abandonment of the euro is necessary to restore competitiveness overnight and, in turn, by deviating from the "gold standard" to engage in inflationary policies. So there seems to be a choice between two clear cut policies: Either devaluation and inflation or austerity measures and structural reforms that will take too long to restore growth. It is not denied that the latter policies will, indeed, be successful in restoring growth but rather that there is no time to wait. As Roubini writes:

> Some argue that Greece's real GDP would be much lower in an exit scenario than it would be during the hard slog of deflation. But that is logically flawed: even with deflation, real purchasing power would fall, and the real value of debts would rise (debt deflation), as the real depreciation occurs. More importantly, the exit path would restore growth right away, via nominal and real depreciation, avoiding a decade-long depression. And trade losses imposed on the Eurozone by the drachma depreciation would be modest, given that Greece accounts for only 2 % of Eurozone GDP.

If that were possible there would, really, be no reason for Greece to stay in the Eurozone. To avoid a decade-long process of adjustment, competitiveness and growth can be restored overnight by devaluating the currency. The structural reforms and the austerity measures are seen as unnecessarily harsh and can be avoided since a process of real devaluation in already taking place—albeit at painstakingly slow rates. What is fundamentally flawed with this argument is that competitiveness can be lost in the short-run once the existing stocks are liquidated in the international markets and prices begin to rise again since supply has not changed. A variety of goods and services can benefit from the devaluation in the short-run but recovery and creation of new wealth require investment to increase capacity if the increase in demand is considered to be lasting. If there is in place a process of real devaluation, which is the result of the re-alignment of relative prices due to the recession, how can a devaluation speed up this process *unless* the government sustains the *temporary* shock by engaging in active fiscal and monetary policies that aggravate the debt problems? A devaluation will be absorbed quickly by the system since the prices of exportable commodities rise more relative to other goods and resources and demand can be met only by existing stocks or by increasing the prices of intermediate goods and resources that cannot be transferred immediately to the new uses. If the government does not engage in active expansionary policies, this temporary shock cannot sustain growth before the increased demand is transmitted to the entire time-distribution of capital. However, this transmission also takes time and it is painstaking. Only goods and services towards the less capitalistic end of the distribution will benefit from the devaluation and before the demand shock is transmitted to the investment and capital-intensive sectors, its effects will vanish as the result of increases in prices and costs.

There is another, perhaps more important, counter-argument that invalidates the theses of the proponents of Greece's exit from the Eurozone. Since it is not inconceivable that the euro will continue to circulate in Greece, and a new currency can circulate only by exchanging euros for drachmas, a competition of currency arises. The question then becomes, what kind of currency will the public choose to hold? As Hayek writes,

> in the long run at least, the effective choice between competitive offers of currencies will be the usual one of competition. The currency that will prevail will be the one preferred by the people who are helped to succeed and who in consequence will be imitated by others Hayek (1990).

Although the government can enforce the circulation of the new currency this can only be accomplished to a certain degree, for example through the means of payment for the wages in the public sector or the immediate conversion of savings in the commercial banks. Even if we discard the "flight from savings" into direct cash holdings in euros, transactions and contracts will tend to be denominates into a stable currency and the euro offers an obvious possibility. As the demand for drachmas decreases right from the beginning, the possible short-run positive effects of the devaluation will disappear faster compared to "full convertibility". Let us follow the argument of Hayek:

> While historically distinct national currencies were simply an instrument to enhance the power of national governments, the modern argument for monetary nationalism favours an arrangement under which *all* prices in a region can simultaneously be raised or lowered *relatively* to *all* prices in other regions. This is regarded as an advantage because it avoids the necessity to lower a group of particular prices, especially wages, when foreign demand for the products concerned has fallen and shifted to some other national region. But it is a political makeshift; in practice it means that, instead of lowering *the few* prices immediately affected, a very much *larger* number of prices will have to be raised to restore international equilibrium after the international price of the local currency has been reduced. The original motive for the agitation for flexible rates of exchange between national currencies was therefore purely inflationist, although a foolish attempt was made to place the burden of adjustment on the surplus countries. But it was later also taken up in countries which wanted to protect themselves against the effects of the inflationist policies of others (Hayek 1990, op. cit., p 114).

In other words monetary nationalism is always and everywhere not an attempt to restore a healthy currency but rather a way to engage into inflationary policies and gain temporary advantages relative to other countries, especially when nominal wages are rigid. Although nominal wage rigidity is less of a problem presently, the fact remains that restoration of international equilibrium requires the *increase* of a large number of prices. The success of the devaluation will depend, naturally, on how long it takes to restore an international equilibrium and, as we have shown, on the extent to which the public will accept the new currency. The restoration of equilibrium in international markets will be swift, and the effects will be mostly nominal, to the extent that the burden of important quantitative adjustments falls upon the long-run. For the most part, the analyses offered by commentators and certain economists, ignore the adjustment of relative prices during a devaluation and, in that way, they fail to recognize monetary nationalism for what it is: An attempt to put the burden of adjustment on the shoulders of others.

> I remain therefore as opposed to monetary nationalism or flexible rates of exchange between national currencies as ever. But I prefer now abolishing monetary frontiers altogether to merely making national currencies convertible into each other at a fixed rate. The whole conception of cutting out a particular sector from the international structure of prices and lifting or lowering it, as it were, bodily against all the other prices of the same commodities still seems to me an idea that could be conceived only in the brains of men who have come to think exclusively in terms of national ('macro') price levels, not of individual ('micro') prices. They seem to have thought of national price levels as the acting determinants of human action and to have ceased to understand the function of relative prices (Hayek 1990, op. cit., p 115).

This is, indeed, an admirable argument in that it places the emphasis on the micro-economic rather than the "aggregate" level. With flexible exchange rates the currency is left to float as the result of all types of misguided government policies that, for example, want to sustain the temporary effects of a devaluation and the "gain in competitiveness". Competitiveness cannot be sustained by changing the currency or changing the aggregate price level. It has to come, necessarily, from changes in supply and demand at the micro-economic level that change the distribution of relative prices in the domestic and therefore the international markets, given a fixed unit of account. The argument of the proponents of a national currency for Greece, is similar to the argument that national wealth can increase simply by printing more money. The idea, however foolish, is accepted by some circles of monetary nationalism who still believe in expansionary policies and the notion that competition of currencies can generate, in some way, wealth for some at the expense of others. It is based on a misguided principle, namely that aggregate price levels exist in practice whereas what exists is a system of relative prices, both domestically and internationally and the idea that a change of currency could shift bodily Greece entirely out of the international system of markets and lift her up to a sustained path of growth. If such a way existed it should have been discovered in the US of the 1930s or Argentina in 2001.

References

Hayek F (1990) Denationalization of money: the argument refined. The Institute of Economic Affairs, London, p 69

Roubini N (2012) Greece must exist, May 17 2012, Project Syndicate

Chapter 37
The Role of the Rate of Profit

Although the rate of interest, as we have emphasized repeatedly plays a fundamental role in the allocation of investment, particularly as the result of cheap credit, in most instances the crucial role is played by the rate of profit. The interest rate, at least in the beginning of business fluctuations resulting from an artificial expansion of credit, facilitates the expansion and in that way it leads to distortions between the distribution of investment plans and the distribution of consumption. Yet the further induced re-allocations of resources are governed by the rate of profit. This shows, in particular, that the rate of interest does not play the significant role that economists trained in thinking about "aggregates" suppose that it plays. With a given rate of profit per annum, which can be obtained proportionately at any subdivision of time such as a month or a quarter, the "Ricardo effect" takes place. As Hayek notes:

> If the price of the product rises this will increase the amount of profit on each turnover in a corresponding proportion irrespective of the length of the period of turnover; and the *time rate* of profit will be increased accordingly much more for labour invested for short periods than on labour invested for long periods. In the case shown by the table the per annum rate of profit is raised, by a rise in the price of the product of only 2 %, from 6 to 7 % on the two years' investment and from 6 to 30 % on the one month's investment. This will, of course, create a tendency to use proportionately more of the latter kind and less of the former kind of labour, i.e, more labour in the last stages of the process and less in the form of machinery or for other work of preparatory character (Hayek 1975).

In other words, "a rise in the price of the product (or a fall in real wages) will lead to the use of relatively less machinery and other capital and of relatively more direct labour in the production of any given quantity of output" (Hayek 1975, op. cit., 1975). The increase of the rate of profit in the consumer-goods industry, coming from an increase of prices, will act as a reduction of the rate of interest which would discourage investment in the more roundabout process. Similarly, when the prices of consumption goods finally begin to decrease in the process of a recession and the rates of profit decrease (since real wages increase and the cost of these sectors increases disproportionately due to their being labor-intensive) a shift of resources to the more roundabout techniques is justified and investment somewhere in the middle of the time-distribution of capital (but close to the

E. G. Tsionas, *The Euro and International Financial Stability*,
Financial and Monetary Policy Studies 37, DOI: 10.1007/978-3-319-01171-4_37,

consumer-goods sector) begins to increase. There is no doubt that the mechanism in question is far more complicated compared to conventional wisdom and it is certainly not true that the demand of investment is derived from aggregate demand:

> it is usually taken for granted that the yield of capital goods in general will move parallel with, or at least in the same direction as, expected final demand. Now this is true enough of capital goods (or rather durable consumers' goods) which without any further collaboration from labour will directly serve consumption. But it is much less obvious in the case of labour-saving equipment; that is, machinery in the ordinary sense of the word; and it is still less obvious in the case of machinery to make machinery and so forth (Hayek, op. cit., p. 13).

For example a fall of real wages which is brought about by direct reductions in nominal wages will make it more profitable to invest money in labour or less labour-saving equipment of low durability and complexity. This tendency will of course follow after more intensive usage of existing equipment, overtime and multiple shifts have exhausted their productivity. In this process the role of expectations is critical:

> If entrepreneurs did expect a very considerable rise of prices to take place at a fairly distant date, say two years ahead, and if they assumed that prices would then remain high for a fairly long period afterwards, this might indeed stimulate long period investments. But the expected distant rise in prices would have to be very considerable indeed to counterbalance the tendency towards less capitalistic investments … (Hayek, op. cit., p. 17).

But since prices in the consumer-goods sector are not expected to rise considerably over a prolonged period of time, long period investment cannot be stimulated and it is quite likely that not even investment of low durability will recover. If need arises this can be accomplished through imports. Overall, the principle of the "multiplier" does not apply because there is no simple relationship between the demand for investment and final demand or consumption. A reduction in nominal wages is likely to intensify the use of labor—along with the use of raw materials and capital of the lowest possible durability—but it does not create the foundation for a long-term recovery of investment in the more capitalistic or roundabout industries. In that sense it does not help to create and sustain a solid industrial structure or new growth patterns. The regulating principle is the rate of profit in the "late" stages of production:

> there can also be little question that in a modern advancing society there are many specialised plants whose labour and equipment are adapted to provide all the other industries with labour-saving devices of one sort or another which it will be profitable to introduce only if the rate of profit earned with the older methods has fallen to a certain level (Hayek, op. cit., p. 24).

To increase investment in the more roundabout industries it would be necessary that the rate of profit decreases in the consumer-goods sector either through a decrease of prices either through a decrease of costs or both. Lower real wages in these sectors certainly cannot help to increase investment as a whole—contrary, perhaps, to popular belief because there is no one "aggregate" investment schedule but rather a whole sequence of stages during which investment sectors produce their goods. The argument that low interest rates should, in principle, have increased aggregate investment considerably misses the important qualification that interest rate affects the cost of borrowing but it does not *guide* investment decisions and, therefore, employment. With relatively high prices in the consumer goods sectors soon the capital sectors that are closer to them will be in the same position, seeing their prices to increase, real wages to fall and, therefore, they will tend to shift to less capitalistic processes:

> in consequence these industries, too, will change to less capitalistic methods of production and shift their demand for capital goods from the types produced by the early stages to the types produced by the later stages. The industries corresponding to the early stages will find that the demand for their products on the part of more and more of the other industries will fall off (Hayek, op. cit., p. 25).

An increase of the rate of interest would have increased the cost of borrowing and would have stopped the "chain reactions" earlier compared to a situation where interest rates are kept stable at low levels. Another factor at work is the price of raw materials which, unlike labour and capital, can move swiftly between the various uses to guarantee high rates of profit. Even during a recession where the consumer-goods sector becomes more labor-intensive, the use of raw materials has to increase, or at least it has to increase in the sectors which supply the consumer-goods industries. Due to their quick turnover they will preclude a swift decrease of prices in the consumer-goods sector or they can even contribute to a raise of prices which has an adverse effect on investment. The other factor at work is that a reduced demand for consumer goods is accompanied by a shift of the supply curves due to expectations. Although the quick turnover of raw materials contributes to a reduction in the profit rates of the less capitalistic sectors this turnover does not contribute to a permanent reduction that would invigorate investment and employment.

> If the rate of interest were allowed to rise as profits rise (i.e., if the supply of credit were not elastic), the industries that could not earn profits at this higher rate would have to curtail or stop production, and incomes and the demand for consumers ~ goods and profits in the consumers' goods industries would cease to rise. In this way the investment for comparatively long periods, for the "sustenance" of which the current supply of consumers' goods is insufficient,. Would be cut out. If, however, as we have assumed, the rate of interest is kept at the initial low figure [...] and investments whose yield is not negatively affected continue in spite of the rise in final demand, the rise of profits in the late stages of production and the rise of costs will both come into play and will produce the result which the rate of interest has failed to bring about. (Hayek, op. cit., p. 33)

Therefore, without an interest rate that is left free to restore equilibrium between savings and investment the rate of profit will assume this role but since nominal adjustments are precluded (that is adjustments in the rate of interest) these adjustments will have to be quantitative in character. Investment funds will have to move to less capitalistic methods of production and previous investments will have to be liquidated along with significant employment effects—if not all labour can move freely between uses because of job-specific skills and expertise. When finally the prices of consumer goods begin to fall:

> The fall in the rate of profit and the rise in real wages will make a "substitution of machinery for labour" profitable, and although at first the effect of this may be small, a point will be reached when the maintenance even of a small capacity of producing final output, corresponding to the reduced current demand for consumers' goods, by the more efficient, more capitalistic methods corresponding to the higher level of real wages, will lead to an increase of investment. Although with the given demand it will not be profitable to produce more consumers' goods (i.e., to produce a final output of greater total costs), it may well be profitable to increase investment beyond current amortisation in order to reduce costs of production. But this in turn will increase incomes and demand and the upward movement will start again (Hayek, op. cit., p. 37).

Hayek offers here an endogenous theory of business fluctuations based on the workings of the rate of profits and the nature of entrepreneurial activity. One important point is that although prices in the consumer-goods sector are notoriously sticky—as he mentioned—the elements of cost are not and may affect considerably the rates of profit. Fiscal policy in the form of taxes and other structural measures like the reduction of nominal wages can set in motion such a business cycle, a fact that is not so well known or understood. This business cycle will take place even when interest rates are freely determined by the markets since the cost of borrowed funds is only one component of the costs. The difference with freely determined interest rates is that some long-term investments would have been proven unprofitable from the beginning and the *quantitative* adjustments that are implied by the re-allocations induced by the rates of profit would have been smaller. What is normally considered "bad" for business, namely high real wages and low rates of profit, *it implies in fact a particular industrial structure* where long-run and roundabout processes are more favored because labour must be substituted for machinery. This does not necessarily mean that international competitiveness is threatened as productivity can still be very high.

> With high real wages and a low rate of profit investment will take highly capitalistic forms: entrepreneurs will try to meet the high costs of labour by introducing very labour-saving machinery-the kind of machinery which it will be profitable to use only at a very low rate of profit and interest. The first increase of investment, induced by the high real wages, would not aim at producing a larger final output. It would entirely take the form of what Wicksell called a growth of capital in height and what Dr. Hawtrey has recently called a "deepening" of capital (Hayek, op. cit., pp. 39–40).

Of course the differential profit rates will set in motion again a business cycle to adjust the industrial structure to the given distribution of demand that cannot be controlled effectively by the rate of interest. At the same time this process cannot take place before unused capacity is exhausted and stocks have been liquidated, that is before prices will begin to increase and re-arrange the constellation of the rates of profit. The income effects resulting from very long-run investments will be very small in the short-run and cannot be expected to have immediate "multiplier"—like effects but rather small effects distributed over a number of years, depending on the durability of investment. In the words of Hayek:

> the lower the rate of profit and the more "capitalistic" therefore the type of investment undertaken, the slower will be the rate at which after any given interval a given expenditure of investment will contribute to the output of consumers' goods (Hayek, op. cit., p. 49).

Therefore, with low real wages and a high rate of profit investment will take less capitalistic forms. This can result in quick recovery of employment and further re-adjustments of the capital structure that will result from the increase of prices and the reduction of real wages that will favor more the less capitalistic techniques. To understand the true causes of the recession the following passage is quite helpful:

> At first the rise in the rate of profit will be confined to the consumers' goods industries. If this led immediately to a similar rise in the rate of interest, marginal rates of profit would everywhere have to be adjusted to this higher rate of interest and activity in the investment good industries would have to be reduced till this was the case. But if the rate of interest does not rise at this stage the increase of profits in the consumers' goods industries will, as we have seen, for some time stimulate investment further [...] We get then the anomalous position that [...] the discrepancy between the demand for consumers' goods and the supply of consumers' goods must get larger and larger. It is this anomaly that the increase in the demand for consumers' goods will for some time increase the output of investment goods more than the output of consumers' goods, and that every further increase in investment will increase profits on consumers' goods still further, that makes the position inherently unstable. *It is a cumulative process, indeed an explosive process, leading further and further away from an equilibrium position till the stresses become so strong that it collapses* (Hayek, op. cit., pp. 55–56, emphasis added).

Although a reduction in nominal wages will put a constraint on this disequilibrium from the demand side it will re-inforce the rate of profit and it is left to the increase of the prices of materials to reduce the profit rate and thus stop the expansion which, as a result of these factors will, eventually, collapse. But the problem with extensive unemployment is not so much in the consumer-goods sectors but rather in the sectors that precede it in the time-distribution of capital and which have collapsed as the result of the large profit margins in the consumption sector. Unless these sectors revive, unemployment will persist and *the way to revive these sectors is to increase, not decrease nominal or real wages.* What for the neo-Keynesians would seem like a straightforward "aggregate demand" policy, it is in fact a much more complicated chain of events which aims at re-structuring the industry in a way that can increase employment, a large part of which is undoubtedly skilled and job-specific labour.

International competitiveness depends on efficiency and productivity factors that are not exclusively related to advantages in terms of wages; instead it depends on the entire industrial structure and the equilibrium configuration of the distribution of capital. In the formation of an industrial structure, the role of expectations is critical since no long-run investment will be undertaken unless the demand for the specific equipment is expected to rise considerably. But once investment has begun the role of interest rate becomes much less important.

> Only for a very small fraction of the total investments-the marginal investments which represent the beginning of new chains of investment-will the demand for funds promptly react to a change in the rate at which capital can be borrowed. For the rest, the demand for capital will be highly inelastic with respect to changes in the rate of interest (Hayek, op. cit., p. 77).

As long as operating costs can be covered the cost from an increased rate of interest can be absorbed due to the further increase in the demand of capital that will be required to sustain the provision of services from the new investment. This implies that an unanticipated increase in interest rates cannot significantly affect—or affect at all—the demand for capital for long-term investments and, indeed, most investment irrespective of its roundaboutness. Therefore, the view that an increase of interest rates is detrimental, particularly during the recession, is seriously misguided. In neo-Keynesian economics there is a vicious circle: How to increase investment when aggregate demand is low and how aggregate demand can boost when incomes are low due to lack of investment and employment. In terms of aggregates there is, of course, no solution to the problem other than artificially increasing aggregate demand through inflationary policies which also reduce considerably the real rate of interest. The fallacies in the neo-Keynesian approach to the problem are many and we will consider them briefly in what follows.

1. Investment of the roundabout type is highly unlikely to increase due to the increase of the rate of profit in the consumer-goods sectors, assuming aggregate demand policies will target first and they will find their effects first in this sector. The increase in prices of raw materials and the subsequent increase of consumer goods prices due to the increased demand, will lower real wages and investment in labor-intensive uses will be more profitable.
2. As the deterioration of investment in the "early" and "middle" sectors continues, unemployment will increase on the main and even maintenance of capital stock will not be undertaken as the structure of capital becomes "thinner" and shallower.
3. Lower real wages will not be able to absorb the increased demand of consumer goods. As prices are sticky, the rates of profit will become lower and investment in the raw materials sector will become more profitable or imports will increase deteriorating the balance of payments—which provides for a straightforward solution to the "twin deficits" phenomenon.
4. At very low interest rates unprofitable investments can be sustained in the medium-term before the rate of profit lowers so much that these investments must be liquidated and resources transferred to more profitable uses. With the passage of time funds will be diverted to uses with very low turnover and higher returns so that the cost of borrowed funds can be repaid and to make up for losses from the earlier periods. The shift in the demand schedules for these uses will increase prices and depress real wages even further leading to an inherently unstable situation which manifests in a wide discrepancy between supply and demand.

5. If and when the prices in the consumer-goods sector begin to decrease, and real wages increase again, funds will have diverted to "earlier" more profitable uses which set in motion another cycle of adjustment and instability. An increase of interest rates could prevent the larger part of the quantitative or real adjustments but with stable interest rates this role will be assumed by the rates of profits.
6. The reasonable way out of the vicious circles created by misguided policies and low interest rates that led to the destruction of a whole industrial structure that could not be sustained, is "growth".

Yet growth cannot be brought about but by rescuing the economy from the depression and, in the final analysis, depression is always and everywhere a shortening of the period of production, the formation of industrial structures which favor the "later" rather than the "earlier" stages of production and investment. Encouraging the more roundabout processes offers the soundest way to sustain investment, employment and production—in the absence of monetary distortions and, in particular, distortions in the structure of interest rates. Investment supported by savings at equilibrium interest rates produces an industrial structure which is inherently stable, unless there are disruptions on an international scale which call for a significant diversion of resources and funds to the "late" stages of production. Such disruptions are extremely rare and, at any rate, few entrepreneurs would expect them to be of lasting importance. Another fallacy regarding growth results from a common misconception:

> While, of course, the relative magnitude of the demand for equipment for a particular industry will depend upon the demand for the product of that industry, it is certainly not true to say that the demand for capital goods in general is directly determined by the magnitude of the demand for consumers' goods (Hayek 1967).

The "derived demand for capital fallacy" can be cleared once we take into account the fact that the services of capital *already in place* have to be provided to many other industries along the time-distribution of capital which have also made investments that are already in place. The continuity of the process of production requires a continuous supply of capital services which, to a large degree, is not determined by the demand for consumer goods but instead by considerations related to the rates of profits and the covering of operating costs along of course with the interest rate for *new* borrowed funds. This fallacy derives from the confusion between the budget constraint for the economy as a whole and the budget constraints of particular industries and firms. In other words, it is due to ignoring the fact that aggregate demand can be sustained via a multitude of techniques of production involving very different roundaboutness and durability of capital.

The "growth accounting" exercises that have become popular in modern economies show a total disregard for the various types of capital and thus for the very different industrial structures that are compatible with aggregate demand. In fact there is a whole configuration of profit rates and degrees of roundaboutness that is feasible given a level of consumption. A mere increase of the "capital stock" in not very informative about growth as it ignores completely the implied configuration of profit rates and growth rates or the implied configuration of degrees of roundaboutness and growth rates that *could* result at rates of interest which equate the demand and supply for loanable funds. Higher and sustainable growth is possible only with the maximum possible degree of roundaboutness in the process of production, and a particular distribution of funds among the different stages of production or the time-distribution of capital. This process need not necessarily take the form of changing completely the techniques of production if interest rates adjust freely. As Hayek mentions in a footnote:

> This lengthening of the structure of production need, however, by no means take exclusively or even mainly the form that the methods used in any individual line of production are changed. The increased prices in the earlier stages of production (the lowered rate of interest) will favour production in the lines using much capital and lead to their expansion at the expense of the lines using less capital. In this way the aggregate length of the investment structure of society might in the extreme case take place without a change of the method employed in any one line of production (Hayek, op. cit., p. 78).

But following a deep recession where much of the investment that has been expanded artificially needs to be liquidated, the economy has to pass through a phase of higher interest rates that favor less capitalistic methods of production, as the necessary adjustment to a long-run equilibrium where the industrial structure will be re-shaped.

References

Hayek FA (1967) Prices and production 1931, Augustus M. Kelley Publishers, New York, 1967, p 143

Hayek FA (1975) Profits, interests and investment, 1939, Reprints of economic classics, Augustus M. Kelley Publishers, Clifton, p 9

Chapter 38
International Industrial Structure

The international structure of industry is no less affected by changes in the rates of profit not only among the sectors of a given economy but internationally. The less capitalistic sectors can move internationally more freely compared to the more roundabout processes but the formation of a national industrial structure is not independent or isolated from the international shifts of funds that take place as the result of changes in all relative prices. On a world scale, economic growth and the dominance of more roundabout processes depends primarily on the prices relative to the consumer goods sectors—or the sectors closer to them in term of durability—and the international relative prices for the same type of equipment. In a frictionless world funds would tend to move to production where prices and profit rates are higher taking into account the variable costs but this movement is limited although it materializes through international trade. A rise in the demand of consumer goods in one country will tend to be supported by raw materials or capital of low durability either from the domestic market or through imports if that proves to be advantageous. During a short-run period which is determined by the time requirements of placing new orders and delivering the local industry can expand to accommodate the increase demand but eventually imports will prevail if the foreign markets can supply at significantly lower prices (after taxes, tariffs, transportation costs, etc.).

The domestic industry will have an advantage if real wages are low and there is considerable unemployment which gives rise to a pattern of recovery of growth that does not burden heavily the balance of payments. As the cost of labour tends to become lower with the increase of prices the domestic industry can expand in depth or roundaboutness but at the same time a tendency is generated to shift funds to the uses whose profit rates have risen more steeply—and these are the sectors nearer to the consumer-goods industry. Technical conditions along with the differential increase of prices will re-adjust the rates of profit and it is likely that the decisions to import will have to be re-evaluated. To gain international comparative advantages, under these conditions, would require significant investment in the more roundabout industries and overall increase of labor-saving techniques. This can happen only when the profit rates in the consumer-goods industries have been reduced considerably and equilibrium interest rates are low.

E. G. Tsionas, *The Euro and International Financial Stability*,
Financial and Monetary Policy Studies 37, DOI: 10.1007/978-3-319-01171-4_38,

In addition, this re-structuring requires that in the right tail or the middle of the time-distribution of capital imports have been substituted by domestic production as the result of a considerable downward pressure of wages and low prices for the "earlier" stages of production. To some extent this will surely be possible, particularly when getting out of a deep recession. If the constellation of interest rates and profit rates is such that import substitution can sustain an increase of investment in the roundabout sectors its effects on employment, production and incomes will be felt for a long time since (1) it is likely that business expectations will have been revised considerably and, perhaps more importantly, (2) due to the lumpiness of investment in the roundabout sectors.

Interest rates will vary and there is no reason why they should to be equal across countries even within the confines of a monetary union, to the extent that healthy financing of net investment has to rely on potentially different rates of time preference and differential marginal rates of productivity of capital in its various uses. A common and stable interest rate for a monetary union is misguided advice. It cannot be maintained and so far as it remains constant it induces significant quantitative adjustments in the real economy. Although it reduces the cost of borrowing, as long as it does not vary with the general tendency of the rates of profit, it creates a disequilibrium that is inherently chaotic, as we described in detail. It induces shifts of resources and funds that will prove unprofitable and tend to re-enforce the gap between consumption and investment. After the sub-prime crisis it seems beyond reasonable doubt that higher interest rates would attract more savings, despite the depression of incomes, and these in turn could be re-allocated more rationally not only across the time-distribution of capital in the depressed economies but also across the monetary union as a whole.

While the cost of borrowed funds would increase, the depression of real wages would offset part of the increased costs. The process of adjustment in the economies that came out most depressed from the sub-prime incident will have to start at the consumer-goods sectors and the capital industries of low durability and high labor-intensity. Exports can be expected to recover first as existing stocks can be sold at competitive prices in international markets. Even if raw materials continue to be imported labor-intensive equipment can be used to a greater extent triggering a recovery of the capital sector with low degree of roundaboutness. The key to recovery is, then, an increase of profit rates in these sectors that would absorb over time a part of funds that were normally diverted to the consumer-goods industries and, in turn, an increase in the rates of profit that goes back to the "early" stages of production. With declining real wages *and* techniques that can economize on imported raw materials, to the extent possible, a new distribution of profit rates will establish itself that can favor indeed investment in the "early" and more roundabout sectors.

One of Hayek's key ideas about recessions in his "Profits, Interest and Investment" was surely that it is "due" to "over-consumption", not under-consumption as economists of his time, but also of today, tend to think. Even more today with constantly low and uniform interest rates across the Eurozone, "over-consumption" is quite prevalent and enforcing it further is no solution to the recession and growth problems of the monetary union. To continue, with declining real wages *in the absence of* techniques that can economize on imported raw materials—whose prices we assume fixed—the effect will be a reduction in costs if interest rates remain low. The effect produces an increase of employment and only gradually, as the profit rate increases, an increase of less durable capital—independently, we should notice of the price margin (price minus marginal costs). The demand for the types of capital used in the consumer-goods sector, either in the form of net investment or maintenance will have to increase.

This demand can be accommodated easily due to the vast stocks of the capital industry and it can do so at lower prices due to depreciation. Although this enforces the profit rates in the consumer-goods sector, soon it will do so in the capital sectors as well although the profit rates will appear to decrease as we move backwards to the "early" stages of production. Although the shift of funds across uses will take some time prices will begin to increase in the capital sectors, the effect of lower specific real wages—that is nominal wages deflated by the product prices of these sectors—will be felt and profit rates will recover. The re-structuring of the industry depends, of course, on the turnover of sector-specific capital. Although the turnover of the "early" sectors is low the existing stocks make up for this fact and employment will rise in many sectors. If new funds were to be invested out of new savings resulting from higher interest, such funds would probably be diverted to the less capitalistic sectors at first. However, the increased interest rates would create excess supply in those sectors and, in the absence of price wages, real wages wound rise decreasing the rates of profit and, therefore, creating the necessary tendency for an increase of funds to accommodate net investment in the capital sectors. Slowly this would raise the demand for capital of more durable type in the "early" stages and would create the foundation for steady growth.

The entire argument rests, of course, on foundations which are foreign to ne-Keynesian or even neoclassical thinking which are predominantly concerned with aggregate investment and interest rates. To these schools the idea that a raise of interest rates could facilitate investment, employment and growth is preposterous and has found its most significant application in a uniform constant low interest rate across the Eurozone. However, the important conclusion is that differential interest rates—determined by the market—can set in motion a re-allocation of resources which, through the mechanism of relative prices, can result in *industrial structures* and *capital structures* that are maximally accommodative to economic growth and prosperity. Aggregate investment or aggregate demand has very little to do with the problem save for the fact that low interest rates contribute to de-industrialization and an artificial expansion of the consumer-goods and services sectors of the economy.

It is well known that Hayek himself favored government interventions of a certain kind. For example he mentions:

> … after the crisis, there appears to be a strong case for measures designed to prevent demand for consumers' goods and prices of consumers' goods from falling too far. Since some movement in this direction is necessary, it would delay readjustment if such measures were taken too early. And as investment and incomes begin to increase again, such extra expenditure should clearly be curtailed at the same rate. But during the later half of the decline a policy of supplementing demand by public expenditure may well be justified. (*Profits, Interest and Investment*, op. cit., p. 63).

This "Keynesian" advice is, however, considerably qualified by the Austrian's school general tendency to recommend reductions in public expenditures and taxes. The question arises then whether "during the later half of the decline a policy of supplementing demand by public expenditure may well be justified". The qualification follows immediately after on the same page:

> Once the rate of profit in the consumers' goods industries has already fallen too far and real wages risen too high, however, the proper remedy appears to be a reduction of wages (op. cit., p. 63).

The conditions under which a Keynesian policy would be effective are, therefore, quite limited. During the depression real wages cannot raise too high first because nominal wages can be reduced and, second, because prices in the consumer-goods industry do not fall quickly but rather they tend to remain rather sticky. If profit rates are not too low and real wages in fact have fallen or remained constant, there is no reason to stimulate "aggregate demand". Hayek's recommendation has the meaning that the rate of profit must not fall too low so as to give incentives for investments of a highly capitalistic type. Nothing of the sort actually happens during the recession—except for firms and industries that had relied too much on the credit and monetary ease. Moreover, investments of a highly capitalistic nature cannot occur due to the significantly revised expectations. The Keynesian argument breaks down for another reason: An increase of public expenditure—apart from its effect being entirely depended on where it goes—that enforces consumption will have to increase in the standard IS-LM model, say.

Superficially, this increase of interest rates accompanied by an increase in aggregate income is a welcome effect. However, if interest rates are fixed, this policy can work only if accompanied by a monetary expansion or an increase of interest rates. The policy cannot also work when the marginal propensity to consumer is very close to unity. On another matter, investment does not depend so much on interest rates but instead on profit rates—one of central arguments of Hayek in his "Profits, Interest and Investment". Irrespective of the Keynesian or neo-Keynesian ideas, if government expenditure goes to the industry in the form of investment funds this effectively reduces the rate of interest and cannot possibly work. If government expenditure goes to the consumers as subsidies, this will help to liquidate the existing stocks at higher prices, lower real wages and thus higher profit rates but it cannot motivate further investment once the stocks have been liquidated unless the government engages in permanent expansion and deficits. This policy is infeasible when government debts are high and, of course, no fiscal stimulus can last forever.

Keynesian or neo-Keynesian ideas miss the essential point that the effect of a fiscal or monetary stimulus does not work through aggregate quantities but rather through the specific structure of the economy. Any positive or negative effects are realized through the intersectoral linkages and the interrelated demand and supply schedules of a myriad of firms and a multitude of industries. Leaving aside the case of a monetary stimulus, whose adverse effects have been analyzed in detail by von Mises,[1] creating a deficit to subsidize consumption ignores the very fact that "over-consumption" was responsible for the recession in the first place. In addition, although the resulting increase of rates of interest is in the right direction it creates an additional burden for borrowing to cover operating expenses or engage in small-scale investment or maintenance. In that sense the real effects cannot be realized and the effects of a temporary fiscal shock will be exhausted long before the "multiplier" predicts. But the fiscal stimulus does not work in a different way than a monetary expansion does, except that it has an additional adverse effect by diverting funds from profitable uses to immediate consumption. Unless the government has a fiscal surplus the additional funds have to be drawn from savings at higher interest rates with temporary effects on employment, incomes and consumption. Overall, only investment in the more capitalistic sectors can sustain a level of growth which is compatible with equilibrium in capital and money markets.

Reducing taxes is better suited to address the multitude of problems from a recession. Raising the rate of profit, however, should remain a constant objective, unless the collapse of the consumer-goods sector is not too severe. Given this qualification, selective tax breaks in the capitalistic sectors nearer to consumption can provide the right incentives for an increase of investment that raises the demand for capital. Tax breaks to consumers will work in the opposite direction and can be used only if the consumer-goods sector experiences very low rates of profit. To some extent, however, this may be necessary if purchasing power deteriorates fast and household debts begin to accumulate dangerously. Although the deficit will worsen, in the short-run, it can recover if the demand of sectors close to consumption begin to raise steadily and expectations are positive.

[1] Even in the Keynesian framework a monetary stimulus decreases interest rates and thus facilitates investments of a too capitalistic type, despite the "immediate" effects that it has on incomes. In that sense it provides an indication that it cannot be a policy in the right direction.

Chapter 39
Capital Structure and Financial Stability

Another important aspect of the problem is that the re-structuring of industry on the European level has important implications for financial stability. Artificially low interest rates created a "bubble" in the durables sector which, when exploded, brought the American and European economies through the most deep recession since 1929. The very idea that interest rates are policy variables that can be changed at will, due to the belief that there is a negative relationship with "aggregate investment" and "aggregate demand", should be abandoned in the interest of international financial stability. The markets operate on a global level not only through real variables but also through various contracts and agreements in the financial markets. Trading of these contracts is extremely easy and anticipates the low turnover of various resources and factors of production, including capital. The underlying forces that led to the sub-prime crisis were in effect long before and the crisis came as a natural outcome of processes that were operating under the influence of movements in relative prices and rates of interest along with rates of profit.

Rates of profit that cannot be realized immediately due to the low turnover of investment can be capitalized by trading in the financial markets, under certain expectations. For the smooth functioning of real and financial markets the expectations have to be mutually consistent and consistent with what will actually happen given all the information that is currently available about the profitability of different investment plans. If these expectations turn out to be "wrong" there is no other way to correct the misalignments but via quantitative adjustments in the real economy and liquidation of certain unprofitable plans. Expectations can be wrong, at least systematically for only one reason; namely that the configuration of relative prices in the capital markets are incompatible with the distribution of resources. In other words, when there are extensive discrepancies from dynamic equilibrium.

The reason why the rates of interest play a more fundamental role than Hayek thought in "Profits, Interest and Investment" is that they determine heavily the formation of contracts and agreements in the financial markets since such contracts need not take into account, immediately, the actual turnover of investment in the real economy. Stock prices are more volatile because they reflect the changing

E. G. Tsionas, *The Euro and International Financial Stability*,
Financial and Monetary Policy Studies 37, DOI: 10.1007/978-3-319-01171-4_39,

expectations of profitability without the requirement that investments are actually fully implemented. Equity premia reflect the expected profitability of such investments (some of which are already in place and others are in an intermediate stage) relative to the rate of interest. The neoclassical "equity premium puzzle", reflects the inability of neoclassical models to account for a high return on equity and a low rate of interest even in models with production. The fact that such models produce counterfactually large risk-free rates and low stock returns implies that, in a certain way, they are compatible with more or less safe investments that, however, cannot be financed in a timely fashion because of the high discount factors of present consumption.

In reality, investment plans are highly uncertain and free financial markets would yield relatively low interest rates and therefore low rates of profit, if these investments were of the more capitalistic type whose return per period is small—but large over a large or an infinite horizon. The neoclassical prediction of high risk-free rates reflects the insufficiency of savings to finance the stream of investments. The prediction of low stock returns is not altogether surprising if production takes the form of high roundaboutness. The real puzzle for the neoclassical models is that they are not concerned with roundaboutness at all since capital is build instantly. Introducing the possibility of large exogenous negative shocks in output, resolves the puzzle, in the sense that the neoclassical model produces higher equity premium and low risk-free rates. Often this is taken as evidence that there is not enough "risk" in the neoclassical model and thus higher stock returns are considered as "pricing" this risk while risk-free rates become lower since they are safer.

The idea that riskier assets should yield today a higher net expected return is well known. But risk, like preferences, is a matter altogether subjective. Different assessments of risk co-exist at the same time and jointly determine the configuration of asset returns. More importantly perhaps, the prediction that net returns of riskier assets are higher *on the average* does not offer much comfort to the individual investor. The average considered relevant in this respect is the statistical sampling average, not the subjectively determined average. But even if the average was of the subjective type, still over a given period of time it would provide no comfort. The statistical "risk" is of less significance once we consider that risky assets derive their risk from their fundamentals which are related to profitability of firms or profitability of new investment. This, in turn, depends on costs and demand—which depend on the "earlier" and "later" stages of production respectively. Although there is inherently almost nothing objectively uncertain about these, "statistical uncertainty" is the form into which precise knowledge of all these factors cannot be possessed by the investors. However, by looking at an index of inputs for a particular industry and the prospects for its demand schedules—however imperfect any aggregate or summary index can be—one can, nevertheless, argue that stock returns vary because it is the assessments of profitability that vary, for the most part, rather than the underlying fundamentals.

Sound investments of the more capitalistic type yield lower dividends per time period and, occasionally, the fluctuations of international demand or the decrease of certain costs can increase their profitability. The stock return of such projects should not be too different from the risk-free rate and, at times, it can even be lower. Investments that are less roundabout and closer to the end of the production processes depend more on the prices of raw materials and the prices of equipment of the less capitalistic variety. If their demand is fairly stable, only the fluctuations in input prices can affect their profits. Their stock prices should be more variable compared to the stocks of the more capitalistic firms, because the input prices of the "earlier" stages are not as stable. Instead of engaging into complex statistical forecasting exercises the investor has to enjoy higher dividends *some* of the time and, possibly, higher stock returns *occasionally* in order to maintain his demand for such stocks. But there is no reason that an investor should maintain his demand if he can switch to the stocks of the more capitalistic industries. However, such demand exists. The reason is that the demand for stocks of the less capitalistic industries shifts so that equilibrium obtains at a much lower price—a price at which, under normal economic conditions—the return should be higher "on the average". By distributing more dividends these industries lower their rate of profit and have the incentive to divert funds to uses where the profit rates are higher. This diversion of funds cannot take place in the short-run or even in medium-run. In addition, by distributing a larger part of profits as dividends the use of own funds for further investment (net or maintenance) is limited and they will either sell stock or borrow which reduces their stock prices even further. The shift of demand will, most likely, re-instate the previous price and the volume of transactions leading to a cycle or fluctuation around a level of stock price that can be considered normal given the supply and demand for the stock and the underlying normal fundamentals under normal economic conditions. This cycle is transmitted to the entire market as the portfolio of investors are re-arranged. As the price of stocks of less capitalistic industries increase, the demand for stocks of the firms "earlier" in the chain of production shifts to the left causing a decrease of stock prices and dividends. The tendency will be reversed as the less capitalistic firm engage in selling stock, etc.

If there were only a single stock which would represent the entire industry it would provide low or even negative excess returns if there were a tendency for its demand to shift to the left that would compensate shifts of the supply schedule to the left; that is if the constellation of underlying fundamentals was such that the demand for the stock would experience a negative shock for a fixed, inelastic supply. This "pessimistic" outcome would be justified by low dividends per time period which is induced by lower rate of profit. In turn, in the case of a single stock, this can be justified only on the grounds that negative "exogenous shocks" to production are more prevalent and unpredictable. But these "exogenous shocks", in fact, can be brought about only by changes in relative prices of the different goods and resources. For the more capitalistic industries or the industries that produce commodities which are used almost universally in the economy, a stable sequence of dividends can be assured, more or less, so there is no reason that they should be priced excessively relative to risk-free assets with the same yield. On the contrary, industries whose output is specific to few other industries and whose demand is also variable, should *occasionally* yield high stock returns, although "on the average" nothing can be said unless we look more closely into the conditions of demand and the factors that affect their rates of profit. The empirical fact that over time horizons that are not too short most stocks yield (daily) *excess* returns that are very close to zero on the average, proves not that they are "risky" but rather that the time-distribution of dividends is more or less stable when they are reduced to the same time horizon that the calculation of excess returns was made.

In the international markets several other financial products will follow the same pattern but their frequent trading will rely on short-run profit rather than a stable pattern of dividend payments. The markets for such products are inherently more volatile but the volatility itself is limited by the underlying components or stocks whose prices are determined by the profitability and the period of production. In the case of public debts, trading can be disastrous as it has been proved in the aftermath of the sub-prime crisis; yet this only reflects the fact that deteriorating profitability and a weak capital structure can only worsen the problems of deficit and interest payments on the debt. Without fiscal discipline and a restoration of equilibrium in the banking and financial markets, primarily an increase of interest rates, the sources of instability in the international markets cannot be eliminated and the resolution of the difficulties and adverse effects remains a political matter, over which the markets can exercise certain pressure but the opposite is also equally true.

The restoration of fiscal discipline and the normal accommodation of debt (in one way or another) solve a problem of international financial stability which, however, has important implications at the micro-economic level. By restoring the confidence in government bonds the stock market will operate smoothly and facilitate the financing of investment that is expected to be profitable and yield dividends to sustain consumption and employment. Confidence should materialize in relatively high risk-free rates for a period of time to increase savings and sustain a sound industrial structure which, in turn, will contribute to fiscal stability and considerably less need to rely on extraordinary austerity measures.

Even with "macroeconomic stability" profitable uses of capital always exist even when deficits, taxes and public debt are high. The primary concerns are the following. *First*, heavy taxation distorts considerably relative prices and rates of profit creating an artificial capital structure that does not correspond to the distribution of consumption. *Second*, large deficits divert resources and savings from profitable uses to the public sector with adverse effects on the economy. *Third*, austerity measures that result from large deficits and debts, although necessary, will temporarily have adverse effects on employment and the demand for capital undermining the sources of growth. *Fourth*, political arrangements of the debt problem are likely to arise which circumvent the markets and the need for structural reforms in the financial markets.

Traditionally, there has been much emphasis in growth theory on changes in aggregate quantities of factors like labour and capital but much less attention on their composition. Even less attention has been placed on (1) the shifts of capital and other resources among uses in the domestic market, and (2) their shifts in the international markets. The potentials for higher productivity and growth are not exhausted, in the confines of the Eurozone, by re-shifting resources before net investment begins to rise or technological innovations are introduced. Although low interest rates still favor a too roundabout mode of production when this has been proven to be unsustainable, profit rates assume the role that the interest rate would normally assume in allocating investment. The relative stickiness of consumer-goods sectors in certain parts of the Eurozone along with the reduction in nominal wages have allowed for cost reductions that can favor labor-intensive uses of funds, in conjunction with the recovery of the rest of the Eurozone which increases prices for consumer goods, raw materials and intermediate capital services.

Clearly, there is a new pattern of industrial structure emerging from the crisis following the configuration of profit rates. This new structure can be supported, at least in the short-term, because of the excess supply of capital and unemployment, so recovery need not be inflationary before the malinvestment of the past is corrected. The recovery will, naturally, have an international dimension as investment and the demand for capital will increase to meet the new requirements of production in Europe and elsewhere. Although "technical progress" per se is quite important for growth, it is not always clear what is meant by the term. It can be understood in the "factor augmenting" sense or in the sense of shifts in the "aggregate production function". The foundations of technical progress are found in the emergence and adoption of labour-saving equipment which can be very sector-specific or of wider applicability. In the latter case it is often the case that capital and labour must be used in fixed proportions while in the former case there can be significant reductions in labour requirements. In both cases the productivity of labour increases and the wider price margins generated, make it highly likely that the diffusion of new technology will be swift. However, this cannot but only happen occasionally and has an impact on long-term growth. In the medium-term growth can be realized not because there is "factor augmenting" or "neutral" technical change but rather because the economy passes through the various stages of *dynamic* equilibrium.

In the course of dynamic equilibrium resources shift among uses until the configuration of profit rates is conformable with the distribution of resources. Hayek pointed out that this would involve an equalization of the rates of profit ("Profits, Interest and Investment", p. 64) but an equalization in the strict sense is not required if there are different economies of scale across sectors, if firms can exercise some form of market power or if there are significant entry costs and time required to shift resources and start production that reaches the market. The potentials for growth that are latent in Europe can materialize in the aftermath of the debt crisis when the landscape begins to emerge more clearly from the clouds of vast malinvestment that has taken place.

Chapter 40
International Empirical Evidence on the ABC's of Recessions

In this part[1] we test the validity of the Austrian theory of the Business Cycle (**ABC**). We use data for major economies over 1980–2006 well before the 2008 financial crisis. We utilize the information available in the most efficient manner through panel unit root panel co-integration analysis. The relationships between variables in the Austrian theory of business cycle are studied with co-integration techniques. We investigate the causality implications of the Austrian theory *at various time horizons* using the method of Dufour et al. (2006). All our results tend to favour the Austrian theory in general terms. The implication is that in *short medium term horizons* (up to 2008) credit expansion had a major role to play in the recession much like as in the 1920s.

Introduction

In this part, we put the Austrian theory of the business cycle to the test. This theory, which lays stress on the role of credit in economic fluctuation, is in the tradition of the neoclassical system, the dominant economic school in the 1920s and 1930s. It was first formulated by the Austrian economist Ludwig von Mises in 1912, in his monumental work "Theory of Money and Credit", where it is developed in great detail. Von Hayek considerably assisted the spread of the theory by publishing two books—"Monetary Theory and the Trade Cycle (1933)" and "Prices and Production" (1935)—in which he worked out further implications of von Mises' theory.

As a first approximation, we posit that the Austrian Business Cycle (ABC for short) theory is based on "misperception of the level of interest rates". The cycle's upward phase results from intertemporal allocation errors due to an interest rate "lower than it should be". It assumes that firms initiate production processes that presuppose the existence of consumers' specific desire to postpone consumption,

---

[1] Based partially on the paper "ABC's of the 2008 recession", with Joanna Konstantakopoulou 2011, Athens University of Economics and Business.

E. G. Tsionas, *The Euro and International Financial Stability*,
Financial and Monetary Policy Studies 37, DOI: 10.1007/978-3-319-01171-4_40,

though this is in fact incompatible with the actual profile of their time-preferences. It is the threat that the processes, once initiated, may be abandoned or cut short that triggers the downward phase of the cycle. This model combines the standard Böhm-Bawerk view of the production process with Wicksell's theory of the relationship between natural and market interest rates.

In Sect. 2 we present the theoretical assumptions underlying the Austrian monetary theory of cycles. In Sect. 3 we deal with the econometric methods used. In Sect. 4 we present our conclusions.

Summary of the Austrian Business Cycle Theory

The Austrian Business Cycle (ABC) theory adopts the natural, or Wicksellian interest rate which is determined by the supply of savings and the demand for loanable funds. In a free market, the clearing price is fully determined by (subjective) time-preference all the individuals of whom the market economy is composed. It should be noted that the term "time-preference" reflects the degree to which an individual prefers the present to the future.[2] This subjective time-preference is therefore an important factor in determining the extent to which individuals save and invest. Obviously when their time-preferences are changed, individuals may tend to reduce their consumption and increase their saving and investment; and the interest rate tends to be lower accordingly (Hayek 1931, 1933).

The crucial question is what happens to the economy when interest rates fall not because of lower time-preference but because of credit expansion. According to Hayek (1935, 1941) the only cause of permanent real change in economic activity is change in individuals' time-preferences (or the productivity of new technology). An interesting concept that defines the foundation of the Austrian school is the "time dimension" of consumption and production. It is this concept that has given rise to the notion of "time-preference" and to the hypothesis that most "indirect production methods" yield the greatest productivity (Hayek 1933, 1935; Böhm-Bawerk 1889).

Production depends at any given moment not only on prior investments but on the temporal sequence in which investments have been made. The temporal structure of the production process, as studied by Böhm-Bawerk, is of the continuous input-point output type. The Austrian theory in fact treats capital almost invariably as "circulating capital". To Böhm-Bawerk's concept of production, von

[2] The product of time-preference is the originary rate of interest, as noted by Mises (1966), who argued that there is always a discount in the price of future goods compared to the price of those same goods in the present. This discounting process is applied to all goods, not just money or capital. "If future goods were not bought and sold at a discount as against present goods, the buyer of land would have to pay a price which equals the sum of all future net revenues and which would leave nothing for a current reiterated income".

Mises and Hayek attached "physical capital". Hayek's "structure of production", can be pictured as a right-angled triangle (an image fully compatible with Böhm-Bawerk's concept of capital as multidimensional in value and time). The horizontal base of Hayek's triangle stands for the time dimension of the production process; and the vertical line corresponds to the value of consumable products. The time dimension is subdivided into several "stages of production," where the output of one stage becomes the input of the next. A single "project"' to convert raw materials, the early stage, into consumables, the final stage, is an *assemblage of the plans of several producers mutually coordinated by the price system*, which of course includes the interest rate (Garrison 2001).

Since capital is heterogeneous, differential shifts in demand by capital type will occur, in response to any change in interest rates. Hayek correlated *directly* the interest rate with the price margins between stages in production.

> The price of a factor which can be used in most early stages and whose marginal productivity there falls very slowly will rise more in consequence of a fall in the rate of interest than the price of a factor which can only be used in relatively lower stages of reproduction or whose marginal productivity in the earlier stages falls very rapidly (Hayek 1967).

A basic assumption of the ABC theory is that when the market interest rate falls below the natural interest rate, investors prefer to turn to capital intensive investment and expand their investment into durable equipment, capital goods, industrial raw materials, and construction (in other words, *more capital-intensive* production processes) than into direct production of consumer goods (in other words, *less capital-intensive* production processes).

Empirical Investigation of the ABC Theory

Introduction

Our econometric analysis is constructed as follows. *First*, we detect the nature of the underlying stationary properties of each time series, using several unit root tests such as ADF and panel unit root tests; the latter are unavoidable, because they suggest a solution to the power problems of single –series based ADF tests. *Secondly*, we conduct a cointegration analysis, following the Johansen procedure (Johansen 1988) to establish how many cointegrating relationships can be found among variables related to the ABC theory. We also conduct panel co-integration tests since they can be more powerful. Co-integration vectors are estimated by means of the fully modified (FM) OLS estimation technique for heterogeneous co-integrated panels (Pedroni 2000). To study for causality at various horizons, we utilize the method of Dufour et al. (2006).

All data are derived from the International Monetary Fund (IFS), for the period 1980:1–2006:4, for USA, Australia, Canada, UK, Japan, Germany, Spain, France and Italy. The variables chosen for our analysis are: Gross domestic product, gross fixed capital formation, Credit, and Interest Rates (see Table 1 for further details).

As we have noted, the ABC theory posits a chain of economic events. The most interesting link in this chain is the one connecting credit with investment and real output. We assume that *artificial changes* of credit influence investment, which in turn boosts economic activity. These *artificial changes of credit* may result from unanticipated changes in money supply or (directly) from changes in interest rates. *Artificially induced credit is in fact the starting up of the business cycle.* Suppose:

$$y_{it} = \beta_{oi} + \beta_{1i} I_{it} + \beta_{2i} c_{it} + \beta_{3i} r_{it} + \beta_{4i} m_{it} + u_{it} \tag{40.1}$$

where y_{it} is output in country i and quarter t, I_{it} is investment, c_{it} is credit, m_{it} is money supply, r_{it} is the interest rate, and u_{it} is an error term satisfying the usual properties.

Testing for Integration

Our first test for integration uses the augmented Dickey-Fuller (ADF) statistic. We also this perform three panel unit root tests: the IPS test, suggested by Im, Pesaran and Shin (2003), the MW test, suggested by Maddala and Wu (1999), and a test belonging to the same category, the Choi test, suggested by Choi (2001). These tests assume non-stationarity in the null hypothesis. The results from the ADF tests (see Table 2) indicate that at reasonable significance levels all the variables are non-stationary, with one exception, money in the UK. The tests shows that first differences of this variable are stationary.

The results from the panel unit roots tests (in Table 3) show that we can accept the null hypothesis (unit root) for all variables at levels, but we can reject it for first differences of time series. So as a working hypothesis all variables can be considered as I(1).

Testing for Co-Integration

Our strategy for investigating the existence of long-run equilibrium relationships between variables is to conduct Johansen co-integration tests (Johansen 1988) and Pedroni panel co-integration tests (Pedroni 1999) on the variables. The country-specific results of the Johansen co-integration test are presented in Table 4. The null hypothesis of at least one co-integration vector is accepted. We ensure conclude that there is a long-run equilibrium to which our variables in each country converge over time. The results of the Pedroni tests are presented in Table 5. They support the hypothesis that there is a single co-integration vector irrespective of the dependent variable (output, investment, money supply and credit).[3]

---

[3] A heterogeneous specific trend is taken into account.

Table 1 Summary of causality relations at various horizons

	United States																					
	h	2	3	4	5	6	7	8	9	10	12	14	16	18	20	22	24	26	28	30	32	34
GDP	← *Investment*	*	*	*	**	**	**	**				**										
	← *Credit*	**	**	**	**	**	*	*	*	*	*	*	*	*	*	*	*	*	*	*	*	*
	← *Interest Rate*	**	**	**	**	**					**	**	**	**	**	*	*	*	*	*	*	*
	← *Money Supply*									**	**	**							**	**	*	*
Investment	← *GDP*	**	**	**	**	**	**	**	**	**	**	*	*	**			**	*	*	*	*	*
	← *Credit*					**	**	**	**	**	**	**	**	**	**	**	*	*	*	*	*	*
	← *Interest Rate*															**	**	**				
	← *Money Supply*									**	**	*	*	*	*	*	*	**				
Credit	← *GDP*	**	**	*	**	**	**	**	**	*	*	*	**					**	*	*	*	*
	← *Investment*	*	*	*	**	*	**	*	*	*	*	**										
	← *Interest Rate*		*	*	*	*	*	**	**													
	← *Money Supply*	**	**					**	**	*	*	*	*	*	*	**	**	**				
Money Supply	← *GDP*							**	**	**	*	*	*	*	*	*	*	*	*	*	*	*
	← *Investment*										**	*	*	**	**							
	← *Credit*															**	**	*	*	*	*	*
	← *Interest Rate*																	**	**	**	*	*
Interest Rate	← *GDP*	**	**	**	**									**	**							
	← *Investment*	**	**	**	**	**																
	← *Credit*	*	*	*	*	*	*	*	*	*	*	*										
	← *Money Supply*	*	*	*	*	*	*	*	*	*	*	*	*	**								

Source: International Monetary Fund, International Financial Statiscs

Note: (*), (**) Signify rejection of the null hypothesis at the 5% and 10% level respectevely

Table 2 Unit Root Tests for the Variables of the ABC Theory

Countries		Levels	First Differences		Levels	First Differences		Levels	First Differences
United States	**GDP**	-2,366	-3,12***	**Money Supply**	-1,673	-3,151***	**Credit**	-1,925	-3,974**
Australia		-2,906	-10,737*		-2,494	-10,862*		-1,702	-2,903***
Canada		-2,635	-3,444***		-1,853	-12,032*		-2,359	-10,987*
United Kingdom		-2,570	-3,81**		-3,412***	-11,008*		-2,159	-3,509***
Japan		-2,254	-5,3*		-1,038	-5,123*		-2,182	-4,635*
Germany		-2,322	-4,244*		-1,758	-4,335*		-2,390	-4,278*
France		-2,598	-5,901*		-1,813	-4,127*		-1,05	-2,592***
Italy		-2,124	-10,321*		-1,783	-3,497**		-2,233	-2,98***
Spain		-1,823	-5,974*		-2,383	-3,456**		-1,820	-2,656***
United States	**Investment**	-2,273	-4,164*	**Leading Rates**	-1,906	-5,974*			
Australia		-2,916	-6,541*		-2,020	-5,921*			
Canada		-2,737	-4,336*		-2,980	-5,36*			
United Kingdom		-3,179	-10,188*		-2,343	-9,087*			
Japan		-2,567	-5,676*		-1,301	-2,88***			
Germany		-1,975	-4,179*		-3,224	-7,218*			
France		-2,837	-10,518*		-1,506	-7,034*			
Italy		-2,902	-10,094*		-1,862	-10,532*			
Spain		-2,315	-5,055*		-1,823	-2,208***			

Note: (*), (**) and (***) signify rejection of the unit root hypothesis at the 1%, 5% and 10% levels, respectively

Table 3 Panel Unit Root Tests for the Variables of the ABC Theory

Variables	IPS		MW		Choi	
	Levels	First Differences	Levels	First Differences	Levels	First Differences
GDP	-0,663	*-13,611*	15,939	*206,981*	-0,558	*-11,162*
Money Supply	-0,126	*-16,574*	16,267	*262,356*	0,086	*-12,691*
Credit	-1,391	*-16,225*	13,104	*270,132*	0,261	*-13,179*
Lending Rate	-0,414	*-22,821*	15,277	*193,111*	-0,338	*-13,372*
Investment	-0,945	*-16,994*	18,179	*291,909*	-0,877	*-14,533*

Note: The critical values for MW test are 37,57 and 31,41 at 1% and 5% statistical level respectively. Italics values signify rejection of the null hypothesis

Table 4 Johansen Cointegration tests

Country		: *rank = r*					
(a) Trace Statistic		*r=0 (69.818)*	*1 (47.856)*	*2 (29.797)*	*3 (15.494)*	*4 (3.841)*	
(b) Max eigenvalue Statistic		*r=0 (33.876)*	*1 (27,584)*	*2 (21,131)*	*3 (14,264)*	*4 (3.841)*	
United States	(a)	**123,183**	**80,690**	**50,744**	**21,188**	3,687	6 lags
	(b)	**42,493**	**29,946**	**29,556**	**17,501**	3,687	
Australia	(a)	**89,532**	**53,311**	25,123	6,255	0,538	4 lags
	(b)	**36,221**	**28,188**	18,868	5,717	0,538	
Canada	(a)	**80,446**	45,252	25,786	8,249	3,006	2 lags
	(b)	**35,193**	19,466	17,537	5,243	3,006	
United Kingdom	(a)	**74,322**	40,937	17,475	9,898	4,310	5 lags
	(b)	**33,985**	23,462	7,577	5,588	4,310	
Japan	(a)	**101,776**	**63,315**	**35,043**	13,304	1,355	6 lags
	(b)	**38,461**	**28,272**	**21,739**	11,949	1,355	
Germany	(a)	**100,335**	**56,495**	**35,062**	**19,303**	**8,350**	6 lags
	(b)	**43,840**	21,433	15,759	10,953	8,350	
France	(a)	**100,818**	**62,208**	29,093	12,689	0,078	5 lags
	(b)	**38,611**	**33,114**	16,405	12,611	0,078	
Italy	(a)	**132,782**	**68,393**	28,002	12,318	0,131	4 lags
	(b)	**64,390**	**40,390**	15,684	12,187	0,131	
Spain	(a)	**87,857**	47,147	24,287	10,323	0,439	5 lags
	(b)	**40,710**	22,859	19,965	9,884	0,439	

Note: Numbers in parentheses represent the 5% critical values of the two test statistics. *r* denotes the number of cointegrating vectors. The eight column contains the optimal lag for the VARs that were selected by minimising the AIC criterion. Finally, boldface values detect evidence in favor of cointegration

Table 5 Panel Cointegration tests

Dependent variable:		no trend	trend
Output	***PP rho-statistic***	1,389	**2,763**
	PP t-statistic	1,230	**3,379**
	ADF t-statistic	**2,863**	**3,967**
Investment	***PP rho-statistic***	1,492	**2,344**
	PP t-statistic	1,112	**2,638**
	ADF t-statistic	1,235	**2,932**
Credit	***PP rho-statistic***	**2,992**	**4,679**
	PP t-statistic	**3,150**	**4,389**
	ADF t-statistic	0,857	**2,422**
Money supply	***PP rho-statistic***	1,274	**2,784**
	PP t-statistic	1,391	**2,859**
	ADF t-statistic	1,420	**2,731**
Interest Rates	***PP rho-statistic***	0,769	-0,038
	PP t-statistic	-1,233	-0,984
	ADF t-statistic	-1,743	-1,271

Note: Boldface values detect evidence in favor of cointegration

Estimating the Co-Integration Vector

To estimate the long-run relationship between variables in the ABC context, there is a choice of estimators. These include within-group and between-group fully modified OLS (FMOLS) and dynamic OLS (DOLS) estimators. FMOLS is a non-parametric approach to dealing with correlation for serial correlation. DOLS is a parametric approach where lagged first-differenced terms are explicitly estimated in which lags and leads are included explicitly.[4]

We follow the fully modified OLS method appropriate for heterogeneous co-integrated panel (Pedroni 2000), in order to estimate (1). This does not have the drawbacks of OLS method of estimation, drawbacks which, as Pedroni notes, are associated with the fact that a standard panel OLS estimator is asymptotically biased and its distribution is dependent on nuisance parameters associated with the

[4] Pedroni (2001) has suggested a between-dimension, group-means panel DOLS estimator that incorporates corrections for endogeneity and serial correlation parametrically. He used the following regression model which includes lead and lag dynamics: $y_{it} = \alpha_i + \beta_i x_{it} + \sum_{j=-K_I}^{K_I} \gamma_{ik} \Delta x_{i,t-k} + e_{it}$ where $\hat{\beta}_{i,DOLS} = \left[N^{-1} \sum_{i=1}^{N} \left(\sum_{t=1}^{T} z_{it} z_{it}^{'} \right)^{-1} \left(\sum_{t=1}^{T} z_{it} \bar{y}_{it} \right) \right]_1$ (*) and z_{it} is the $2(k+1) \times 1$ vector of regressors $z_{it} = \left\{ (x_{it} - \bar{x}_i), \Delta x_{it-k,\ldots} \Delta x_{it+K} \right\}$; $\tilde{y}_{it} = y_{it} - \bar{y}_i$; the subscript 1 outside the brackets in (*) indicate that only the first element of the vector is taken to obtain the pooled slope coefficient.

dynamics underlying the data generating processes of variables. To eliminate the problem of bias due to the endogeneity of the regressors, we use the Group-Means FMOLS estimator, by incorporating the Phillips and Hansen (1990) semi-parametric correction into the OLS estimator. We also allow for heterogeneity in short-run dynamics and via fixed effects.

Consider the following co-integrated system for a simple two variable panel of $i = 1,\ldots,N$ members,

$$y_{it} = a_{it} + \beta x_{it} + \mu \tag{40.2}$$

$$x_{it} = x_{it-1} + \varepsilon_{it} \tag{40.3}$$

where the vector error process $\xi_{it} = (\mu_{it}, \varepsilon_{it})'$ is stationary with asymptotic covariance matrix Ω_i. The FMOLS estimator is:

$$\hat{\beta}_{i,FMOLS} = N^{-1}\sum_{i=1}^{N}\left(\sum_{t=1}^{T}(x_{it}-\bar{x}_i)^2\right)^{-1}\left(\sum_{t=1}^{T}(x_{it}-\bar{x}_i)y_{it}^{*} - T\hat{y}_i\right) \tag{40.4}$$

where

$$y_{it}^{*} = (x_{it} - \bar{x}_{i}\_ - \frac{\hat{\Omega}_{21i}}{\hat{\Omega}_{22i}}\Delta x_{it} \tag{40.5}$$

$$\hat{\gamma}_{it} = \hat{\Gamma}_{21i}\_\hat{\Omega}^{0}_{21i} - \frac{\hat{\Omega}_{21i}}{\hat{\Omega}_{22i}}\left(\hat{\Gamma}_{22i} - \hat{\Omega}^{0}_{22i}\right) \tag{40.7}$$

where the $\hat{\Omega}$ and $\hat{\Gamma}$ are covariances and sums of autocovariances obtained from the long-run covariance matrix for the model. Heterogenous time trends, allow for more general structure (Harris and Sollis 2003). Fully modified OLS estimates of the cointegrating relationships are presented in Table 6 on a per country basis and for the panel as a whole.

From the *panel estimates*, including general time effects, we see that the coefficients of all variables are statistically significant when normalizing with respect to output. The effect of investment on output turns out to be positive, the estimated coefficient being 0.68 with a t-statistic of 32.32. Credit is also found to have a positive impact (0.18) on output. Money supply is statistically significant for output with a t-statistic of 2.94. Interest rates are found to have a negative impact (−0.08) on output.

On a *per country basis*, investment has a positive impact on output, though the relationship is not statistically significant in Australia. The impact of credit on output is positive in all countries, but the relationship is statistically insignificant in Italy and Spain. In the US, the estimated coefficient of credit is 0.22, with t-statistic of 2.76. In Japan, the corresponding estimated coefficient is 0.41, with t-statistic of 3.67. Money supply is statistically significant for output in nearly all countries, with Australia the only exception. In detail, money supply has a positive impact on output in the US, Canada, Germany, France and Italy, but a negative impact on

Table 6 FMOLS Results

Fully modified OLS estimates (dependent variable is output)

common time dummies included

	Investment		Credit		Lending Rate		Money Supply	
United States	0,67	[13,51]	0,22	[2,76]	-0,05	[-3,93]	0,13	[3,45]
Australia	0,01	[0,42]	0,08	[1,35]	-0,09	[-4,25]	0,01	[0,42]
Canada	0,72	[10,94]	0,14	[1,93]	-0,03	[-3,38]	0,04	[2,16]
United Kingdom	1,01	[8,94]	0,08	[2,52]	-0,08	[-2,52]	-0,13	[-2,75]
Japan	0,70	[7,27]	0,41	[3,67]	0,00	[-1,88]	-0,17	[-4,83]
Germany	0,36	[4,56]	0,02	[3,28]	0,01	[2,92]	0,15	[3,53]
France	0,62	[6,37]	0,06	[1,87]	0,00	[-2,37]	0,06	[2,59]
Italy	0,56	[3,92]	0,08	[0,4]	-0,15	[-5,72]	0,08	[1,53]
Spain	0,69	[23,07]	0,02	[0,43]	0,00	[-2,2]	-0,02	[-7,31]
	0,68	**[32,32]**	**0,18**	**[4,46]**	**-0,08**	**[-5,95]**	**0,11**	**[2,94]**

Fully modified OLS estimates (dependent variable is investment)

common time dummies included

	GDP		Credit		Lending Rate		Money Supply	
United States	1,28	[12,3]	0,07	[2,68]	-0,05	[-4,52]	0,08	[1,67]
Australia	1,19	[17,44]	0,06	[2,17]	-0,01	[-4,71]	0,00	[-0,04]
Canada	1,20	[11,87]	0,00	[-0,05]	-0,04	[-2,78]	-0,05	[-1,88]
United Kingdom	0,78	[9,34]	0,06	[1,96]	0,01	[4,14]	0,08	[1,75]
Japan	0,96	[7,75]	0,08	[3,55]	0,00	[0,54]	0,23	[6,18]
Germany	1,08	[4,34]	0,36	[2,53]	0,01	[1,61]	0,11	[2,72]
France	0,96	[6,39]	0,43	[3,12]	0,00	[2,23]	-0,12	[-3,71]
Italy	0,56	[3,66]	0,64	[3,49]	-0,03	[-1,87]	-0,11	[-1,99]
Spain	1,39	[22,87]	0,01	[0,19]	0,01	[2,06]	0,03	[8,87]
	1,04	**[31,99]**	**0,23**	**[3,41]**	**-0,03**	**[-4,16]**	**0,04**	**[3,89]**

Fully modified OLS estimates (dependent variable is credit)

common time dummies included

	GDP		Investment		Lending Rate		Money Supply	
United States	1,60	[2,53]	0,22	[1,68]	-0,02	[-1,78]	0,31	[6,15]
Australia	0,45	[0,49]	-0,21	[-0,29]	0,00	[-0,68]	-0,27	[-1,89]
Canada	0,83	[1,38]	0,03	[0,07]	-0,11	[-3,12]	0,01	[0,2]
United Kingdom	2,71	[2,83]	-1,08	[-2,1]	0,04	[2,4]	0,92	[3,81]
Japan	0,94	[3,88]	-0,20	[-1,81]	0,00	[-1,21]	0,26	[2,34]
Germany	0,03	[0,06]	0,68	[2,77]	-0,04	[-3,17]	-0,10	[-0,73]
France	-0,10	[3,37]	0,63	[3,37]	0,00	[0,09]	0,21	[10,05]
Italy	0,04	[0,23]	0,48	[3,31]	0,00	[2,25]	0,21	[6,14]

(continued)

Table 6 (continued)

Fully modified OLS estimates (dependent variable is credit)

common time dummies included

	GDP		Investment		Lending Rate		Money Supply	
Spain	0,64	[0,8]	-0,05	[-0,09]	0,00	[0,07]	0,02	[1,91]
	0,79	**[3,95]**	**0,15**	**[1,85]**	**-0,08**	**[-1,84]**	**0,21**	**[9,00]**

Fully modified OLS estimates (dependent variable is money supply)

common time dummies included

	GDP		Investment		Credit		Lending Rate	
United States	0,78	[2,11]	1,12	[0,81]	1,23	[4,43]	-0,09	[-2,35]
Australia	0,98	[0,8]	-0,23	[-0,23]	-0,01	[-1,40]	-0,51	[-1,97]
Canada	4,37	[2,58]	-2,82	[-1,99]	0,07	[0,11]	-0,08	[-2,28]
United Kingdom	-1,94	[-3,18]	1,41	[1,93]	0,32	[3,13]	0,02	[1,26]
Japan	-1,86	[-5,4]	2,67	[6,23]	1,16	[2,53]	-0,01	[-1,54]
Germany	1,75	[3,20]	0,32	[0,94]	-0,28	[-1,04]	-0,06	[-5,64]
France	1,90	[[1,81]	-2,50	[-3,27]	3,65	[9,68]	0,00	[0,65]
Italy	0,91	[1,47]	-1,11	[-1,84]	2,69	[6,01]	0,01	[0,92]
Spain	-2,99	[-7,07]	22,21	[8,69]	0,20	[0,12]	-0,11	[-3,82]
	-0,58	**[-2,58]**	**2,34**	**[3,75]**	**1,07**	**[6,33]**	**-0,09**	**[-4,55]**

Fully modified OLS estimates (dependent variable is leading rate)

common time dummies included

	GDP		Investment		Credit		Money Supply	
United States	-60,02	[-2,71]	53,02	[3,71]	-0,46	[-0,07]	-2,83	[-1,17]
Australia	72,73	[-3,47]	66,33	[4,22]	-4,88	[-0,92]	-4,92	[-1,24]
Canada	-7,41	[-0,63]	9,93	[1,05]	-2,46	[-0,60]	-2,12	[-1,73]
United Kingdom	-18,64	[-2,58]	32,13	[4,13]	3,22	[2,37]	2,47	[1,18]
Japan	18,10	[0,99]	5,86	[0,36]	-14,55	[-1,17]	-6,30	[-1,36]
Germany	41,99	[2,71]	18,24	[1,97]	-25,51	[-3,88]	-20,08	[-5,37]
France	-10,80	[-3,09]	80,33	[2,82]	3,21	[0,13]	4,43	[0,78]
Italy	-66,14	[-5,68]	8,46	[0,57]	3,12	[0,70]	49,83	[3,42]
Spain	58,63	[-1,89]	40,62	[1,90]	1,62	[0,90]	-2,47	[-3,22]
	-36,83	**[-5,45]**	**34,99**	**[6,97]**	**1,11**	**[-0,18]**	**-3,19**	**[-3,81]**

Note: Figures in brackets are t-statistics

output in UK, Japan and Spain. *Interest rates are statistically significant in all countries without exception.*

When *investment* is chosen as the dependent variable, we see that all other variables are statistically significant. The impact of credit on investment is positive (0.23) with t-statistic of 3.41. Interest rate has a marginally negative effect (−0.03) on investment. Output and money supply have positive effect on investment -the estimated coefficients are 1.04 in the case of output and 0.04 in the case of money supply. The t-statistics are 31.99 and 3.89, respectively. Per country, we find that there are some differences from the results above. For Canada and Spain, Credit is statistically insignificant. For Japan, interest rate is statistically insignificant. For Australia, money supply appears statistically insignificant.

When *Credit* is chosen as dependent variable, all variables are statistically significant. The estimated coefficient of money supply is 0.21, with t-statistic of 9.00. Output has a positive effect (0.79) on credit. Investment also has a positive impact on Credit. The sign of the estimated coefficient of interest rate, on the other hand, is negative. *Per country*, we see that money supply is insignificant in Canada and Germany but in Australia money supply has a negative and significant impact on Credit. In Australia, Japan, France and Spain Credit is not influenced by interest rates. In Australia, Canada and Spain, Credit is not influenced by investment while also in Australia, Canada, Italy and Spain, Credit is not responsive to output.

The estimated coefficient for money supply which the FMOLS estimate gives is statistically significant irrespective of the normalization. The corresponding coefficient for credit is 1.07, with t-statistic 6.33. Interest rate has a marginally negative effect on money supply. The effect of investment is positive, 2.34. By examination of our per country results we see that there are significant differences from the overall panel results: In Australia, Canada, Germany and Spain, Credit has no effect on money supply. In the UK, Italy and Spain interest rates have no effect on money supply.

The findings from panel estimates accord with the sequence of events predicted by the Austrian business cycle theory. Specifically, investment has a positive impact on output and, *more importantly, the impact of Credit on output and investment is also positive.* Credit, is found to be positively influenced to a significant degree by money supply. Per country, our findings reveal minor differences. *The ABC theory is fully verified in the US, UK, Japan, France and Italy, whereas in Spain, Canada, Australia and Germany there are some parts of the chain of the ABC theory that do not seem to be significant.*

Testing for Causality

The issue of causality is important for our analysis. To test for causality we adopt the method of Dufour et al. (2006), based on running vector autoregressions at different horizons. Dufour et al. (2006) use a finite order vector autoregressive model to provide tests for examining whether there are causal relationships between variables *at various horizons.*

Consider a *VAR* (*p*) process of the form:

$$W(t) = \mu(t) + \sum_{k=1}^{p} \pi_k W(t-k) + \alpha(t), t = 1, \ldots T \tag{40.8}$$

where $W(t) = (\omega_{1t} + \omega_{2t}, \ldots \omega_{mt})'$ is a random vector, $\mu(t)$ is a deterministic trend, and $\alpha(t)$ is a white-noise process of order two with a non-singular covariance matrix Ω. The common specification for $\mu(t)$ is that it is constant, although other deterministic trends –such as seasonal dummies- could also be considered.

This autoregressive form can be generalized to allow for projection at any horizon h given the information available at time t. Hence, the observation at time $t+h$ can be computed recursively from Eq. (40.8) and is given by:

$$W(t+h) = \mu^{(h)}(t) + \sum_{k=1}^{p} \pi_k^{(h)} W(t+1-k) + \sum_{j=0}^{h-1} \psi_j \alpha(t+h-j) \tag{40.9}$$

where $\psi_0 = I_m$ and $h<T$. The appropriate formulae for the coefficients $\pi_k^{(h)}$ and $\mu^{(h)}(t)$ are given in Dufour and Renault (1998), and the ψ_j matrices are nothing but the impulse-response coefficients of the VAR. Equation is an autoregression of order p at horizon h or a (p, h)-autoregression. Let us consider Eq. (40.9) written in matrix form:

$$W(t+h) = \overline{W}_p(h)\Pi^{(h)} + U(t+h) \tag{40.10}$$

We can estimate this equation by OLS, which yields the estimator:

$$\Pi^{(h)} = \left[\overline{W}_p(h)'\overline{W}_p(h)\right]^{-1}\overline{W}_p(h)'W(t+h) \tag{40.11}$$

Hence

$$\sqrt{T}\left[\hat{\Pi}^{(h)} - \Pi^{(h)}\right] = \left[\frac{1}{T}\overline{W}_p(h)'\overline{W}_p(h)\right]^{-1}\frac{1}{\sqrt{T}}\overline{W}_p(h)'U(t+h) \tag{40.12}$$

Under usual regularity conditions, $\sqrt{T}vec\left[\hat{\Pi}^{(h)} - \Pi^{(h)}\right]$ converges in distribution to a normal distribution with a non-singular covariance matrix. We are interested in the hypothesis that a variable ω_{jt} does not cause another one, ω_{it}, at horizon h, and the restrictions related to that hypothesis take the form:

$$\mathrm{H}_0^{(h)} : \pi_{ijk}^{(h)} = 0, k = 1, \ldots p, \tag{40.13}$$

where $\pi_k^{(h)} = \left[\pi_{\iota\xi\kappa}^{(h)}\right]_{i,j=1,\ldots m}$ comes from the (p, h)—autoregression defined in Eq. (40.9). In other words, the null hypothesis takes the form of a set restrictions on the coefficients of the matrix $\hat{\Pi}^{(h)}$. Under the hypothesis $\mathrm{H}_0^{(h)}$ of *non-causality at horizon h* from ω_{jt} to ω_{it}, the asymptotic distribution of the Ward statistic $W\left[\mathrm{H}_0^{(h)}\right]$ is $\chi^2(p)$. In order to get an appropriate distribution, we have to take in account that the prediction error $\hat{u}(t+h)$ follows an *MA (h-1)* process. We use the Newey-West procedure, which provides a general purpose positive-semidefinite covariance matrix in this instance.

The normal asymptotic distribution may not be reliable in finite samples. This may especially be the case for a VAR system with a large number of variables and/or lags. An alternative to using the asymptotic Chi square distribution of $W\left[\mathrm{H}_0^{(h)}\right]$ is to use Monte Carlo or bootstrap techniques. Since the asymptotic distribution of

$W\left[\mathrm{H}_0^{(h)}\right]$ is nuisance-parameter free, such methods yield asymptotically valid tests when applied to $W\left[\mathrm{H}_0^{(h)}\right]$, and typically give better control of the test level for finite samples.

In our empirical study, ***p-values are computed using a parametric bootstrap***. The procedure can be described as follows: An unrestricted VAR(p) model is fitted for the horizon one, yielding the estimates $\hat{\Pi}^{(1)}$ and $\hat{\Omega}$ for $\Pi^{(1)}$ and Ω.

1. An unrestricted (p, h)- autoregression is fitted by least squares, yielding the estimate $\hat{\Pi}^{(h)}$of $\Pi^{(h)}$.
2. The test statistic W for testing non-causality at the horizon h is computed.
3. N simulated samples are drawn by Monte Carlo, using $\Pi^{(h)} = \hat{\Pi}^{(h)}$ and $\Omega = \hat{\Omega}$ (given the hypothesis that $\alpha(t)$ is Gaussian); we then impose to $\hat{\Pi}^{(h)}$ the constraints of *non-causality*.
4. The simulated p value is obtained by calculating the rejection frequency.

The results of per country causality tests, following the method of Dufour (2006), are reported in Table 1. Here, we are investigating whether the ABC theory chain of events is really valid. Particularly, in the first stage, we test whether the interest rate is influenced by money supply. We note that the "chain" can function straight from interest rate, since this constitutes a monetary policy tool.[5] In the second stage, we test whether credit is affected by money supply or interest rate. We then investigate causality between credit and investment, the crux of the matter for verification of the ABC. In the third and last stage, we test whether investment affects output.

We first apply the test to the **US**. The results indicate that interest rate is influenced by money supply, in short and medium term horizons. Credit in the medium term horizons is *caused* by money supply and Credit in short term horizons is *caused* by interest rate. ***The crucial link of the Austrian chain is clearly in place, since credit causes investment from horizon 6 onwards*** (up to 34). Moreover we detect robust evidence of causality from investment to output, as expected. ***The behaviour of Credit, nevertheless, is remarkable because it causes output over all horizons***. We therefore conclude that the ABC theory is strongly validated for the US economy.

For Australia, it is money supply that seems to cause interest rate, which itself clearly causes credit in the short and medium term horizons. We also observe a bi-directional causal relationship between money supply and credit. ***The evidence supports causality from Credit to output. Here, again, the ABC theory appears to be verified***.

For **Canada**, the chain of events in the ABC theory starts from the interest rate, which causes credit over any horizon. Investment and output, are significantly

[5] However important the causality relation between money supply and interest rate, it *cannot* on its own nullify the ABC theory.

	Australia																					
	h	**2**	**3**	**4**	**5**	**6**	**7**	**8**	**9**	**10**	**12**	**14**	**16**	**18**	**20**	**22**	**24**	**26**	**28**	**30**	**32**	**34**
GDP	***← Investment***	**	**	**	**	**																
	← Credit						**	**	**	**	**	**	*	*	*	*	*	*	*	*	*	*
	← Interest Rate	**	**	**	**	**	**															
	← Money Supply															**	*	*	*	*	*	*
Investment	***← GDP***	**	*	*	*	*	*	*	*	*	**		**	*	*	*	*	*	*	*	**	**
	← Credit					**	**	**	**	**	**	*	*	*	*	*	*	*	*	*	*	*
	← Interest Rate	*	*	*	*	**	**	**							**	**	**					
	← Money Supply				**	**	**	**	**	**				*	*	*	*	*	*	**	**	**
Credit	***← GDP***		**	*	*	**	**	**														
	← Investment	**	*	*	*	*																
	← Interest Rate	*	*	*	*	*	*	*	*	**	**	*	*	**	**							
	← Money Supply	*	*	*	*	*	*	*	*	*	**	**	**	**	**	**		**	**	*	*	*
Money Supply	***← GDP***	**	*	*	*	*	*	*	**	**												
	← Investment													**	**			**	**	*	*	*
	← Credit	*	*	*	*	*	*	*	*	*	*	*	*	*	*	*	*	*	*	*	*	*
	← Interest Rate	**	*	*	*	*	*	*	*	*	**				**	**	*	*	*	**		
Interest Rate	***← GDP***	**	**	*	*	*	*	*	**	**					**	*	*	*	*	*	**	
	← Investment															**	**	**	**			
	← Credit											**	*	*	*	*	*	*	*	*	*	*
	← Money Supply					**	*	*	*	*	**			**		**	*	*	**			

Source: International Monetary Fund, International Financial Statiscs
Note: (*), (**) Signify rejection of the null hypothesis at the 5% and 10% level respectevely

	Canada																					
	h	**2**	**3**	**4**	**5**	**6**	**7**	**8**	**9**	**10**	**12**	**14**	**16**	**18**	**20**	**22**	**24**	**26**	**28**	**30**	**32**	**34**
GDP	← ***Investment***	**	**	**	**																	
	← ***Credit***								**	**	**	**	**	**	*	*	*	*	*	*	*	*
	← ***Interest Rate***	**	**	**	**	**	*	*	*	*	*	*	*	*	*	*	*	*	*	*	*	*
	← ***Money Supply***																	**	*	*	*	*
Investment	← ***GDP***	**	*	*	*	*	*	*	*	*	*	*	*	*	*	**						
	← ***Credit***																					
	← ***Interest Rate***	**	**	**	**	**	**	**	**	**	*	**	*	*	*	*	*	*	*	*	*	*
	← ***Money Supply***																					
Credit	← ***GDP***	**	**	*	*	*	*	*	**	**	**	**	**									
	← ***Investment***										*	*	*	**								
	← ***Interest Rate***		**	**	**	**	*	*	*	**	**	**	*	*	*	*	*	*	*	*	*	*
	← ***Money Supply***	**	**	**	**																	
Money Supply	← ***GDP***						**	**	**	**				**	**	**						
	← ***Investment***																					
	← ***Credit***																**	*	**	*	*	*
	← ***Interest Rate***				**	**	**	*	*	*	*	*	*	*	*	*	*	*	*	*	*	*
Interest Rate	← ***GDP***	**										**	**	*	*	*	*	*	*	*	*	**
	← ***Investment***																					
	← ***Credit***															**	*	**		**	*	*
	← ***Money Supply***																	**	**	**	**	**

Source: International Monetary Fund, International Financial Statiscs

Note: (*), (**) Signify rejection of the null hypothesis at the 5% and 10% level respectevely

	United Kingdom																					
	h	**2**	**3**	**4**	**5**	**6**	**7**	**8**	**9**	**10**	**12**	**14**	**16**	**18**	**20**	**22**	**24**	**26**	**28**	**30**	**32**	**34**
GDP	← ***Investment***	**	**	**	**	**																
	← ***Credit***			**	**	**	*	*	*	*	*	*	*	*	*	*	**	**	*	**	**	**
	← ***Interest Rate***																					
	← ***Money Supply***																					
Investment	← ***GDP***	*	*	*	*	*	*	*	*	*	*		*	*	**	*	*	*	*	*	*	*
	← ***Credit***	*	*	*	*	*	*	*	*	*	*	*	*	**	**							
	← ***Interest Rate***			**	**	**	**	**	**	**	*	*										
	← ***Money Supply***																					
Credit	← ***GDP***			**	**	**	**	**	**	**	**	**		**	**				**	*	*	*
	← ***Investment***		**	**	**	**	**	**	**	**	**						**	**	**	**	**	**
	← ***Interest Rate***			**	**	**	**	**	**	**	**	**	**			**	**	*	*	*	*	**
	← ***Money Supply***																					
Money Supply	← ***GDP***																		*	*	*	*
	← ***Investment***	*	*	*	*	*	*	*	*	**									*	**	**	**
	← ***Credit***	*	*	*	*	*	*	*	*	*	*	*	**	**	**					**	**	**
	← ***Interest Rate***	*	*	*	*	*	**	**	**	**	**	**	**				**	*	*	*	*	*
Interest Rate	← ***GDP***					**	**	**	**	**												
	← ***Investment***	**	**	**	**	*	*	*	*	*												
	← ***Credit***				**	**	**	**	**	**	**	**										
	← ***Money Supply***													**	**							

Source: International Monetary Fund, International Financial Statiscs

Note: (*), (**) Signify rejection of the null hypothesis at the 5% and 10% level respectevely

	Germany																				
	h	**2**	**3**	**4**	**5**	**6**	**7**	**8**	**9**	**10**	**12**	**14**	**16**	**18**	**20**	**22**	**24**	**26**	**28**	**30**	**32**	**34**
GDP	← ***Investment***				**	**	**	**	**	**	*	*	*	*	**	**	**					
	← ***Credit***	*	*	*	*	*	*	*	*	*	*	*	*	**	**	**	**	**	**	**	*	**
	← ***Interest Rate***																					
	← ***Money Supply***	**			**	**	**	**	**	**	**	**	*	*	*	*	*	*	*	*	*	*
Investment	← ***GDP***								**	**	*	*	**									
	← ***Credit***	*	*	*	*	*	*	*	*	*	*	*	*	*	*	*	**	**	**	**		
	← ***Interest Rate***																					
	← ***Money Supply***	**	**	**	*	*	*	*	*	*	*	*	*	*	*	*	*	*	*	*	*	*
Credit	← ***GDP***							**	**	**	**	**	**									
	← ***Investment***						**	**	**	**	*	*	*	**	**	**	**					
	← ***Interest Rate***																					
	← ***Money Supply***			**	**	*	*	*	*	*	*	*	*	*	*	*	*	*	*	*	*	*
Money Supply	← ***GDP***				**	**	**	*	*	*	*	*	**									
	← ***Investment***							**	**	**	**	**	**									
	← ***Credit***																					
	← ***Interest Rate***												**	**	**	**	*	*	**	**		
Interest Rate	← ***GDP***				**	**	**	**	**	**				**	**	**						
	← ***Investment***						**	**	**	**	**	**	**	*	*	*	*	*	*	**	**	
	← ***Credit***	*	*	*	*	*	*	*	*	*	*	**					*	*	*	*	*	*
	← ***Money Supply***																					

Source: International Monetary Fund, International Financial Statiscs
Note: (*), (**) Signify rejection of the null hypothesis at the 5% and 10% level respectevely

	Japan																					
	h	**2**	**3**	**4**	**5**	**6**	**7**	**8**	**9**	**10**	**12**	**14**	**16**	**18**	**20**	**22**	**24**	**26**	**28**	**30**	**32**	**34**
GDP	← ***Investment***	**	**	**	**	**	**															
	← ***Credit***	*	*	*	*	*	*	*	**	**	*	*	*	*	**	**	**	**	**	**	**	**
	← ***Interest Rate***	**	**	*	*	*	*	*	*	*	**							**	**	**	*	*
	← ***Money Supply***		**	**	**	**							**						**	*		*
Investment	← ***GDP***																					
	← ***Credit***	**	**	**	**	*	*	*	*	**	**	**	**	**	**	*	**					
	← ***Interest Rate***								**	**	**											
	← ***Money Supply***												**	**	**							
Credit	← ***GDP***														**	**						
	← ***Investment***															**	**	**				
	← ***Interest Rate***						**	**	*	*	**	**				**		**				
	← ***Money Supply***							*	*	*	*	*	*	*	**	**	**	**	**	**	*	*
Money Supply	← ***GDP***								**	**	**	**	**									
	← ***Investment***	**										**	**	**							**	**
	← ***Credit***								**	**	**	**	**	**	**	**	**	*	*	*		
	← ***Interest Rate***	**	**	**			**	**	**	**	**	**	**	*	**		**			**	**	
Interest Rate	← ***GDP***														**	**	**	**	**	**	**	**
	← ***Investment***																	**	*	*	**	**
	← ***Credit***					**	**	**	**					**	**				**	**	**	**
	← ***Money Supply***	**	**	**	**	**	**	*	*	*	*	*										

Source: International Monetary Fund, International Financial Statiscs

Note: (*), (**) Signify rejection of the null hypothesis at the 5% and 10% level respectevely

	France																					
	h	**2**	**3**	**4**	**5**	**6**	**7**	**8**	**9**	**10**	**12**	**14**	**16**	**18**	**20**	**22**	**24**	**26**	**28**	**30**	**32**	**34**
GDP	← ***Investment***	**	**	**	*	*	*	*	*	*	*	**	**	**	*	*	*	**				
	← ***Credit***	**	**	*	*	*	*	*	*	*	*	*	*	*	*	*	*	**	**			
	← ***Interest Rate***									**	*	*	*	*	*	*	**	**				
	← ***Money Supply***								**	**	**	**	**	**	**	**	**	**	**	**	**	*
Investment	← ***GDP***													**	*	**	**	**	**	**	**	*
	← ***Credit***	**	**	**	**	*	*	*	*	*	*	*	*	*	*	*	**	**				**
	← ***Interest Rate***			**	**	**	**		**	**	**	**	*	*	*	*	*	**				
	← ***Money Supply***																					
Credit	← ***GDP***	*	*											**	*	*	*	*	*	**	**	*
	← ***Investment***	**	**	**	**	*	*	*	*	*	**	**	**	**	**	**						
	← ***Interest Rate***												**		**	**	**					
	← ***Money Supply***	**	**	**	*	*	*	*	**	**												
Money Supply	← ***GDP***	**	**								**	**	**					**	**	*	*	**
	← ***Investment***						**	**										**	**	*	*	*
	← ***Credit***	**	**		**	**	**	*	*	*	*	*	*	*	*	*	*	*	*	*	*	*
	← ***Interest Rate***							**	**	**	*	*	**	**	**	**	**					
Interest Rate	← ***GDP***										**		**	**	**	**	**					**
	← ***Investment***	**	**	**													**					
	← ***Credit***	**	**	**	**	**	**	**									**					
	← ***Money Supply***	**	*	*	**	**	**															

Source: International Monetary Fund, International Financial Statiscs
Note: (*), (**) Signify rejection of the null hypothesis at the 5% and 10% level respectevely

	Italy																				
	h	**2**	**3**	**4**	**5**	**6**	**7**	**8**	**9**	**10**	**12**	**14**	**16**	**18**	**20**	**22**	**24**	**26**	**28**	**30**	**32**	**34**
GDP	← ***Investment***																	**	**			
	← ***Credit***						**	**	**	**	**	**	**	**	**			**				
	← ***Interest Rate***										**	**										
	← ***Money Supply***										**	*	**	**	**	**	**	*				
Investment	← ***GDP***																					
	← ***Credit***	**	**	**	*	*	*	*	*	**	*	**	**	**	*			**	**	**	**	**
	← ***Interest Rate***																					
	← ***Money Supply***					**	**	*	**	**	*	*	**	**	**	**						
Credit	← ***GDP***																			**	**	
	← ***Investment***	*				**	**	**	**	**												
	← ***Interest Rate***	**	**	**	**	**	**	**														
	← ***Money Supply***	**	**	*	*	**	**	**	**													
Money Supply	← ***GDP***													**	**							
	← ***Investment***										**	**	**	*	*	*	*	**	**	*	*	**
	← ***Credit***	**	*	*	*	*	*	**	*	**	*	*		*	*	*	*	**				
	← ***Interest Rate***																					
Interest Rate	← ***GDP***	*	**	**				**	**	**										**	**	
	← ***Investment***	**	**	**	**																	
	← ***Credit***	*	*	*	**	**																
	← ***Money Supply***	**	*	*	*	*	**	**	**	**	**	**	*	*	**							

Source: International Monetary Fund, International Financial Statiscs

Note: (*), (**) Signify rejection of the null hypothesis at the 5% and 10% level respectevely

	Spain																				
	h	2	3	4	5	6	7	8	9	10	12	14	16	18	20	22	24	26	28	30	32	34
GDP	← ***Investment***	**	*	*	**	**	**	**	**													
	← ***Credit***									**	**	**	**	**	**	*	*	*	*	*	*	*
	← ***Interest Rate***									**	*	*	*	*	*	*	*	*	*	**		
	← ***Money Supply***										**	**	**	**	*	*	*	*	*	*	*	
Investment	← ***GDP***	**	**							**	**	*	*	*	*	*	**	**	**			
	← ***Credit***												**	**	**	*	*	*	*	*	*	*
	← ***Interest Rate***										**	**	*	*	*	*	*	*	**	**	**	**
	← ***Money Supply***	**	**	**	**	**	**	**	*	*	*	*	*	*	*	*	*	**	**	**		**
Credit	← ***GDP***							**	**	**	*	*	*	*	*	**	*		**			
	← ***Investment***								***						**	**	*					
	← ***Interest Rate***				**	**	**	*	*	*	*	*	*	*	**	**	**	*	**	**	*	**
	← ***Money Supply***			*	*	*	*	*	*	*	*	*	*	**	**	**	**	**	**	**	**	**
Money Supply	← ***GDP***										**	**	*	**	**	*						
	← ***Investment***															**	**					
	← ***Credit***	**	**	**	**	*	*	*	*	*	*	**	**	**								
	← ***Interest Rate***									**	**	**	**	**					**			
Interest Rate	← ***GDP***		**	**	**	**	**	**						**	*							
	← ***Investment***					**	**	**	**					**	**				**	**	*	**
	← ***Credit***														**	**	**	**	**	**	**	
	← ***Money Supply***										**	**										

Source: International Monetary Fund, International Financial Statiscs
Note: (*), (**) Signify rejection of the null hypothesis at the 5% and 10% level respectevely

affected by interest rates and output by credit. There seems to be no causal relationship between credit and investment; the main mechanism of the business cycle is apparently the interest rate.

In the **UK**, Credit is caused by interest rates, a variable which has a significant causal relationship with investment. In the UK, the main links of the ABC chain are closely connected. Output is caused by credit, and investment affects output in the short term. In **Germany**, ***the results also seem to support the ABC theory***. The main force is money supply. It is this that causes credit, which in turn causes investment, and output. Not surprisingly output is affected by Credit. The evidence for Japan again testifies in favour the ABC theory. There are significant causal relationships from credit to output and from credit to investment, over any horizon. The sequence of events in ABC seems to be valid for **France** as well. In particular, we detect evidence in favour of causality from credit to investment and from investment to output. Credit is caused by money supply in the short term. In **Italy**, *investment does not cause output over any horizon*. The role of credit is crucial though, since it causes output and investment in medium term horizons so the ABC theory is fully valid. In **Spain**, the chain of causal relationships functions only in the medium and long horizon. This is not true for the causal relationship, between investment and output, as output seems to be caused by investment only in short term horizons.

The causality findings from our application of the method of Dufour et al. (2006) to major economies, confirm the crucial role of Credit in ABC theory so we have to consider it as a plausible explanation of the business cycle alive today as was in the 20's.

Summary of Findings

In this part we set out to examine, for major economies, whether the Austrian theory of the business cycle is verified. For this purpose we combined cross-sectional and time series data, and we used reliable econometric methods.

We find that investment has a positive impact on output; credit has a positive impact on output and investment, and credit is positively influenced to a significant degree by money supply. Per country, our findings showed minor differences. For the US, the UK, Japan, France and Italy the ABC theory is fully verified. In Spain, Canada, Australia and Germany, certain parts of the ABC chain do not seem to "match".

We examined the causal relationship between variables at various horizons by means of the method of Dufour et al. (2006). Our results differ slightly from country to country but the ABC theory holds in general. The implication is that in short and medium term horizons (up to 2008) credit expansion had a major role to play in the recession much like as in the 20's as the Austrian School predicted.

References

Böhm-Bawerk (1889) Kapital und Kapitalzins. Zweite Abteilung: Positive Theorie des Kapitales. Innsbruck: Wagner. 2nd edn, 1902; 3rd edn in two volumes, 1909 and 1912; 4th edn in two volumes, 1921, Jena: Fischer. Translation of 1st edn as The Positive Theory of Capital, London: Macmillan, 1891. Translation of 4th edn as Capital and Interest, vols. 2 and 3, South Holland, IL: Libertarian Press

Choi I (2001) Unit root tests for panel data. J Int Money Financ 20:249–272

Dufour J-M, Renault E (1998) Short-run and long-run causality in time series: theory. Econometrica 66:1099–1125

Dufour J-M, Pelletier D, Renault E (2006) Short run and long run causality in time series: inference. J Econometrics 132(2):337–362

Garrison R (2001) Time and money: the macroeconomics of capital structure. Routledge, London

Harris R, Sollis R (2003) Applied time series modelling and forecasting. Wiley, Applications

Hayek FA (1931) Prices and Production, New York

Hayek FA (1933) Monetary theory and the trade cycle. Harcourt, Brace & Co., New York

Hayek FA (1935) Prices and production, 2nd edn. Augustus M. Kelley, New York

Hayek FA (1941) The pure theory of capital. University of Chicago Press, Chicago

Hayek FA (1967) Prices and production, 2nd edn. Augustus M. Kelley, New York

Johansen S (1988) Statistical analysis of co-integrating vectors. J Econ Dyn Control 12:231–254

Konstantakopoulou, Ioanna, Efthymios G, Tsionas (2011) ABC's of the 2008 recession: Robust and Reliable international Evidence on the Austrian Theory of the Business Cycle, KEPE Discussion Papers, Athens

Maddala GS, Wu S (1999) A comparative study of unit root tests with panel data and a new simple test. Oxford Bull Econ Stat 61:631–652

Mises L (1912) The theory of money and credit. Yale University Press, New Haven, Conn

Mises L (1966) Human Action: A Treatise on Economics, 3rd rev. ed. Chicago: Henry Regnery,

Pedroni P (1999) Critical values for cointegration tests in heterogeneous panels with multiple regressors. Oxford Bull Econ Stat 61:653–678

Pedroni P (2000) Fully modified OLS for heterogeneous cointegrated panels. In: Baltagi BH, Fomby TB, Hill RC (eds) Nonstationary panels, panel cointegration and dynamic panels, advances in econometrics, vol 15. Elsevier Science, Amsterdam

Pedroni P (2001) Purchasing power parity tests in cointegrated panels, Rev Econ Stat 83:727–731

Pesaran and Shin (2003) Testing for Unit Roots in Heterogeneous Panels. J Econometrics 115:53–74

Phillips PCB, Hansen BE (1990) Statistical inference in instrumental variable regression with I(1) processes. Rev Econ Stud 57:99–125

MIX
Papier aus verantwortungsvollen Quellen
Paper from responsible sources
FSC® C105338

If you have any concerns about our products,
you can contact us on
ProductSafety@springernature.com

In case Publisher is established outside the EU,
the EU authorized representative is:
Springer Nature Customer Service Center GmbH
Europaplatz 3, 69115 Heidelberg, Germany

Printed by Libri Plureos GmbH
in Hamburg, Germany